Kilvert:
The Hom less Heart

700020

D1649822

Kilvert:
The Homeless Heart

by

John Toman

WORCESTERSHIRE COUNTY COUNCIL
CULTURAL SERVICES

For though we wander out of the way oft in this wilderness.
Our faces still are set toward our home.

'The Pilgrimage', Kilvert

If there is rest within the breast,
'Tis where the heart is holy.

'Happiness', one of Kilvert's favourite poems by William Barnes

B KILVERT, F

Logaston Press

LOGASTON PRESS
Little Logaston, Logaston, Woonton,
Almeley, Herefordshire HR3 6QH

First published by Logaston Press 2001
Copyright © John Toman 2001

All rights reserved. No part of this publication
may be reproduced, stored in a retrieval system,
or transmitted, in any form or by any means,
electronic, mechanical, photocopying, recording
or otherwise, without the prior permission,
in writing of the publisher

ISBN 1 873827 37 7

Set in Times and Baskerville by Logaston Press
and printed in Great Britain by
Antony Rowe, Chippenham

Cover illustrations:
Refer to plate section

Contents

To live over other people's lives is nothing unless we live over their perceptions, live over the growth, the varying intensity of the same—since it is by these they themselves lived.

Henry James

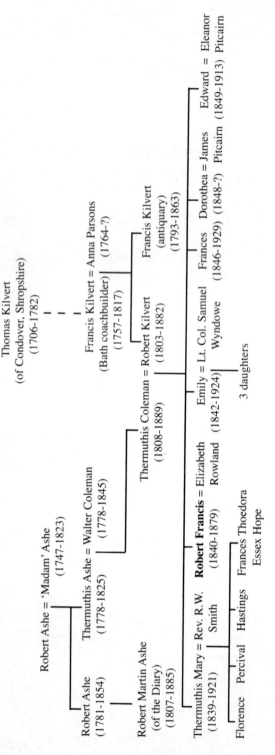

Thomas Kilvert
(of Condover, Shropshire)
(1706-1782)

Francis Kilvert = Anna Parsons
(Bath coachbuilder)   (1764-?)
(1757-1817)

Francis Kilvert
(antiquary)
(1793-1863)

Robert Ashe = 'Madam' Ashe
(1747-1823)

Thermuthis Ashe = Walter Coleman
(1778-1825)   (1778-1845)

Thermuthis Coleman = Robert Kilvert
(1808-1889)   (1803-1882)

Robert Ashe
(1781-1854)

Robert Martin Ashe
(of the Diary)
(1807-1885)

Emily = Lt. Col. Samuel   Frances   Dorothea = James   Edward = Eleanor
(1842-1924) Wyndowe   (1846-1929) (1848-?) Pitcairn   (1849-1913) Pitcairn

3 daughters

Thermuthis Mary = Rev. R.W.   Robert Francis = Elizabeth
(1839-1921)   Smith   (1840-1879)   Rowland

Florence   Percival   Hastings   Frances Thoedora
                                 Essex Hope

Robert Francis Kilvert's family tree

vi

Acknowledgements

Many people have contributed to the search for Kilvert. Without the support and encouragement over eight years of my wife, Elizabeth, the book would never have been written. My publisher, Andy Johnson, had faith in the approach I adopted and his guidance during the book's evolution has always been spiced with perceptiveness and humour. My friend and former colleague, Ray Acton, saw an early draft and made wise, helpful comments on it.

I am particularly grateful for the friendship and interest of the late Edward West, Kilvert scholar and former secretary of the Kilvert Society. I should also like to thank the following: John Harnden for his research into the Cornewall family, Mrs. Penelope Hatfield, Archivist of Eton College, for making me welcome there and answering innumerable queries; Mrs. Julia Hopton for her great kindness in allowing me to see Baskerville family papers; Lady Delia Venables Llewelyn for permission to quote from the Llysdinam Collection; Random House for allowing extensive use of Kilvert's published diaries, Rev. Dr. J.N. Rowe, Archivist of the Kilvert Society, for much valuable help and information; Mrs. Persis Wiltshire for her research into the life of the Baskerville family in Wiltshire.

Thanks are also due to: Mary Abbott of Anglia Polytechnic University; Elizabeth Boardman, Archivist of Oriel College, Oxford; Helen Burns of Llandrindod Wells Archive Office; Mrs. S. Cole of the Radnorshire Society; Rev. Derek Cooper, Rector of Camerton, Somerset; Judith and Mark Curthoys, Archivists of Christ Church College, Oxford; Professor Leonore Davidoff of the University of Essex; Dr. C.S.L. Davies, Archivist of Wadham College, Oxford; Mrs. Dianne Foster, local historian, Llandrindod Wells; Michael Gray, Administrator of the Merchant's House, Marlborough; Mrs. Hood of Clyro Post Office; John Hudson, editor of the Bristol Diocesan Newspaper; Ian Knight of the Victorian Military Society;

Michael Marshman, Local Studies Librarian, Trowbridge Library; Dr. T.K. Maurice, who helped to fill in the history of the Baskerville family in Wiltshire; Joan Phillipson of Historical Research Associates (Belfast); Chris Price, Local Studies Librarian, Brecon Library; Canon D.T.W. Price of Lampeter College; Mary Roberts, local historian of Rockley, Wiltshire; Matthew Steggle, Archivist of Trinity College, Oxford; John Till of the Shrewsbury Historical Society; Philip Walmsley, local historian of Stroud; Dr. John Wroughton, formerly Headmaster of King Edward VI School, Bath; staff of the National Library of Wales, the British Library, Lambeth Palace Library, the public libraries of Lincoln, Bristol, Hereford, Trowbridge, and of the universities of Leicester, Cambridge, Nottingham, Bristol, and of the Archive Offices of Hereford, Lincoln, Llandrindod Wells, and Trowbridge.

Preface

It fell to William Plomer to 'discover' Kilvert's Diary in 1937 when, as a publisher's reader, he was sent two old notebooks by the Diarist's nephew, Perceval Smith. He was immediately struck by their quality and recognised that they were the work of a man of unusual gifts. He sent for the remainder of the notebooks—22 of them in all. They contained, he wrote, 'a detailed picture of country life in the 1870s which is, so far as I know, unmatchable. It is a perfect piece of social history ... and is the work of a rare and graphic artist'.[1] Plomer made a synopsis of the notebooks and they were published in three volumes in 1938, 1939 and 1940 by Jonathan Cape. They were welcomed by the public from the beginning.

The published Diary is, of course, only a fragment of the original. The two typescript versions Plomer made of the whole work were lost—one when the offices of Cape were destroyed in the Blitz, the other thrown away by Plomer when clearing out his house. The manuscript meanwhile had passed from Perceval Smith to his sister, Mrs. Essex Hope, who told Plomer one day that she had destroyed it because of its private nature.[2] Between five and six notebooks, in addition to the 22 Plomer received, had already been destroyed by Kilvert's widow, because, it is assumed, she did not wish entries dealing with his relationship with other women to be seen by anyone else. Our picture of the Diarist would have been much more complete if all of the original Diary had been published. Plomer estimated that it would have amounted to well over a million words, and he underlined that it is through the Diary that we can get to know Kilvert; it is, he said, 'his own monument', there he 'speaks for himself'.

The Diary is in part a random collection of what are often trivial events, dictated by the passage of time. When Kilvert paused in one entry to ask himself why he kept his Diary, he justified his effort by the modest claim that even his 'humble and uneventful life' should have some record, 'which may amuse and interest some who come after me'.[3] The remainder of the entry, however, indicates that it was also his intention to provide a record of a community whose existence was represented by the country house. His concern was prompted by his strong identification with that community and his awareness that it was threatened by change. Many Diary entries go beyond casual jottings; they are very full and show signs of careful shaping. It is clear that Kilvert must have taken detailed notes of some events while they were happening or as soon as possible afterwards, to be worked up in a considered way during many evenings. The result is an elaborate, sustained view of life, and a kind of narrative of his own life in which he can be discerned pursuing a dream of happiness symbolised by a notion of 'home'.

In the absence of family papers that would provide the basis of a conventional biography, I have exploited the Diary itself as the major source of insight into Kilvert. It is, after all, a very large document and constitutes a full statement by the Diarist himself of his experiences and views on a wide range of topics. It is from the Diary that we learn what experiences moved him to joy, anger, indignation, and tears. In order to make those responses more coherent, I have shown their origins and the way in which they make connections with each other, with other sources of information about Kilvert's life (principally the memoirs of his father and his sister, Emily), with events that he witnessed, and with things that he read. His responses have been placed within their contemporary context in the belief that that is the means of understanding them better. His background and education have been explored, as well as his relationships with a number of people who had significant meaning for him. Some examination is made of literary and artistic influences on him, including the part played in his life by certain 'heroes'. A number of chapters explore his attitudes to certain key aspects of life—property, politics, national education, manliness, and country house society.

From its first publication, an important element in the Diary's appeal was the way in which it revealed, as The Observer put it, 'a character ardent, likeable, and now and then of quite unlooked-for complexity'. In 1945, the critic and historian, A.L. Rowse, was observing: 'What is the secret of Kilvert? Ah! - if only one knew that... But there, Kilvert has this mark of genius, among others, that he has the faculty of making us insatiably curious about him. We want to know all about him...'.[4] My book is an attempt to reveal, if not the 'secret' of Kilvert, which in any case does not exist in one particular fact, at least the major factors which together constitute his 'unlooked-for complexity'.

'Robert Hewitt was a young farmer of the old school; honest, frugal and industrious; thrifty, thriving and likely to thrive; one of a fine yeomanly spirit, not ashamed of his station, and fond of following the habits of his forefathers, sowing his own corn, driving his own team and occasionally ploughing his own land. As proud, perhaps, of his blunt speech and homely ways as some of his brother farmers of their superior refinement and gentility... To the full as proud as any of them was Robert, but in a different way, and perhaps a safer'.

M.R. Mitford, *Our Village*, p.266

[The landed interest is] 'a partnership not only between those who are living, but between those who are living, those who are dead, and those who are to be born'.

Edmund Burke, quoted in F.M.L. Thompson, *English Landed Society in the Nineteenth Century*, p.6

'The possession of land is the guarantee of respectability, and the love of respectability and land is inveterate in our race'.

T.H.S. Escott, 'England: Her People, Polity and Pursuits, 1879', in *Culture and Society in Britain 1850-1890*, edited J.M. Golby, p.27

PROLOGUE

The World of Sleeping Beauty: Kilvert Enters Chieflands

Kilvert's account of his visit in May 1876 to the small farm of Chieflands, near Corsham, Wiltshire, occurs well into the published version of his *Diary*. Over 1,100 pages of it (out of a total of 1,300) precede the Chieflands account yet so central is it to the way he saw his society that it might have introduced the whole work. He was born in 1840 and when he became a curate to the Rev. Richard Lister Venables in the Welsh border village of Clyro in January 1865, that society, remote as it was, was changing. One writer on Kilvert, Laurence Le Quesne, attempted to draw closer to his experience by living for some years in the house occupied by the Diarist in Clyro and by seeing 1870 events in the *Diary* through 1970 eyes. Discussing Kilvert's world on one occasion with friends who, like Le Quesne, were roughly of the Diarist's social class, Le Quesne found that they all hated their own society. Behind their antipathy lay two main reasons: 'radical insecurity on a global scale, and ugliness'. An element in the former was the Cold War but there was also their awareness as upper middle-class professionals that the status of their class had declined. Kilvert, they recognised, was accorded much more automatic respect for who and what he was. Their effort to explain their feeling that his world was a 'paradise', and their nostalgia for it included the rationalisation that in spite of its disease and premature death, it represented 'a stable historical order',

1

whereas they enjoyed health in 1970 but lived within 'a total historical uncertainty'.[1]

Kilvert, indeed, found his world a paradise but in his perception of
it there was anxiety, a consciousness of turning away as many modern
readers of the *Diary* do from their own time and society, a deliberate,
if temporary, living in the past. The modern reader is very aware that
Kilvert's society has gone. When Kilvert became curate in Clyro, part
of it had already gone and other parts were in the process of going.
The second Reform Bill of 1867, which gave some urban workers the
vote, the 1870 Education Act, and the establishment of a trade union
for agricultural labourers in 1872, were some of the factors in the
change. The mystery as to why Kilvert suddenly began keeping a diary
in January 1870 may be explained, at least partly, by a need he felt to
record a traditional society that was changing forever, as though its
passing could thereby be arrested for a while so that he could savour
it longer. How far that need was conscious is an open question. His
Diary suggests that he felt relatively at ease with his society and
contemporary evidence indicates that society felt at ease with itself.
1850-1865 was a period of calm and there was an acceptance by 'the
greater part of every particular social group of a hierarchical social
order', though certainly some social hostility was repressed.[2] People
continued to be deferential to their social superiors. Bagehot was
saying just before the second Reform Bill that Britain was the
supremely deferential country.[3] A modern historian, however, noted
that in 1867, 'the surface of things could seem almost intact'.[4] He also
observed that if one lived in the country it was much more possible to
believe in social harmony because the landed gentry still controlled
the countryside. He warned too that the England of the mid-1870s
was vastly different from that of the 1850s and even the 1860s. In the
1850s, he noted, overmuch confidence was placed in the virtues of
independence and energy as means to solve social problems, whereas
from the 1860s onwards the role of central government increased
and with it the role of the professional bureaucrat, who saw much
more clearly the need to reform such institutions as elementary and
public school education, the civil service, the universities, and the
army. As the power of the Church and of the aristocracy decreased,
that of the press, the professional bodies, and the trade unions
increased. Kilvert himself reflected the change in his highlighting of
the arrogance and amateurishness of generals in the Crimea and of

administrators at home.[5] At the time of the Crimean War, Oakfield, the hero created by W.D. Arnold, one of Dr Arnold's sons, was stating firmly: 'Social Reform is becoming the cry of the world'.[6] By the time Kilvert died in 1879, progressive rather than conservative opinion was influencing political events.

In May 1876, therefore, when Kilvert walked to Chieflands through the Wiltshire countryside that had exploded into the glorious fresh greenery of spring, his mind may have been unusually conscious of change. As it happened, various things that day had reminded him of change and mortality. He had received news that one of his favourite patriarchs had had a seizure and Kilvert went that afternoon to see how he was. Another old farmer, Austin, was also seriously ill and Kilvert went by Hardenhuish village, the site of his own old home, to check on his condition. There he learnt that his old nurse had had to be taken to Devizes lunatic asylum. The visit to Austin at Corsham may have put in Kilvert's head the idea of visiting the nearby Chieflands, where the Frys, relatives of Mrs. Austin, lived. In the second volume of the *Diary* he had already introduced the Fry family, who lived at this ancient farm.[7] On 17 October 1872 Kilvert, who had by then left Clyro to help out again as curate to his father at Langley Burrell, Wiltshire, met old Isaac Giles, who had known Kilvert's grandfather, Squire Coleman. Kilvert was proud of his genteel forbears but was particularly proud of the quality that Giles found in Squire Coleman. He was a very plain man, he told Kilvert, 'there was no pride about he'. The Squire used to rail against the pride of mere farmers, Giles recalled, and it was then that he reminded the Diarist that there was one local farmer left who was free of that sin—Mr. Fry of 'Clievelands'.[8]

The Frys, John (aged 64 in 1876) and Mary Ann (aged 58), were brother and sister. Their parents had lived at the farm before them and they themselves had lived all their lives there. This sense of continuity and indeed of timelessness permeates Kilvert's account of his visit. Circumstances combined to induce in him a readiness to find deep joy in everything he experienced. The contacts he had with country folk prior to arriving at Chieflands were all pleasing. The labourer who gave him directions to it was very courteous; the boy who came by with a pitchfork on his shoulder was whistling cheerfully and Kilvert could hear the voices of people engaged on their farming tasks. All was colour, light, and fragrance. The May sunlight imparted a golden glow to the scene. The spring foliage had a wonderful richness and the meadows were green and gold. The sun was 'a mighty minstrel playing upon a beautiful instrument a sweet melody and harmonious air'. Bluebells had never appeared so beautiful before with sunbeams filtering through 'skylights' in the foliage to tip 'the rich and heavily hanging clusters of bells with a brilliant azure gleam and blue glory'. Kilvert saw it all with 'the heavenly alchymy of a quiet eye and contented mind', and by the time he reached the farmhouse his responsiveness to it was heightened. It seemed to fit into the landscape as though it too had simply grown there over centuries. He had expected to see something squalid and run-down but he beheld 'a tall fair mansion, that had once apparently been the residence of a gentleman and lord of the soil'. The house was to some degree decayed but this was an essential piece of its charm.

Decay characterised the farm too. Details of neglect proliferate through Kilvert's description of it. The orchard was overgrown and the garden 'lay waste, overrun and trampled down by a multitude of fowls'. Flower beds were devastated and farm buildings 'strange and deserted'. Pigeons were everywhere. Yet on a 'ruinous wall... sat a magnificent peacock which would have adorned the terraced lawns and gardens of a palace'. The fairy-tale note struck by this last detail is the key to Kilvert's vision of Chieflands for it conveys the timelessness which he loved to discover in English landscape. Time at Chieflands had come to a stop: 'The whole place bore a strange quaint old world look which took one back a hundred years. The Sleeping Beauty might still be sleeping there and waiting for the magic touch and kiss of the Prince. It looked like a place that had been forgotten and left unvisited for a hundred years. And meantime life had gone sleepily on and the people of the farm had moved about the yards and fields and ploughed and sowed like figures in a dream'. Kilvert included the fairy-tale convention of natural creatures, in this case guinea fowl, which are gifted with speech and call out a warning, 'Go back, go back', to the tale's hero. Nothing threatens here, however, nor is Kilvert likely to wake the place's inhabitants from their congenial dream into some unwelcome, alien reality. He is given an extravagantly warm welcome by Mary Austin, niece to the Miss Fry (Mary Ann) of Chieflands. The latter is herself a figure from a folk-tale: she was a 'stout middle-aged woman in a russet-brown working dress, [with] a round weather-beaten good-humoured face...'. She was in her working dress even though Mary Austin and her niece, Ada Collett, had been invited there for their dinner and their tea. Kilvert was invited 'very courteously' into the parlour by Miss Fry but he insisted on going into the kitchen where the rest of the company were sitting. As he sat on the oak window seat he observed all the 'motley assemblage of living creatures' outside waiting to be fed, and the servant girl preparing tea (she, like Miss Fry, is another timeless figure, who could have graced a prosperous farm any time in the previous 400 years).

The talk concerned one of Kilvert's favourite topics—Squire Coleman, his maternal grandfather. In the *Diary*, he regularly forms a contrast with the then current Squire Ashe of Langley Burrell,[9] who seemed to possess the cold and tyrannical nature of his forbears who had bitterly opposed the marriage of their daughter, Thermuthis, to (Squire) Walter Coleman. Walter's marriage to her was in fact an unhappy one but that did not seem to affect his dealing with other people for he was known for his kindness and warmth. Kilvert referred to him as 'a good and easy landlord'.[10] Kilvert was reminded as he sat waiting for tea at Chieflands that the farm had been in the Coleman family since the reign of Queen Anne. The link between it and the Colemans went back further than that: an indenture of 1620 shows it passing into the hands of William Coleman of Hullavington.[11] Another, dated 9 April 1847, records its sale by Squire Coleman, Kilvert's grandfather, to Joseph Neeld of Grittleton House, Chippenham. John Fry's father, Edward, had been tenant since very early in the 19th century. Miss Fry complained that the current owner, Sir John Neeld,[12] did no repairs to the place. Her brother praised Squire Coleman for the consideration he had shown them when they were *his* tenants. He used to worry about the state of their crops at time of drought because their soil was light and well drained.

John Fry's appearance is conveyed in the phrases that Kilvert reserved for the sons of the soil he so much admired: 'He was a tall stout fine-looking man, black-haired, with a smooth face and a quiet pleasant countenance... very fond of all his pets and dumb creatures, fowls, rabbits and pigeons'. His father had sat, crippled with rheumatism, for so many years by the fireside that his feet had worn two holes in the stone of the kitchen floor that went right through to the earth beneath. As he listened, Kilvert was moved by these 'simple family records' and the story they told of continuity and harmony, the 'quiet plaintive peaceful uneventful monotonous life in the old farmhouse in the fields generation after generation, the few cares, the simple anxieties, the narrow interests, the limited horizon'.

The even pattern of this existence had bred certain virtues in these people and the remainder of Kilvert's account of his visit to Chieflands makes clear what they are. 'How kind and courteous they were, the brother and sister with the simple graceful dignified patriarchal hospitality. "Please to make use of what there is in our poor way. You are kindly welcome"'. They were not gentry yet their manners lacked nothing in terms of gentility. The hospitality they offered amounted to very little but he felt as honoured as someone would who had been entertained with extreme sumptuousness.[13] Their essential grace did not derive from fine clothes, expensive furniture or a retinue of servants. Their modest, decayed country house could not have conveyed more of an air of venerable tradition than if it had been in truth a grand and imposing mansion. John and Mary Fry had communicated to Kilvert as great a sense of civilised values as he could have gained from the nation's noblest aristocrats, and it had been achieved without the scaffolding of wealth, rank and education. It had also been achieved without affectation, vulgarity and artificiality. Victorian society by 1876 was one of rigid class divisions and all-pervading class consciousness yet Kilvert had experienced an occasion entirely devoid of class tensions. The relationship between the Frys and their old landlord was potentially fraught with class tension and therefore destructive of social harmony. However, instead of a conflict of interests and a distance created by rank, there was interdependence and community. (In his poem 'Honest Work', Kilvert underlined 'The golden rule of neighbourhood - that each may share the common load', which demonstrated 'how hearts are linked to hearts by God'.)

The Frys come across as prime example of the yeoman farmer who was once a key element in agricultural society. Froude, the Victorian historian, traced the emergence of the independent yeoman: the medieval villein originally had no rights and was his lord's property; gradually custom gave him the rights of a free man; custom became law and villein tenure became copyhold tenure.[14] Copyholders were those with a lease on their property (ie. not freeholders), of which they held a copy. In a normal medieval village there would be the lord of the manor, freeholders, both large and small—known collectively as 'yeomen', copyholders, tenant farmers, cottagers, squatters, and farm servants. No clear distinction could be made between the small farmer, whether freeholder, copyholder or tenant, and the cottager because the cottager might own or rent some strips of land. A line could be drawn, however, between those who farmed and those who obtained their living by labouring. This situation lasted until the 18th century. 'The most important social fact about this system is that it provided opportunities for the humblest and poorest labourer to rise in the village'.[15] However, it was not a golden age because the village was under the shadow of the squire and the parson, and the farmers often tried to encroach on the commons. But the village was a community and each villager had some independence. It was, however, destined to change as a result of the Enclosure Acts, the urge for greater productivity, and the desire of men with new wealth for country estates. The yeoman class experienced its highest point in terms of status and independence around 1650. The freeholding yeoman tended to disappear in the 18th century, to be replaced by the three tier system in which landowners leased farms to tenants, who in turn employed labourers.[16] Gone was the paternal concern that was a feature of the previous structure. Capitalist agriculture had arrived and paternalism was in retreat.

The landed class in which the yeoman had his honoured place was hierarchical but before the 19th century the sense of divisions was softened by its common interests, harmony, and relative absence of a hard, materialist outlook. For Kilvert, John and Mary Fry represented the survival of these values, which had apparently flourished most strongly some generations before but were still felt to be a force in the time of Squire Coleman. Various tributes have been paid to yeomen as a group. Colloms wrote of the pre-enclosure yeoman, owning a plot of land which he worked with no other labour than his own family, and enjoying a large measure of independence. He might prosper, employ labourers and live the life of a gentleman.[17] The independence shown by these small landowners included a resentment of the great.[18] In the 19th century the press was usually hostile to farmers as a class, making little distinction between the size of tenant farmers' holdings, although those with the largest acreage did merit special attack. The freeholding farmer, or yeoman, however, generally had a good press. This may have been due to the fact that his kind had been dying out since the 18th century and the attitude to him contained an element of nostalgia.[19] For Colloms, his demise had far-reaching consequences for village life. Since he had 'the instincts of the good steward', taking care of his land and buildings, he passed on an improved asset to posterity. He was above the exclusive concern for profit that dominated life in the town. He was the kind of farmer that the older type of squire favoured and when he passed, the change 'broke the large and durable social relationship between yeoman and squire'.[20] Of the small proprietors in the rural community none worked harder than the yeoman. He had to possess great physical toughness because essentially he was a labouring farmer and had to be capable of the great variety of jobs on a farm. He had to be very disciplined over the long hours the work required and had to have frugal habits.[21]

John Fry, farming the 84 acres of Chieflands,[22] did not have the full independence of the yeoman in that he was a tenant rather than an owner-occupier. Nevertheless, he symbolised the type well enough because he farmed the land himself,[23] cared deeply for it, and regarded it primarily as a source of income rather than of status. Moreover, for centuries the word 'yeoman' covered both tenants and owners.[24] Kilvert's own home county of Wiltshire was not, in fact, rich in yeomen. It was notable rather for the number of its great estates (those in excess of 10,000 acres; yeomen's holdings were generally between 1,000 and 100 acres). Wiltshire also came high among English counties in terms of numbers of aristocratic mansions and of peers. The other 'Kilvert' counties of Herefordshire and Radnorshire came well below Wiltshire in these respects. These facts supply some corroboration for the view, expressed by the Kilvert scholar Frederick Grice, that Kilvert was not as happy in Wiltshire after leaving Clyro because he was aware of 'certain social tensions' that did not exist on the Welsh border.

The most overt statements in the *Diary* about social injustice occur when Kilvert had returned to Wiltshire society and Grice saw these as evidence that Kilvert was troubled by the intolerance and lack of generosity of the upper-classes there, and drew attention to the high-handed Squire Ashe of Langley Burrell as compared with the apparently genial and tolerant Squire Baskerville of Clyro.[25] Certainly the Welsh border area showed features that differentiated it sharply from Wiltshire. Raymond Williams, who was himself a Welsh border man and deeply aware of its special character, underlined the special place in the development of agriculture held by all border areas. They resisted longer than other areas the pressure exerted by agrarian capitalism towards the aggregation of land into the hands of a few landlords and the reduction of workers into wage labourers. What is found in those regions is 'a relatively isolated rural community... conscious... of its hard but independent life'.[26] It was easier to resist that pressure in Radnorshire because the country was a mixture of arable and pasture and not, as large areas of Wiltshire were, predominantly corn country. Wales as a whole had been described as 'a bastion of peasant culture'.[27] Because its farms were small, generally family-run and raised all kinds of produce, they could the more easily survive hard economic times and the trend towards larger units. They not only employed fewer labourers than English ones on average, but retained longer the practice of boarding outdoor labourers. This resulted in a closeness of community and a relative absence of disaffection among labourers. These facts go some way to explain why Wiltshire and other southern English counties were centres of labourers' riots in 1830, whereas Welsh counties remained quiet. However, the Welsh border-land was not entirely free from social tensions: there was poverty and a demand for land aggravated by 'a cultural and political divide between landowners and peasantry'.[28] Many Welsh radicals believed that the backward state of farming was the result of the division between the anglicised, Anglican, and Tory landowners and their Welsh-speaking, Nonconformist, and Liberal tenants.[29] Kilvert's *Diary* records manifestations of that conflict, though he himself took every opportunity to underline the extent to which he valued the warmth of the Welsh people and felt at home among them.

Kilvert did write tributes in his *Diary* to Welsh farmers whose spirit and independence he admired; they contain much that is revealing about his attitudes to the land and to rural society. None of them, however, has the depth and comprehensiveness that make the Chieflands passage such a central and unique vision. Kilvert had several reasons for choosing John Fry's farm as its vehicle rather than a farm in the Radnorshire hills. Landowners on occasion elicited Kilvert's praise and he could have chosen any one of many as the subject of a portrait so full of love and respect as that of the Frys. Their houses were grander and more beautiful than Chieflands. His visits to Bowood and Yaverland,[30] for example, provided him with opportunities to describe picturesque settings and individuals whose authority and influence were at the centre of rural life. Those passages lack, however, the intimacy of the Chieflands visit; the dimension of people is absent from them. He was friendly for seven years with the very approachable Baskerville family of Clyro Court but did not single them out for special tributes.

It was the social relations of the people at Chieflands, as well as the people themselves, that were the focus of Kilvert's interest, and their house was important only in so far as it signified those relations. The interest derived from the intermediate position the Frys occupied between the larger landowners on the one hand and the mass of landless labourers on the other. What mattered about John Fry was the harmonious relationship that had existed between him and his landlord. It was obviously relevant to Kilvert that the landlord in question was his own beloved grandfather, Squire Coleman; Fry had had long, friendly and honourable dealings with one of his own. But Kilvert's involvement in that relationship went beyond that because his background included not only the landlord element but also the yeoman element. His great, great grandfather, Thomas Kilvert, was steward in the 1730s to the Lady of the Manor of Condover, near Shrewsbury. Thomas' forbears, back in the 17th century, were yeomen and his brother was a tenant farmer of a substantial kind. The relationship between Thomas and his employer was a close one with very little sense of subordination in it. She regarded him as a friend as well as an employee. His wife was in charge of the domestic routine of Condover Hall and worked at tasks that would have been familiar to Mary Fry.[31] One side of his ancestry, therefore, placed him firmly within the intermediate group of the landed interest. His involvement in and concern for the life of the land was thus reinforced by both sides of his ancestry. Being a country clergyman and the son of one also meant he was involved in country affairs. Ironically, it was by virtue of becoming, shortly before his death, Vicar of Bredwardine in Herefordshire that Kilvert himself became in effect a yeoman because with the position went certain freehold lands. He was quite pleased, too, to record that as a freeholder he could now be placed on the register of voters.[32] When his father wanted to find something complimentary to say about another clergyman, who was otherwise deeply unprepossessing, he found it natural to acknowledge that he was 'an honest yeoman-like sort of man'.[33]

The history of the yeoman, sketched in earlier, placed emphasis on his industry, independence and integrity. It was an honourable tradition and he had as much right to be proud of it as any social superior had to be proud of his. It was founded on solid worth whereas it was often the case that landlords had no real care for the land and its duties, or were over-conscious of their rank and status, and devoted themselves simply to the pleasures of their estate. Sir John Neeld, Fry's current landlord, was neglectful of the repairs needed at Chieflands.[34] It was the stewardship of the dutiful landlord and the yeoman farmer that gave rise to the notion that the landed interest constituted 'national civilisation' (the phrase was Disraeli's from a speech of 1843), and served causes above self-interest and profit. To Kilvert, the Frys were eminently 'civilised' even though they lacked the background that would have given them a higher form of taste and manners. They could rival the nobility in the pedigree of their virtues. 'Honour, dignity, integrity, considerateness, courtesy, and chivalry were all virtues essential to the character of a gentleman, and they all derived in part from the nature of country life'.[35] The Frys possessed all these virtues, which could be summed up as the qualities of 'heart'.

They had another virtue, too, which was legitimate pride. They and Kilvert knew about the illegitimate pride that made empty claims for recognition based on rank, family name, exclusive education, money and possessions. The yeoman traditionally deplored that kind of pride in aristocrats just as Squire Coleman deplored it in farmers, who based it on much lower claims. Kilvert, in his Chieflands account, had drawn attention to the 'strange quaint figure' of John Fry's brother from Bath who happened to be at the farm that day. He had been sitting for three hours in a ditch, gun in hand, hoping to shoot rabbits. The existing Game Laws prohibited John Fry from shooting rabbits or any other game on the land he rented, declaring them to be the property of the land's owner. What his brother was doing was, therefore, illegal and Kilvert probably knew it but declined to mention it as though he thought it a perfectly natural and right thing for a tenant farmer, or his brother, to be doing.[36] The Game Laws stood as the most glaring example of the false pride that arrogated the right to shoot game to a privileged few. Kilvert's visit to Chieflands was about to end when someone urged the company to go to the door to see the peacock with his tail full spread. 'Ah', said his mistress, 'this is his pride'. Neither she nor any of the others would have challenged his right to his pride.

The people of Chieflands and the society of which they were a part, represented the qualities of tradition, self-sufficiency, and harmonious interdependence. The beautiful spring weather of the Chieflands passage was a chance element that gave Kilvert the opportunity to include a picture of Nature in harmony with herself alongside the pictures of man in harmony with Nature, with himself, and with other men. It was the beauty and order of Nature that produced the 'alchymy' of the 'quiet eye' and the 'contented mind' that were both the means of realising the vision of Chieflands and the blessings of it. They themselves belonged to an earlier age which Kilvert, in company with many others, imagined was free from the strains and pressures of modern life. The source of inner calm was for Kilvert, as it was for Wordsworth, Nature. Apart from being, as he was, a lover of Wordsworth, Kilvert had discovered that he too obtained profound satisfaction from the river Wye to which Wordsworth had so often turned in times of depression. Wordsworth had written of how his 'eye [was] made quiet by the power/Of harmony, and the deep power of joy', and how 'the weary weight/Of all this unintelligible world' was lightened by it.[37]

The achievement of the 'quiet eye' and the 'contented mind' has proved elusive from the time of Wordsworth onwards. Matthew Arnold's 'Scholar-Gipsy' was seeking an escape from 'this strange disease of modern life' in 1853. Kilvert's *Diary* has offered, in addition to its other delights, an escape route from modernity to its readers ever since its publication in 1938. Its editor spoke in his Preface to the first volume of the way it soon became 'an escape route' from the 'public alarms and private anxieties' of the Second World War. It took its place, therefore, in a tradition of writing about the English countryside. Writers of the late Victorian and early 20th century period, by interpreting the countryside in particular ways, created a version of England which English readers have found significant and reassuring for well over 100 years. A gentleman farmer's house in Wiltshire fitted perfectly into this picture of England and was expressive of a certain kind of 'Englishness'. Within the picture '...the land, "peasant proprietorship", even country life itself, were coming to represent order, stability and naturalness... the country and country people were seen as the

12

essence of England... uncontaminated by... the false values of cosmopolitan urban life'.[38] Even the name of Kilvert's Wiltshire farmhouse, 'Chieflands', becomes symbolic in relation to these understandings. An important part of what its culture stood for was a certain kind of classlessness, which is part of its political dimension. Inequalities did exist in rural society, of course, but the fact that the different groups which made up the landed interest were involved in the same activities, had lived for generations in the same locality, and had reciprocal obligations, meant that the divisions among them could be transcended more easily than those of urban society. It was just this sort of classlessness which was claimed for foxhunting by its defenders. Kilvert often celebrated it when he described social events in the country in which all classes participated in apparent harmony.

It is not accidental that this vision of a harmonious rural England takes on the associations of a beloved home where one could be totally at ease, nor that it is located in his own home county. Chieflands, above all, was a home, and the nostalgia for it, inextricably linked as it was in Kilvert's mind with his own forbears, was a nostalgia for childhood, which was of profound importance for Victorians. The historian Houghton spoke of the way love of Nature merged for them into a nostalgia for 'a lost world of peace and companionship, of healthy bodies and quiet minds', as memories which most of them had of country life took on increased importance during England's transition from a rural to an urban society.[39] Williams noted that the idea of 'country' is so often an idea of childhood and, furthermore, that 'the common image of the country is now an image of the past', and represents a pull towards 'old ways, human ways, natural ways'. That was, in essence, the appeal to Kilvert of Chieflands and the Frys. By contrast, the pull of the city is towards 'progress, modernisation, development'.[40] The tension is very clear in *The Wind in the Willows* where Rat, Mole and Badger stand for the country whereas Toad, while still nominally a squire, has irrepressible leanings towards such toys of progress as motor cars and aeroplanes.

Howkins, a modern historian of the countryside, found that the 1870s, the period of Kilvert's *Diary*, were significant as the time when a tradition of writing was established which habitually represented the country in a nostalgic way. However, he was aware as Williams was, that the tendency to develop an image of an idealised rural past pre-dated that time. Literature abounds in pictures of earlier, happier rural England but establishing a clear point where it existed proves difficult; it depends where one stands on the moving 'escalator' (Williams' word) of time. There had, nevertheless, been a transfor-mation of rural life but it took so long, was so complex, and varied from region to region, that it is impossible to locate a simple point where it occurred. But that finally becomes unimportant, as Williams pointed out; what is important is the fact of the reaction, its nature and the reasons for it. This is one of the ways in which Kilvert's *Diary* is important and interesting. It exhibits in the Chieflands passage the idealisation of 'an order based on settled and reciprocal social and economic relations'[41] in which feudal values loom large. It is no coin-cidence that so many idealisations of the rural past focus on the period when the capitalist agrarian revolution was changing the tradi-tional order. Cobbett, for example, who was a boy in the 1770s, wrote of that time: 'In the whole world there was not so happy a country as England was'. There was the reassuring continuity that marked Chieflands: 'Men lived in the same cottage from the day of their marriage till the day of their death. They worked for the same master for many years... without any legal engagement and without any other dependence than that occasioned by respect, and goodwill'.[42]

Central to the nostalgia was a notion of an ideal village community that partook of the nature of myth. 'To say it was "myth" is not to say it was all false; rather, it is a montage of memories...'.[43] When Flora Thompson wrote of the existence in her village of ancient rhymes that would have 'spoken to the discerning... of an older, sweeter country civilisation than had survived', she was adding one more memory to the montage.[44] When the Sleeping Beauty of Chieflands fell asleep, to remain preserved for Kilvert's pleasure and reassur-ance, it was also the 1770s, the time of his grandparents.[45] As Chieflands drowsed through its never-ending afternoon, he was inclined to overlook its neglect and decay,[46] as modern readers of his *Diary* can overlook the harsher realities of Clyro and Langley Burrell. Obviously the contrast between a pre- and a post- agricultural revolu-tion farm can be exaggerated and the older institution romanticised out of all proportion. It is noticeable that from the idealised rural community that Kilvert presented, one important group was missing—the labourers on whose labour the whole structure rested.

They are taken for granted.[47] That Kilvert characterised Chieflands as 'a tall fair mansion... once... the residence of a gentleman...' is another indication of his desire to idealise it. It was important for him to establish that John Fry was a gentleman. The farmhouse is certainly a substantial one, a 'mansion' it is not.[48]

Kilvert was one of many who, living in the country and loving its ways, tried to believe that it hadn't changed, yet every time they asserted the superiority of country life over that of the town, they acknowledged that it had. The possibility, raised and given specific focus in the Chieflands passage, of being able to hold back time, receives more general expression in the *Diary* as a whole. The one is a microcosm of the other.

'A very little literature, and a modicum of classical learning, went a long way'.

Mark Pattison, writing of the qualifications needed to establish an Oxbridge reputation in the early years of the 19th century, *Memoirs*, p.69

'I have but little to record about my life at Oxford. It was very uneventful. Probably few undergraduates spent the three or four years in a more quiet or even course'.

Robert Kilvert, *Memoirs of the Rev. Robert Kilvert*, p.58

'To what stratum of society the undergraduates of any college belong... what social status they maintain - this is the most patent fact about any college...'

Mark Pattison, writing on Oxford in 1830, *Memoirs*, p.17. He became a student at Oriel two years later

'The Victorian middle-class... was ridden by fear: fear of radical politics (manhood suffrage as well as socialism) because it threatened the bourgeois state of 1832; fear of atheism because it might dissolve the moral sanctions on which society rested; fear of sensuality because it threatened the family'.

W.E. Houghton, *The Victorian Frame Of Mind, 1830 - 1870*, p.398

CHAPTER I
Kilvert and his Father

Social harmony was not a feature of Kilvert's background; conflict was an inescapable element of his father's world, both local and national, though one would not think so from his account of his times. This chapter draws out some key elements of Kilvert's family background principally by focusing on the religion, the education, and the society that shaped his father, for Kilvert was very deeply influenced by him and he remained a hero to him throughout his life, even though Kilvert was aware of his faults.

Robert Kilvert was born in 1803 and grew to maturity in the difficult years that followed the end of the Napoleonic War in 1815. 'We lived', he recalled, 'in... Widcombe, a pleasant and populous suburb of Bath, in Caroline Buildings, a row of houses fronting South Parade...'. He knew from the beginning that the family was poor as a result of the double blow of the failure of his father's coachbuilding business and of the bank in which his father's and his grandmother's money were invested.[1] This lady was grandmother Kilvert, not the haughty Madam Ashe of Langley Burrell, who had disapproved highly of her daughter's marriage to the genial Walter Coleman. Kilvert dwelt a great deal in his *Diary* on his Coleman roots and particularly on the way Walter was resented by the Ashes, who were extremely conscious of their social standing. The Kilvert family's poverty explains in part why Robert Kilvert was sent in March 1811 as a day boy to King Edward VI Grammar School in Bath.

There were at the time several schools in Bath offering blends of commercial and classical education designed to appeal to farmers and tradesmen. Robert's father was a tradesman but he sent Robert and his eldest brother, Francis (who was 11 years older), to a school for gentlemen. After his years as a pupil there, Francis became an assistant teacher to King Edward's headmaster, Nathanael Morgan, who had died a short time before Robert was entered. '[Morgan] had been a Fellow of King's College, Cambridge, and of course an Etonian', Robert recorded in his *Memoirs*, 'and was considered an excellent scholar'.[2] In noting that Morgan was 'of course an Etonian', he was registering a pattern of which most gentlemen would be aware: King's College had been founded at the same time as Eton and only Eton boys could become its Fellows. Together they signified social exclusiveness. Morgan had become headmaster of King Edward's in 1778 during Bath's heyday as a fashionable resort, and one of the school's historians noted that he was responsible for the 'pinnacle of prosperity and fame' that it reached.[3] Morgan's father was an Etonian and he too had enjoyed the comfort and prestige of a Fellowship at King's. It was so important for Morgan junior to obtain a Fellowship that he actually started at Trinity College, Oxford, while he waited for the vacancy that would bring him one. Fellowships were awarded not to the ablest Eton pupils but merely the oldest and were worth £3,000 in the middle of the 19th century. They were widely recognised as sinecures. Morgan's success in managing King Edward's can be seen chiefly in changing its social ethos from that of a grammar school into that of a minor public school. The school's charter stated that the incomes from its property should provide for ten poor boys of Bath to be admitted without fees.[4] Robert might well have qualified as one of those poor scholars but there had been none at the school for generations. Instead of the mixture of sons of tradesmen, farmers, and minor gentry that had traditionally attended grammar schools, the boys of King Edward's in 1811 were 'from the county families as well as from the professional ranks of the neighbourhood'.[5] Robert noted that 'some of the boys were rather low class, and their grossness was something horrible'. He also referred to the moral depravity of the school (his phrase was 'atrocious evils').

Morgan's policy of maintaining a totally classical curriculum and a predominantly boarding establishment would have discouraged local farmers and tradesmen from sending their sons to the school. He had copied Eton by having a boy deliver an annual oration in Latin on the occasion of the swearing in of the new Mayor of Bath.[6] It had become common at this time, when social classes were pulling apart, for status-conscious parents to transfer their sons to schools where only fee-payers were admitted.[7] Morgan's successor, the Rev. Thomas Wilkins, emphasised the 'convenient accommodations for numerous boarders' in his reply to a questionnaire about endowed grammar schools in 1816, the year Robert left. The dormitories were in fact grossly overcrowded and there was one outdoor toilet for 100 boys.

However helpful Morgan had been to boys struggling with learning, Wilkins was a man of a different mould.[8] He had not flogged anyone during his first weeks as headmaster, Robert observed, but on the latter's second day as a pupil, Phipps Major felt Wilkins' 'swishing strokes on his naked skin' for the crime of singing.[9] Robert conceived a terror of Wilkins that haunted him for the rest of his life. He froze when his turn came to say his lesson and made mistakes for which he was severely flogged. That, and the sight of boys being flogged for such trivial offences as singing, were the basis of his awareness of 'the sad mismanagement of justice towards boys' displayed by the regime. He managed, however, to turn that feeling of resentment into a morally beneficent experience, declaring that the beatings did him 'an immense deal of good' because the public shame involved made him determined that he would never again be guilty of the offence that provoked them. It was a stance that was part of the age and was adopted by many, though not all. It is of some significance that in the recurrent dream that Wilkins inspired in him, he had become Wilkins' curate and the brutal headmaster was preparing to flog him in front of the congregation because he had lost the place in the service, as he used to lose it in his lesson book. The dream bears close resemblance to the one that his son, the Diarist, had in relation to his vicar, the Rev. Venables (the second dream is dealt with in a later chapter). In both there is a terrifying, righteous authority figure, a failure to perform a social duty, and a shameful, public retribution. In important ways, the ethos of King Edward's was representative of these things—it stood for the traditional authority of a ruling class and for the education that confirmed its right to rule.

Robert spent five years at the school. In assessing its influence on him several factors need to be borne in mind. The most obvious is that he was just seven years old when he was first left by his father to face 'the vortex of dust and noise' of the school-room. One enduring impression was the general wildness of the place. We hear of 'barbarians' and 'barbarism', of 'hurly-burly', of boys wrestling, of floggings and injustice. One of the school's historians noted that bullying and fighting were rife. Robert found it intimidating and looked forward to holidays. The fact that he noted the presence of some lower-class boys indicates his awareness of the superior social tone which the school had cultivated. New money from trade and industry was, in this period, demanding a voice in the education of its sons but King Edward's had elected to serve those who belonged to, or aspired to belong to, traditional 'good society'.

Robert was removed from the school in 1816 probably because he was unhappy, and went to the school run by his brother Francis at Claverton Down, Bath. The Kilvert family's need for money prompted Francis to set up his own establishment as soon as he was able. He had also recently become curate at Claverton. Robert recorded that he was 'truly glad... of the change to my brother's study, and the quieter and more humanising life there'.[10] Perhaps another reason for Robert's removal from King Edward's was that he wasn't learning. He remarked that he made 'some considerable progress' under his brother's instruction, so much so that at the age of 15 he had himself started to tutor boys who were the results of his brother's contacts.

He learnt from his brother the value of useful social connections. It was the influence of two of his brother's friends that secured him a scholarship to Oriel[11] and he was learning the importance of being a gentleman and of mixing with gentlemen. He was impressed by the social eminence of some of his brother's pupils and by the fact that through them he himself met 'some of the leading people of Bath'. His own pupils were well-to-do. He enjoyed his visits to the Marriotts, friends of the Kilvert family, who lived in nearby Claverton. Mrs. Marriott was 'of the old school, refined and autocratic', her son was Rector of Claverton, the daughters were 'used to the best society', and the younger sons were 'thorough gentlemen'. Robert's private tuition was grounded on knowledge of the classics and he recalled being flattered that, young as he was, his 'aptness for Latin and Greek' helped him to win pupils and ensured that he was 'deferred to beyond the common'. Furthermore, his scholarship was, he recognised, the reason for his being able to mix with the Marriott sons and other young men. Ultimately, it was the means by which an Oxford education came his way and that, of course, would set him up for life. On a knowledge of Latin and Greek rested the entire claim of Francis Kilvert, Morgan and Wilkins to wealth, respectability, status, and authority. It was that background and his respectability which enabled Kilvert the Diarist to obtain his position in Clyro with the

Rev. Venables. It continued to be, virtually till Kilvert's death, the mark of distinction which separated the gentleman of traditional mould from inferior beings who might challenge his position.

Robert's experience at his brother's school and as a private tutor confirmed an aspiration already present in his family background to identify closely with the gentry class: in that direction lay his future and his hope of establishing his own fortune and re-establishing that of his family. Social connections were to be the means of realising these objectives. There is a strong awareness in Robert's *Memoirs* of influential, often titled personages, who might prove to be the source of patronage.[12] King Edward's had played a part in developing this awareness, as had the genteel city of Bath. By 1822, when Robert was about to go to Oriel, it was a town of faded gentility; the wealthy and fashionable had deserted it for Brighton and it had become middle-aged and middle-class. It continued to be prosperous but its wealth had little to do with trade or industry.[13] It is easy to see why in some ways it suited the Kilvert family. However, not even Bath was immune to the enormous social changes going on in the rest of the country. A commercial spirit, which was the inevitable accompaniment of industrialisation and capitalist agriculture, permeated society, and in the middle-classes coalesced with a passion for respectability.[14] Wealth, said the writer John Sterling in 1828, was the god of the early 19th century. 'There never was a time when it was so necessary for comfort... To succeed in life is to make a large fortune...'.[15] To be unsuccessful was to be poor and despised. There was a mania for 'getting on' and a new phenomenon—social mobility. The Kilvert family was caught up in the rush to establish respectability and its sons knew that their duty was to fend for themselves in a highly competitive world, (there had been six sons apart from Robert but two had died by 1819). A society had developed that was 'all elbows, jostling, pushing, snubbing, presuming'.[16]

Oriel College, which Robert entered in late October 1822, was one of three that made some efforts to raise the academic standards of the university (the others were Balliol and Christ Church). For the most part the other colleges functioned as they had in the 18th century when 'professors who never lectured, tutors who never taught, students who never studied, were the rule rather than the exception'.[17] Studies were still regulated by Elizabethan statutes that were totally out of date, and examinations had become empty rituals. The manners, morals, and sports of students were barbaric. Courses had something to offer only to those intended for the Church or the law. 'Heading the college undergraduate lists were the noblemen and gentlemen—or fellow-commoners... —a tiny minority of privileged students, who dined at the high table, hired the cocklofts for their servants, were exempt from the vulgar scrutiny of college and university exercises, and received honorary MAs after a comparatively brief residence'.[18] The conservative state of the university was largely the result of its being the preserve of the clergy, who provided the heads, tutors, and Fellows of colleges.

Robert Kilvert's account of his time at Oriel College is a painful one, shot through as it is with the awareness, in both social and intellectual terms, of his own unworthiness. From the moment his journey to Oxford began he was reminded of his lowly social position. At Cirencester, his coach was kept waiting two hours, as it always was, for the arrival of the Duke of Beaufort's letters. On arriving in Oxford, he was pleased to find an old school friend, who invited him to his lodgings. However, Robert couldn't help noticing that his friend measured out tea 'very sparingly from the caddy with an extremely small teaspoon'. That sort of invidious comparison was more worthy of Oxford's supercilious scouts and bedmakers, who often sneered at students who lacked the means to live with some style, than of a gentleman. Robert had gone to university backed by what he called 'a valuable exhibition' but it is evident that he had to live a very frugal existence. He had been warned by his eldest brother before he went of the danger of giving wine parties he couldn't afford and gave none, refraining even from buying himself decanters or glasses, and went through his entire college life without drinking a single glass of wine. The strictness with which he observed his brother's advice and refrained from indulgence indicate an Evangelical streak that seems to have been part of him when he went to Oxford. Perhaps he also recognised that it would be unwise to be seen as competing socially with his wealthier student colleagues.

The business of rank dominated Oriel life. The College records show that he was entered as a 'Bible clerk'. Bible clerks had been for centuries part of the Oxford scene and were poorer students willing, in exchange for lower fees, to perform Bible readings and other duties during chapel services. Even lower categories of students had existed earlier, who actually waited on those of superior social status. By the end of the 18th century, however, these had been abolished and Bible clerks occupied the lowest place in a college's hierarchy. Out of a total of 300 students at Oriel over the years 1818-1830, Robert was one of nine Bible clerks. In addition to paying lower fees, they also paid only £10—whereas all others paid a minimum of £30— in 'caution money', a sum exacted by the College as insurance against student debt or damage. It did not accord with Robert Kilvert's sense of status to record those facts. That he felt able to despise the unscholarly Latin pronunciation of the Oriel tutor, Hawkins, who conducted him through the oath-taking ceremony, compensated a little for these petty humiliations, though doubtless he felt guilty about it. After the ceremony was over, the satisfaction he felt on having become 'a member of the first university in the world' included the sense of having been admitted to a club distinguished socially as well as academically. Nevertheless, his lodgement in the club was a very inferior one. 'The only accommodation I could get was two very miserable rooms at the top of a winding staircase, close to the college bell, which rang with deafening noise four or five times a day'.[19] His inferior accommodation was the result partly of his not being able to afford anything better, though it may also have denoted his status as a Bible clerk. There certainly was severe competition for places. Behind his own observation that he was fortunate to get in, lay an awareness of Oriel's reputation, both social and academic. Mark Pattison, who went there shortly after Robert left, described it as 'a fashionable college, the resort of gentlemen of old family', and its popularity was confirmed by Thomas Mozley, who was for four terms a fellow student of Robert.

The scholarship that enabled Robert to go to Oriel was the result of a recommendation by a friend of his brother Francis to John Keble, one of the College's tutors, and it was awarded by Copleston, the Provost. Copleston was an outstanding Latin scholar, becoming an Oriel Fellow at the age of 19. He came from one of the oldest landowning families in Devon. The seriousness and discipline of Oriel's High Church tutors owed something to the influence of Evangelicalism, which had already had a profound impact on society by the time Robert went to Oxford.[20] We have no evidence that indicates a specific source of Evangelical influence on his family that he might have assimilated in his youth. However, there are grounds for believing that the family would have been very likely to have adopted that religious outlook. In its early years, Evangelicalism was contained within the Anglican Church but long before the end of the 18th century a group had split off which adopted the name of Methodists and achieved a particular following among the working-classes. Those who remained in the Church were called Evangelicals and they felt a special mission to convert the upper-classes to piety. The movement made most progress among the middle-classes, which had adhered to religion in the 18th century when it was in decline.[21] It was very popular among merchants, manufacturers, professionals, and farmers, and some of its main supporters came from the upper middle-class.[22] Its appeal lay in its emphasis on individual spiritual salvation and moral duty during a period of enormous social unrest and anxiety, when industrialism and radicalism were challenging traditional social values.

It is possible that the turning point in the attitude of the Kilvert family towards religion was the bankruptcy that blasted its fortunes in 1794. The father of Evangelicalism, William Wilberforce, had produced his *Practical View of the Prevailing Religious System of Professing Christians in the Higher and Middle Classes* in 1797 and it immediately became a best-seller. Bishops, aristocrats and royalty heaped praises on it. Its message was that most people were Christians in name only, content merely to attend church and observe the outward forms of religion. In reality being a Christian involved hard discipline, a concentration on the inner spiritual life and on values that should permeate every aspect of daily living. Its appeal was partly a matter of timing: 'It was written by a national figure at a time of national emergency. Disaster had followed disaster in the continental war and the French had rejected peace on any terms that could be acceptable'.[23] Beset by fear and the prospect of sterner tests ahead, the nation was ready to turn to religion. The suspension of all payments by the Bank of England just prior to the book's publication, with all the direct relevance which that event bore to his own personal case (his bank too had failed), could have been the clinching factor that influenced Robert's father to take up religion with renewed fervour. The concern of most professing Christians was, Wilberforce insisted, with temporal things; the true believer learnt to make light of 'the buffets of fortune'. It is not hard to imagine a bankrupt tradesman finding in such notions deep comfort, a renewed sense of personal honour, and the discipline to face family duties. The ethos of Oriel College confirmed and deepened that influence upon his son.

Evangelicalism was an element in the movement for reform but where it attracted the support of the clergymen it often took the form, as it did in the case of Copleston, of a renewed emphasis on the importance of traditional institutions. A student of his observed that the atmosphere of Oriel in the early years of the century inclined to Conservatism, which was 'rather the fashion among our best-bred and best-connected men'.[24] Conservatism marked the outlook of most of the other tutors during the period in which Robert was a student. John Keble is described by the *Dictionary of National Biography* as 'a tory of the old school'.[25] Though unprepossessing in appearance, voice, and manner, he nevertheless inspired reverence in Robert, who noted his reputation for 'talent and excellence of character', and his aura of 'simple goodness'. It was he who urged Thomas Arnold, a Fellow of the College, to give up 'reading and controversy' and to take up 'holy living' as a curate in a parish.[26] Robert's tutor was Edward Hawkins and he, too, recommended to students the acceptance of traditional belief and avoidance of intellectual controversy. Though basically a kind man, he was dull and authoritarian in outlook. Newman, another Oriel tutor, said of him that 'he could not endure free and easy ways' and any show of humour 'produced a strange rigid expression in his face'.[27]

Robert's account of his own intellectual progress gives clear insights into the nature and quality of the education provided at Oriel. It is evident that students were not always inclined to take their studies seriously. There were men 'who were up to anything in the way of frolic and irregularity', and he distanced himself from them as he did from those who declined to attend dutifully to the mechanical tasks he found satisfying. One was the weekly essay, or 'theme', to be written in either Latin or English on a prescribed topic. Each Thursday, the best essay of the previous week would be read by its author before the whole College, who had been led in procession to the Hall for this purpose by the Provost and Fellows. When the student had read his essay, 'he walked up through the thronged benches to the Provost and presented his composition to him... This was much thought of and I repeatedly had the honour of reciting my essay in this somewhat formidable presence'.[28] His reverence for Oriel's rituals contrasts with the attitude of Mozley, who remarked that in his time only a handful of students took pains with their themes.[29] He also applied himself conscientiously to an even more limited intellectual exercise: the summarising of the daily sermon that was required of all students. Most of the students resented the sterility of this exercise, too, especially because, as Robert admitted, its chief purpose was to secure attendance at chapel. He, however, 'took great pains with it', and valued the approval he gained from tutors 'as something really worth having'. It seems he had the task, as a Bible clerk, responsible for what he called 'the discipline of the chapel', of noting the names of absentees. He found 'disgraceful' the way other students cribbed notes made of the sermon by one of their number who had attended church.

There is a distressing, servile quality about Robert's deference to the authority of the College and to its rituals and demands. The reasons for it lay in his extreme nervousness and uncertainty, his humble social position (relative to that of fellow students), his religious outlook, and his need to make a success of his university career because of financial problems at home. The distance between teachers and taught, the relatively empty nature of tasks imposed on students, and their formality, all compounded the authoritarian ethos of Oriel during Robert's years there.[30] The weekly staple of 'lectures' made a significant contribution to this ethos. A 'lecture' took the form (in classics) of the explication of a text by a tutor. Students were asked in turn to construe part of the chosen text but the learning of the tutor was paramount. 'Lectures' were, therefore, designed so that authoritative readings could be laid down. In addition to dry, narrow studies, authoritarian teaching, and a fear of ideas, there was emotional frugality, for the Oriel tutors were men of such seriousness that they 'so suspected feeling that they appeared at times to have no religious feelings'.[31] Robert's attitude to them was generally one of awe. Keble was the most likeable and approachable but Robert was overwhelmed, he said, by 'the smallest note of approbation' from him. His sense of unworthiness, loneliness, and homesickness produced a crisis in the lecture room: 'One day at lectures a feeling of desolation and misery came over me so powerfully that I almost fell off my chair'.[32] He had not been able to afford the private tutor that was essential to compensate for the university's inadequate tuition and he missed the close supervision of his brother. He had 'read a great many books' but his studies lacked guidance and structure. After a week of exams, he was 'sick in head and heart', and his career at Oxford culminated in a nervous breakdown and a third class degree instead of the first he had, somewhat optimistically, hoped for. This was source of deep disappointment to him. He was a highly-motivated, hard-working, and serious student, whose respect for Oxford could not have been greater, but its system failed him, though his failure was due in part to faults in his own nature.

His dutiful application to his duties as Bible clerk and to his work must have appeared to some students like toadying to the authorities and would have set him apart from them. His lack of money and his own personality—nervous, easily overawed, deferential to a fault—meant that he was an outsider socially, so that he could assert, almost with pride, that he had 'one or two friends, very few acquaintances', and had spent no time 'lounging in other men's rooms'. No less than three of William Wilberforce's sons were college contemporaries and one wonders whether any were his 'acquaintances', in spite of being his social superiors. To give no wine parties, and to refrain even from taking a single glass, must have made him contemptible for, as Pattison observed, 'it belonged to the commoner of Oriel to invite his friends to drink wine with him'.[33] But, of course, Robert was not a commoner but a despised Bible clerk, at the bottom of Oriel's social hierarchy. To the gentlemen-commoners at the top if it, he would be a social cypher, worthy only of their scorn, whilst they, in turn, excited his condemnation for their unprincipled behaviour. It is characteristic of him that his reference to students' moral laxity is limited to horse-play in the lecture-room and the cribbing of sermon notes. He omitted to mention the dissipation of the College's wealthy set, which had become a blot on its name before his course ended. Mozley thought that they were 'perhaps as bad as any in the University'.[34] One of their leaders was James Howard Fitzharris, later Earl of Malmesbury; another was Sir Charles Murray. Both were in the College for much of the time that Robert was. 'We were a merry set of fellows', wrote Murray, 'fond of singing late into the night over suppers'.[35] Newman complained to them about their conduct but was in a very difficult position partly because he was the most junior tutor, but chiefly because the aristocratic group was favoured by both Copleston and Tyler, the Dean. He was especially appalled at the contempt they showed towards the compulsory end of term communion when some of them were, on occasion, drunk.

In this ethos, any man from a humble background might easily be intimidated, even if he had a confident, dominant personality, which Robert certainly had not. But what became of the humanising influence exercised by his brother, Francis, at the Claverton Down school? Where was his own love of literature, his passion for the novels of Sir

Walter Scott, during his years at Oriel? When he criticised his fellow students his target was not their lack of 'inner life', or of a feeling for beauty, or of intellectual curiosity, for which Pattison criticised them. It was not even their rowdiness, childishness, and dissipation. He found fault only with their failure to show proper respect for authority, their refusal to conform. The fact that the institution in whose name respect and conformity were demanded was, to a high degree, shallow and heartless, was irrelevant. So, too, was the fact that its highest authorities shamelessly pandered to the spoilt, arrogant sons of gentry families. These young men insulted Newman, both in and out of the lecture room. What humiliation was inflicted by them on the mere Bible clerk, and what contribution did it make to his 'desolation and misery'?

One bitter irony in Robert's situation was that he had always identified himself closely with the country house society represented by Oriel's gentlemen-commoners.[36] The 'nice, well-appointed' country house had, he wrote, 'through life been to me like a second home', and he expressed delight at the 'liberty to roam, gun in hand, through well-stocked covers'.[37] No one knew that experience better than Fitzharris, whose father, the second Earl of Malmesbury, was one of the most fanatical game-preservers in the country. He had started his game book in 1798 and maintained it for the next 40 years, and when he closed it, boasted that he had shot 54,802 head of game on his estate. His well-stocked covers no doubt kept his son amply supplied at Oxford, whose tables were, in any case, 'loaded with game, and a young man is told he may have as much as he please from the college kitchen...'.[38] The contribution made by the Earl's son to the country house ethos of Oriel ensured that it was, for Robert, a bleak social environment in which to grow. His son, the Diarist, shared his love of the country house but he, too, was to find that it did not always provide hospitality for the human heart.

Robert had not looked forward to an intellectual awakening at Oriel, and certainly did not experience one: 'it was very uneventful', he noted in his *Memoirs*. The only praise he bestowed on a tutor was in recognition, not of intellectual, but of moral gifts. If the implicit pressure of Oriel was not the Evangelical one towards a life of seriousness and pious activity, it was the worldly one towards social ambition and social pleasures. He himself resisted the coarser appeal of the latter and plodded away at tasks that had changed little in the previous 50 years. He accepted them as he accepted without complaint or criticism the authority of his tutors. Acceptance of all lawful authority, irrespective of its integrity or justice, was a central Evangelical doctrine and he had shown an adherence to it at King Edward's School in Bath. To the individual bent on piety, there was valuable discipline in acquiescing to harsh authority, as there was to irksome tasks.[39] The son of the Bath coachbuilder had to accept at Oriel subordination and even humiliation that was different only in degree to that suffered by the poor scholars at King Edward's who were made to sit in a wooden pen by a headmaster (Wilkins' successor) who justified his policy by declaring that 'Pride and Tyranny are in continual action in those of superior Rank, Fortune or Strength... Most men who have been at a public school will know this to be true'.[40] Morgan had learnt this truth at Eton and it came to dominate his school. Fitzharris had learnt it there too and carried it with him to Oriel. Robert's religion also told him to despise pride and tyranny in those of high rank,[41] but because he needed to establish a career for himself in the class-conscious world of the 1820s, in which social connections were everything, he was forced to submit to them.

Thus, in the father's early life was established a tension that was to dominate the experience of the son. Both accepted and admired aristocrats as the natural leaders of society and were keen to see that leadership continue, but at the same time they could be critical of rank and had to suffer its arrogance. Kilvert in the Chieflands passage was attempting to determine the proper place for pride and an acceptable relationship between those of high rank and those who were lower in the social scale. However, change was in the air, driven by increasing criticism of Oxford's outdated practices. Such reforming spirit as existed in Oriel was directed at revitalising the Church so that it could retain its power and increase its effectiveness as a force making for stability and order. Hawkins and other Oriel tutors were at one with Copleston in believing that the Church was 'the cement of the whole social structure'.[42] One would never have guessed from Robert's account of his student life that any part of the social edifice stood in need of pointing.

He was perhaps a good example of the young man, pictured by G.M. Young, who attained his majority in 1831 with the ground rocking under his feet. Revolts had broken out all over Europe. 'At home, 40 years of Tory domination were ending in panic and dismay;

Ireland, unappeased by Catholic Emancipation, was smouldering with rebellion; from Kent to Dorset the skies were alight with burning ricks. A young man looking for some creed by which to steer at such a time might... hold by the laws of political economy..., he might simply believe in the Whigs, the Middle Classes, and the Reform Bill; or he might, with difficulty, still be a Tory'.[43] One looks in vain in Robert's *Memoirs* for a reference to any of these events and movements. The chief explanation for their absence from his record of the period lies in its atmosphere which, as Young noted, was more powerful than any particular set of political beliefs. A young man then was likely to find himself 'at every turn controlled, and animated, by the imponderable pressure of the Evangelical discipline...'. This was the situation of Robert. He was no more a political animal than was his son and, one suspects, found little difficulty in spite of the tumultuous times, in retaining his Tory certainties. They, in combination with a naturally retiring, rather timid personality and a religion which had its focus firmly on personal salvation, kept him from close involvement with the affairs of his society. His Oxford education had also contributed significantly to that state of affairs.

Oriel, like all Oxford colleges, had church livings to bestow, but Robert had to look elsewhere for preferment. It was through a good word spoken on his behalf by an old Oriel friend that he obtained the curacy of Keevil in Wiltshire in 1827. Its circumstances exemplified much that was wrong with the Church before the Reform Bill. 'The incumbent, a Canon of Winchester... had never resided, and (good easy man!) allowed the outgoing curate to recommend his successor'.[44] Kilvert had found that 'good' and 'easy' expressed precisely what he admired in his grandfather's attitude as a traditional landlord. Robert's Oriel friend was known to the curate, who was happy to accept his recommendation. Robert's comment, 'good easy man!', indicates his uncritical acceptance of the practice by means of which a man of influence could be incumbent of several livings (as Morgan of King Edward's was), pocket their stipends and pay curates a fraction of them to perform their duties. While Robert seemed to accept that he would have to spend some years as one of the Church's lowly paid drudges, doing what Sidney Godolphin Osborne, clergyman and fierce critic of the 19th-century Church, called the 'slop work' of the profession, it is clear that he felt some resentment of his situation in Keevil. In that respect, too, he had been let down by an aristocratic Church. He complained '...there was no one... to give me the smallest scrap of direction'. He recorded that in addition to the 500 souls in that parish, there were 300 in the hamlet of Bulkington, one and half miles away, who were also his responsibility. Furnishing the small vicarage, which he received rent-free in addition to the stipend of £70 a year, absorbed all his meagre savings. 'Of course we could not have lived on the proceeds of my curacy',[45] he observed, and proceeded to do what scores of other impoverished curates of the time did—he took in pupils. Robert had embarked on his career in the Church.

His approach to his parishioners was the Evangelical one that had been encouraged at Oriel. His *Memoirs* recount his satisfaction at occasions when the sick and the dying embraced religion. Mozley had remarked on the influence on his Oriel contemporaries of Wood's *Death-bed Scenes and Pastoral Conversations*, a book seen by young men intended for the priesthood as a 'promising novelty' because it filled a gap in the Church's resources.[46] It is likely that Robert learnt of this work before he left Oriel. A typical example of the pastoral experience in which he delighted was the case of a local farmer's wife whom he had visited many times during her bouts of illness. She had always coldly rejected his ministrations but on one occasion she begged his forgiveness for her former behaviour. He 'cried and sobbed unrestrainedly' as he went home through the fields, so grateful was he to have been the means of reconciling her to God.[47] To the man of simple piety, spiritual conversions of this kind were always going to be of supreme importance.

Their importance was communicated to Kilvert partly through his father's sermons. After one of them, Kilvert remarked that hearing him was like hearing 'a spirit preaching without a body'.[48] Robert's text on this occasion was 'Wisdom cries aloud in the open air' (Proverbs 1.20-22) and its theme is the need to hear warnings about sinful lives because 'I in my turn will laugh at your doom ... when terror comes upon you'. Rejection of sin and the quest for spiritual grace was a regular theme of Robert's sermons and in this he was thoroughly Evangelical for Wilberforce had laid down that 'man is tainted with sin ... radically and to the very core'.[49] Among texts Robert chose were Matthew 8.11-12: 'give us this day our daily bread, forgive us the wrong we have done'; Ecclesiastes 9.6: 'For the dead, love, hate, ambition are all over' (the text just before this states 'the hearts of men are full of evil'); Psalm 25.10: 'All the ways of the Lord are loving and sure to men who keep his covenant'; preceding verses refer to the Lord teaching sinners the path of righteousness. One sermon of his father's which Kilvert found particularly 'beautiful and touching' was from Luke 18.9 on the Pharisee and the Publican. The former boasted of his respectability while the latter acknowledged his sinfulness. Kilvert continued: 'When he spoke of the Fountain of Blood over which is written for ever "Wash and be clean" the tears were in the preacher's eyes and trembled in his voice and I think some hearts in the Church were not unmoved nor their eyes dry'.[50] In these moments we see exemplified the 'religion of the heart' in whose precepts Kilvert was raised. It formed the basis of his simple piety as it did his father's. It was responsible for, among other things, Kilvert's impatience with theological debate. Because such debate was, as he saw it, irrelevant to the prime purpose of religion, he found it a waste of time, just as he did discussions about church ceremony. While a curate to his father in Langley Burrell, he attended a meeting of clergymen on proposals to change the rubrics of services, and though he noted that others were interested, he found the proceedings 'rather futile'.[51]

In his remark about the disembodied nature of his father's sermons may be discerned a recognition that his father's piety was of a purer, more strictly Evangelical kind, than his own. This is in some measure the deference that a son was expected to show to his father but it also underlines that Robert belonged to an earlier time when the need for a religious and moral regeneration was felt to be that much greater. Nevertheless, it is clear from the *Diary* that Kilvert too had assimilated all the basic precepts of Evangelism, as later chapters will show. Though he brought a human, sympathetic approach to his parishioners' problems and their spiritual journeys, sin remained a terrible reality for him all his life and he never lost sight of the importance of repentance and of the need to remind himself and his parishioners of it. (In his poem, 'Pandora's Box', Eve's eating of the fatal apple is seen as a day of 'ruin, grief, and dark dismay' and the source of all human ills). He rejoiced when he came across cases where individuals had triumphed over sin. While a curate in Langley Burrell, he chose at an evening lecture to read from an account of 'John Wesley's Cornish preachings and John Nelson's conversion told by himself from *Mrs Kitty Trevelyan's Diary*'.[52] When John Ducket, an octagenarian parishioner died, Kilvert remembered that 'he was wild when he was young, but after the change came over him he was quite an altered man'.[53]

In his concern for a very young female parishioner can be seen both the kindness and gentleness characteristic of him but also the relentless determination to play a full part in her struggle against what was probably sexual promiscuity. It was Boxing Day 1874 when he heard that the condition of Hannah Williams had worsened. She had slipped and injured her back carrying a bucket of water and Kilvert saw in her accident retribution for her sinful ways. He visited her in the morning first and 'the proud haughty beautiful face was laid low at last and flushed with pain ... the poor wild beautiful girl is stopped in her wildness at last and perhaps by the finger of God'.[54] He sat by her bedside repeating the hymn 'Sun of my soul' in the afternoon and made a third visit that evening. The next day he went before church to see how she was, while in the afternoon he spent more than an hour constantly turning her in bed in an effort to make her more comfortable. He talked to her 'very seriously about her past wild conduct' the following day, and stayed for a long time reading several texts among which was Keats' 'St. Agnes' Eve'. (This was highly characteristic of Kilvert; that romantic, sensuous poem in which a beautiful girl escapes from tyrannical and decrepit authority into the arms of her passionate lover would not have figured in his father's repertoire of texts for sinful young girls, but Hannah was young and attractive and Kilvert was always susceptible to female beauty.) Almost daily visits continued until the middle of January. On the 14th, he took her hand in his and 'looking earnestly and lovingly upon her I said "You do like me a little bit, don't you?" ... "Yes", she said ... "You will try to be good and steady now, dear, won't you?" "I will try", she said humbly but firmly'.[55]

Kilvert made use of her affection for him in his effort to shame her into repentance. For him, as for his father, shame played an important part in a sinner's spiritual journey, as did the thought of punishment. This is well illustrated in the dream Robert had during his schooldays at King Edward's, Bath. Kilvert's firm belief in the value of whippings and the attraction it held for him may have had its origin in his early experiences at home and at school. His *Diary* contains numerous references to whippings and towards the end of a life that was destined to be short, he mused half-seriously on the perennial nature of 'that threatening promise - "I'll whip your bottom"'. The phrase in that form was, he thought, 'probably as old as the English language and in some form is perhaps as old as the world'.

In the *Diary* the bottoms that suffer chastisement are always those of young girls and it is evident that Kilvert experienced much guilt over his desires in this regard. On one occasion a pretty girl whom he had put on a swing, slipped forward off the seat and, wearing no drawers, her bottom was exposed to view.[56] He delighted in her 'plump and smooth' flesh, which he declared was 'in excellent whipping condition'. However, he also felt a pang of guilt because he had hurriedly placed her on the swing and had left her clothes pulled up round her waist. The accident had revealed his desire.[57] At those moments in the *Diary* when awareness of his own sinfulness emerges explicitly, the connection between it and his attraction to young girls is often made clear. One Sunday in March 1873, he wrote; 'The madness, cloud and delirium ... has passed away at length. "And it came to pass that when the devil was gone out the dumb spake". I can write again now'.[58] His activities the previous day suggest the reason for the guilt that he felt that Sunday. While visiting parishioners, he had caressed and kissed three girls and witnessed the bathtime of several others. At the end of it all, he was exhausted 'with different emotions'. Another entry reads: 'Though I be tied and bound with the chain of my sin yet let the pitifulness of Thy Great mercy loose me'.[59] Again, the clue to the sin lies in the rest of the entry, which concerns a pretty girl in a carriage whose hat was set coquettishly. 'The old, old story,' Kilvert commented.

The guilt he acknowledged in these passages seems excessive if only lustful thoughts of girls were involved. A constituent element of the mysterious sin may have been masturbation, which provided relief from his erotic experiences. Exacerbating his guilt too was his strong sense of the sexual innocence of women, especially young girls. He had assimilated the image of the 'pure woman', as well as the associated notion of the uncleanness of sex, that were widespread in the years during which he grew to maturity.[60] In his attitude to his mother and sisters there is a consistent note of reverence. He was often attracted to pretty girls in classes he taught, the prime example being 'Gipsy Lizzie' in Clyro. He sought to counteract the keen awareness he had of her 'indescribable beauty' by praying that she should 'grow up as good as [she was] fair'.[61] In the masturbatory fantasy he wrote up in his *Diary* about a Clyro farm girl, the guilty pleasure of dwelling on her 'bosom that heaves half-uncovered' was balanced by the earnest hope that she remained 'ever good ... pure and true'.[62] This tension is clearly evident in the entries concerning Hannah Williams and other attractive girls.

Just as he could see in Hannah Williams' illness punishment for her sin, especially the sin of pride, so he had a tendency, as many clergymen (and others) of the period did, to see poverty as a consequence of it and this made him more accepting of poverty. Material success, conversely, could be viewed as proof of living a good life, and those who failed to achieve it could find in poverty a beneficial discipline in the search for salvation. Sin was certainly a real issue for Kilvert in his own spiritual struggle. One Monday in July, with the weather searingly hot, he was sitting reading under a tree. 'As I sat there my mind went through a fierce struggle. Right or wrong? The right conquered, the sin was repented and put away ... And I thought I heard the harps of the angels rejoicing in heaven over a sinner that had repented'.[63] He does not explain what the sin was but a factor in his state of mind may have been guilt at being thus idle when others were working. In the entry for the following day, when again he sat under a tree reading, he found that he was driven to pity 'the poor haymakers toiling in the burning Common where it seemed to be raining fire'.[64] Kilvert believed that both poverty and hard work were necessary if one was to lead a Christian life. In his poem 'Honest Work', which he copied and passed out to the labouring poor, he talked of the value of the 'school' of work, of how Christ worked as a carpenter, and how therefore 'toil is sanctified'. God was 'ever looking on, counting all the toil and cost'.

But this is to look ahead at Kilvert's ministry; more needs to be said here about his father's early years as a curate in Wiltshire. When Robert accepted the Keevil curacy, he was very aware of its difficulties. Rural Wiltshire was not an easy place for clergymen at that time. Relationships among landlords, farmers, and labourers were under great strain because of the recession that followed the boom years of the Napoleonic War. Unemployment, hunger, and poaching were widespread; the poor rates soared. In 1824, labourers' wages were at their lowest point in the period since Waterloo. Fear of workless labourers had led to the brutal Night Poaching Act of 1816, which prescribed seven years' transportation for the taking of a rabbit. Sir Samuel Romilly called it 'a cruel absurdity' and expressed concern at the increased class antagonism to which it would give rise: 'The game laws have the effect of exciting a ferocious spirit not only among the lower-classes but also among those in the higher walks of life'.[65] The only hint of local tension to be found in Robert's *Memoirs* is the reference to 'broken windows at the Vicarage, and the need of fire-arms', but he attributed this to clergymen's wives interfering too much in the lives of labourers.[66] Cobbett, who was touring southern counties in this period, thought Wiltshire labourers 'the worst used... on the face of the earth', and said he had never before witnessed human wretchedness to equal theirs.[67] A harsher regime had been introduced in Wiltshire jails as part of the increasingly severe repression being brought to bear on the nation's labouring population in order to discourage revolution.[68]

Wholesale revolution did not come but 22 southern and eastern counties witnessed the rising of labourers that became known as the Swing riots, and Wiltshire was one of the worst affected. Crime had risen ominously in those counties in the period 1819-1829, whilst 1829-1830 saw a huge increase in crimes of arson, a clear index of labourers' discontent. Game law offences, another such index, reached a peak nationally and in Wiltshire at this time.[69] Rioting began in Kent in June 1830 and reached Wiltshire by November. With the destruction of their property staring them in the face, the squires of Wiltshire were suddenly queuing up to insist that their labourers, whom they had kept on starvation wages for 20 years, had to be paid 10s a week. *The Times* for 29 November 1830 declared that oppression of the peasantry arose 'from the endeavours of men of property to squeeze out of the bodies of the labouring population a larger share than justice or humanity would have permitted on the general profits of land and labour'. Kilvert's grandfather, Walter Coleman, and Thomas Clutterbuck, a Widcombe neighbour of the Kilverts, promised labourers at Christian Malford that they would receive the rise in wages they requested. The riots were suppressed everywhere with vindictive ferocity. The Wiltshire judge sentenced 50 labourers to death, 150 to transportation, and 46 to prison.

All this was happening while Robert Kilvert worked away in his Keevil parish, but he preferred to record other events which for him had more profound implications—occasions when his parishioners repented of their sins and embraced God. However, his failure even to register the Swing riots is intriguing and requires exploration. His son did make one reference to them: Squire Ashe, he wrote, had led a nocturnal patrol to frustrate machine-breakers, '45 years ago',[70] but the *Diary* entry is the excuse for him to tell a funny story about an old man out at night collecting straw who was mistaken for a machine-breaker. It is more understandable that the younger man, for whom the event was distant, should have seen it in terms of a bit of comical, local history. His father's case was different. It is inconceivable that the riots did not impinge on him in his work because he was surrounded by labourers and their families and would have been aware of their poverty and misery. In the nearby parish of Melksham, for example, 50 single men were working for 8d a day each prior to the riots—a circumstance that found its way into *The Times*. The clergyman of that parish was not only one of Robert's 'chief acquaintance', as he put it, but one of the two landowners who exploited these unfortunate labourers was almost certainly the Mr. Long whom he referred to as his local landowner.

In spite of this, the sensitive, anxious, young curate stated that the five years he spent in Keevil were ones 'of great happiness generally'. Shortly before he left there in the summer of 1832, a period of enormous agitation over the Reform Bill, he found things 'going on pleasantly and smoothly'. Why this insistence on internal and external calm when two of the most violent convulsions of the age were shaking society to its foundations? He left Keevil because the new vicar intended to reside in the parish and he chose to go to nearby Melksham to become curate to the Rev. Hume, who was, as he was, of Evangelical bent. The signs for a happy stay seemed, therefore, propitious, but in a mere three months his health collapsed and he left. 'The work was too much for me', he recorded vaguely, which seemed odd because he had coped for five years in Keevil alone and with a large work load. It seems very likely that for one of his temperament and beliefs, the events of the Swing uprising would have proved all too disturbing. He may actually have had his authority challenged by disaffected labourers.[71] The riots, especially in combination with the revolution signified by the Reform Bill, when traditional aristocratic leadership was challenged, may have produced a breakdown similar to that which overtook him at Oriel, where again he had been subjected to experiences that threatened his personality and beliefs. The fact that his *Memoirs* end abruptly at 1832, and that we have little information about him between then and 1835, lends weight to the idea that the breakdown he suffered was serious.

No doubt his Evangelical faith kept him going then as it did in the difficult Keevil years, but the social and political events of the 1820s and 1830s were at the same time especially taxing for men of his kind. The Evangelical revival had been in part a reaction to the French Revolution, which served as an example of what could happen when people strayed from the path of righteousness, ignoring the duties of their class and challenging the authority of aristocracy and Church. Political conservatism was a key feature of all Evangelicals, who tended to see matters of wages, unions, political rights as manifestations of spiritual corruption and lack of piety. 'What is socialism', asked one Evangelical preacher, 'but opposition to all moral and religious control?'[72] Evangelicalism appealed to a wide spectrum of society because it reflected the fears and aspirations of the age and Robert and his father may have been drawn to it along with many others anxious about a society undermined by so many new forces. Population increase, the factory system, demands for reform, the huge growth of towns and cities, class conflicts—all contributed to social unrest.

To the Evangelical mind, the panacea for these problems was for each individual to live a more pious life, to fulfil punctiliously the duties prescribed for one of his class and to exert moral influence in his own circle by example. A concern with politics was a distraction from all of this. The letters of another Evangelical Wiltshire clergyman, the Rev. William Money, indicate how it was possible to ignore most political events: they contain no reference to Peterloo, the Swing riots, or the Reform Bill. His wife, Emma, remarked that elections were not for the pious clergy. However, local newspapers reveal that, in common with other north Wiltshire clergymen, William was a supporter of the anti-slavery movement. He chaired a meeting in Calne on 7 November 1830 that had the object of petitioning the government for the abolition of slavery. A month earlier there was a meeting at Melksham of Friends to the Abolition of Negro Slavery with Robert's friend, the Rev. George Hume, in the chair. Robert himself was not present at either meeting. Emma also exhibited the ambivalent attitude to the gentry that was characteristic of Robert and his son. On a visit to Cheltenham in 1824, she was censorious of its grand society while simultaneously enjoying mixing with it: 'Their dress, manners, and idle habits, to us sober people are really disgusting, and... what is of much greater consequence, sinful in the sight of God'.[73] Wilberforce, in his *Practical View*, had condemned the 'luxury' and 'frivolity' of the rich.

The contempt felt by Kilvert for the idleness and luxuriousness of the rich had its origins in attitudes such as these. The account of his father's education has shown how important it was for him to secure by hard work a position that would enable him to contribute to the family income. He could only deplore the irresponsibility and dissipation of the sons of landed gentry who dominated Oriel College. The ambivalent attitude of worthy middle-class families towards landed property was a notable feature of the period; it was to become more pronounced later in the century. Though land-ownership did not figure extensively in the middle-class scheme of things in general (though in fact for the Kilverts it had above average importance), it was a significant symbol for a class that believed whole-heartedly in the importance of property. The middle-class had other sources of wealth and would often despise income that proceeded simply from a rent roll. That was but one of the differences between middle-class and upper-class life which gave rise to a political stance among middle-class folk which defined itself by opposition to an aristocratic code of values. Basic to that opposition was disapproval of aristocratic extravagance and vice.[74] Families whose existence depended on moderation and industriousness were bound to look askance at lives marked by luxuries, gambling, and the reckless accumulation of debt, just as Robert disapproved of the 'neglected property' of the Hicks-Beach family in Keevil.[75]

If anything summed up Robert's stance both towards aristocratic excess and the disturbing changes going on in society, it was the Queen Caroline affair, which was the only political event on which he commented. It came to a head in 1820 and centred on whether the King would recognise the woman he had married but had grown to hate. She was backed by Whigs who stood for reform and a majority of the common people. Robert was not only shocked by the 'nauseous divulgements' at her trial of her licentiousness, but at the fact that the press should report them in detail and thereby provoke civil disorder. He wrote of gangs of ruffians with the rallying cry of 'Queen, Queen!' attacking her opponents, indicating 'dangerous symptoms of disturbance throughout the country'.[76] To him, as to many others, cheap newspapers, which were one manifestation of democracy, were a counterweight to aristocratic power, and the more they revealed of the vices of the rich, the more that power was undermined. The affair was recognised, therefore, as a watershed between the old world and the new, and those of conservative mind, such as Robert, were afraid of the passions unleashed by it in the mob, of the erosion of authority, and of the power of the popular press.[77]

Many clergymen were setting up prep schools in the century's early years in order to catch the tide which flowed steadily towards a separation of classes that began with, and was confirmed by, separate school systems, which reflected the social relations existing between classes. By the late 1820s, education had already become of supreme significance in the rivalry between classes that was expressed through status and respectability. Schools not only reflected the hierarchical structure of society, but accentuated social distinctions.[78] Robert became part of this social process when he established his small private school at Keevil in 1827. At his brother's school in Bath, he had perceived the opportunities that existed to provide tuition for the aspiring upper middle-class. When he became Vicar of Hardenhuish (commonly known as 'Harnish') near Chippenham in 1835, he was able to set up a proper school in the Rectory specially enlarged for him by his patron, Mr. Clutterbuck, formerly his Bath neighbour, who had the living in his gift. Wealthy and influential, Clutterbuck had moved from Widcombe in 1822 and established himself in the grand Hardenhuish House. Once again, Robert's career had moved forward as a result of social connections. It was an important move, not because the living was a rich one (it paid little more than Keevil), but because it enabled him to contemplate marriage. He married Thermuthis Coleman in 1838, and Kilvert was born on 3 December 1840, the second of the Kilvert children, all of whom were born at Harnish.

Robert had attended two schools in Bath: King Edward VI Grammar and his brother's school at Claverton Lodge. The one he depicted as brutal and austere, the other as ordered and humane. Yet from the evidence of Augustus Hare, one of his Harnish pupils, the regime he copied was that of King Edward's. The links between the Hare family and the Kilvert family were deeper and more extensive than is initially apparent. The first was made in the 'lost' part of Robert's career between leaving his Melksham curacy, probably in autumn 1832, as a result of his breakdown, and spring or summer 1833. He would have been looking with some anxiety for a position in Wiltshire in which he might hope to recover his health and earn some money. He must have heard that a curate was wanted in the parish of Alton Barnes about 16 miles from Keevil on the other side of Devizes. The Rector there was Augustus Hare, uncle of the Augustus Hare who later became a pupil at Robert's Harnish school. The Rector had become ill in 1833 and it was felt he should winter abroad, so he left his rectory and 'a Rev. Robert Kilvert came thither as his temporary curate', in the words of the younger Augustus, who will henceforth be referred to simply as Hare.[79] Unfortunately, the Rector died in Rome on 14 February 1834 and, in a bid to comfort his sister-in-law, who was only 41, the Rector's brother promised she would become godmother to his own unborn child, who was named after her late husband. The child was born a month later and was actually given to his uncle's widow to bring up as her own. Thus, Mrs. Augustus Hare became Hare's adoptive mother, was always regarded by him as his only real mother, and will be referred to as such in what follows.

Robert probably remained at Alton Barnes only until a new Rector could be appointed but it proved important to have made the acquaintance of Mrs. Augustus Hare, who had married into a very well-connected family.[80] Kilvert recorded in November 1870 being told by Mrs. Venables of Clyro that Mrs. Augustus Hare had died and he observed: 'My Father I know will feel her death', so it is evident that Robert regarded her with some affection.[81] This affection origi-nated partly in the gratitude he felt at being offered the Alton Barnes curacy when he badly needed it and partly in the fact that she supported the school he set up in Harnish. When her son was nine, she sent him, accompanied by his two cousins, to Robert's school. The cousins, Marcus and Theodore, were the nephews of Julius Hare, Archdeacon of Lewes in Sussex and incumbent of Herstmonceaux, the family's rich living in that county.

Hare lived nearby with his mother; uncle Julius, who had a formi-dable reputation both as a churchman and an academic, deputised for his absent father. Julius had been the Cambridge tutor of F.D. Maurice, famous later as one of the Christian Socialists and had married Esther, Maurice's sister, while Maurice had married Julius' half-sister. Hare detested the religiosity of the Maurices, who went in for what he called 'an intensive life of contemplative rather than active piety'.[82] He believed that Christianity should manifest itself in good living, kindness to others, and not in inward-looking spiritual discipline. Esther and her sister were forever seeking out others' spir-itual faults, as well as their own. Hare felt more kindly disposed towards their brother, F.D. Maurice, whom he thought 'a truly good man', although he too was self-absorbed, always 'maundering over his own humility' and lost in mystical speculations. Hare's mother was greatly influenced by the Maurices, especially the sisters, who, Hare said, were 'a fearful scourge to my childhood'.[83] Esther was allowed to bully and harry him because Mrs. Hare had, under her influence, developed such an Evangelical mania, that she was convinced that he benefited from harsh treatment. She believed literally in turning the other cheek so that, if Esther abused her son, it was right that he gave her the chance to abuse him again.

Another scourge was uncle Julius, who possessed no tender feelings towards children and always spoke to them sharply. Hare's mother believed it necessary to break the will of a child and Hare, who had become particularly naughty as much out of sheer terror as anything else, was deemed by her to be in need of severe chastisement. Because she was terrified of over-indulging him, she accepted the savage floggings given him by Julius. From this picture of Hare's home life we can see what kind of boy he was, what kind of mother he had, and the attitude of mind he took with him to Robert Kilvert's school. Having met Robert in 1833-4 at Alton Barnes, and presumably recalling his piety and seriousness, when the time came for her son to go to school, Hare's mother chose Harnish as a place where he could experience further disciplining. Hare certainly believed that he had been sent there to cure his 'terrible fits' of naughtiness, partly on the urging of the Maurices.[84] He was taken there on 28 July 1843 and had his first taste of what he called its 'reign of terror'.

Hare described Robert in these terms: 'Mr Kilvert was a good scholar, but in the driest, hardest sense; of literature he knew nothing, and he was entirely without originality or cleverness, so that his knowledge was of the most untempting description... [he] was deeply religious, but he was very hot-tempered, and slashed our hands with a ruler and our bodies with a cane most unmercifully for exceedingly slight offences'. As a schoolmaster, he behaved exactly like Wilkins, the head of Bath Grammar. Although we have no evidence which suggests that Kilvert himself was ever beaten by his father, he nevertheless believed, as has been noted, that erring children should be subject to severe chastisement. He expressed hearty approval of a man, whom he thought might have been a gardener, exerting simple, direct parental authority by threatening to smack the bare bottom of his 12 year-old daughter in the street. On two occasions he expressed concern at inappropriate or excessive beatings of girls by their fathers. On another occasion, he was disturbed that a young girl was beaten by her brothers but he believed that she 'merited her flogging richly' and that 'her parents very wisely have not spared her nor the rod'.[85] Kilvert even offered to whip her himself. In addition to the prurient interest that is usually evident in these passages, there is a note of puritanical righteousness that stemmed from Evangelicalism and from the example of his father's school. Hare described the lessons as 'trash' and believed that, in this three and a half years at Harnish, he had learnt 'next to nothing - all our time had been frittered away learning Psalms by heart, and the Articles of the Church of England, ...Our history was what Arrowsmith's Atlas used to describe Central Africa to be... "a barren country only productive of dates"'. And, as was typical of many similar prep schools and public schools, the teaching of classics, their curricular jewel in the crown, was shockingly deficient: 'I could scarcely construe even the easiest passages of Caesar'.[86]

The contrast between this and what Robert himself tells us of the school run by his brother, who was a learned antiquary, and what is known about the latter as a man and a teacher could hardly be more obvious. He was very active in the Bath Literary Club, knew all about the city's literary associations and read papers on them to an appreciative audience. There was no reflection in Robert's teaching of his brother's love of literature or of the exchange of ideas. A former pupil of Claverton Lodge, Warde Fowler, described Francis Kilvert as a scholar and a man of letters, and as kindly and benevolent, though apparently austere. Fowler was in no doubt as to how different his school was from most private schools. There was an 'entire absence of the pressure of cramming'; instead there was a curriculum structured on the love of books and the well-motivated search for information.[87] Robert's model of learning, on the other hand, was the authoritarian one of Mr. Gradgrind; all imagination and pleasure had been excluded from it and there was an emphasis on facts, rote learning and drills.

Some Kilvert scholars have cast doubt on the accuracy of Hare's picture of the Harnish school. Lockwood, for example, asks whether it is possible to reconcile the 'amiable' father with the terrifying schoolmaster depicted by Hare, and implies that, since the Kilvert family appears in the *Diary* and in Kilvert's sister's *Recollections* as 'happy and united', the amiable picture is the truer one.[88] This view, however, overlooks the fact that it was very common for Victorian fathers to display an amiable side and yet be figures of terrifying authority to their children. Emily Kilvert in her memoirs highlights her father's geniality but there are also hints that he could be very stern as for example when he sent her weeping to the corner of the Harnish schoolroom to learn her lessons again. Kilvert, during the period of his Clyro curacy, tended to make his vicar, Venables, into a father figure compounded of exactly those apparently contradictory elements of amiability and austere authority. An expert on Victorian biography, Peter Abbs, underlined in the preface to Edmund Gosse's *Father and Son* the psychological mechanism that made this possible and common: 'The agony of the Victorians resided in the schizoid split between public and private, between the large formal gesture and the intimate personal actuality'.[89]

Gosse had underlined the way Victorian biographers deliberately concealed those aspects of their subjects that they felt would offend the public's notion of propriety. Hare, who was a particularly open and clear-sighted individual, was himself capable of this deception in relation to his tyrannical uncle Julius: the editor of Hare's book, *The Years With Mother*, commented that it was typical of the period that Hare could write 'laudatory passages' in the *Dictionary of National Biography* about the uncle who had flogged him so severely when he was only five and quite delicate.[90] This duality of attitude explains why he could write what Kilvert called 'a nice letter' to Kilvert's parents, full of 'affectionate' reminiscences of his schooldays at Harnish, when his mother was ill, in November 1870. Is it conceivable that Kilvert, when writing his *Diary*, remained somehow free of this duality, this 'mutual complicity' that shaped Victorian autobiography, in which 'language became a screen to shelter the vulnerable egos of writers and readers alike'?[91] As a pupil at his father's school, he must have witnessed, as Hare did, the assaults on pupils with rulers and canes and experienced the dreary lessons, yet there is not one reference in his *Diary* to life in the school.[92] All he allowed himself in the entry dealing with Hare's letter to his parents was a mention of 'dear old Harnish' and, even though he quotes Hare's detailed comments on schoolboy games and adventures, lessons, and teachers at the school, he refrains from matching them, as one might have expected him to do, with recollections of his own. He had the opportunity there to pay tribute to his father as he does at many other points in the *Diary*; in relation to life at Harnish school, he declined to take it. Abbs stresses that the modern reader, who is used to explicitness in literature, can detect hidden meanings in Victorian autobiography, 'can read the private underground of the text as well as the polite public surface'.[93] (Chapter 4, in its examination of a particularly disturbing dream Kilvert had, takes further this issue of the pressure to conceal unpleasant facts).

Gosse's *Father and Son* provides further insights into both Hare's case and Kilvert's. Gosse's father had an extreme religiosity more akin to that of Hare's mother than that of Robert Kilvert, however, though there was not the 'struggle between two temperaments, two consciences' that Gosse said his book recorded, there existed marked differences of personality between Robert Kilvert and his son. Unable to accept the picture of the former presented by Hare, another Kilvert scholar stated that it was probably 'a distorted one'.[94] He argued that his school 'cannot have had a bad reputation' because a number of pupils who attended it had aristocratic connections. This, too, ignores contemporary realities, in particular the tendency for parents to select a school on the basis of its social, rather than its academic reputation. Hare noted that the boys were 'rich middle-class' and the list of them supplied by Emily Kilvert bears this out.

As far as Hare's mother was concerned, it was equally important that the school provided stern moral discipline, and he was in no doubt about what guided his mother's choice of school: 'my mother, thinking it of far more importance to select "a good man" than "a good master", determined to send me there'. Ironically, as it turned out, 'all infantine immoralities were popular' there and Hare was shocked at the sexual experiences into which he was inducted at the age of nine.[95] Knowing as we do, the religious opinions she held, it is clear what meanings she attached to the concept of 'a good man'; she would have regarded Julius Hare as one. We also know what Hare's concept was. He was not opposed to religion *per se* but 'the pleasantness of religious things', he said, 'depends on the person who expresses them'.[96] Robert Kilvert's Evangelical conscience would have rejected vehemently the idea that a religious life was in any sense a matter of 'pleasantness'. When he invited Mrs. Hare to be his daughter Emily's godmother he must have known that she was a woman who had embraced wholeheartedly the Evangelical premise that a true Christian's life was one of strict spiritual discipline. It was typical of Hare's generous, forgiving nature that he remained devoted to his mother in spite of the torments he suffered for which she was largely responsible. Though he was a snob, it was widely acknowledged that he was friendly, affectionate, likeable, loyal, a lively storyteller and a good listener.[97] This is important to bear in mind when we consider the validity of his portrait of Robert Kilvert. Hare already knew when he went to Harnish school about the harshness that could result from misconceived piety and he categorised its headmaster with those he referred to as 'so-called "religious" people', to whom he had a profound and entirely understandable antipathy. There are good grounds, therefore, for believing that his picture of Robert is a true one.

As the number of public schools increased in the middle of the century, so the prep schools multiplied to meet the demand. Robert's little school, humble though it was, was part of this trend. It must have catered well to the current demands because it turned out products which even Eton found acceptable. Almost a third of the families represented at the school (according to the list supplied by Kilvert's sister)[98] could boast that one of their boys went on to Eton from there in the 1850s. Harnish school was no different from and no worse than the majority. It is worthwhile to attend to particular emphases in Hare's picture of it to see how far they correspond to whatever can be deduced of the personality of Robert. When Hare referred to him as 'deeply religious', he was registering that he was Evangelical, and that it permeated the atmosphere of his school. It appears that he was in the habit of referring to his pupils as his 'little flock in Christ's fold'. The Evangelical bias can be seen more clearly in Hare's observations that Robert was 'strangely impractical with no knowledge whatever of the world'. It was a large claim and might seem exaggerated until we recall the unworldly and slightly fussy tone that informs his *Memoirs*. At Oriel he was particularly admiring of the gentle, retiring Keble, with his 'simple goodness' and 'unsullied child-like nature, which put to shame all indelicacy or irreverence'.[99] Robert presented something of that character to his contemporaries at the College: Newman spoke of how he left 'a fragrant memory behind him' there. He never really settled into university life because he was deeply homesick, especially in his first year. He had never been away from home before except for a few days and confessed he was 'shy, shrinking, sensitive... to a ridiculous degree'. Later, he partially overcame these feelings but never mixed with other students and was always relieved when he could escape from the strangeness of the College to the comfort and reassurance of his family circle. It is also perhaps of significance that Thomas Mozley, his contemporary at Oriel, with its very small student body, made no mention of him.

Another apparently large claim of Hare's was that 'of literature he knew nothing' but this too fits in with the picture we have, given by Robert himself, of the nervous Oriel student with no ideas of his own, always inclined to believe that the truth of texts was what eminent tutors told him it was. In any case, for many Evangelicals, the only text of importance was the Bible, and literature was regarded as productive of delusions and the titillation of the senses. Carlyle's father, for example, used to tell him that 'Poetry, Fiction in general [was] ...not only idle, but false and criminal'.[100] It might be objected that there is evidence of pleasurable experience of literature provided by Robert for his children. 'What an enjoyable "raconteur" Papa was!' his daughter, Emily, recalled. 'He used to tell us such splendid stories round the fire on winter evenings'. Shakespeare and Sir Walter Scott were the authors she particularly remembered. Some Dickens was also read by her mother, though not to the children. It is clear, therefore, that their father was at ease with some literature at a period which coincides roughly with Hare's years at the Harnish school. Other fiction deemed acceptable in the household were the Evangelical novels of Grace Aguilar. Kilvert's sister, Emily, recalled their mother reading to them Aguilar's *Home Influence* (1847) and its sequel, *A Mother's Recompense* (1851). The theme of the former was spelt out thus in its preface: 'The author's aim has been to assist in the education of the HEART, believing that to be of infinitely greater importance than the mere instruction of the mind'. Robert Kilvert had, therefore, achieved a compromise position with regard to imaginative literature: Shakespeare and Scott were acceptable and could be considered 'improving' like the works by Aguilar. It is quite conceivable that Robert felt able to present Shakespeare and Scott to the known and trusted audience of his own family, for whom some pleasure was appropriate, but regarded them as too risky and inappropriate for his pupils. He himself had access to Shakespeare as a young boy and took part in family theatricals. In all of this he had the example of Wilberforce to guide him. Wilberforce did not object to the reading of novels and was fond of them himself. He was highly critical of the theatre, largely because the theatres of the late 18th century were immoral places but he did not object to children performing in school plays.

The dominance of Scott's Waverley novels in the repertoire of Kilvert senior also has some significance, bearing in mind Kilvert junior's romantic attachment to the past. We are told that his father knew all of the Waverley novels by heart. Though Scott was, in a general sense, a contemporary writer for Robert, his novels did not at all engage with contemporary social realities. Shakespeare, too, was safely in the past and represented a similar unchanging literary canon. Many of Robert's political ideas would have come to him via Scott's novels, which made accessible, to those members of the public who like him declined to involve themselves in politics or to read political works, the views of Burke in particular, who encouraged the maintenance of traditional social structures, the defence of property, and a disregard for the poor.[101] Those Victorian novelists who did engage with relatively contemporary social realities remained unread by Robert and his son. Neither was going to have much to do with the likes of Dickens, Thackeray, Charlotte Brontë, or George Eliot if it were true that 'it is our lay writers who are moulding the character and forming the opinions of the age', thus superseding '...the clergy in the direction of the thought of England'.[102] What Hare meant by literature was works that reflected the ideas and movements of the age, an emphasis totally absent from the Oriel curriculum.

Robert's love of Scott, which he may have developed as a schoolboy, was probably boosted through contact with Oriel students, one of whom, Patrick Boyle, was a close friend of Charles Scott, the novelist's son. Charles was at Brasenose College from 1824 and used sometimes to visit Boyle, whom he had known at school.[103] Mozley listed 'a son of Sir Walter Scott' among members of 'the Family', the drinking club of Oriel commoners who met nightly.[104] This may have been Charles Scott, visiting from Brasenose. It is unlikely that Robert would have met him because he would not have been a member of 'the Family', though several students who later became clergymen were, but he would have heard of the prestigious visitor. Is the absence of any reference in Robert's *Memoirs* to Scott, or to his son Charles and his link with Oriel, and to 'the Family', to be explained in terms of their not being seemly in a serious clergyman? Scott's novels, nevertheless, had a special place in the experience of those of conservative temperament growing up in the turbulent times of the 1820s and 1830s. The more the social order seemed threatened then, the more such people turned to the Waverley novels for their reassuring portrayal of a society of fixed ranks, heroic qualities, and submissive lower orders. The novels also had a great appeal for the authoritarian temperament, which the Kilverts, father and son, possessed in large measure. The authoritarian character tends to worship the past and is relatively uninterested in contemporary social and political events. Coleridge and Wordsworth were advising country gentlemen at this time to ignore social changes and to reassert feudal values as a means of counteracting pro-democracy forces. Scott's novels played a key part in this movement: 'In conservative - aristocratic circles, where the dread of bourgeois democracy was strongest, heroic literature acquired the value of a political symbol. Medieval romance in particular could be read as the image of feudal society in striking contrast to the new order that was pushing it aside...'.[105] Heroic literature fulfilled the same function for conservatives of the middle-class.

It is possible, therefore, to reconcile Hare's charge that Robert knew nothing of literature with evidence that shows that he undoubtedly had some taste for it. Of more importance is the *nature* of the literature he chose for himself and his family. It is evident that Kilvert's romantic vision of the past derived in some degree from his father.[106] His love and knowledge of poetry most likely came from his uncle Francis and the Claverton school. Kilvert went into no details about the influence, literary or otherwise, of the school he attended, until the age of 11, at Harnish Rectory; he would never have been critical of it. He was glad to endorse the warm, nostalgic comments made about it by Hare in the letter he wrote to the Kilverts. Kilvert would tolerate no criticisms of the father who was in many ways his hero and his inspiration. In his *Diary*, he always spoke of him with tenderness and reverence; invariably he was 'my dear Father'. Apart from enjoying working together as vicar and curate, son and father were very close. They went for walks, worked in the garden together, and regularly fished together.

Kilvert confided in his father over such sensitive issues as his hopes of marrying and of having his poems published. His father, however, advised against publication and in this we may discern a fundamental difference between the two men. In the *Diary* entry reflecting this moment, Kilvert was emphatic about publication: 'I wish to do so'. Writing was important to him and, in addition to his poems, he had by this time been writing his *Diary* for well over four years, a fact which, revealingly, he had never communicated to his father. In the effort to secure his father's agreement, he had enthused about the poet, William Barnes, whom he had visited the previous day but his father was unmoved. (It should be borne in mind here that Barnes' poetry had special importance for Kilvert because of the compassion it exhibited for the poor, a point taken up in chapter 9, and because it was written by a clergyman). Kilvert was understandably angry. Robert's hostility to the idea was another reflection of his Evangelicalism. Carlyle's father regarded poetry as 'idle' and 'false', as has been noted. In the novel *Home Influence*, chosen by Robert Kilvert for reading to his children, we are told that poetry is 'a dangerous gift', the pursuit of which could, unless carefully restrained, usurp the space which the serious concerns of life and religion should occupy. Indulged in too intensely it led to excess of feeling, which resulted in seeing things in a romantic and unreal light.[107]

Is this the explanation for the stance towards writing that Robert adopted in the preamble to his own *Memoirs*? He is at pains there to indicate in no uncertain terms that he was deeply opposed to writing them and only 'an earnestly expressed wish on the part of one whom I could not well refuse has set me on the task'. This unnamed person (Mrs. Kilvert?) had apparently settled on the idea that he should write 'a family history', but far from responding with enthusiasm to such a reasonable request—the Kilverts were, after all, people who set much store by family history and family relations—he underlined that not only did he take 'no pleasure in the undertaking', but found it 'actually distasteful'.[108] He raised ancillary objections about the 'trifling' interest of anything he might say and the likelihood of repeating stories that the family had heard often, but these clearly do not equate with his basic antipathy. If his antipathy to writing family history did not stem from a conviction that it was not the sort of thing a serious clergyman should be found doing, then it is difficult to see what its origin was. He undertook it only because of a request from someone who mattered much to him. Perhaps the fact that he was not writing fiction, something 'false', also helped to persuade him. Whatever the reason, he did not care to make public even within his own family what he was doing. He began the task in 1866 and finished it in 1879, during which period his son was writing his *Diary* unaware that his father was simultaneously writing his *Memoirs*. Furthermore, his son was living at home for almost a third of that period. On other occasions during his son's lifetime, Robert must have revealed his hostility to writing, especially of the imaginative kind, undertaken by clergymen, and the extent to which resentment over it and other differences of opinion between them festered in the consciousness of Kilvert will be examined in a later chapter.

Kilvert made a point of writing to his father on each and every birthday, and was ever solicitous for his health and comfort. Whenever Robert was complimented, as he was for example by a Radnorshire farmer for his skill in catching trout, or for his work with the Church Missionary Society, Kilvert was as pleased as though he himself was the subject of the compliments. In his *Diary* he pictured his father in the way the latter pictured John Keble: as a man of 'simple goodness', humble, sincere, dignified. He admired the way he struggled for independence, enduring poverty and loneliness to do God's work in trying circumstances. As Robert grew old, his son was admiring of the fortitude with which he endured illness and worried about how he would cope when he left him to accept the living of St. Harmon. On his 75th birthday, Kilvert wrote, 'My dear Father's seventy-fifth birthday. May it please God to spare him to us for many years to come'.

A desire to hold back time has been identified as a characteristic stance of Kilvert, and it is necessary to have a full picture of the father whom he wished to live forever because he was so deeply influenced by him, and because the circumstances which shaped his father's early experiences had clear implications for the way in which he viewed the world. Robert had to defer to rank and to model himself on men of rank because that was the way his career and his family's respectability could be established. Wealth and respectability were then two sides of the same coin, a circumstance which was an important feature of a new society, characterised as never before by fierce class antagonisms. To progress in this hostile society required social background and social connections, and Robert was sent to a school and a university where both mattered a great deal. The Kilvert family found it comforting to highlight their social origins. Robert remembered that his brother Thomas had a seal marked with the family's armorial bearings; the way in which Kilvert continually returned to them is discussed in the next chapter.

No matter what those origins were, at the socially exclusive Oriel College Robert found himself at the bottom of the heap, and had to endure isolation and some humiliation as a result. Excessive pride had particular importance for the Kilvert family: it had marred relationships within the family between the Colemans and the Ashes, and the family religion taught that aristocratic pride was both wicked and contemptible.[109] However, that religion also counselled respect for all lawful authority and aristocratic authority still ruled society, in spite of movements to reduce its power. Robert deferred to it, partly out of expediency and partly because, as a natural Tory, he could tolerate no other worldly authority.

An Oxford education was for him both an avenue to social success and a further training in piety and seriousness. The Kilvert family, largely because its forbears were countrymen, felt a powerful attachment to the landed interest, which was reinforced by contacts with landowning families and with rural clergymen at various points in its history. Robert's choice of the Church as a profession, was a natural one. It was the path his eldest brother had taken; Oxford University was ruled by clergy and was their training ground; and the position of a clergyman, especially in the countryside, commanded social respect. Many clergymen had gentry backgrounds, however, and the Church at this time was 'a patronage-ridden structure' and there was a steady bias against the man without social connections.[110] Mrs. Hare had extended patronage to Robert and he acknowledged it by inviting her to become godmother to his daughter Emily. Rural clergymen were also part of the landed interest and Robert discovered to his cost that Oriel College was both a reflection of the power of the landowning class and of the 'ferocious spirit' that it manifested in the 1820s. He encountered there its fierce adherence to the notion of rank which, as later chapters will show, was the cause of many painful experiences for his son. Both men, nevertheless, maintained a loyalty to the country house and all it stood for. The fact that Robert chose not to support the anti-slavery movement is a further indication of his solidarity with the landed interest, which was heavily involved in slave plantations and the sugar trade. For one family of landowners—the Clutterbucks—Kilvert developed an almost mystical reverence, which must have had its origin in his father's obligation to it. Kilvert, in celebrating the Clutterbucks' paternalist role at the centre of the Harnish community, was thereby upholding the traditional privileges of landowners, the hereditary principle, and the rights of property as against human rights. His notion of the community, as was noted in the Prologue, rested squarely on the fulfilment by each class of its traditional responsibilities, and for landowners this meant the care of their dependants. It was by their charity, and not by radical changes in the structure of society, that the sufferings of the poor were to be ameliorated. The poor had the duty of deferring to their betters, and, through their industriousness, of striving to attain the independence that brought respectability.

Robert was bound to condemn labourers who rebelled against their poverty in 1830 because he was a conservative, an Evangelical, and because his own social position was insecure. Those were reasons enough why he appeared indifferent to their sufferings. An additional one was that his ministry was not of the thoroughly 'active' kind which Hare favoured and Kilvert practised. Such indifference seems to the modern mind reprehensible in a clergyman whose principal duty was care of his flock, especially in one whose brand of Christianity placed so much emphasis on heart rather than head. In order to understand it, one needs to recognise the great fear that people of Robert's background had of labouring people: 'The sensibility of the Victorian middle-class was nurtured in the 1790s by frightened gentry who had seen miners, potters and cutlers reading *Rights of Man* ...It was in these counter-revolutionary decades that the humanitarian tradition became warped beyond recognition'.[111] In an age which carried the seeds of revolution, that fear was very real, and was productive of the 'ferocious spirit' demonstrated by the repressive measures imposed by the authorities in the early decades of the century. In Kilvert's personality, too, there lurked a vestige of the 'ferocious spirit', and it helps to provide an answer to a question which readers of his *Diary* have often found baffling: how a man, otherwise notable for his kind, good heart, could be so accepting of poverty and the social injustice that gave rise to it. One clergyman was so concerned at how hard, selfish, snobbish, and materialistic society had become by 1830, that he began to doubt people's very capacity to register basic sympathy.[112]

Kilvert's own anxiety was less great than that of his father partly because he lived in a less threatening age, partly because his Christianity had a more human face, and partly because he was more at ease with himself. However, as later chapters will show, he experienced very similar tensions over his ambiguous social position and important personal relationships were blighted as a result of it. Father and son both feared change because the new society which was remorselessly shaping itself during their lifetimes was eroding those traditional institutions which, especially when suffused with nostalgia, helped to buttress their social and psychological identities.

'I was born under circumstances particularly fortunate... for happiness. Those of an English country gentleman of the XIXth Century... Such a position at such a date, 1840, was perhaps as good a starting point for a happy life as could well have been afforded me'.

Wilfrid Scawen Blunt in Elizabeth Longford,
A Pilgrimage of Passion, The Life of Wilfrid Scawen Blunt, p.4

'every home ...is [the] nearest approach to perfection of beauty that is ever attained on earth'.

Robert Kilvert, *Trevellyk*, in *More Chapters from the Kilvert Saga*, p.75

'The real strength of Evangelicalism lay not in the pulpit or the platform, but in the home'.

Canon Charles Smyth, 'The Evangelical Discipline',
in *Ideas and Beliefs Of The Victorians*, p.103

'...the people of this country look to their aristocracy with a deep-rooted prejudice - an hereditary prejudice, I may call it - in their favour'.

Cobden in a speech to Parliament in 1845

'I am, and my father was before me, a violent Tory of the old school; - Walter Scott's school, that is to say...'.

John Ruskin, *Praeterita*, p.13

CHAPTER 2
Kilvert and Home

When Robert married Thermuthis Coleman in 1838, he knew he was doing well for himself in all respects. Some neighbours were doubtful about the social distance between them. He, however, was entirely confident about the step he was taking because 'no two people could have been less anxious what the world said about them. They themselves both thought that they were acting right'. At least one neighbour was confident that Robert had married 'a nice wife' and was 'the happiest of men'.[1] Kilvert always had before him in his parents' marriage an example of sensitivity and selfless concern. His father characterised his relationship with his wife in these terms: 'There was a depth of fervent love between them, founded on mutual respect and entire devotedness to each other. If anything ever went wrong, the unhappiness was of that best kind which showed itself in each feeling distress chiefly on the other's account, and being more concerned about that than anything else in the world'.[2]

Kilvert's admiration of his mother was founded partly on his conviction that she had made an excellent choice in marrying his father. Robert had married above himself just as, in the opinion of Madam Ashe, Kilvert's great-grandmother, her daughter had married beneath her in marrying Walter Coleman, Kilvert's grandfather. Though that marriage turned out to be an unhappy one, Kilvert always approved of the marital choices that his grandmother and his mother had made. He had love for his mother as well as respect for her integrity. He took much care over birthday presents for her. On her birthday in May 1870, he sent her Miss Molesworth's *Stray Leaves from the Tree of Life*, a Pilgrimage that he had specially written for her, and a copy of his 'Honest Work' poem. It was with her, rather than with his father, that he had frequent talks about the family background and the whole business of choosing marriage partners. He could open his heart to her about his love for Daisy Thomas. She was very keen in September 1871 to know the name of his intended and shortly afterwards received from her 'a nice long letter with a good deal about Daisy' about whom she had heard from Kilvert's letter to his father a few days before.[3] He enjoyed tut-tutting with his mother over the scandalous behaviour of Miss Long, the heiress of nearby Draycot, and her infatuation with and disastrous marriage to the worthless rogue, Wellesley. (William Wellesley was related to the Duke of Wellington and his life provided the Kilverts with a further example of aristocratic wickedness. *Burke's Peerage* said of the marriage: 'Of the miseries which followed this marriage and of the subsequent scandals of [Wellesley's] career, it is better to say nothing'.) He accompanied his mother on outings and on her frequent visits to the neighbouring family of Mr. Large, whom Kilvert was pleased to call a 'yeoman'. He showed his affection and concern for her on New Year's Eve 1871 when he was anxious that his conversation with his sisters would disturb her as she slept 'the sleep of the just'.

Kilvert's father had Harnish particularly in mind when he observed that a country parsonage provided the best chance for a happy married life. The account of his sister Emily Kilvert, which is the only one we have, of life in the Harnish years (1835-1855) pictures a family living a comfortable existence and feeling comfortable about itself. Its financial and physical needs were provided for, although it was not particularly well off because the Harnish living was a poor one. However, the Church was a gentleman's occupation and the Kilverts lived in a gentleman's house, thanks to the patronage of a very important local gentleman, Thomas Clutterbuck. His generosity had provided extensions to the Rectory, as well as a school-room and a nursery above it, which enabled Robert Kilvert's school to grow beyond its original eight pupils. It was possible also to afford some servants. There was a nurse, who later served as a cook, and an under-nurse to look after the six children, all born between 1839 and 1849, as well as a housemaid and a manservant, who probably also tended the garden.

The household was very full at this time. Apart from the Kilvert children and the servants, there were (after the extensions) 12 pupils and a tutor boarding. During the week various additional masters— for music, French, and drawing—visited the house, while on Saturday came Sergeant Reeves, the drill master to drill the boys in front of the house, and 'the tuck man', who timed his arrival to coincide with the moment the boys received their weekly pocket money. Kilvert himself ceased to live at home from 1851 onwards, apart from holidays, because he had gone to be a pupil in his uncle's school at his home, Claverton Lodge, near Bath. Emily remembered this house as formidably grand and highly ordered, with a drawing room always kept locked and used only on very important occasions. Hardly less intimidating were the large bookcases with glass fronts, holding valuable books belonging to her aunt Sophia, the daughter of a Czech count and a refugee from the French Revolution. In spite of this, it was clear to Emily that there was a more liberal atmosphere at Claverton Lodge than at Harnish largely because uncle Francis was an intellectual and not of Evangelical persuasion. The home of the Kilvert children was, however, happy enough. The boarding pupils supplied built-in playmates and there was a succession of tutors and servants, so there was a wide range of adults to whom they could relate. The monthly Church Missionary Society working parties were 'great events in our quiet lives', Emily remembered, and she and her sisters were expected always to be engaged in some work of their own that would contribute to the general effort. Before each working party, there was a meeting of Evangelical clergymen: 'My father being an Evangelical, none of the High Church Clergy in the neighbourhood would have anything to do with these meetings'.[4] This circumstance, plus the fact that the Kilvert children had almost no friends except the boarders, meant that their existence was sheltered. Every summer, the family took a holiday at the seaside, usually to Weston-super-Mare, but also to resorts in Devon.

The Kilvert children never lost their awareness of what was owed to the Clutterbucks. They were in awe of 'our Squire, Thomas Clutterbuck', as Emily called him. They had the privilege of being allowed to walk to church through the grounds of Harnish House, though expressly forbidden to use the Clutterbuck's private path. Her father's pupils were allowed to play cricket in a field belonging to the family, and they and the Kilverts were invited to Hardenhuish House one evening in 1856, shortly after the end of the Crimean War, and were treated to the sight of Captain Hugh Clutterbuck, a hero of the charge at Balaclava, 'wheeling himself about in a self-propelling chair'. The 15 year-old Kilvert was also impressed at how grown-up his eldest sister Thersie (Thermuthis) looked on this important occasion, with her hair 'dressed... in a new fashion with a velvet bandeau round her head...'.[5]

The event that provoked the move from Harnish in 1855 to Langley Burrell was the death that year of Robert Ashe, squire and Rector of that village. The ill-health of his son, Robert Martin Ashe, who was also a clergyman, prevented him from fulfilling both roles and he decided to offer the living, which was in his gift, to Robert Kilvert, who was the husband of his cousin, Thermuthis Coleman. Robert must have felt that this was an opportunity he could not decline. It meant moving out from the sheltering wing of the Clutterbucks but he not only had a new source of patronage, this time from within the family, but a living that paid £350 a year as against the £100 of Harnish. He could afford to give up his school and to inhabit a grander, more spacious rectory. Many of the family's old contacts could be retained because Langley Burrell was only a few miles from Harnish.

The preceding chapter has indicated that the Kilvert family maintained an ambivalent attitude to the aristocratic class that stood at the top of the social pyramid, and that this was a matter not simply of general political outlook but reflected its individual social and economic circumstances as well as its basic religious values. Middle-class Evangelicals of the early 19th century, of which the Kilverts were a fairly typical rural example, set out to evolve a version of the home and family in opposition to that of the upper-classes, and central to this was a notion of manliness. It was still accepted that a husband should command the obedience of wife, children, and servants, just as all in society should acknowledge the authority of those above them in rank. However, in addition to that traditional injunction, it was necessary to develop new understandings of masculinity that were different from the gentry model, which expressed itself through field sports, military discipline, duelling, and drinking in male company. Robert had experienced this model at Oriel College and had kept aloof from it. Evangelical man sought spiritual objectives and spiritual discipline instead of these physical challenges. He took pride in work, philanthropic endeavour, and in his concern for the welfare of the weak and poor.[6] Work was virtually synonymous with the moral earnestness that characterised the Kilvert family religion. It was Newman's moral earnestness, his 'appeals to conscience, the sincere conviction of purity and generosity' that, according to A.P. Stanley, drew students to him at Oriel.[7] Celebration of work necessarily implied some criticism of those who, like many of the landed gentry, lived a life of idleness and pleasure. Work had to be defended against the contempt of those who despised it because they had no need of it. It was the means of providing honestly and honourably for the family and thus was to be respected. Whenever Kilvert left copies of his 'Honest Work' poem with parishioners, he was endorsing this ethic.

His admiration for the Evangelical Moule family is indicative of his acceptance of this model of behaviour. The Rev. Henry Moule was a friend of Kilvert's father. Born in 1801, he was curate of Melksham in 1823 and was the means by which Robert heard of the vacancy at neighbouring Keevil. Moule became Vicar of Fordington, Dorset, in 1829. When Kilvert visited him at Fordington in April 1874, he noted that he had been vicar there for almost half a century. His long tenure, record of pious endeavour, and dynamic personality had made him an institution in Dorset and a hero in Kilvert's eyes. Kilvert referred to him as 'a universal genius' and his visit to him was a kind of tribute.[8] Moule worked untiringly in the cholera epidemics there in 1849 and 1854. The educational and moral conditions of the people naturally excited his concern, too. Kilvert told of their woeful ignorance of church ceremony and tradition. Moule's tendency to challenge gentry values can be seen in his campaign to force the Duchy of Cornwall, which owned many of the slum cottages in Fordington, to acknowledge its responsibility for the misery and immorality of their inhabitants. He also worked to obtain a ban on Dorchester race meetings (Kilvert called them 'low bad races'), even though they had the support of the lady of the manor. For this he suffered abuse locally. Kilvert mentioned that Moule and the respectable church-goers were insulted as they went to church by mobs of young men and that their gardens were vandalised. Kilvert, and presumably his father, admired Moule's actions.

He was not only an exemplar to the Kilverts, but his household in several ways reflected the Kilvert one. He took in private pupils, as Robert Kilvert had done, and his son, Handley, served as his curate, just as Kilvert did to his father. Handley had a reverence for his father that was akin to that felt by the Diarist for his. To Handley, his father was 'a gentleman so true, a Christian so strong', and the relationship between them resembled that of father and son in the Kilvert home: 'Father had been an object of such reverence as perhaps to check a little on both sides, the easy demonstration of affection'.[9] Nevertheless, though Handley recalled a strongly Evangelical home, the piety of it was never in conflict with the warmth of parental affection, which again reflects the situation in the Kilvert home. Handley, like Kilvert, had no interest in field sports, because he too could find no pleasure in killing. He relished, as did the Diarist, the close contact with neighbours and parishioners granted to the son of a vicarage, enabling him to understand 'the home-like ties..., the family affections, that gather themselves round the "pastoral house"'.[10] Evangelical families were noted for the strength of their family affections.

Kilvert had developed something of a passion for a Mrs. Hockin, lately married, who became a neighbour at Langley Lodge, Langley Burrell, in 1867, and he probably visited her there. The Hockins moved to Cornwall later and he was delighted to be once again in their home and in the presence of Mrs. Hockin when he was invited to holiday there in late July 1870. He found it hard not to behave like a lover during his stay, recording once that he scrambled up some rocks in search of ferns for her. 'Not very successful and H (Mr. Hockin) had got her some much finer ones, but she did not despise mine'.[11] The visit was one of ecstatic happiness for him, and when the moment came to depart, he was heartbroken. He wrote passionately of 'the withering of tendrils torn from their grasp' and of the 'bitter moment when the Tamar was crossed ... the wild restless longing, the hopeless yearning ...'. His stay had been 'happiness, how great, unbroken sunshine, unclouded blue ... I thought, was it so, that there were tears in those blue eyes when we parted'.[12] When he was asked, in February 1871, to be godfather to the Hockins' daughter, he was overjoyed, and wrote about her almost as though she were his own child: 'It was the thing I have been longing for. Now I shall have a real right in the child. Silver and gold have I none ... but such as I have she shall have ...'.[13] Mrs. Hockin had the kind of womanliness which Kilvert especially favoured and her family was one of several which for him had all the right qualities.

It was the 'home-like ties' and 'family affections' important to Handley Moule and to Kilvert that Kilvert's sister, Emily, found worth recording. She chronicled the comings and goings of those—private pupils, their tutors, neighbours, members of Missionary working parties[14]—who constituted the 'pastoral house' and extended its influence. Her account conveys the sense of a strict and spartan upbringing: the children had few toys and 'cake was almost an unknown luxury, and buns even a treat we only had on birthday evenings'.[15] It is important to examine the children's books available in the nursery at Harnish in order to assess the strictness of the upbringing. Edmund Gosse recalled that 'no fiction, religious or secular' was admitted into his home, a prohibition stemming from his mother, who believed strongly that it was sinful. 'Story books were sternly excluded' and Gosse never had one read to him in his entire childhood.[16] By comparison, a much more free and easy approach operated with regard to the Kilvert children's books, though some control in the direction of piety was exercised, as is clear from the list provided by Emily Kilvert. Nevertheless, she recalled that of picture books, 'really good ones', there was no shortage.[17] Some appear religious in character, for example, *Dr Kitts' Sunday Book*, *Food for Babes*, and *Prince of Peace*. Emily thought the first of these 'delightful' because of its good pictures, but she disliked the other two, which were perhaps more serious and moralistic, and were gifts of her godmother Mrs. Augustus Hare. That Mrs. Hare occupied a position of such importance at that period and in such a religious household as the Kilverts', is another indication of the strong influence of the Hare family on it. (Another instance of close links between the two families is that some time between 1843 and 1845 Robert Kilvert was invited by the father of Marcus Hare, Hare's cousin who also attended Harnish school, to stay at their home, Corsley House, near Longleat.)

Children's books of the period were both imaginative and well-written and though more strongly Evangelical in tone in the early part of the century, they never lost their didactic element; it merely became more subtle.[18] In the 1840s, the period of which Emily was writing, there was clearly much pleasure to be had from books, as is evident from others given to her by Mrs. Hare, such as *The Honeysuckle*, a book of poems most of which Emily memorised, *Spring Blossoms*, which she loved, and the *Playmate*, which she nearly wore out with reading. Another of Mrs. Hare's gifts was Mrs. Trimmer's *History of the Robins* (1786). In the late 18th century, Mrs. Trimmer began to write books for charity schools and they were approved by the Church and the Society for Promoting Christian Knowledge. Her approach to education, founded on the belief that 'reasoning and gentle reproof and encouragement' would improve children's behaviour, conflicted somewhat with that of Mrs. Hare! Mrs. Trimmer disapproved of fairy tales and her books have strong moral content, of which *History of the Robins* is a fair example, being designed to improve children's treatment of animals. Good family relations is another element in its moral stance and its preface underlines a parallel between a human family and the family of robins in the book, who have names like Dicky, Flapsy and Pecksy. It recommends that animals should not be 'wantonly killed, nor treated with the least degree of cruelty'.[19] A later chapter deals with Kilvert's kindness towards animals and hatred of field sports and the story of the *Robins* must have played a part in the development of his attitudes.

Another book in the Kilvert nursery was Mary Howitt's *The Children's Year* which was probably bought by Mrs. Kilvert as it is not included among those—the majority—listed by Emily as gifts of her godmother. Mary Howitt came from a strict Quaker family and Mrs. Trimmer's *Robins* was her favourite book as a child. The books of Mary Howitt and of her husband, William, were 'early-Victorian favourites' in the moral movement in children's fiction.[20] The Howitts moved in a circle of eminent people that included Wordsworth, Tennyson, Louisa M. Alcott, Augustus Hare, and Hans Christian Anderson, whose stories Mary Howitt translated. In *The Children's Year* she recounted what her own two children did in a year. The speech of the children is natural and as characters they are quite free of artificiality so that child readers could easily identify with them and enjoy their everyday activities. They are not there simply to reinforce moral lessons. Howitt sought to convey in her books her beliefs that an over-strict upbringing was dangerous for children and that moral instruction should be combined with enjoyment.[21]

The Kilvert children experienced sternness but, as in the Moule home, it was similarly balanced by affection. Family prayers were taken seriously but if Robert Kilvert found one of the children misbehaving during them, his method of reproof was to throw his silk handkerchief at them. However, it seems certain that the children felt his reproof keenly, such was his authority, especially as the miscreant had to retrieve the handkerchief and return it to their father when prayers were over. There was a severe Evangelical feel to the family Sunday for the children—in spite of being allowed to join their parents for supper, at which roast potatoes appeared as a great treat.

Kilvert's mother's role, as seen in Emily Kilvert's account, was typical of that which women came to fulfil in the early decades of the century. Just as man was the source of all strength and authority in the home, so woman was the epitome of dependence. She achieved her full potentiality only in a family, by being a wife and a mother. There she could exert the powerful moral influence that came from her purity, gentleness and more refined nature. A clergyman's wife had special responsibility because of his prominent position in the community. It was of the utmost importance that his conduct and home should be without blemish. Emily Kilvert shows her mother supporting her husband's work and guiding the upbringing of the children in exactly the way contemporary manuals prescribed. She also maintained the open house required to meet the needs of parishioners.

In the socially and politically disturbed 1820s and 1830s, authors of domestic manuals were advancing the concept of the family as the source of stable values. Earlier accounts had emphasised the role of religion in relation to home and the woman's role, but by this time it was no longer taken for granted that religion would be the focal point, nor that homes would combine workplace with living space as rural homes, which had been the norm for the majority, traditionally did. More and more people were living in towns and were favouring homes separate from places of business.[22] In the 'pastoral house' of Harnish Vicarage, working and living could continue side by side, and it also clung to a model of domestic relationships—Grace Aguilar's *Home Influence*—which placed great emphasis on religion. Aguilar's intention in the book was to illustrate 'the spirit of true piety' and the Christian virtues that emanated from it. Her story was aimed chiefly at mothers because they wielded the greatest amount of 'home influence'. She also underlined that 'it is the heart, not the mind, which is required for the comprehension of self-devotion',[23] an emphasis which echoed Evangelicalism's determination to define itself as 'the religion of the heart'. We are told in the novel that the influence of the home has only one basis—God's holy word—and that domestic pleasures are the sweetest and most enduring. In Kilvert's poem 'The Hill Home', he indicated that the 'beacon light of love' was the key domestic pleasure: 'Sweet world of home, thy sacred bond contains the purest joy'. Victorian writings on the home indicated that it was particularly a woman's task to make it the place of peace and security, which the Kilvert home was. This is a constant theme of Emily Kilvert's recollections. Home was to be a source of moral values in a society increasingly taken up with materialistic concerns: '...men could operate in that amoral world only if they could be rescued by women's moral vigilance at home'.[24] The division of the individual's world into private and public spheres was the result of the increased domination of society by capitalism and its work ethic.

The conscious association of the home with security often found its expression in the idealisation of childhood. 'The home became the place where one had been at peace and childhood a blessed time when truth was certain and doubt with its divisive effects unknown'.[25] In all of Kilvert's references to the home of Harnish, these notes are continually sounded. As he walked there in February 1875, 'tears came into my eyes as a thousand sweet and happy memories swept across my soul'. Once he imagined he saw a single star like a guardian angel watching over the 'old sweet home... of my childhood'.[26] He expressed a longing to return to its security:

O that one peaceful happy day I might rest in they sweet arms,
O that the little child after his weary pilgrimage might come home
     as last...[27]

The desire to return to a home seen as a haven, even as heaven itself, recurs repeatedly in Kilvert's poems. Death, pictured as 'The Welcome Home', is the theme of the poem of that title, and those who meet death have attained a 'haven safe within the harbour bar'.[28] In his powerful attachment to the concept of property, Kilvert was entirely Victorian and entirely representative of his class. It was one subject that could arouse in the mild-mannered Diarist, with his strong aversion to argument, passions of the fiercest kind, as is evident from the following *Diary* passage: 'Got into an argument with Mr Latimer Jones about people's legal and moral rights over their property and he spoke in such an insolent overbearing contemptuous way that my blood was up, and Mrs Bevan said afterwards she feared we should have fought'.[29] We shall never know what view Mr. Latimer Jones held of the legal and moral rights attaching to property. It has proved impossible to identify either him or his background. His name suggests he was Welsh and one factor in the argument that developed may have concerned estates in Wales held by the

English. Perhaps another was the denial of the vote to those who had no property. A large element in Kilvert's Oxford course was the law of personal property; the next chapter provides details of it. Something of Kilvert's own view can be gathered from an entry concerning 'My Harden Ewyas' (Harnish). It was his he argued 'by a higher right than the bare possession of houses and fields'. It was his 'by the ownership of the spirit', by the 'inalienable right' of being his birthplace.[30] Mr. Jones' interpretation of property rights was probably much more prosaic and rational than the romantic attachment which lay behind Kilvert's. His had been derived from his home background, from his university course, and from the ethos of the time, which was dominated by aristocratic influence.[31] It showed itself in relation to property in his tendency to see the landed estate and its relationships as the supreme form of social organisation.

Henry Brougham, the Whig politician and reformer, had used the phrase 'romantic attachment' in 1818 to designate the sentimental feelings of English gentlemen towards their public schools. Mack in his history of the public schools regarded 'romantic attachment' as integral to the irrationalism that he believed was a characteristic feature of upper-class sensibility. Other constituent elements of it were patriotism, yearning for the past, reverence for authority, and passivity.[32] They were all strongly entrenched in the Kilvert household, and manifested themselves clearly in the special place occupied by the novels of Sir Walter Scott. Aguilar's novels also contained a vein of rich romanticism which links them to the contemporary interest in medievalism and antiquarianism that was focused and fed by Scott. One character in Aguilar's *A Mother's Recompense*, after a visit to Scotland, expresses the fervent wish that Sir Walter Scott was still alive and able to feature her and her husband in a new novel so that they could experience romantic scenes and situations.[33] The length to which people would go to feed their Scott obsession is well illustrated by Mrs. Hughes,[34] grandmother of the author of *Tom Brown's Schooldays*. The record of her journey to the novelist's home of Abbotsford in 1824 is remarkable for showing the attitude of mind that focused only on those places and buildings that reflected its interest in its own class and in antiquities. Places were of note to her either for the gentry seats which enhanced them or for their fine churches (her husband was a Canon of St. Paul's). She showed a steady antipathy to anything connected with trade. 'I rejoice to see that trade flourishes', she wrote, '[but] I hate to see the process'.[35] Anything that was new wounded her sensibility. All in all, her account reveals a mind in danger of finding every human scene dull and disappointing that did not find its counterpart in the Waverley novels.

Kilvert was not so extreme as Mrs. Hughes in his penchant for ancient, romantic scenes but it was a very strong element in his make-up. It was noted in the last chapter that the genteel, leisured city of Bath, with its relative lack of industry, suited the Kilvert family, and this is generally true. However, a coach-building business was part of the family history, and the family religion admired industriousness and self-help. Something of this element appears in the *Diary* entry for 23 October 1872 that deals with a visit to Bristol: 'It is a grand city. How much grander than Bath. I breathe freely here. Here is life, movement and work instead of the foolish drawl and idle lounge'. His attitude had no doubt been learnt from his parents and helps to explain the otherwise puzzling comment by Emily Kilvert about her mother's 'horror of what she called "Bathy" people'. Mrs. Kilvert didn't believe Bath people applied themselves enough to work. The *Diary* passage is particularly significant for the fact that he underlined that he felt more at home in Bristol ('I breathe freely here'), even though Bath had actually been home and he found, in general, that the countryside suited him better than cities. He had a similar impression of a similar city—Liverpool. He enjoyed especially the bustle and activity of its docks, which, piled high with merchandise from all over the world, gave a vivid idea of the 'vast commerce of the country'. He was fascinated by other scenes of work, describing iron forging as 'very interesting' and the working of machinery as 'beautiful'. His final impression was of exhilarating contrasts of wealth and poverty, of 'wildernesses of offices' and 'palatial warehouses', and of 'bustling pushing vulgar men, pretty women and lovely children'.[36] When a carriage of the train in which he was travelling came off the line, he showed a real interest in the screw jack by which it was returned to it: 'this marvellous implement'.[37] Similarly, he enjoyed a chat about 'Professor Tyndall's discoveries in science and sound' with a clergyman he met on a London train.[38] It is evident, therefore, that he did not turn completely away from the thrusting commercial and technological world of the 19th century in favour of a rural dream.

Nevertheless, throughout his *Diary* there is a steady pull towards the past, especially the romantic past of myths and legends, of battles and chivalry, of castles and kings. He had a particular love of the English Civil War and there are frequent references to Charles I. He saw a play entitled 'Charles I' at the Lyceum in February 1873 and found some parts 'particularly touching'.[39] Highly characteristic of his love of romantic history was his visit in June 1874 to Nunwell Park and Yaverland on the Isle of Wight. He had obviously read about the Oglander family whose name links both houses. He knew enough to regret that, though the family had been seated at Nunwell since the Conquest, 'the last of the old race ...has just passed away, leaving no heir... His place knows him no more and a stranger ...sits in his seat'.[40] The passage expresses the importance for Kilvert of rank and title, lineage, tradition, and the fear of extinction, of ultimate anonymity, which was a factor in his desire to keep a diary. 'Romantic attachment' appears again a few pages later in his description of Yaverland: 'Today I went to Yaverland. Yaverland to my imagination has always been a romance and a paradise since a quarter of a century ago I read a beautiful and touching story of the old manor house. And this, my soul, is Yaverland... The dream has come true'.[41] Gentle assertion of his status as a clergyman won him admittance to the dream house and his soul was fed.

It bore some similarities to another which had been part of his childhood experiences. Mrs. Hamilton, in *Home Influence*, had established a home, called Oakwood because of the superb oaks in its park, which was notable for its happy relationships and wholesome moral atmosphere. Physically it recalled Yaverland. It was a 'castellated mansion' with deeply recessed windows that corresponded to the 'low broad windows with heavy mullions' of Yaverland. Both had oaken staircases. Yaverland had a Norman church in its grounds while the other had the ruins of a chapel, burnt by Cromwell's soldiers. A powerful sense of history permeated both and they had been lived in by one family for generations. Oakwood had comfortable modern apartments, which had been provided without spoiling its antiquity. In a detail that recalls Mrs. Hughes' mania for the antique, we are told that these rooms were saved from being 'disagreeably modern' by their oak panels.[42] Oakwood and other country houses in Aguilar's novels express two qualities—'a pure sense of poetry in the Universe and Man' and 'a constant, unfailing piety'[43]—that sum up much of what Kilvert stood for. The former can be equated with the romantic sensibility that found deep comfort in ancient, beautiful places; the latter depended on infusing the material and worldly with a spiritual sense that stemmed as much from an appreciation of natural beauty as from religion, though Mrs. Hamilton did emphasise, too, the way 'the presence of the living God is so impressed on His works'. She also cultivated an awareness of beauty in the arts and human character. Beauty of this latter kind could be found 'in the struggles, faith and heroism of the poor...'.[44]

Kilvert's attitude to the beauty of the country house can be illustrated further in the *Diary* entry for 3 November 1874. He had gone to Bowood, home of the Marquis of Landsdowne, especially to admire the autumn colours of its magnificent beeches, but trees of all kinds held a deep fascination for Kilvert. He had been familiar with Bowood since childhood: the Kilvert children were given special permission by the Marquis to walk in the grounds.[45] They were raised with a constant sense of what they owed to the condescension of aristocrats and other gentry. Bowood's 'natural' features—its plantations, its lake with its cascade, its beeches—are those of a created landscape. Its beauty and associations stimulated Kilvert's composing eye. 'To eye and ear it was a beautiful picture...'. Its symbolisation of traditional England led him on significantly to question the entire purpose of his diary-keeping: 'Why do I keep this voluminous journal?' Though his answer was 'I can hardly tell', the juxtaposition of the query with the symbol of Bowood implicitly suggests that the 'humble and uneventful life' that he said was his gained in significance because it had, no matter how peripherally, been linked to that aristocratic house. It represented traditional, ordered social relations, the harmony that came from everyone knowing their place in a unified world. Kilvert did not see the 'Nature' of Bowood as the creation of generations of labourers, nor that its tradition went back only to the 18th century and was a product of capitalist agriculture. 'What would the noblest estate be without the hands that turned its soil to profits?' Sidney Godolphin Osborne had asked. Bowood was in fact the creation of the modernising forces which were steadily subverting Kilvert's rural community.[46]

In relation to another estate, that of Moccas, the home of Kilvert's Bredwardine squire, Sir George Cornewall, Kilvert adopted a similarly romantic and unhistorical stance. Again it was, significantly, oak trees that he saw as symbolic of the country house tradition. From the second half of the 18th century, trees had been used to signify social order and the power of property. Oak trees, in particular, possessed powerful symbolic associations; they were claimed to be 'venerable, patriarchal, stately ...and quintessentially English'.[47] Great trees represented great families. In another of those *Diary* entries that Kilvert had obviously put together very carefully, he indicated that he knew and accepted these meanings. Moccas Park had outstandingly fine and ancient oaks and Kilvert simultaneously admired their great age while resenting the way in which they rendered his own mortal life meaningless. 'I fear those grey old men of Moccas', he wrote, 'those grey, gnarled, low-browed, knock-kneed, bowed, bent, huge, strange, long-armed, deformed, hunch-backed, misshapen oak men that stand waiting and watching century after century, biding God's time with both feet in the grave and yet tiring down and seeing out generation after generation, with such tales to tell...'.[48] One thing which stands out in this remarkable description is that almost all of the epithets used to convey the human, yet strangely inhuman, quality of the oaks could be applied to labouring people, whose physical appearance differentiated them so markedly from gentlemen. Whenever Kilvert met fine-looking labourers, he made a point of noting it.[49] Contemporary moral attitudes to the poor were conditioned by the repulsion felt at their physical appearance. Morality was layered, just as society was, and was the result of breeding: 'the upper-class inherited qualities just as their horses inherited fine fetlocks or a good wind. And the reverse was true - the inheriting of poor qualities, moral defects'.[50] An element in Kilvert's characterisation of the alien old men of Moccas was his fear of the 'waiting and watching' working-class and the power they might one day possess.

He likened one tree, the 'king oak of Moccas Park', to 'a great ruined grey tower', and noted how, in a manner that he found sinister, the ancient tree, while giving some appearance of being dead, was actually pushing out new growth. In a passage which, as a whole, is highly romantic and Wordsworthian, he refused to acknowledge that the Moccas trees were the product of human activity: 'No human hand set those oaks. They are "the trees which the Lord hath planted". They look as if they had been at the beginning and making of the world, and they will probably see its end'. The story of the oaks was both less romantic and less mysterious. Over a period of almost half a century from 1793, the Moccas gardener, Webster, had planted nearly 300,000 oaks on the estate. Large numbers were felled at various times to pay off family debts and shipped down the Wye and Severn to Bristol, where many would have been made into slave ships that sailed from there to Africa and the West Indies. The Cornewall family owned a sugar plantation, worked by slaves, on the island of Grenada. Kilvert was, however, unable to make an easy, automatic identification with the political/commercial tradition symbolised by these ancient trees, even though it was a tradition he revered. The reason was partly that he had to give expression to his own, unique imaginative experience of the trees and the Wordsworthian terror they inspired. In them, he encountered what Wordsworth had called 'huge and mighty forms, that do not live like living men', which 'moved slowly through the mind/By day, and were a trouble to my dreams'.[51] Another reason was, as noted earlier, that they reminded him too much of alien working people. Perhaps another was that he resented the way they stood for an aristocratic tradition which could give a kind of immortality to some chosen beings, while others had to face total extinction. Kilvert's astonishing claim that he was related to the Cornewall family, and that his forefathers had owned the Moccas estate, becomes more significant when seen in this connection.

The first time the claim surfaces in the *Diary* is in the entry for 10 April 1875 when Kilvert was being shown Moccas Church by Sir George Cornewall and Kilvert showed special interest in the tomb of a medieval knight, Sir Reginald Fresne. Kilvert had the idea that, because Fresne was a corruption of the Latin word *Fraxinus*, which is the generic name for trees of the ash family, the Ashe family, from which he was descended on his mother's side, was related to the Cornewalls. He apparently had no other evidence for this flimsy conjecture but it took root in his mind for he was still pursuing it nearly three years later. On this later occasion he was rash enough to state it publicly when circumstances gave him encouragement. By this time he was Vicar of Bredwardine and Sir George's neighbour. On New Year's Day 1878, Kilvert had met his churchwarden, Davies, and was invited to his farmhouse, which he rented from Sir George. Made comfortable by Davies' old-fashioned courtesy and a glass or two of his home-made cider, Kilvert listened to an account of how the Davies family had been tenants of the Cornewalls for nearly 100 years, yet so close was the bond of trust between tenant and landlord, that no lease had ever been thought necessary. However, Cornewall landlords had over the years failed to maintain the farmhouse properly: Davies described it as 'worse than a cottage'. Earlier that morning, Kilvert had visited the cottages of his tenants (as Vicar of Bredwardine he was entitled to rent out his glebe land to locals).[52] It was this fact, plus the similarity of the story of the Davies' farmhouse to the story of Chieflands, that pushed Kilvert into stating openly that he was the social equal of Sir George, whilst at the same time reflecting privately that the tradition of care for tenants represented by his grandfather, Squire Coleman, made him Sir George's moral superior. Kilvert then launched into an account of the tomb of Sir Reginald de Fresne in Moccas Church. 'He was an ancestor of mine,' he confidently declared, 'and my forefathers owned the Moccas estate'. The church-warden, Kilvert noted, opened his eyes 'almost incredulously at first' (as well he might) but after Kilvert had gone through the pedigree, of which he gives no details, Davies was (so Kilvert believed) more convinced because he had heard of the name *Fraxinus*.[53] A few days later, Kilvert was at Squire Ashe's home seeking more information about the link between the Ashes and Cornewalls. However, Mrs. Ashe had 'unfortunately mislaid the only book which would throw light on the subject'. He had by then broached the subject with Sir George because he said he was 'much interested' in it.

This fanciful connection increased Kilvert's interest in the Moccas estate. The meanings which he read into the scene he beheld as he descended the hill and entered Sir George's Park were precisely those that Thomas Hearne had intended, among others, in his painting, 'Moccas Deer Park with a large oak tree' (*c*.1788/9). He had done a series of views of Moccas to celebrate both the ancient features of the Cornewall estate and the improvements that were being undertaken by the Sir George Cornewall of the time. The 'large oak tree' is the 'king oak' with which Kilvert was so taken. Hearne depicted the pollarded tree, with its vast girth and a hollow in its trunk, very much as the 'great ruined grey tower' described by Kilvert. Kilvert also commented 'that the tree may be 2000 years old', as though he had read or heard about it. Hearne's picture had appeared as one of six 'Picturesque landscapes' in *Antiquities of Great Britain*, volume two (1807), edited by Hearne and Byrne, and the accompanying text draws attention to the two features which particularly impressed Kilvert. The age of the Moccas oak was, the commentator tells us, 'supposed to equal, if not exceed, any other tree'. He made no esti-mate of its actual age, and Kilvert may have obtained that from

Bishop, the Moccas curate, who had told him all about the Moccas oaks in August 1872. The *Antiquities* commentator also noted the way in which the combination in an oak tree of decay and vigorous growth was a true mark of the picturesque.

It is evident that Kilvert's antiquarian interest had led him to make some study of the picturesque fashion in nature and art, which was in vogue when Hearne was painting. His visit to Yaverland and Nunwell is informed by an awareness of the picturesque. It is also to be found in several passages in his account of his Cornish holiday.[54] His sister Emily stated that the volumes of *Old England* were 'a never failing source of pleasure' in their childhood. This work contains a romantic account of English history and features hundreds of pictures of ancient buildings. Its full title reflects its nostalgic tone: *Old England. A Pictorial Museum of Regal, Ecclesiastical, Municipal, Baronial, and Popular Antiquities.* Robert Kilvert recalled in his *Memoirs* that he had developed a taste for antiquities from a similar book he found in his grandmother's house. '*Old England*' was in the tradition of what David Morris calls 'the rising demand for visual images and information related to British history'.[55] There was a great upsurge of antiquarian interest from the 1750s onwards, with many antiquarians becoming members of the Society of Antiquaries. This body supported the publication of Hearne's *Antiquities,* which is a collection of prints of picturesque ruins. Kilvert's uncle Francis, an influential antiquary in the south-west, would certainly have possessed a copy, though he was not a subscriber to it and for him, Hearne would have been a local luminary. Born in 1744 at Marshfield, only eight miles from Bath, Hearne had done a painting of the Old Toll House in Widcombe, the Bath suburb in which the Kilvert family lived. His reputation as a watercolourist remained high until the mid-19th century. Kilvert's interest in the picturesque must have been greatly stimulated by his uncle and by the books in his library when a pupil at his Claverton Lodge school. For many like Kilvert and his uncle 'the interest in the picturesque and in antiquities were often indistinguishable from one another'.[56] It is evident from Kilvert's visits to historic buildings, visits that were very frequent in the later part of his life when he was intensely preoccupied with the past, that he had read guides similar to Hearne's *Antiquities,* which aimed to provide the public with 'visual souvenirs of well known sites'.[57] Historical texts accompanied each print in *Antiquities* and Kilvert's accounts of visits to, for example,

Malmesbury Abbey Church and Llanthony Abbey, show that he had read beforehand something of the history of these sites, both of which appear in Hearne's book. There are signs too of the reflection on the 'moral content ... related to rural life' that Hearne sought to encourage in those who viewed his prints.[58] Much picturesque theory favoured resistance by the rural and the traditional to modern life,[59] which is a strong element in Kilvert's stance towards the past.

He showed detailed, explicit awareness of the picturesque when he visited Tintern Abbey at the end of June 1875. The possibility that he had seen Hearne's painting of the Moccas oak, and had read the commentary on it in the *Antiquities* volume, is made all the more likely when one sets the commentary to be found there on Tintern Abbey against Kilvert's own.[60] Throughout much of the latter there is the strong sense that he was intent on establishing his own point of view on this famous building and its picturesque credentials in opposition to an official or accepted one. He begins by asserting 'Tintern Abbey at first sight seemed to me to be... almost too perfect to be entirely picturesque...', in contradiction to the claim made in the *Antiquities* guidebook that 'no monastical ruin in Great Britain presents a more beautiful perspective'. The guidebook claimed that 'the arches were obscured by foliage, edged by tendrils of ivy', whereas Kilvert declared '[it] seemed to be bare... one wants a little more... ivy and the long line of the building should be broken by trees'. He also wanted 'more ruin', while the guidebook confidently stated that 'everything impresses the mind with the idea of decay'. Kilvert was prepared to accept what the commentator had to say about 'clustered columns and divisions of aisles'. He liked the Abbey's 'narrow aisled vistas' and the 'graceful lightness of the soaring arches', which, with the 'perfect tracery of the east and west windows [were] singularly beautiful'. The *Antiquities* commentator had declared the Abbey's perspective to be 'uncommonly beautiful'.

Moccas Court would, of course, have been another place where Kilvert had access to the *Antiquities* volume and Hearne's paintings. He was a regular visitor there and on occasion dined with Sir George Cornewall, who extended the facilities of his library to local gentry. Kilvert once met his friend Tomkyns Dew returning from lunching at Moccas and from consulting botanical books in the library. Hearne's painting contained, as was noted earlier, a strong political as well as a picturesque dimension. It shows a young man, probably a member of the Cornewall family, seated with the vast bulk of the oak tree towering up reassuringly behind him. The series of views of Moccas, of which it formed a part, 'conveyed a sense of local rootedness and cohesion',[61] which was the impression which the current Sir George Cornewall wished to project of himself. It was a time of agricultural and industrial expansion, as well as a time when it was prudent, with the memory of the French Revolution still very fresh, to underline the power and usefulness of traditional authority. Kilvert had always valued the sense of 'local rootedness' supplied by the Clutterbuck family in his own locality. It was that concept of community, with all its suggestions of order and stability, which provided the framework in which his notion of the secure home of childhood, unchanged and unchanging, found its place. His concern with his armorial bearings (they are mentioned three times in the *Diary*) are linked to this notion. In addition to their romantic overtones, they also indicated for him 'local rootedness', and a desire to assert equality of a kind with such as the Cornewalls.

It is not accidental that he chose to characterise both Yaverland and his Harnish home as 'paradise'. The association of home with heaven was an entirely conventional Victorian one. It was given classic, memorable expression by J.A. Froude, the Victorian historian. In his comments on home, there is the vein of melancholy which is characteristic of so much Victorian writing and which is particularly strong in the later parts of Kilvert's *Diary*. Houghton noted it in Browning, in Tennyson's earlier poems and in 'In Memoriam', in Matthew Arnold, Clough, Sterling, Maurice, Kingsley, and J.S. Mill. It was, he said, felt to some extent by 'nearly all educated Victorians'.[62] Froude's mood of futility and frustration is reflected both in the tone of Kilvert's *Diary*, especially after he had left Clyro, and in the frequent passages where he reflects on mysterious, unnamed illnesses and the imminence of death.[63] Gripped by an illness to which he did give a name on this occasion (congestion of the lungs) in March 1878, he reflected: 'How calm bright, peaceful and homelike is the dear old home. How long will it last? So going forward'. Froude similarly talked of journeying through life accepting its routine joys and sorrows but, as the end approached, there was an increasing sense of dissatisfaction when the heart cried out that it could find 'no rest here, no home. Neither pleasure, nor rank, nor money, nor success in life... can satisfy'.[64] The unquiet soul had to accept that the earth could never provide the sense of belonging it craved. Its impulse was towards the 'one last reality', identified in Froude's mind with his birthplace. 'We call heaven our home', he said, because it was 'the best name we know to give it'. He believed that 'God has given us each our own Paradise, our own ...childhood... to which our own hearts cling, as all we have ever known of Heaven on earth', and he saw human beings, as Kilvert did, as 'earth's weary wayfarers'. Kilvert's poems reiterate the idea of men as pilgrims searching for a final resting place, an idea encapsulated in the motto he invented to go with the family's armorial bearings: 'Peregrinamus... we are pilgrims'. His further comments on it are immensely revealing of what it signified for him. 'It hath a solemn, lovely, melancholy sound', he said, made up of four elements: '"We are pilgrims". "We are strangers". "We are foreigners". "We are sojourners"'.[65]

Kilvert derived this view of home from the general ethos of his family: its relationships, its religion, the reading it allowed and encouraged. It also came from the example of his father, whose near breakdown at Oriel was partly the result of a homesickness in which deep melancholy and the experience of 'strangeness and loneliness' played a significant part, as well as the departure of his brother, Richard, for Canada and 'our removal just at this time from the old home where I was born'.[66] Of course, there were reasons for his unhappiness which had to do with Oriel's atmosphere, but his alienation can be seen, as can that of his son, against the background of social and economic changes that continued through the century.

The authority of the Church and of the ruling class was being steadily weakened by the combined effects of industrialism, radicalism, reform, and religious scepticism. By the time Kilvert was born, the process was already well advanced in the towns, where the social relations that existed on the landed estate had no place. Working people there were not under the eye of squire and clergyman, and many lived in a state of perpetual conflict with their employers over wages and working conditions. The factory system, as Robert Owen had noted as early as 1815, had changed 'the general character of the mass of the people'.[67] Relations between employers and workers in industry were increasingly subject to state interference and state legislation, and bureaucracy came more and more to influence the way things were managed. People's lives were transformed further by the experience of urban living. By the middle of the 19th century, more people lived in towns than in the countryside and the character of home life was changed by the split between home experience and work experience that was noted earlier. The social and physical mobility that had enabled people to move into towns in the first place was disruptive of traditional ways of living and thinking, and one of its consequences was rejection of religion by the working-class. Even in the countryside, the Church had virtually lost its control over labourers when Robert Kilvert was in Keevil, and his son knew that his influence on his poorer Clyro parishioners was limited to women, children, and the old. When Kilvert gives us portraits of peasant piety in his *Diary*, his subjects are invariably elderly men and women. From the 18th century onwards, the Church's role lay in social work with the 'non-combatants and... the wounded, not in inspiring the main army'.[68] This effectively sums up the nature of Kilvert's parochial work, apart from his involvement with village schools, which forms the subject of a separate chapter.

His nostalgia for childhood included an attachment to the idea of the simple peasant of traditional society, who, though he might suffer from hunger and oppression, had the comfort of knowing that he had an unquestionable place in the village community and did not experience the 'homelessness' and anonymity of his town-dwelling brother. Long before Kilvert took up his post as curate in Clyro in 1865, this had already become a myth. Enclosure Acts which denied access to common land, permanently low wages, and hostility from landlords and farmers, made labourers aliens in their own communities. For ten years before 1865, many landlords had pursued a steady policy of pulling down cottages on their estates in order to reduce their liability to pay poor rates for the pauperised labourers who lived in them, so that it was true to say that 'people do not desert villages, villages nowadays desert people'.[69] Those cottages that did remain were usually unfit for human beings: 'The majority of cottages that exist in rural parishes are deficient in almost every requisite that should constitute a home for a Christian family...'.[70] Kilvert also romanticised the work done by agricultural labourers. To anyone who did not enquire too closely, it might appear that their work was more satisfying and fulfilling than that of factory workers, but most jobs were hard, monotonous, dirty, and had to be performed in all weathers on an inadequate diet. When Kilvert celebrated 'Honest Work' in his poem of that name, it was the traditional jobs of the countryside—milking, ploughing, caring for animals—that are featured. Work of that kind came into his mind when he became nostalgic for home during absences from it:

> I seem to scent the new mown hay,
> And in the mornings blythe
> I hear across the ocean gray
> The mower whet his scythe...[71]

At the Chieflands farm of the Frys, home and work appear as a unified whole in a vision of a society which was integrated by a number of over-arching meanings missing from life in the town. That vision was fundamental to Kilvert's concept of landed property, which not only provided incomes for rich and poor, but defined one's social position and its attendant duties. Coleridge in 1816 had reminded landowners of the weight of their responsibility in connection with property: 'This land is not yours, it was vested in your lineage in trust for the nation'.[72] It was a view of property Kilvert had absorbed, as the anecdote he told about the Clutterbuck family, the local gentry in Harnish, makes clear. We are told that in 1814 when Mrs. Clutterbuck was newly married to the 'old Squire', Thomas Clutterbuck, he was showing her round his estate and remarked, 'All this is ours'. She replied, 'Only lent to us'.[73] Integral to her concept of landed property as trust was awareness of the needs of its dependants.

Kilvert was brought up in the knowledge that his family were dependants of the Clutterbucks. When he sought to give expression to his deepest feelings about home, a landed family, secure in its property and its traditions, was a central element in his vision. His heart ached over the void the Clutterbucks' absence from Hardenhuish made: 'All the cry seems to be for the old family, the beloved and honoured family, the Clutterbucks, to come back to their own again'. What was absent for Kilvert with the Clutterbucks gone was not simply their name and personalities, but the tradition and the relations that they had built up. They had (so it seemed to him) a personal knowledge of the villagers and they of them. A new gentry family could inhabit the Clutterbuck home but could neither recover nor recreate the power of the contacts developed over generations. It was impossible to take shortcuts to achieve these fruits that were the harvest of organic change. A thoroughbred horse was the result of generations of breeding. Apart from providing tenants with farms, labourers with work, and the poor with charity, the gentry supplied the entire community with the opportunity of living vicariously their own privileged lives. In their balls and celebrations, the gentry symbolically lived for their less fortunate neighbours, who, with a varying degree of participation, were able to share in those events as though they were momentous events in their own lives. The commonest example was the coming of age of the son or daughter of a gentry family. The case of Miss Long is recorded in the *Diary*. 'When Miss Long became heiress of Draycot and Wanstead and came of age there were great rejoicings. An ox was roasted whole in the park and a troop of yeomanry cavalry guarded it, riding round the roasted ox to keep the people off it... thousands of people gathered from far and near to see the rejoicing'.[74] A squire and his authority did become deeply impressed on the minds of some country folk. Kilvert, visiting the mad Mrs. Watkins and trying to focus her mind on serious thoughts, asked her whom she prayed to, and she replied 'Mr Venables'. Venables was Kilvert's vicar at the time. Kilvert commented: 'It was the dim lingering idea of someone in authority'.[75] Another of Kilvert's authority figures, Squire Ashe of Langley Burrell, had become identified with God in the minds of the village children. When asked in school, 'who made the world?' they replied 'Mr Ashe'. Though he found these episodes amusing, Kilvert liked to see authority given its due. At the chaotic opening of a new chapel in Radnorshire, the crowd had been inattentive during the addresses of earlier speakers, 'but directly the Squire of Nantmel began to speak, a man whom they knew and respected, there was instant silence and attention'.[76]

The attitude towards Nature which Kilvert assimilated from his home background incorporated the landed estate and its integrating order, but that order was steadily being eroded by railways as well as by social and political changes. Kilvert's ambivalent attitude to the modernity represented by rail travel is seen in his general love of it, which was counter-balanced by his hatred of tourists and of missing trains. There were a number of issues that roused Kilvert to almost insane fury; one of them, as has been shown, was property rights. Another was the British tourist. This is seen most startlingly in the *Diary* passage that concerns his visit with his Clyro friends, Bridge and Morrell, to a favourite spot of Kilvert's—Llanthony Abbey. Taking Morrell's carriage to a point where their walk could begin, they arrived at the Abbey ruins only to find that some tourists were there already. 'What was our horror on entering the enclosure to see two tourists with staves and shoulder belts all complete postured among the ruins in an attitude of admiration, one of them of course discoursing learnedly to his gaping companion and pointing out objects of interest with his stick... Of all noxious animals... the most noxious is a tourist. And of all tourists the most vulgar, illbred, offensive and loathsome is the British tourist'.[77] What exactly was the offence caused by the Llanthony tourists that merited this intemperate outburst? It seems that they had offended simply by being there at all: clearly he regarded such places as his, or meant exclusively for people of his class. It would be good to know the identity of these tourists. It is most unlikely they would have been working men because the day in question was a Tuesday, and would probably not have chosen Llanthony Abbey as their destination in any case. Perhaps they were clerks or shop assistants from Hereford, who had a day off and had taken the train to Hay and then walked the 12 miles up the valley to Llanthony. One of the chief consequences of the coming of the railways was that they spread a taste for visiting places of interest beyond the tiny minority of upper-class people to whom it had formerly been restricted. It was plain to Kilvert at least that the offending tourists were not gentlemen.

He was quite unable to find any reasonable basis for his resentment of them. By picturing them in 'an attitude of admiration', he implied that their interest in the ruins was false, and that the knowledge displayed by one was spurious. In spite of the fact that he had studied history at Oxford, he was dismissive of a genuinely historical approach to local places such as was taken by the Woolhope Naturalists' Field Club at this time in the locality. He distanced himself from it and its activities with great care. Such historical interest as he had was more of an antiquarian and romantic character,[78] while another reason for remaining aloof was his preference for solitary wanderings. On one occasion, he expressed interest in a site the Woolhope Club was investigating near Hay but observed in his *Diary*: 'I did not go as I hate going about in a herd...'.[79] The two tourists at Llanthony were innocent of being either numerous or noisy, yet Kilvert still managed to identify them with tourists, whom he generally found 'vulgar' and 'illbred'. He convicted them of lack of breeding on these most illogical and unjust grounds: 'The most offensive part of their conduct ...was that they had arrived before us and already ordered their dinner, so we had to wait till they had done...'. His cup of wrath ran over when he discovered, as he scanned the Visitors' Book to pass the time, that the pages bearing entries from October 1865 to May 1866 had been cut out; the entry of his own last visit was one of the missing ones. For Kilvert there was only one possible culprit—the British tourist.

When the landlord was free to serve Kilvert's party, he told the servant girl to prepare 'plenty of ham and eggs *for the gentlemen*',[80] who had been kept waiting an hour for their food. The real nature of the tourists' offence is thus revealed: in keeping their betters waiting (the fact that they were not waiting when the tourists ordered their own dinner was irrelevant), they had shown a conceit, a presumption, a failure to know their place. The attitude recalls that of another country-bred clergyman's son—J.A. Froude, who has already been mentioned in this chapter—towards people he met from the colonies. For Froude, colonials represented, just at Kilvert's tourists did, certain unfortunate tendencies of emergent democracy, as his comments on those he encountered on a ship returning from New Zealand makes clear: 'They were, as a rule, vain, ignorant, under-bred, without dignity, without courtesy and with a conceit that was unbounded. Middle-class democracy is not favourable to the growth of manners'.[81] Moreover, they declined to acknowledge the superiority of a 'gentleman' and to show him the deference Froude expected. In Kilvert's idealised rural community, landowners, farmers, and labourers, though separated by rank and station, should live together in perfect harmony.

Railways, and the era of cheap, mass travel which they ushered in, boosted the spread of democratic attitudes. European trains continued to demarcate the classes into separate carriages, whereas in the U.S.A., that former colony, carriages were open to all. Railways made it possible for the less well-off to travel beyond the limited horizons of their villages, which in itself put them on a par with the rich, who had previously been the only ones who could travel regularly and any distance. There was a staggering increase in the number of passengers. Between 1842 and 1847, it rose from 23m a year to 51m. By 1851 the figure was 79m, by 1860 it was 160m, and in the year Kilvert died it was 604m.[82] Travel by horse-drawn carriage had always involved a highly conspicuous display of wealth in the shape of the carriages themselves, the grooms, and the fine horses, but even for the very rich rail travel was necessarily a much more anonymous business and in spite of the different grades of railway carriage, inevitably there was some mixing and levelling. Railways brought to villages the newspapers which Kilvert's father had seen as a dangerous organ of democracy. By the 1860s, the isolation and self-sufficiency of village communities was beginning to break down as a consequence of the spread of the railways. Kilvert's lifetime coincided in fact with the most rapid development of the network. After the initial boom of the 1830s, there was a second one in the mid-1840s, by which time most of the major cities had been linked. A new boom came at the time Kilvert took up his Clyro curacy, the total length of lines doubling between 1850 and 1870.[83]

Railways represented all the forces there were destined to disrupt traditional rural ways. One historian called the navvies who built them 'the shock troops of industrialism'.[84] They were synonymous with progress. When the railway came to the village of Williton in Somerset, a banner with the words 'Hail, Steam the Civilizer!' was stretched across the main street.[85] This was the keynote of the Grand Gala Day that marked the completion of the line from Hereford to Brecon a few months before Kilvert arrived in Clyro. It had officially been opened on 19 September 1864, and on the 26th 400 people crowded on to an excursion train (tickets 1s 9d), which called at all the little villages on the route. Some people competed with each other in sticking their heads out of the windows, while others consumed sherry and biscuits. One traveller expressed the view that going to Hay by rail was attributable to 'the genius of the age', and said he had read in the newspapers a claim that 'before we dies we may actually fly through the air!' Another marvelled at being able to travel from Hereford to Hay for 1s 9d when the old coach used to cost 10s and take the best part of a day. When the train arrived at Hay, a Mr. Jennings, in a toast to the chairman of the railway company, observed that some tradesmen naturally feared the extra competition that railways brought but such people would have to change and adopt the 'new-fangled' notions of the new age. In a field near the station, two marquees had been erected—one for refreshments, one for dancing—and they were filled with a thousand day-trippers. It is as well that Kilvert missed this Grand Gala Day—he would have hated it, not least because the phenomenon it celebrated encouraged a restlessness among poorer country folk, which was disturbing because it led to their being dissatisfied with their station in life. Country traditions also died away because of the impulse towards commercialisation and 'new-fangled' notions and new habits.

Kilvert, in his romantic attachment to the land, preferred to ignore economic realities. His attitude is exemplified in the episode when he met a farmer in Dorset who declared he was 'a slave'. Kilvert tried to cheer him by pointing out that he had a farm but the man stubbornly and gloomily repeated that he was a slave and had been one all his life. Kilvert seems not to have enquired further into the farmer's situation, but the point the latter was making was that he was a mere tenant and owned nothing. He also drew attention to his limited horizons, which was another aspect of his slavery. 'He regretted that he had never travelled or been far from home'. He offered Kilvert some cider and Kilvert asked him if he had heard of William Barnes, the Dorset poet, and his praise of Dorset hospitality, but he had not. Kilvert had not come to the district to hear any of this. He was seeking 'the ruined ivied tower' of Holditch Court and 'the grand old days' of the nearby castle. (Experts on the picturesque regarded ruined towers with particular favour.) The limited knowledge, including local knowledge, of the farmer was replicated in a country boy of whom Kilvert later sought directions to the old tower and the way to Hawkchurch, barely two miles away; the boy knew the location of neither. The tower was, Kilvert observed, 'within a stone's throw' of where the boy stood. He obviously thought it deplorable that the boy knew nothing of the tower which he had come to see, but he was as unwilling to examine the reasons for the boy's ignorance as he was the reasons for the farmer's slavery. Nor could he romanticise this tenant farmer as he had Mr. Fry of Chieflands, whose 'narrow and limited horizons' Kilvert had represented as virtues.

In what has already been said about Kilvert's attitude towards nature, emphasis had been laid on its romantic character, its love of the ancient and traditional, its veneration for the landed estate as a symbol of community and for beauty as evidence of the existence of a benevolent creator. It remains now to indicate more of the part that literature and painting played in its development. Account has already been taken of the influence of Sir Walter Scott's novels. In what Kilvert read and retained from the pastoral tradition of English poetry can been seen the nostalgia that is central to his vision.[86] It is there in the choice of readings he made for himself at the Clyro Penny Reading on 27 November 1871. 'I recited some passages from the Deserted Village, the Village Ale House, the Village Schoolmaster and the Village Clergyman'.[87] Goldsmith's portraits of the Schoolmaster and the Preacher (revealingly Kilvert altered the word to 'Clergyman'; perhaps 'preacher' smacked too much of Dissent and lacked dignity) are affectionate. The former was immensely learned in the eyes of rustics and, though severe where learning was concerned, was basically kind and jovial. The latter might have been Kilvert himself.[88] Goldsmith's Village Ale House had a benign aspect which appealed to the Diarist, but which he could not find in Clyro's New Inn. The one provided rest from 'smiling toil', the other was the haunt of the disaffected and unrespectable poor for whom work was a bitter experience. Kilvert, like Goldsmith, declined to engage with the actual nature of labourers' work. Nor did he choose to read those parts of the poem which indicated that the Schoolmaster, Clergyman, and Ale House were elements of an older village spoilt by enclosures.[89] Goldsmith had been specific about the process that created a mansion and estate (such as Bowood):

> ...the man of wealth and pride
> Takes up a space that many poor supplied;
> Space for his lake, his park's extended bounds...

Kilvert did his 'Deserted Village' reading before he read an article on the work of another poet in the pastoral tradition—George Crabbe.[90] In it were many emphases Kilvert would have found pleasing. The writer noted that Crabbe was loved by all women and children, and died 'little affected by change'. There was also a warm picture of Crabbe's uncle, 'a sturdy yeoman', in whose house master and servants dined together (as they probably did at Chieflands), and of an idyllic rural society in which labourers' trade unions had no place. However, the article noted that Crabbe's poem, 'The Village', was written as a 'corrective' to 'The Deserted Village', and aimed at giving 'the bare blank facts of rural life, stripped of all sentimental gloss'.[91] The poor in 'The Village' are not, 'as rich men fancy, healthy and well fed. Their work makes them premature victims to... rheumatism'. Their ultimate end was the workhouse.[92] In spite of this realism, Crabbe finally took comfort, as Kilvert did, in the moment when rich and poor 'Die and are equal in the dust at last'.[93]

Kilvert had made a hero of William Barnes, the dialect poet of the Dorset countryside, about whose work he had quizzed the Holditch farmer. Kilvert made a pilgrimage to see the poet in April 1874. 'I told him I had for many years known him through his writings and had long wished to thank him in person for the many happy hours his poems had given me'.[94] What he valued above all in Barnes' work was his human sympathy: 'All his poems are overflowing with love and tenderness towards the dear scenes and friends of his youth'. Barnes' poems, however, maintain a realistic and critical stance towards their subject matter, which Kilvert largely ignored. Barnes knew, and was prepared to admit, that the rural society of his youth had changed. His poem, 'The Happy Days When I Wer Young', presents a picture of a blighted Arcadia. It begins with the reflection, by a labourer, that when he was young he felt no weight of care pressing on him, and was content and fulfilled by his daily work. He and other labourers had health and adequate food and shelter. In the community there was harmony and an absence of fear and hostility. Conversation then, either at work or in the home, did not take the line that it commonly did in more recent time—the need to despise the laws of God and man. The poison that destroyed this idyll came from human society:

> Vrom where wer all this venom brought,
> To kill our hope an' taint our thought?
> Clear brook! thy water coulden bring
> Such venom vrom thy rocky spring.

Other of Barnes' poems indicate that some of the venom came from enclosures and the greed that encouraged the swallowing up of small farms by larger ones and by estates. One poem, 'Eclogue: The Times', locates the source of the venom in the Corn Laws, which helped to keep labourers poor, and in labourers' lack of political representation, which left them vulnerable to laws made by the rich for the rich.

Barnes' deep love of country ways links him to Wordsworth. In the belief, perhaps initially absorbed from Aguilar's *Home Influence*, in the power of natural beauty to awaken a spiritual sense, Kilvert was truly Wordsworthian. Wordsworth urged experiencing Nature in calm and 'meditative cheerfulness', because he 'Who, in this spirit communes with the Forms/Of Nature, who with understanding heart/Both knows and loves such objects... needs must feel/The joy of that pure principle of love' which would make him seek out affectionate natures in his fellow human beings.[95] In Wordsworth, Kilvert found another element to which his nature responded: the sense of the countryside as a retreat from human society, seen most clearly in his determination to be alone when walking. He expressed intense dislike of meeting people on walks and his love of 'a deserted road'.[96] His solitary wanderings were a means of expressing and relieving his melancholy. 'I like wandering about these lonely, waste and ruined places. There dwells among them a spirit of quiet and gentle melancholy more congenial... to my spirit than full life and gaiety and noise'.[97] Wordsworth had attributed to 'Visions of the hills/And souls of lonely places' the power of evoking primal emotions of joy, hope, and fear, which became the foundation of his youthful character.[98] Complementary to Kilvert's love of solitude was the interest he shared with Wordsworth in solitary figures. For both Wordsworth and Kilvert they promoted a deep fellow-feeling, the result of the 'pure principle of love', of which the former had spoken. William Barnes, too, represented this principle and it is noticeable that Kilvert referred to him as 'half hermit'. Kilvert was fascinated by the Solitary of Llanbedr, a clergyman who lived in a squalid cabin near Clyro, though he was a 'Master of Arts of Cambridge University'. Local people 'touched their hats to his reverence with great respect' and 'recognised him as a very holy man...'. Solitary beings had political significance, too, for both Kilvert and Wordsworth in that they made clear that the true sources of man's happiness were entirely separate from his social and political existence. Wordsworth's leech-gatherer represented for him the triumph of individual integrity over material circumstances. He did acknowledge that it was an unjust society that created such figures, but his interest in the man was based on his fortitude and honest labour.[99] Wordsworth had abandoned his youthful radicalism and become an orthodox Tory and the reverence in his poems for order and established institutions were Tory elements that appealed to Kilvert.[100] The moral issues of human happiness presented themselves to Wordsworth in terms of traditional obligations:

> The primal duties shine aloft like stars;
> The charities that soothe, and heal, and bless...
> The generous inclination, the just rule...[101]

It was an essentially paternalistic vision, which, as the subsequent chapter on Kilvert's relationship with the poor will show, represented in all essentials the approach adopted to rural poverty by him and other gentry clergy.

From Tennyson, another of Kilvert's favourite poets, the Diarist derived a number of things, some of which complemented and extended literary influences that have already been registered. Tennyson had all of Scott's interest in the medieval and the heroic and Kilvert was born into the period when the cult of the hero was at its height.[102] Tennyson deepened Kilvert's awareness of the beauty and mystery of Nature that he had learnt from Wordsworth. He also expressed a Wordsworthian moral optimism that became part of Kilvert's outlook.[103] Tennyson's attitude to rank was, like Kilvert's, highly ambivalent: 'Tis only noble to be good./True hearts are more than coronets/And simple faith than Norman blood', Tennyson had written.[104]

In his choice of novelists Kilvert was very much middle-of-the-road Victorian. Instead of Jane Austen, Thackeray, Dickens, the Brontés, George Eliot, he read Adelaide Sartoris, Charles Kingsley, Mrs. Gaskell, Lady Verney, and Trollope. One might have expected that Dickens, with his faith in natural love, in the basic instinct to do good and to experience beauty, would have made him a favourite with Kilvert, but the *Diary* contains nothing to indicate that he ever read Dickens. Kilvert's sister, Emily, recalled seeing serialised parts of *Bleak House* in her mother's possession. What is perhaps significant is that the head of the Kilvert household never read Dickens aloud to the family. His objection to the popular author may have been at bottom religious. Although Dickens frequently declared he was a Christian, he had no time for formal religion, for the Church and its authority. Where his characters are motivated by the pursuit of goodness, there is no clear religious impulse behind what they do and their aim is to spread happiness, not faith. The greatest obstacle to his acceptance in the Kilvert home was probably that he rejected the notion of original sin.[105]

When we come to Kilvert's taste in paintings, we find that he was as selective about the realities portrayed in them as he was about those portrayed in fiction and poetry, and again provides us with a 'microcosm of middle-class taste'.[106] His choices were determined largely by subject matter, and he found it easier to admire older artists than contemporary ones. Landseer, for example, whose anthropomorphised animals were admired by Kilvert, had been painting in that style long before the Victorian age began. Kilvert was not taken with 19th-century landscape painting as represented by Constable, Turner, and the Impressionists. Their 'individual physical vision' and 'spiritual insight' was lacking in Victorian landscape, in the view of Humphry House; the kind of vision favoured was the 'vision of ordinary life' because 'the world of Victorian art is the world of the plain practical man'.[107] Rather sentimentalised portrayals of children and animals were for Kilvert, as for many Victorians, the most appealing subject matter. He admired Murillo's 'The Good Shepherd', in which a child with lambs is depicted in a sentimental way. Patriotic subjects were also important to him. He saw Elizabeth Butler's 'Roll Call' and called it 'striking', although was slightly disappointed by it. He liked paintings that told stories and indicated time passing, again a very Victorian taste.[108] The sentimentality of some Victorian paintings was a means of investing factual representations of people and scenes with moral and emotional significance, added as an embellishment.[109]

This is seen very clearly in those works depicting the rural simplicity that in fact belonged mainly to the pre-Victorian genre of George Morland, David Wilkie, and William Collins. Kilvert indicated his sensitivity to calm, peaceful, pastoral scenes when he saw in Langley Burrell 'the old grey manor house and Church Tower ...framed as in a picture by the golden elms'.[110] A hillside in Radnorshire reminded him of William Collins' picture, 'Come Along', which showed 'two barefooted, gleaning girls fording the brook on stepping stones'.[111] Collins' work dominated the early Victorian period when Kilvert was young. He was born in 1788, studied with Morland, who specialised in the painting of animals, and was a friend of David Wilkie.[112] Collins was in fact at one with those contemporary critics of Morland's paintings of the rural poor who found them disturbing because they were too realistic.[113] Collins' early success was built on his 'Disposal of a Favourite Lamb' (1813), which achieved huge popular success; 15,000 small prints of it were sold that year. He knew he had hit a rich vein and continued to exploit it with a public for whom 'a prettily sentimental view of country life' was an escape from the squalors of urban living.[114] The genre owned something to Murillo, another of Kilvert's favourites. Collins' paintings often featured landscapes with incidents involving children. 'Happy as a King' shows fresh-faced children, happy and clean despite their rags, playing on a five-barred gate.[115] Two other highly popular paintings of his were likely to have had a strong appeal for Kilvert, 'Cottage Hospitality' (1834) and 'Rustic Civility' (1832). He made much in *Diary* entries of hospitality and courtesy encountered in the cottages and farms of the lower classes.[116] 'Rustic Civility' shows a barefoot child, who has been gathering sticks, touching his forelock in deference as he holds open a gate for a gentry rider, who appears only as a shadow in the foreground.

The issue of Kilvert and painting cannot be left without some reference to his response to Holman Hunt's 'The Shadow of Death', which he saw in London in June 1874. He had been warned not to go and see it (perhaps by the Venables with whom he had dined the previous evening), and he found that those who had warned him had been right. He pronounced it 'theatrical and detestable', and 'a waste of a good shilling'. He was no doubt put off by its symbolic nature but there were reasons other than aesthetic ones for his finding it so 'detestable'. There *is* a theatrical element to it but so many others that he liked were just as theatrical.[117] The chief reason for his hostility is that Hunt's painting portrays Christ as a working man and sets him firmly in his carpenter's shop. Hunt had declared his intention of showing something of historical reality: 'my picture is strictly... historic with not a single fact in it of a supernatural nature'.[118] This was too much for Kilvert, whose attitude was akin to that of the Cambridgeshire gentry lady with whom the Rev. J.W.E. Conybeare was discussing the current agricultural labourers' strike. Conybeare's wife soon realised that this haughty lady was deeply opposed to the strike and hurriedly changed the subject to the Hunt painting. This was no better, for the lady had seen it and condemned it. 'I do not like having forced upon me that our Lord was a working man...', she explained frostily.[119] The painting was nevertheless extremely popular and clearly appealed to many who could accept its historical fact.

The tension evident in Kilvert's attitude to the Hunt painting is in some ways symbolic of the Kilvert home. To judge from his father's and his sister's accounts of it, it was a happy home, but it was beset by a variety of conflicts. It deferred in a general way to its social betters yet a sense of its own identity and values as middle-class people bred an opposition to landed power. Basic to that opposition was Evangelicalism, which cherished the fundamental conviction that one's worth resided in one's spiritual self and not in rank or wealth. The Kilvert home stood for stable Christian values and for warm emotional relationships and was bound to disapprove of country houses dominated by excessive pride in rank and by manly sports. Though the country house tradition appealed to the Kilverts because of its history, romance and stability, its authority was steadily being weakened as democratic, bourgeois forces gained ground. The decline in religious belief and in deference had not been confined to the town. From other disturbing features of the town—competitiveness, materialism, radical politics, overt class conflict—it could be pretended that the countryside was still free. However, the Kilvert clergymen, were, nevertheless, required to minister to and to control, as far as possible, the disaffected and property-less rural poor. The institutions of land and Church, on which the Kilverts depended for their livelihood and status, as least provided some of the unifying values that the new society lacked. In order to assert its status and to resist a society whose tendencies it deplored and feared, Robert and his son were driven increasingly to exalt the virtues of an idealised 'earlier world of country peace and unifying belief',[120] which could serve as a comforting home. Railways and tourists were unwelcome intruders into that home. In other respects, too, the Kilvert home was backward-looking and anachronistic. Evangelicalism had been the inspiration for a new image of family life in the late 18th century, but this had ceased to be the case by the time Kilvert was born. Though he favoured a hierarchical and authoritarian society, his romantic, passionate, artistic nature may have chafed against the restrictions of a tightly regulated Evangelical household. The earlier set of values it represented still had meaning for Kilvert, as his admiration for the Moule family showed, but he himself expressed his sense of home more through secular and literary symbols and associations. In his determination to identify perfect domestic values with a rural idyll of Tory paternalism and sentimental images, he was, however, embracing the past. His need to escape from the uncongenial aspects of modernity was even greater than his father's and his awareness of a feeling of homelessness was much more acute and disturbing, partly because he experienced it with the imaginative intensity of an artist.

'I remember well... the strong tendency of an Oxford life upon any one who is justly fond of Oxford, to make him exceedingly venerate those who are at the head of Oxford society...'

Dr. Arnold in a letter of 17 August 1840 to an old pupil

'[Wadham was] some great Elizabethan or Jacobean country-house turned into a college, splendid yet homely...'
Patrick Wright Henderson, *Glasgow And Balliol And Other Essays*, p.58

'In 1855 modern Oxford may be said to begin'.

J. Wells, *Wadham College*, p.185

CHAPTER 3
Kilvert at Oxford

As Kilvert grew to manhood, and the prospect beckoned of following his uncle and his father to Oxford, awareness of his secure and substantial home must have instilled confidence. During the years in which Kilvert's family was re-establishing its finances and its social position in Wiltshire, the country, too, gradually began experiencing greater harmony than it had known for many decades. An important element was the absence of talk of class divisions, which had been so prominent in the 1830s and 1840s. Recent reforms had settled the demands of the poor and of radicals for greater social justice. By the time Kilvert was born in 1840, there had been 25 years of peace, people in general had become more prosperous and the worst of agricultural recession was over. The repeal of the Corn Laws in 1846 proved not to be the disaster many landowners predicted it would be, and agriculture entered into a period of growth from the early 1850s. There were clear signs that the middle-class values of independence and respectability had taken hold of large sections of the working-class, and as prosperity and knowledge grew, so did a belief in a progress that ultimately all would share, reflected in the 1851 Exhibition to which Kilvert was taken as a boy. Palmerston had assured the nation in 1849 that 'every class of society accepts with cheerfulness the lot which Providence has assigned to it'.[1]

When Kilvert went up to Oxford in autumn 1859, therefore, he had every reason to feel confidence in the situation of his country, his class, and his family. When G.M. Young wrote that 'by 1860 the whole world was the Englishman's home...',[2] he was emphasising that Britain's confidence stemmed from its empire, which was the greatest the world had seen, and Kilvert, perhaps because Church Missionary work had steadily brought into his home information about African and Indian territories, had a strong interest in Empire. To him, as to most Victorians, the empire could only grow from strength to strength, both because that was Britain's destiny and because its responsibility to bring Christianity to native peoples was clear. While working as his father's curate in Langley Burrell, Kilvert involved himself with missionary work, as he did when he was Vicar of Bredwardine. A visiting speaker to a missionary meeting in Langley Burrell impressed Kilvert with the size of the task facing the Church in India: 'He illustrated in a very striking way the number of the heathen. If 5000 should pass through Langley every day it would take 400 years for all the 800,000,000 to go by'.[3]

It was easy in 1859 to feel that Oxford, too, would go on forever, unchanged as the home of the Church, although by this time the public schools had begun to dominate both universities and were changing their character. During the previous 50 years, public schools had changed but only in a slow, haphazard manner. They were not responsive to change 'because the upper-classes were for psychological and political reasons attached to the past *per se*, and satisfied with the traditionalism, ...the class character, the narrow classical training, and above all, the free boy life, with its escapades and its inculcation of manliness and patriotism which schools exhibited'.[4] However, Kilvert's own class, especially the urban, industrial sector of it, had begun to make new demands on them and to make them reflect their own values. It was entirely because the middle-classes felt so confident of their values and their power in the middle of the century that they sought to bring both the public schools and the universities into line with their ideals and aspirations. They demanded a wider curriculum, in which some more useful subjects—modern languages, maths, some science, and modern geography—appeared alongside the Latin and Greek which Nathanael Morgan of King Edward's, Bath, had been determined to retain. Following the example of Dr. Arnold's Rugby, they expected schools to have a greater moral dimension and to be less barbarous places. The growth of empire led to schools developing an emphasis on organised team games to prepare the future army officers and administrators for the rigours of their jobs. As fewer and fewer boys made the career choice that Kilvert was to make, and more and more saw the opportunities overseas, the clerical domination of Oxbridge was challenged.

Kilvert took to Wadham College the same serious attitude his father had taken to Oriel: profound respect and deference towards its traditional authority and scholarship, and an intention of working hard to achieve academic success. He demanded something more than the schoolboy escapades and the field sports that satisfied many of Oxford's ex-public schoolboys. When he went up, it was probably already his intention to enter the Church, though Oxford was more than the means to a career. It was important to him, as it had been to his father, because it signified social acceptance. Kilvert's *Diary* shows that he shared the anxiety of the time about who was and who was not a gentleman. In the mid-Victorian period when he was a young man, the social mobility that was already breaking up fixed social ranks in his father's youth, had made the problem of who was a gentleman especially difficult. Kilvert must have asked himself many times whether he was a gentleman, or sufficient of one. His background, which included yeomen, tradesmen, squires, and clergymen, provided no clear answer, although to some the possession of armorial bearings was in itself proof of gentlemanly status.[5] In 1859, when his son was preparing to go to Oxford, 'the short answer [seemed] to be, that you could not be sure until judgement was delivered in your favour by the appropriate social authority—the particular élite group by whom you were anxious to be recognised'.[6] Achieving respectability had been vital to the Kilvert family after the loss of its business and its wealth. To be a gentleman was to be respectable, but while many could claim respectability, not everyone could claim to be a gentleman because gentlemen formed an élite group. Oxford was undeniably the home of gentlemen, and Kilvert achieved the same sense of satisfaction as his father had when he knew that he too had attained the education that marked him in most people's eyes as a gentleman. Revisiting Oxford in May 1876, he referred to the way in which its towers aroused in him an 'indescribable thrill of pride and love and enthusiasm'—a phrase that was possibly half-remembered from Grace Aguilar's *Home Influence,* where she referred to 'a love of and a pride in' Oxford. For someone with such an attitude to Oxford and with such a love of beautiful, historic places, it is very odd that Kilvert does not reminisce in his *Diary* about his student days. The only entries that concern Oxford are those which centre on return visits he made in 1874 and 1876.

His father had not been able to choose which Oxford college he entered, but had gone to the one whose doors were opened by patronage. Oriel was, nevertheless, very acceptable both academically and socially. There are reasons for believing that Wadham was chosen for Kilvert. The outstanding fact about it, apart from a sound academic reputation, was that it had been known for many years as the most Evangelical of Oxford colleges, largely owing to the influence of Benjamin Parsons Symons, who had become Warden in 1831. 'He was a courageous witness for Evangelical divinity in the days when Evangelicals were not popular in Oxford...'.[7] He was known as a very keen supporter of the Church Missionary Societies, which were a feature of the Kilvert home. His uncompromising stance made the College even more popular than it had been and men went there simply because the Warden and tutors were Evangelicals. T.G. Jackson, who was a student there just before Kilvert went and who also came from an Evangelical family, described Symons as 'a bulwark of conservatism', a reputation which may have been another reason for Wadham's appeal for Kilvert's father.[8] Kilvert, in gaining admittance to the gentlemen's club of Oxford, was implicitly acknowledging the validity and survival of traditional pre-democratic values that were enshrined in the landed gentry and the public schools. In the judgement of one who was a Fellow of Wadham and later its Warden, the College had all the beauty of a country house. It was regarded, he said, as the most beautiful of all the colleges, largely because it was open to countryside on two sides for a long period, including the years Kilvert was there, and was known as 'the Country College'. Thus, it and Oxford as a whole appealed to those who were 'Conservatives at heart' because of its traditions and its ethos, which existed in 'the charm of its old buildings and old gardens and old customs preserved with singular tenacity...'.[9] Kilvert expressed his love for Wadham's semi-wild gardens when he visited it again in May 1874, commenting particularly on trees he had known as a student that were still there.

Kilvert had to accept, however, as his father had years before, that country house beauty at Oxford would be accompanied by country house arrogance and extravagance. For those who had never been insiders at Oxford, it could exercise a fascination that G.M. Young called 'exasperating' because, beautiful as it was, it was also the home of so much idleness, dissipation, and snobbery. Thackeray was infuri-

ated by the student uniforms denoting different social classes; they
were 'absurd and monstrous' in a place of education, and belonged
to the 'brutal, unchristian, blundering, feudal system'.[10] The pinnacle
of the Oxford social pyramid was Christ Church College. It was the
largest and wealthiest college and the bulk of its students came from
Eton, Harrow, and Westminster. Unlike all other Oxford colleges, it
had no statutes and its Dean and Chapter were its law and its
authority, and a very powerful, prestigious body. They administered
the College's vast estates and paid themselves, as they were entitled to
do, two-thirds of its annual income. They had control of its 90 livings
and 100 Studentships. One third of the latter went to relatives and
friends of Christ Church Canons in 1854. Between seven and eight
Students were appointed every year by a system of nomination which
had nothing to do with merit, examination, or competition. The
Dean and Chapter rejected criticism of the system by pointing out
that Studentships were not to be regarded as prizes but as means of
enabling morally deserving young men, many of whom might be too
poor to afford a university education, to gain positions in the Church
and government. They were worth only £90 a year but, since they
could be held for life, they were eagerly pursued.

To proceed from Eton to Christ Church was an established pattern
for aristocrats and those who aped them, as Kilvert well knew.[11] No
words capture the significance of Oxford's most aristocratic college
better than those of Lord Willoughby De Broke. Of his father, who
left it in 1865, he wrote: 'For him and his set the University of Oxford
simply did not exist. It was just Christ Church... To them [it] meant
Bullingdon... fox-hunting, racing, a not too serious form of cricket,
and no end of good dinners... What better can the world give? They
may have heard, with a vague sensation of pity, of the University
Debating Society. They supposed that there were other colleges than
their own'. On occasion they might be summoned into the presence
of a don from 'so obscure a place... as Wadham'.[12]

Kilvert's *Diary* is blank about many aspects of his life and experience and is maddeningly so about the Christ Church career of Walter
Mynors Baskerville, the squire of Clyro, with whom he had a close
relationship. They were close in age, though Walter was slightly older,
having been born in January 1839. Kilvert was often invited to Clyro
Court and met Walter frequently at Clyro Vicarage. Walter asked
Kilvert to be his Chaplain when he was High Sheriff of Radnorshire

in 1868. The two men were actually at Oxford at the same time and it seems likely that they would have compared notes about their experiences. It also seems likely that if the *Diary* had contained entries about such exchanges, Plomer would have included them. However, the knowledge that his squire had been at Christ Church and had wasted his time there may have decided Kilvert against recording any conversation they had on that subject. Certainly Walter's farcical career at Christ Church is a case-study of exactly the kind of irresponsible, spendthrift attitude to privilege and opportunity that Kilvert had been brought up to deprecate. Walter's own father, Thomas, had set a bad example. In 1808, when he went to Trinity College, Oxford, a gentleman's approach towards university education was casual, but Thomas's seems to have been more than usually negligent. He began on 22 November, a late start that meant he never even signed the college's admission register and had in effect missed half the autumn term. He declined to appear at all the following term and maintained steady attendance for only the next two terms. Needless to say, he left without taking a degree. Walter's Oxford career followed the same pattern. He came into residence at Christ Church in autumn 1858 with the status of Gentleman-Commoner, which gave him the 'privilege', among others, of paying higher fees. He occupied one of the larger and most expensive (five guineas a term) rooms in Peckwater Quadrangle, noted as the place where the richest and rowdiest undergraduates lived.[13] He attended during the spring and autumn terms of 1859 but was absent for the summer term of 1859 and the spring term of 1860. He rejoined the university again in summer 1860. Some of his absence may be accounted for by the possibility that his father's ill-health necessitated his being at home, as the eldest son, to help to manage the estate.[14]

Such idleness and lack of application were, in fact, encouraged by his college, because the dons rarely took students to task for neglect of their studies. Not surprisingly, the carefree attitude of Dean Gaisford was rewarded with a feeling of reverence among students.[15] In Walter's case, his interest in cricket (something else he shared with Kilvert) had much to do with his intermittent attendance. He had written from Oxford in late April 1860 pledging his support for the newly-founded Hay Cricket Club, 'composed of gentlemen resident in the town and neighbourhood', with a promise to subscribe two guineas to its funds. From August 1860, cricket became Walter's life, at least in the summer months. He seemed useful with the ball but was a poor batsman and did not play in Oxford's Bullingdon Club matches. Playing for Hay against Hereford in August 1860, he bowled out two players in Hereford's first innings and caught and bowled a third. He took three wickets in the second innings, too. He batted only once in this game—at number five—and made only one run. So great was his desire to play cricket, that his name is to be found in the lists of other local teams, including, on occasion, his own eleven, and sometimes he played for Radnorshire. He was playing cricket the weekend before his father died on 9 September 1864.

When the Mordaunt case hit the newspapers in February 1870, Kilvert was able to obtain additional information from Walter. Kilvert recorded that he was reading about the 'Mordaunt Scandal Case', with its 'horrible disclosures of the depravity of the best London society'. This divorce case, which revealed intimate details of Lady Mordaunt's adultery with several men, including flirtation with the Prince of Wales, had something of the same significance for Kilvert that the Queen Caroline case had for his father and he brought to it the same Evangelical disapproval, while simultaneously relishing the scandal. Sir Charles Mordaunt, Lady Mordaunt's husband, was known to Walter from their Eton days and he preceded him to Christ Church. From this 'insider' position, Walter was able to illustrate the case with what Kilvert called 'some extraordinary stories' of the world of the aristocracy. Walter had probably met Lady Mordaunt because she sometimes attended the Hereford Hunt Ball, as, for example in January 1862 when Walter's mother and sister were in the assembly, though he was not (he spent the day hunting in Radnorshire with his own pack of hounds).

Kilvert had a deep respect for aristocracy as an institution but the ethos of Christ Church stood for everything he loathed about it. At various points in his life, he kept on coming into collision with gentry values he deplored; his father had experienced the same conflict at Oriel and to a smaller extent at King Edward's, Bath. For both of them, the conflict had to be borne because they needed Oxford to confirm them as gentlemen. In attempting to assess what Kilvert brought to Oxford and what he took away, it is important to know to what extent Christ Church was representative of the university as a whole, and whether its excesses were contained within its own walls and had little influence on students of other colleges. To some extent Kilvert had gone to Oxford in search of its immemorial traditions and charms but reform had in fact begun to change it some years before. The middle of the century had seen some fundamental reforms, as mentioned above, which brought into conflict two views of learning: the Church's, which saw education as a matter of the inculcation of Christian morals and a training in judgement for the clergy, and a secular one, which emphasised the advancement of learning and some preparation for the professions. The university extended the range of studies in 1850 and one of the courses introduced was Law and Modern History, which Kilvert took. To that extent, he was prepared to accept innovation. In order to push forward the process that had begun with these internal reforms, a Royal Commission, composed of liberals, was set up in 1852 to enquire into the 'State, Discipline, Studies and Revenues of the University and Colleges of Oxford'.

Its report identified the outstanding vices of the student body. There was 'sensual vice', for which the villages around Oxford provided ample opportunity, and there was gambling. More prevalent than either, however, was the habit of extravagant expenditure. A minority over-spent on a disgraceful scale. Between them and the majority, who showed restraint, there was 'still a considerable number of young men who spend far more than they have any right to spend...'. In his evidence to the Commission, one professor said that the best way of discouraging these vices was to make study and not amusement the rule at Oxford. The amusements on which money was spent were dining and drinking at inns, the 'excessive habit of smoking', driving, riding, and hunting.[16] Hunting was the cause of most expense, and the keeping of horses was connived at by several colleges, though it was also easy for students to hire horses. It was common to spend four guineas a day on hunting. The report estimated that the total cost for a parent of his son's university course, including supplying his clothes and supporting him during vacations, was at least £600, or £200 a year.

This figure for the early 1850s matches another available for the period when Kilvert was a student. The author of an 1865 *Cornhill Magazine* article said that £200 a year was needed for a tolerable existence at Oxford. Less than that and a man was in danger of running into debt and would be unable to maintain the social life of his fellows, which was as much a part of his education as classics and maths.[17] This, most probably, would have been Kilvert's situation because his father could never have spared £200 out of his annual stipend of £350, and he would have had to manage on a figure nearer to the £130 which the *Cornhill* writer said was the irreducible minimum. Even this would have imposed a severe strain on the family income, which, as far as is known, had no additional supplement. The need to live a very frugal existence amid so much wealth and extravagance, would have been a further source of tension for Kilvert, in addition to that which proceeded from the spectacle of so many students declining to study in favour of country house frolics. Moral disapproval would have turned to indignation at the privileged position of the Gentlemen-Commoners. 'Young noblemen', noted the 1852 Commissioners, 'wear a distinctive academic dress, take precedence of their academical superiors, are permitted to take degrees at an earlier period than other students, and in general treated in a way that seems to indicate too great a deference to rank in a place of education'. Baronets and Knights could also graduate earlier. The report found it particularly offensive that the deference was shown not merely to rank but 'notoriously' to wealth *per se*.[18]

Those students who had no appetite for or had no need of serious study did not take the honours course and were content with an ordinary degree or no degree at all. The attainment required for an ordinary degree was, the report noted, small, and at Oxford the number who failed it on average over the four year period 1845-8 was 100 out of an entry of 387—far more than at Cambridge or Dublin. A great disincentive to hard work was the absence of any real professional value in an Oxford education. Courses to prepare students for the professions of Law and Medicine did not exist, and as for that of the Church, which might be said to be the reason for Oxford's existence, 'no efficient means at present exist in the University for training candidates [for it]...'.[19] Kilvert had come to Oxford to take an honours degree and to be prepared for entry into the Church. He would be denied any contact with Christ Church students and could choose not to follow the example set by its wilder spirits, but the disease which was most virulent at Oxford's most aristocratic college had infected all the others to a disturbing degree.

Wadham was reasonably typical of the others, as is evident from the testimony of men who were there just before and just after Kilvert. Wright-Henderson, who became a Fellow there in 1867, observed that its tone was set by the wealthiest students and that there was considerable 'worshipping of persons ranks and wealth'.[20] In his own student days at Balliol in 1861 there was much wine-drinking and running up of spectacular debts. Frederic Harrison, a student at Wadham from 1849 to 1853, was one of its most outspoken critics. He was very conscious later in life how priggish his comments on student society, while still a student, sounded, but he stood by them. He was appalled at the puerility and shallowness displayed by students, the majority of whom had come from public schools. He himself had attended an excellent London day school, which was free from the meaningless rituals of public school education. There *was* intellect among his fellows at Wadham but too often it was used to sneer at serious purposes and serious study. Books were not evaluated but categorised simply as 'slow' or 'amusing'; there was no interest in ideas; conversation generally was silly, trivial, and unreal. Harrison's group of friends were by nature opposed to 'the more hilarious spirits who glorified the Boat, the Eleven, sports, and convivialities'. It was in order to escape from the inane banter of those with schoolboy mentality and from those who were too dull to join either in the banter or in serious discussion, that he formed a protective alliance with Edward Beesly, John Bridges, and George Thorley—the three who later became his fellow Positivists. As a group they had been influenced in this direction by the brilliant history tutor, Richard Congreve, who had come to Wadham from Rugby.[21] He was a follower of Comte, the founder of Positivism, a 'Religion of Humanity' in which man and his noblest works replaced God as models for behaviour in order to fill the vacuum created by religious doubt.

For other Wadham tutors, Harrison had nothing but contempt. They lived, he wrote, 'by themselves and for themselves', with the result that they became 'the most refinedly selfish men on the face of the globe'.[22] They were obsessed with jealousy and hatred for their colleagues and had no real friends among them. On Kilvert's return visit to Wadham in May 1876, he dined with his friend Mayhew at the High Table with the Fellows—'an object of my undergraduate ambition realised at length'. It was something Harrison actually experienced as an undergraduate and he was so bored and frustrated by the experience that he gave a satirical account of it in a letter to a friend. The Dean, he said, was well-meaning but so utterly silly as to be incapable of stimulating conversation. He was too conscious of his position to be able to relax in the company of undergraduates but, more seriously, was so afraid that they would drag him out of his intellectual depth, that he confined himself largely to observations on the weather and the progress of some beans in a colleague's garden. The College Chaplain was too keen to humour and to defer to the Dean to be able to contribute conversationally. Kilvert had different expectations from Harrison's when he dined with the Fellows. He was not looking for stimulating conversation, a meeting of minds, and seems to have approached the occasion with the attitude of the College Chaplain in Harrison's account. One of the Fellows was George Thorley, one of Harrison's close friends from his student days; he had stayed on and had become Subwarden by the time of Kilvert's visit. All that Kilvert had to say of him was that he was 'very agreeable'. Of the conversation at dinner he gave no details. Just like his father at Oriel, he was all respect and deference, overwhelmed at the thought of being in such élite company. Harrison had referred sarcastically to the Dean and Fellows as 'Olympians' but for Kilvert they were worthy of the name. 'I sat on [Thorley's] right hand', he wrote, 'and we had an exceedingly pleasant dinner and evening over the dessert in the Common Room. I had never been in the Common Room before'. Apart from Fellows, it was only Gentlemen-Commoners who had use of the Common Room.[23]

It was the sense of being at the heart of Oxford tradition, as well as being the recipient of a social honour, that explains Kilvert's joy. Wright-Henderson described the Common Room as 'a typical specimen of the old-fashioned kind', which had changed less than most common rooms up to 1867, the year he became one of its Fellows, because until then the Fellowships had been closed to members of other colleges. He was the first non-Wadham man to be appointed. He characterised Wadham's Common Room in ways that would have appealed to Kilvert: 'Its traditions were uniform and unbroken, like traditions handed down from generation to generation in a family...'. This was what Kilvert loved about rural society, as exemplified by Chieflands. In Wadham's old-fashioned atmosphere, Wright-Henderson continued affectionately, characters could flourish and become contented rather than merely dull. In this totally male (Fellows were only permitted to marry as from 1870), 'semi-aristocratic' society, there was an atmosphere like that of a cathedral town, completely dominated, prior to 1860, by Toryism. Tradition had retained Bible clerks at Wadham up to and beyond Kilvert's day, but they were discontinued after 1872 because it was assumed that the social distinction was resented, especially by the clerks themselves.[24]

The teaching provided by the dons was also traditional and dull. It was not likely to be otherwise with Warden Symons at the helm. Since he had spent his entire life at the College, 'it was no wonder that his mental range was limited and his horizon rather narrow'.[25] He was a very sound authority on church doctrine but an infuriating man. Some believed he was by nature genial. However, in his management of the College, he was autocratic and suspicious of any suggestion of change, while with undergraduates he was 'utterly without a sense of humour'.[26] From the high incidence of smoking at Oxford and from the fact that Symons would not tolerate it, came, perhaps, Kilvert's own detestation of the habit. Kilvert's father had once been poisoned by the smoke of a cigar he tried as a young man and probably warned his son off tobacco. The practice of requiring from students an analysis of the Sunday sermon, which Kilvert's father had taken pride in at Oriel, was rigidly enforced by Symons. When the University Commissioners were seeking information about colleges, he was one of several wardens who refused to answer their questions. 'By the 1850s [he] was increasingly out of sympathy with the modern world'.[27] College lectures under his leadership belonged to the past and were identical in form to the ones Kilvert's father had known, with students taking turns to construe a classical text. Honours students sought to be excused from them and hired private tutors. At Oriel Robert had been unable to afford a private tutor, which was probably the situation in which his son found himself, and one reason for his obtaining a fourth. Kilvert's College tutor was Walter Waddington Shirley, who was one of those men who had come to Wadham from Rugby. He had a first class degree in maths and was lecturer in maths at Wadham until 1863, when he became professor of ecclesiastical history at Christ Church.[28] He had steadily developed his studies in (mainly medieval) history prior to this and would have tutored Kilvert for a range of subjects. He was regarded as brilliant, though a stern disciplinarian, and was described as 'the most relentless of our dons' because of the way he once apprehended a student for rook-shooting and had him sent down.[29]

The course in Law and Modern History taken by Kilvert was the result of the Oxford statute of 1850, which laid down that an Arts degree henceforth was to consist of two Schools: the traditional Literae Humaniores had to be one, while the second could be chosen from Maths and Physics, Natural Science, or Law and Modern History. Honours students like Kilvert studied English History from the birth of Christ to 1789, the Laws of England, the Law of Nations, Adam Smith's *Wealth of Nations*, and Blackstone on the law of Personal Property. Though the School had 'law' in its title and involved some study of law, it was much less a course in law in the modern sense, than the modern Philosophy, Politics, and Economics course, and in some respects was an extension of the philosophy studied in the Lit. Hum. School. Those who introduced the course had in mind the average country gentleman, who was coming to Oxford in increasing numbers and who required to know the basics of political, economic, and legal thought in order to discharge his local administrative duties more effectively. Walter Baskerville took the course and was a typical candidate for it, although it was also considered appropriate for country clergymen. The first point to be made about the course is that its content and values were backward-looking. Its study of history ended significantly at 1789 with the French Revolution, an event which demarcated the old world from the new more completely than any other. The second important point is that the course was much concerned with property. The view of property that dominated the course's law element was largely the 18th century one which held property to be the basis of social order and the source of prosperity. The two central texts, *Commentaries on the Laws of England* (1765) by Sir William Blackstone and *The Wealth of Nations* (1776) by Adam Smith were a powerful influence on a number of Kilvert's basic attitudes in ways both general and specific. In particular, they will be seen to make strong connections with the key statements that he made on property in the *Diary*. This is especially the case with *Wealth of Nations*.

Smith assumed that each man had his station with its own particular responsibilities and the chief duty of property owners was to fulfil their obligation to lesser folk. An important part of Chieflands' merit as a property was that it existed as an indispensable unit in a larger whole. It represented economic and social usefulness, productivity, and contentment. Its yeoman tenant, John Fry, fitted well into Smith's picture of a countryside that offered beauty, pleasure, tranquillity of mind, and independence—'charms that ... attract everybody'.[30] The merits of yeomen are extolled in *Wealth of Nations* Book II, Chapter 3. Fry discharged his responsibilities dutifully but was let down by his landlord, Sir John Neeld. It had not always been so, for Kilvert's grandfather, Walter Coleman, exemplified the disinterestedness which, according to Smith, identified with the joys and sorrows of others and counteracted selfishness. Landowners who saw land solely in terms of power and prestige as Neeld did, neglected both the needs of their tenants and of the land itself. Smith had noted in *Wealth of Nations* that great landowners were seldom great improvers of their land. They were unable to apply the 'exact attention to small savings and small gains' of which small owners were capable. It was partly also pride that produced this carelessness.[31] Kilvert had underlined the damaging effect of such pride and such carelessness in relation to Chieflands. He was keen to see honest and industrious labourers aspire to become small farmers, as is shown in chapter nine. Smith too had written of 'the natural effort of every individual to better his own condition'.[32]

Interdependence among landlord, tenant and labourer was the rock on which the landed interest was founded and produced the notion of land as a trust which Kilvert endorsed. (The last chapter noted the *Diary* entry in which the wife of old Squire Clutterbuck insisted that her husband's estate was 'only lent to us'.) Kilvert was sharply critical of landowners who used their estates for their own selfish ends, as later chapters show.[33] It was because the Clutterbuck family had this beneficent approach to the larger community that he missed them when they left Harnish. Behind the *Diary* entry in which he saw landlord and peasant essentially united in the same enterprise lay a similar notion of community.[34] When Kilvert argued with Mr. Latimer Jones over people's legal and moral rights to property, one can be sure that these notions of responsibility, disinterestedness, and sympathy for the needs of others informed his views. The existence of rich and poor in a community did not, in the opinion of Adam Smith, make social cohesion more difficult because wealth provided employment and prosperity in which others could share. He contrasted manufacturers unfavourably with landowners in this respect. The former were, he said, 'unproductive' as a class. 'The expense, on the contrary, laid out in employing farmers and labourers ...produces a new value, the rent of the landlord. It is therefore a productive expense'.[35] Smith also wrote that the people of nations such as England, which consist in large measure of landlords, farmers, and labourers were likely to exhibit the characteristics of 'liberality, frankness and good fellowship'.[36] These were precisely the qualities Kilvert found in Squire Coleman, John Fry, and Squire Clutterbuck.

Property as a topic loomed large in the examinations for the course. One dealt with real property, another with the rights of persons and personal property, and both were based on a study of the relevant parts of Sir William Blackstone's *Commentaries on the Laws of England*. This monumental work contained one of the classic accounts of the English Constitution, which was regarded in the 18th century as a perfect system because the balance of power it achieved among King, Lords, and Commons guaranteed individual liberty. In Blackstone's formulation, the House of Commons represented, not the wishes of the people, but the reasoned judgement of the MPs who had been elected to it. It was, therefore, basically un-democratic, if not anti-democratic. This vision of the Constitution had great appeal for the conservative-minded because it ruled out the need for, and the desirability, of change. Radically-minded souls, such as Jeremy Bentham, regarded Blackstone's *Commentaries* as 'a masterpiece of obfuscation and an apology for reigning abuses'.[37] Blackstone gave particular endorsement to the political *status quo* in his account of the link between property and the right to vote. Those without property had to be excluded from voting because, having no stake in the country, they were incapable of exercising judgement. Such a view, which was widely held in Victorian times, naturally lent itself to an aristocratic conception of society since aristocrats, by virtue of being the largest property holders, were generally hostile to the extension of the suffrage.

It seems likely that the 18th-century view of social order that Kilvert assimilated at Oxford received reinforcement from the works of William Paley. Though his *Principles of Moral and Political Philosophy* (1785) was not a set textbook at Oxford as it was at Cambridge, it was hugely influential and was a standard item in the education of gentlemen in the first half of the 19th century. Property is the central element in its account of the relationship between law and society and the role of punishment was not to satisfy the demand for justice but to deter assaults on property. It emphasised natural as well as social order and Kilvert may have picked up from Paley (and from Wordsworth) the idea that behind all natural phenomena was a benign intelligence. Kilvert's poem, 'Honest Work', which expresses the essence of his conception of social and moral order, contains these lines addressed to the poor:

> Envy not the rich, the great,
> Wealthier in your low estate,
> Nobler through your workful days,
> Happier in your simple ways.

In this, there is an echo of Paley's words: 'I have no propensity to envy any one, least of all the rich and great'. He added that if he did envy any one it would be the healthy young man, 'going forth in a morning to work for his wife and children'.[38] To have an occupation was, therefore, both a blessing as well as a duty to the poor; idleness was the curse of the rich.

This summary of Kilvert's law course goes far to explain, *inter alia*, the harshness of his attitude to the poor and to social justice, an attitude that received further stiffening from a religion which urged acceptance of authority. And the crucial point, perhaps, about the content of his Oxford education is not only that it looked backward and had at its centre a static view of society, but that he was expected to be passive in his approach to it. He was not required to make a critical evaluation of its ideas for his examinations, which required only short answers to a large number of questions. 'The questions were all what would be now called "book work" and called for nothing but intelligent reading and a reasonably good memory'.[39] The standard was set deliberately low in accordance with the aim of those who designed the course to be 'an easy School for rich men'.

It was not only the University Commission that had produced changes which Kilvert would have felt at Oxford, though that was the means by which the door was opened to other agencies, influences, and events. According to Wright-Henderson, after the university reforms of the 1850s, Oxford became a place of reforms and ideas. Not only Comte, but a whole variety of intellectual leaders—Jowett, Mark Pattison, Mill, Herbert Spencer, and Huxley—won adherents among the student body. During Kilvert's university career, two major events, one international, one national, sent shock waves through

Oxford. The first was the American Civil War, which not only aroused political awareness in both Oxford and the country as a whole, but split British opinion into two fiercely opposed camps. The war was significant because it represented the threat by the industrialised, democratic North to overwhelm the agrarian, patrician South. British intellectuals, liberals, and the working-class supported the former; aristocrats, rural gentry, Tories, and most likely, Kilvert, the latter. There was much anti-democratic feeling in Oxbridge.

The national event, which by comparison was a storm in a teacup, but which had particular importance for Anglican Oxford, was the publication of *Essays And Reviews*. Dean Stanley, one of the Oxford liberals, said that the book had its origin in a scheme originally proposed in 1835 by Dr. Arnold and Archdeacon Julius Hare to establish a journal in which theological subjects could be discussed in a liberal atmosphere. One of its objects was to encourage Biblical criticism. *Essays And Reviews*, which came out in early spring 1860, was a venture in this tradition. Several scholars and divines were asked to contribute but only seven finally did and they were mostly unknown to each other. They consisted, *inter alia*, of Frederick Temple, Headmaster of Rugby, Rowland Williams, Professor of Hebrew at Lampeter College, Professors Baden-Powell and Jowett of Oxford. Baden-Powell, in his essay, argued that many people found serious difficulties with the evidence for Christianity but they met with a lack of sympathy from those who refused to think about the difficulties themselves and thought it wrong even to do so. Reason and intellect alone, rather than conscience and feeling, were, he argued, the proper judges of matters of 'external fact' (as opposed to revelation).[40] Frederic Harrison was deeply aware of these difficulties while at Wadham, and made efforts to hang on to his faith, but spoke of how 'the heartfelt perplexities of earnest men' were forever bearing down on 'fixed religious belief'.[41] The points that Baden-Powell made in support of such men were fair and reasonable but they, and similar ones expressed by his fellow essayists, were too much for the Anglican establishment. At first the volume made little impression but by autumn there was 'the first muttering of a coming whirlwind'.[42] Oxbridge was suddenly accusing the authors of *Essays And Reviews* of a concerted attack on belief and conservative elements were vilifying 'intellectuals'. The authors were called upon to resign their positions in the Church of England. Meetings of clergy were held to condemn the book. Kilvert would have been stirred by the controversy, but would not have sympathised with those who had apparently challenged belief and would have found it reassuring to side with the traditionalists.

Charles Kingsley had, some years before, challenged tradition and had later recanted, and Oxford was most likely to have been the place where Kilvert conceived his admiration for him. On the occasion of Kingsley's death in January 1875, Kilvert made an entry in his *Diary* which suggested both that the energetic clergyman of Eversley in Hampshire meant a great deal to him and had done so for much of his life: 'So Charles Kingsley is dead. "His body is buried in peace, but his name liveth for ever more". We could ill spare him'.[43] The earlier part of the entry concerns the imminent death of an old man of the village whom Kilvert had known many years. Kingsley had steadily taken up most of the sensitive questions of the day and had turned the majority of respectable people against him in the period in which Kilvert grew to manhood. In his novel *Yeast* (1848), he exposed the dreadful living conditions of the rural poor and attacked landowners' greed and oppression, which he thought were their cause. He made a particular target of their game laws, which in his view made cottagers into poachers, and rebuked those landowners who squandered their wealth on 'liquor and harlots'.[44] Each instalment of the novel in *Fraser's Magazine*, a journal favoured particularly by rural gentry, produced increasingly hostile reaction. Kingsley expressed similar views in his sermons. He asked one wealthy congregation to consider whether it was right that land was cultivated by paupers. Subsequent chapters will show Kilvert advancing identical criticisms of landowners.

Kingsley turned his attention to the injustices suffered by industrial workers, particularly those in tailoring sweat shops, in his novel *Alton Locke* (1850). Its hero is a Chartist. Chartism was a direct response to the economic crises of 1838 and 1842 when there was widespread poverty and starvation; working people became angry and the well-to-do became alarmed. The Charter of the people's leaders demanded reform on the basis of six principles: universal manhood suffrage, voting by ballot, equal electoral districts, annual parliaments, no property qualifications for MPs, and payment for MPs. *Alton Locke* chronicles the high hopes of the Chartist cause and its ultimate defeat with the failure of the great demonstration on

Kennington Common in London in 1848, when formidable numbers of special constables were deployed to protect property and preserve law and order. A character in Kingsley's novel states that the hope for reform lay with the people of the cities because the rural poor 'are too weak to resist their own tyrants'.[45] We are told that in the countryside the National schools for the poor were ruled over by parsons who imparted only 'a smattering of information' in order to ensure that children remained 'slaves and bigots'.[46] By showing support in the novel for Darwin's theory of evolution, Kingsley indicated that he was out of step with the great majority of bishops and clergy. His outspoken sermons, several collections of which were published in Kilvert's lifetime,[47] and his active involvement in the 1848 Chartist demonstration had not endeared him to the Church. Shortly after that event, he joined with the Christian Socialist, F.D. Maurice and others in founding the magazine, *Politics for the People*, which urged that all the burning social and political questions of the day should be the concern of everyone, including clergymen. At one meeting addressed by Christian Socialists in April 1849, Kingsley, sensing the hostility of the audience, rose to his feet and declared: 'I am a Church of England parson ... and a Chartist'.

It was actions of this kind, plus his sermons, letters to newspapers, and novels that gave him national notoriety. An article in the 1851 *Quarterly Review* attacked both *Yeast* and *Alton Locke* and called their author a socialist, even a communist, and underlined how deplorable this was in a clergyman. Some clergymen accused him of heresy. Part of his notoriety was undeserved because not everyone who condemned him bothered to read what he wrote. The *English Churchman*, for example, stated that he was 'somewhat notorious as the author of "Alton Locke", a book of doubtful principles, we understand, but which we have never seen'. That novel and *Yeast* were especially read by young men. Frederic Harrison told how *Yeast* and the writings of Maurice and other Christian Socialists changed his orthodox religious views, and said that Kingsley 'woke up' young people in all sorts of ways. Another student at Oxford in the 1850s, William Morris, stated that he was greatly influenced by the works of Kingsley.[48] Some people wrote to Kingsley's widow explaining that they had declined to read his works while he was alive because of his reputation, but felt happy to read them once he was dead. Kilvert was not one of those: we know that he read *Alton Locke* in March 1873, nearly two years before Kingsley died and it is possible he read other of the novels and some of the sermons while he was at Oxford, as many other students did.[49] Kingsley was to remain a thorn in the Establishment's side. His wife, writing in 1854, said: 'For at this time, and for some years to come, all parties in the Church stood aloof from him as a suspected person...'.[50]

One cannot imagine his being anything other than a suspected person in the Kilvert household in these years. It seems that Robert Kilvert did not care to commemorate Kingsley's death in his church, even though it was marked in many other churches all over the country, on the Sunday following the event (Kingsley died on Saturday 23 January 1875). Kilvert makes no mention of any commemoration at Langley Burrell in his entry for 24 January. Perhaps if he had been master of his own church there would have been one but he served his father as curate at this time. Kilvert did not record Kingsley's death in fact until the next Sunday. Kingsley represented so many of the things that Robert Kilvert despised and feared and it seems likely that he would have been one of those who condemned Kingsley without daring to contaminate himself by reading his books. However, a pious and conservative clergyman could, as we have seen, gather quite enough from reports in the press. Robert's religion ruled that the faithful were not to involve themselves with political and social problems, yet here was a clergyman not only making political speeches and writing political novels, but urging all clergymen to recognise that politics were part of religion. (As chapter 1 has shown, Robert was distinctly uneasy about clergymen becoming authors). Kingsley, moreover, gave his support to a revolutionary working class organisation which incited men to acts of disorder. He trumpeted his views in the newspapers that Robert had feared since he was a young man, making himself no better than a demagogue. Through him the pulpit was defiled and the figure of the clergyman stripped of all dignity. Worst of all, he attacked the authority of Church, landowners, government, universities, and property, all of which were guarantees of the status of the Kilvert family. Not having lived through the Swing and the Chartist riots, Kilvert had no experience of the deep anxiety over property that his father had but his background ensured he grew up with it. Kingsley was advocating that the property qualification on which the right to vote depended should be abandoned and the suffrage extended to the unlettered and potentially violent mass of working men. Kingsley's favourite cause of sanitary reform also threatened property owners because it raised difficult questions of property rights.

Yet it was the issue of sanitary reform that led to his reinstatement in the public mind and to the enhancement of his social position. Prince Albert had long believed in the necessity for better water and sewage systems if persistent outbreaks of cholera were to be avoided. He had also long admired Kingsley's writings on this topic. The shift in Kingsley's reputation had, however, occurred in 1855 when his novel *Westward Ho!* was published to mainly favourable reviews. The Crimean War was occupying the nation's attention and Kingsley's tale of adventure set in the Elizabethan age and its brave, uncomplicated hero, Amyas Leigh, caught the public mood. It sold in large numbers and was enjoyed by the respectable classes, including Prince Albert. Kingsley's new status was given clear recognition in 1859, the year Kilvert went up to Wadham: Kingsley was invited to preach before the Queen and Prince Albert at Buckingham Palace. Shortly afterwards, he was made one of Her Majesty's Chaplains and preached at the royal chapels. The Palace could afford to favour him because it was above party politics and Prince Albert was instrumental in Kingsley's appointment as Professor of History at Cambridge in 1860. To Kilvert, who had just gone to Oxford to study history, the appointment would have been significant for that reason and as confirmation that the worth of a good and pious man had at last been recognised. Any hesitation he might hitherto have shown in acknowledging Kingsley as a hero would have disappeared once he had received official approval. Nor was Kingsley the radical he had once been. During the 1850s he had gradually abandoned his democratic opinions, partly because he had seen the conditions of the poor improving and partly because he saw good in existing institutions. He would, therefore be politically acceptable to Kilvert and would become more so after 1860.

Kingsley's change of tone is clear from the preface he wrote to *Alton Locke* when it was reissued in 1862, by which time Kilvert was at Oxford. (The reissue of this, and other of his novels, at this time indicated the new opinion of him held by the public). In the *Alton Locke* preface he asserted that the British upper classes had undergone 'a noble change'; gone was their old self-interest and arrogance. Statesmen were more enlightened, philanthropists and clergy had ameliorated social ills, and, apart from a handful of backwoodsmen squires, there was among the ruling class an attitude of trust and even affection towards the working-class. Trade unionists were also to be trusted and working men needed and deserved the vote. Those who had bothered to read what Kingsley actually wrote could see that he was no revolutionary, merely a radical Tory. Kilvert did take the trouble to read *Alton Locke* and was able to recognise that, in spite of its concern with revolutionary material, there was much in it to reassure the conscientious clergyman that he still had an important role. Not many thoughtful Christians could quarrel with Lady Ellerton's statement near the end of the book that real worth consists not in property but in the grace of God, or with her belief that men should look for 'a state founded on better things than acts of parliament ... [on] the eternal promises of God'.[51] She points out the futility of revolutions and insists that Christ is the only hope of salvation for men. Another character, Eleanor, states a religious position which, as later chapters will show, was substantially that of Kilvert and goes a long way to explain why he was particularly impressed by the novel. She declares that the 1848 Charter was an illusion, out of which workers had made 'a selfish and self-willed idol'. They should abandon it in favour of social reforms that could be achieved by moral living, by 'the means which God puts in their way'. Men had to show that they could live like brothers. The selfishness, violence and atheistical tendency of the Chartist cause had defiled it 'in the eyes of the wise, the good, the gentle', among whom, of course, could be found the clergy. Alton Locke, the novel's hero, protests to her that the clergy seem to him 'as ignorant, as bigoted, as aristocratic as ever', but she points to the 'miraculous, ever-increasing improvement in the clergy'. It is their role to 'christianise democracy'; without them there could be no freedom for the people. First, however, they must be 'truly priests of God ... priests of the people ... priests after the likeness of Him who died on the cross'.[52]

The ministry that Kingsley had established at Eversley was a very close reflection of these principles. He became rector there in 1844, following a man who had signally failed to fulfil his duties: Kingsley's widow described the parish as 'sorely neglected'. Few people attended services and the church had not been repaired for over a century. He attacked the needs in earnest, establishing boot clubs and coal clubs, a loan fund, a lending library, and an infant school. Hardly any of the parishioners could read or write so he ran an evening class for men in his rectory, a summer writing class for girls, and cottage lectures for the old and infirm in outlying districts. Believing that a clergyman should communicate with every individual in his parish, he became known for regular and devoted home visiting on a scale very rare in those days, according to his wife. 'It was not simply that he cared [for the poor] exceedingly, was kind, feeling, sympathetic ... It was far more than this. There was in him a delicate, deep respect for the poor'.[53] His parish work occupied his days and six evenings a week and the strain of it, coupled with his literary work, led to a breakdown of his health in 1849. Reading the *Diary*, we receive the impression that Kilvert's was a far less strenuous pastoral regimen, which is the result largely of Plomer's editing. As will be seen later, Kilvert's ministry in many ways resembled Kingsley's and probably received inspiration from it via the latter's publications, rather from anything he received from his formal Oxford education.

On a number of key political questions, Kingsley expressed views that are basic to Kilvert's outlook. He was loyal, to the point of being feudal, towards royalty, as was Kilvert. During the 1871 crisis when the Prince of Wales was ill and thought to be dying, Kilvert was in agony lest the 'Child of England', as he called him, would be lost as Prince Albert, of whose death ten years before the current crisis was a reminder, had been. When the Prince rallied, Kilvert wrote in his *Diary*: 'I love that man now, and always will love him... God bless him'.[54] Kingsley's complete faith in aristocratic leadership is plain from a letter he wrote in 1866 in which he acknowledged that as a younger man he used to believe the 'revolutionary doctrine' that argued that all men were born equal yet some were denied their political rights by an unjust society. A quarter of a century teaching his own parishioners had led him to recognise, however, that 'there are congenital differences and hereditary tendencies which defy all education...'. Political power could not be given to those born 'fools and knaves'. It was natural and right that every man in the country looked towards the Peerage for leadership; political democracy was tainted by materialism and secularism.[55] Kilvert had his criticisms of aristocracy but Kingsley expressed there precisely why Kilvert revered it and why he distrusted democracy. Kingsley had attacked selfish squires in *Yeast* but had great faith, as Kilvert had, in the force for good they could be. One man who knew Kingsley said that Kingsley believed that 'a hearty English squire who does his duty' to all his dependants 'is the nearest thing to a saint which the world can produce'.[56] For Kilvert, his grandfather, Squire Coleman, was certainly the salt of the earth, if not a candidate for canonisation.

When Kingsley became professor of history, Kilvert was a student of history, so it is relevant to ask whether the latter's reverence for the former was based partly on his approach to the subject. It is unlikely that Kilvert journeyed to Cambridge to hear him lecture but he would surely have read in newspapers of the tumultuous joy with which his lectures were received in the sister university. Kingsley's inaugural lecture indicated his view of history. It was, he said, primarily about understanding men and women, 'for History is the history of men and women, and of nothing else...'.[57] He played up the importance of biography, drama, story, and romance, which were the elements that had most appeal for Kilvert. Kingsley once gave a lecture to shopmen and middle-class lads on the Norman Conquest and was pleased to record that they were delighted with what he told them of the 'doughty deeds, and grand old Norse blood of their own ancestors'.[58] The Cambridge students, too, were delighted with history taught this way, though academics there and at Oxford sneered. The imaginative bond between Kingsley and Kilvert on the matter of history can best be illustrated by the visit Kilvert made to the church of Moccas on the estate of his neighbouring squire, Sir George Cornewall. 'The thing that interested me most', wrote Kilvert, '...was the beautiful tomb of Sir Reginald de Fresne the Crusader, ... The shield upon his arm was pure. His good sword slept in its sheath by his side...'.[59] It is pure romance, pure Sir Walter Scott, and pure Kilvert.

In Kingsley's attitude to games, too, there was an elevated, romantic quality because he was convinced of their moral, as well as of their physical, value. They developed, he said, 'not merely daring and endurance but better still, temper, self-restraint, fairness, and honour...'.[60] The cult of games was only just beginning to take root when Kilvert went to Oxford. Until 1850, 'sports' at Wadham meant field sports, even though such sports as rowing had been part of its life since the 1830s and a boat club was in existence by 1837. By 1849, the Wadham Eight were winning cups at Henley. Throughout the 1850s and 1860s, the College's oarsmen were pre-eminent, and during Kilvert's period three of its cricketers played for the

University Eleven. Harrison was nettled by the tendency of some students to hero-worship members of the Eleven and of the Boat, and, a little later, Wright-Henderson noted that there was considerable admiration of those who excelled at sport. However, while there was much enthusiasm for sport, it was pursued in an amateurish way as compared with the more organised, more obsessive, and more self-conscious approach that was the norm by the 1870s. When that approach came, however, it lacked the moral element admired by Kingsley.

The evidence suggests that Kilvert took no part in sport at Wadham. In his account of one return visit to Oxford, he expressed a good deal of excitement over 'the old scene bright and busy... [with] the river alive... with all sorts of boats...', but he wrote as if he had always been a spectator of boat races,[61] (the record of Wadham's Debating Club shows that he was a spectator there too; he never proposed or seconded a motion and never spoke in a debate). He makes no mention in the *Diary* of rowing or of playing cricket, his participation in the latter being confined to scoring for the Langley Burrell village team. He did record on 5 August 1874 that 'we played tennis... in a drizzling rain', but his poor eyesight ruled him out of a hard ball game. It is not difficult to account for the appeal of cricket for Kilvert. It was patronised by royalty and aristocracy and approved by the Church as wholesome recreation and a moral training ground, since it particularly involved the qualities Kingsley had claimed for games in general. Though it encouraged some mixing between the classes, class distinctions were rigorously preserved. And finally, in an age of rapid social change, it was a stable institution.[62]

Lack of participation in sport would not enhance Kilvert's position at Wadham because those who did participate were looked up to, as has been noted. It would hardly raise Kilvert's stock in the eyes of other students that Warden Symons strongly disapproved of sport. T.G. Jackson, who was at Wadham just before Kilvert, suffered as he did from short-sightedness. 'I think', he wrote, 'due weight is not given to the effect of short sight on a boy's character... Partly cut off from what goes on about him he stands on his guard and becomes reserved and stand-offish'.[63] Jackson, too, was unable to play cricket but he did row at Wadham, and believed it helped him break though 'the crust of reserve'. Sport would not, then, be a means by which Kilvert was able to fraternise with other students or to gain their respect and making relationships was not easy at the Oxford of the 1850s. According to Wright-Henderson, students were 'stiff and diffident' and the tone of classrooms was characterised by 'decorum and dignity, approaching dullness'.[64] In 1858, Dean Stanley commented that 'The stiffness of undergraduates in social intercourse is only surpassed by their marvellous lack of interest in... theological study'.[65]

It was for the Church's version of 'liberal education', if not specifically for theological study, that Kilvert had gone to Oxford.[66] Account has been taken of various aspects of Wadham—intellectual, moral, political, social and athletic—in order to assess its impact on him, but little had been said of the professional. A pamphlet of 1839 proposing reform at Oxford, and not considered particularly conservative at the time, made these statements among others: 'Of course in the 19th century few persons require to be taught that a liberal education necessarily means a religious one'. It went on to register a protest against physical science, law, history, and even theology being studied until students had passed the traditional Oxford course of classics and maths. Any attempt to allow those subjects to be taken at honours level was similarly to be outlawed. To give them status as 'liberal' studies would be 'the ruin of English education'.[67] Ten years later, the University Commissioners were stating unequivocally, as has been noted, that the training for the Church provided by Oxford was totally inadequate.

Frederic Harrison, who graduated in 1853 shortly after the Commission began its work, contemplated entering the Church but decided against it, not because of doubts about his own faith, although he had turned increasingly to Positivism, but because of a profound disillusionment with the Church as an institution. Oxford had been a catalyst in his decision because, since it was to all intents and purposes the seminary of the Church of England, it afforded him a unique opportunity to study its hierarchy, ethos, training methods, and recruits. The men he most admired there shared the misgivings that he expressed in a passionate, painful letter to his mother. 'I think its whole constitution and working rotten and wrong', he told her. He saw it as essentially a rich man's Church, narrow, worldly, jealous of its wealth and political power. As a profession, it was sought out by rich men, its top positions and choicest livings were highly paid, many livings were in the gift of wealthy families. The sources of its wealth—

tithes, land, investments—were morally dubious. On this last point, the Commissioners had been particularly critical of the way wealth was deployed to the disadvantage of the University. They attacked Fellowships that were confined to 'natives of particular localities, to members of particular families, and to those who are or have been Scholars in the College...'. The wealth of the great landed estates owned by Colleges only benefited the Colleges, and not the University. It might have provided for many to study and to teach but as it was, it went only to handful of Fellows, who were elected without any reference to merit.[68]

Those who were recruited to the Church from among Oxford's undergraduates were, in Harrison's experience, the sons of rich men. That might not matter so much if they were the best men but they were the dullest and the most selfish. He had witnessed 'miraculous conversions' of some of the most immoral undergraduates, 'conversions' winked at by Bishops. Nor were these the exceptions, although he knew there were clergymen of real worth. Clergy who were the sons of rich gentlemen inevitably retained the class feelings of rich men and expected livings of at least £300 a year. They were not likely to be able to win the confidence of the poor, although if they were in the rural livings they had a better chance of doing so than their urban colleagues, who complained that no working men attended church.[69] Harrison cited the case of one friend who had taken a country curacy (and who actually shared his view of the Church) and complained that he had no one to talk to of his own social level. This was the situation of Kilvert's father, who observed of his Keevil living that 'the class of men were rather below the average, so that I had no society in the place'.[70]

While Kilvert did not approve of the arrogant assertion of rank nor of the abuse of privilege, he did approve of gentlemen and of a gentlemanly Church, and it may have been an awareness that some of that atmosphere had gone from Oxford that gave rise to his extraordinary feeling of sadness when he revisited it in May 1874. 'All was as usual', he observed, as far as Wadham's natural surroundings were concerned, 'but all else was altered... The familiar friendly faces had all vanished... Strange faces and cold eyes came out of the doorways and passed and repassed the porter's lodge. One or two of the College servants remembered my face still, almost all had forgotten my name... I felt like a spirit revisiting the scenes of its earthly existence and finding myself strange, unfamiliar, unwanted'.[71] The intensity of feeling here can be explained largely in terms of Kilvert's romantic attachment to the idea of 'home'. His family home was the centre of particularly close relationships. The family motto he had created for himself contained, it will be recalled, the elements 'we are foreigners, we are strangers'. All his life, he would seek the perfect home, the place of ultimate security. Oxford was an approximation to it, but like all earthly homes, it would change, fall short of the ideal.

His sadness in 1874 was occasioned, not simply by the fact that Wadham was filled with a new generation of students and that only a few College servants remembered his name, but because the nature of the place had changed. The Oxford he had known in 1859 was still in most important respects the home of the Church of England; Kilvert knew that in 1874 this was no longer the case. He would also know that the majority of its graduates then were choosing some other career than the Church. Twelve other students were admitted to Wadham when he was. Six became clergymen; two became lawyers, one a master at Winchester, another at a private school in Brighton. The profession of the others is not known. Perhaps he even suspected that many of the undergraduates he saw in 1874 were not as gentlemanly as those who had been his contemporaries. Though there were still many sons of squires and of rural clergymen at Oxford when he revisited, the close connections between it and the landed gentry, which made Wadham like a country house in more than appearance, had been significantly weakened, just as the landed interest itself had been. The phrase that he used to sum up his impression of changed Oxford was 'the place thereof shall know it [ie. his name] no more', which was how he had expressed his sadness that the Oglander family of the Nunwell estate were to pass into oblivion in the absence of an heir. It was the impulse which led him to keep his *Diary*.

The transformation at Oxford was the same as that which threatened all landed families, including his own landless one. One landowner's son, Lord Redesdale, who had revelled unashamedly in the deference paid to rank while a student at Christ Church in the 1850s, loved the 'old world atmosphere about the place, ...a sort of elusive aroma of the cloister and the monk'. He believed it right that Fellowships went to men of 'good' families, with 'no damned nonsense of merit about it',[72] and he regarded it as a retrograde step when this was changed. Reform ruined Oxford for him: 'what was once [one of] the strong places of Christianity [is] now held by the heathen'. Oxford 'ceased to be a place of learning for English gentlemen of the ... Christian faith', and, in a highly significant parallel, he likened the profound nature of the change to that which overtook the House of Commons after the 1867 and 1884 Reform Bills, which destroyed, once and for all, the power of the landed gentry.[73] Frederick Meyrick, who was both a (Wiltshire) landowner's son and a clergyman/tutor at Oxford, had the same romantic attachment to Oxford's past. He lamented the victory of the Oxford liberals, which severed the connection between the Church and the University. He resented the transformation of Fellowships into straight forward teaching and research posts and the way in which Oxford became an academic instead of a religious institution. Oxford lost, he said, 'the old characteristics of an English University' and became more like a German one.[74] He resigned his post as a tutor at Trinity in 1858 in protest and became an HMI the year Kilvert went to Wadham. His summing up of the worth of the traditional clergyman tutors would not have satisfied Frederic Harrison but Kilvert would not have quarrelled with it: 'They did not inspire into young men enthusiasm or strong devotion, but they made them into upright, natural gentlemen'. Even Harrison confessed in 1910 to a nostalgia for 'the pathos and music of [Oxford's] traditions', which had changed after the reforms of the 1850s.

Is it possible, given the state of Oxford and of Wadham in the early 1860s, and with the predicament of such an honest and earnest critic as Harrison to guide one's speculations, to come close to Kilvert's frame of mind when he made his decision to become a clergyman? It was never likely that Kilvert would think the way Harrison did, nor experience what he experienced. The Positivist influence at Wadham that had begun with Congreve was short-lived,[75] and though Oxford was beginning to change, it was still perfectly possible to live at Wadham as if nothing was different. Harrison had had a religious upbringing but not an Evangelical one. He was city-bred, had attended a school which encouraged liberal speculation, and lived in a family with cultivated tastes. Kilvert had been brought up in the country, in a family overawed by tradition and authority. In spite of his uncle's teaching, Kilvert's was not a sophisticated intelligence. He had not been reared to have Harrison's 'horror at our social miseries' nor his 'zeal to correct abuses', and whereas the latter had steeped himself in the writings of the Christian Socialists, especially Kingsley, it seems very likely that Kilvert could embrace Kingsley only when he had abandoned his radicalism. Harrison knew that the correction of abuses required fundamental political change, as well as increased moral fervour; Kilvert wanted things to remain the same. Harrison was angry that 'men like... Kingsley... [who] do what they can to meet their duties, ...are silenced—driven out—maligned. Narrow minds— feeble hearts—are all that are wanted in the Establishment'.[76] If Kilvert had been one of Harrison's Wadham contemporaries, he might have been included in this last judgement. His heart was by no means feeble but he was one of those Victorians who exemplified the paradox identified by G.M. Young: why, he asked, in a money-making age, did people look up to birth more than money, why, in a socially mobile age, did people prefer immobility? The question implied its own answer: people disturbed by change, preferred the past, they preferred the old money that was associated with tradition, good breeding, the land.[77] They believed, as Kilvert and Warden Symons did, in preserving the differences between classes. Ironically, Symons was so wedded to them that he really resented having to admit Commoners like Kilvert (as opposed to Gentlemen-Commoners) to Wadham at all. He told the Oxford Commissioners that he was under no legal obligation to accept Commoners, and that everything he did for them was done out of kindness and condescension.[78]

As to whether Kilvert was happy with the Wadham of Symons, it is difficult to be sure in the absence of *Diary* entries that deal directly and fully with his student days as opposed to those that concern return visits, but their absence is in itself significant. The simple fact that when he went back to Oxford he spoke of it with affection proves nothing, and overlooks the power of romantic attachment. It was very common in the 19th century for men to revisit with powerful feelings of nostalgic affection their public schools where they were deeply unhappy. Kilvert spoke of the 'merry laughing breakfast' he had with his old Wadham friends, Mayhew and Laing, and of how it was 'spiced with many college stories and recollections of old days', but that does not necessarily mean they were happy recollections for him and he gives no details of them. Since he was no intellectual leader, loathed field sports, did not participate in athletic sports, and had neither the money nor the inclination to be a social butterfly, the conclusion seems irresistible that he would experience much the same social isolation as his father did at Oriel. While deferring to his social superiors, their idleness and extravagance would have troubled him. Concern over his own slender means would have been ever-present. He would have found the work a strain, yet would have been anxious to succeed, and always slightly afraid of the learning and authority of tutors. Wadham provided him with no more of an intellectual awakening than Oriel had for his father, and his studies would have tended to confirm his conservative attitudes and his attachment to the past. At the end of it all, he had a fourth class degree but some confirmation that he was a gentleman.

'It is of the utmost importance that men in high rank should find standing beside them in the ranks of the Church their equals in birth and their fellows in education, and, if anything, it is still more desirable that the poor of England should be ministered to by English gentlemen. What we mean by gentleman is just this - it is the habit of putting self down and of exalting those to whom he is ministering'.

Bishop Samuel Wilberforce, writing in 1864, the year Kilvert was appointed curate to the Rev. Venables

'He was often the patriarch of the parish, its ruler, its doctor, its magistrate, as well as its teacher, before whom vice trembled and rebellion dared not show its head'.

Dean Church on the well-connected parson

'...bad consciences were not bound to make very generous minds'.

M.K. Ashby, writing of landowners who knew the wages they paid to their labourers were inadequate, *Joseph Ashby of Tysoe*, p.73

'Few will doubt that the Church of England greatly needs the help of divine grace to preserve it from an undue reverence for station and property'.

Rev. Llewelyn Davies at the 1873 Bath Church Congress attended by Kilvert

'In the afternoon I had the happiness to have all the poor people to myself. None of the grand people were at Church by reason of the snow. So of course I could speak better and more freely'.

Kilvert's *Diary*, Vol. 2, p.157

CHAPTER 4
Kilvert and Venables

In 1865, the year in which Kilvert became Venables' curate, Trollope was working on his book, *The Clergymen of the Church of England.* It consists of fictional sketches of clergymen, which display the precision and irony of the fully developed creations of his novels.[1] Trollope found much to admire in his figure of 'The Parson of the Parish', describing him as 'the proper type and most becoming form of the English clergyman. He is pure parson and nothing else, and in the daily work of his life ... he cannot but feel that he is devoting himself to those duties which properly belong to him'. Trollope noted that until recent times the 'Parson of the Parish' was 'almost necessarily' educated at Oxford or Cambridge. It was felt by all that he was a gentleman 'who had lived on equal terms with the highest in the land in point of birth, and... that the occupant of the parsonage was as good a man as the occupant of the squire's house'. Then changes, 'not for the better', occurred. Theological colleges were established, producing what were called 'literates'. Such men might be, Trollope conceded, as capable as the old-style parson of teaching God's word, but would never equal him. They would inevitably be 'less attractive, less urbane, less genial', they would not, in a word, be 'gentlemen'. Country people needed a gentleman and would recognise instinctively whether they had one in their parson; they would automatically obey and respect and believe in the gentleman. The ideal man would probably be the younger son of a squire, or his father would have been a parson. He would have deep knowledge of rural affairs.[2] As Trollope's picture develops, it begins to resemble Venables more and more, until it becomes hard to detach oneself from the absurd idea that he must have had in mind the Vicar of Clyro.

When Kilvert became his curate, Venables was a widower and was probably glad of his company. Whatever feeling of closeness the older man had for the younger because of loneliness was probably reciprocated; Kilvert no doubt felt lonely too at being far from home in a strange locality. During the previous year, he had acted as curate to his father at Langley Burrell and there are distinct signs in the *Diary* that Kilvert regarded Venables with that mixture of awe, love, and veneration that he felt towards his own father. He had the same authority, dignity, and, to some extent, austerity, possessed by Robert Kilvert. Kilvert served them both as curate. Kilvert quaked at the thought that he might have been in the shoes of Mr. Irvine, his replacement at Clyro, who had made the 'terrible mistake' of confusing the day on which he was supposed to take the Clyro Church service while Venables took the one at Bettws. Irvine was about to begin at Bettws when he heard the terrible voice of Venables saying, 'Are you aware there is no one at Clyro Church?'[3] Venables was not only an authority figure for Kilvert as formidable as his father, but to a large extent became his second father, and Clyro Vicarage became a second home. He and Kilvert's father were of the same generation[4] and had experienced the same changes in society, viewing them from the similar positions of public school, Oxbridge, rural parsonages, Tory politics, and a love of the novels of Sir Walter Scott. Venables had been sent in 1820 to Eton, the most aristocratic school in the land, though he stayed only three years, probably because its ethos was too barbaric, and was transferred in 1823 to Charterhouse, then at the height of its popularity as the school for the moderately rich where drilling in classics could be had for lower fees.

We have virtually no evidence of the subjects Venables and Kilvert discussed[5] but one feels sure that the former's visit in 1867 to Scott's Abbotsford home must have been one of them. Le Quesne's examination of parallel passages in the diaries of Venables and Kilvert led him to the conclusion that the younger man was heavily influenced by the older: '... it is as though Kilvert is seeing with the vicar's eyes and thinking with his mind'.[6] It was the result, Le Quesne believed, of Venables' dominating personality and of Kilvert's passivity. An additional reason may have been that Kilvert shared his vicar's outlook to a large extent. He certainly spent a vast amount of time in Venables' company; there was no one in Clyro whom he saw more often. He virtually lived for half his time at the Vicarage, dining on average four times a week over a period of seven and a half years.[7] In that time, he also made a dozen visits, some as long as a week, to

Venables' Llysdinam mansion. He accompanied him, too, on many dinner engagements to homes of other gentry and they went for innumerable walks and rides together. There was, therefore, ample opportunity for him to assimilate Venables' opinions, and, because Venables so much resembled Kilvert's father and Kilvert was young, impressionable, and away from home, every incentive to be guided by the older man.

Kilvert's paternalist, Tory conception of society would receive much reinforcement in the Clyro Vicarage of Venables: his approach to property, to the landed gentry, to the poor, and to political changes was very similar to that of his vicar. For Kilvert, the Venables family fulfilled the same role in Radnorshire as the Clutterbucks in Wiltshire. Venables had given a full account of what the landed estate meant to him in the book *Domestic Scenes in Russia*, which he wrote shortly after his visit in 1837 to the relatives of his first wife. (He had married the daughter of a Russian general). He found Russian gentry worryingly deficient in their awareness of the importance of rank, particularly of the way it could be asserted through ownership of land. The Russian gentleman failed to see the symbolic value of a country estate, viewing it, Venables observed with incredulity, merely as a summer residence. He had no family pride in its inheritance, which, in any case, was dissipated by the absurd, in Venables' view, Russian system which demanded that an estate must, at the death of the father of a family, be sub-divided among his children. Venables was a firm believer in primogeniture; as an eldest son, it would have been surprising if he were not. If all children had a share in an estate, it was pointless to spend money on its embellishment, he argued, because the eldest son would lack sufficient means to keep it up. 'Why should one build a house suited to a fortune of £5000 a year, when the son who inherits it will have but £1000...?' he asked.[8] It was right and proper that the bulk of a family's fortune be directed towards one individual and the preservation of a seat commensurate with that fortune and the family name. In addition to prestige, estates brought power and 'influence of property', unknown to the Russian landowner. He had few public duties, Venables observed, and no influence beyond that over his serfs, who, since they were their master's property, could not feel the English labourers' 'sincere and voluntary attachment' to the landed family. The house of the Russian landowner lacked luxury and amenity; there were not even field sports to induce guests to visit; there was no park. In fact, 'the handsome, substantial, well-arranged country seat is unknown in Russia', Venables concluded.[9] His phrasing echoed Robert Kilvert's praise of the 'nice, well-appointed' country house which he regarded as his second home.

In the matter of history and lineage, the Venables' prestige stood as high as any family in the land, notwithstanding the fact that they were not titled. They were of Norman origin. Gilbert de Venables came from a town of that name in Normandy and was first cousin to Duke William of Normandy. Kilvert, on a visit to France, sought out the town especially, and reported on it to his vicar. Gilbert came to England in 1066 with the Conqueror and established the Barony of Kinderton in Cheshire. After this promising beginning, the Venables family continued to acquire property in Shropshire and Montgomeryshire. Venables' father, Richard Drake Venables, married Sophia Lister of Girsby Hall, Lincolnshire. From 1830, when he was 21 years old, Venables' family home was the mansion of Llysdinam, near Clyro, and his father, who held several church livings, added to his estates over the years by acquiring mountain land in lieu of tithes. Venables himself had further embellished and extended Llysdinam ready for his retirement. That Kilvert would take the trouble while on holiday to search out the town of Venables is indicative of the importance lineage and country house traditions had for his romantic nature. The Frenchman, Hippolyte Taine, who wrote a book based on his observations of English gentry life in the period 1860-70, said it was the park of the English country house, rather than the house itself, which revealed 'the poetic dream of the English soul'.[10] To Kilvert it was both, though he was particularly attracted to parks. He tried to make Llysdinam, after it had been extended, into a monument of feudal power: 'it now looks inspiring, almost like a castle...'.[11]

He both recognised and approved of the fact that country houses were about power and authority, as well as about history, romance, and tradition. Venables had emphasised that the English landowner had duties his Russian counterpart had not. He himself served on various committees that dealt with the affairs of the poor and followed his father in being for many years Chairman of Radnorshire Quarter Sessions. Nothing, unless it was the Game Laws, epitomised the rule of the landed gentry more than the magistracy, which has been described as 'the most aristocratic feature of English government'.[12] Kilvert gave his whole-hearted support to this institution. He recorded a rabbit-poaching case that concerned the Wye Cliff property in Clyro owned by the Crichton family. Rev. Venables, who was on the bench and knew the Crichtons, declined to hear the case so as to ensure impartiality. Kilvert clearly thought this was not only unnecessary but that the absence of Venables' judgement and authority exposed the incompetence of the other JPs, who 'made a mess of the whole thing, giving a much too severe sentence which they had ignominiously to reconsider'.[13] The episode illustrates the extent to which those brought before the bench were subject to its amateurishness and caprice. Kilvert may have been right that on this occasion an unduly severe sentence was initially given but harsh and unjust sentences were the norm. Injustice in sentencing was often the result of vindictiveness and a willingness by JPs to bend the rules: '...very great irregularities and injustices were committed by the magistrates under the game laws', stated the Home Office representative to the 1846 Select Committee on the Game Laws. The Home Office had to order the release in one year of 40 poachers who had been wrongfully imprisoned and had commuted the sentences of 14 others.[14]

Kilvert was content that, not only justice, but all the care of the poor, be left in the safe hands of the traditional authority figure. He believed with Venables that labourers' attachment to such figures was, or should be, 'sincere and voluntary', and that the different classes of the social hierarchy were ordained by God. To Venables, as to all paternalists, the large difference of wealth between gentry and labourers was a matter of the natural order of things. His sermon of March 1855 was based on the text: 'The Lord maketh poor and he maketh rich; he bringeth low and he lifteth up'. He went on to declare that people were too prone to claim that they themselves were responsible for the wealth they obtained, not remembering that it was God who gave the power that resulted in wealth. It was up to all to use properly the talents given to them, as well as to fulfil the duties assigned to them.[15] He chose the Sunday before Christmas in 1849 to deliver a similar message. Every opportunity to do good reminded us, he said, that we were God's stewards and that we should be called upon to give an account that would show whether we had wasted God's goods or whether we had employed them in His service. We were employing them well whenever we used them for the benefit of

others. That opportunity, that blessing, was within the reach of all—
the poor as well as the rich.[16] This view of property as a trust, it will be
recalled, Kilvert had heard expressed in the words of Mrs.
Clutterbuck. Kilvert accepted that one important duty of property
holders was charity. Venables saw himself as the father of the poor
and was praised by Thomas Baskerville, the squire of Clyro, for his
management of the Clyro Coal and Clothing Clubs.[17] Another duty
was the provision of education and here again the two clergymen of
Clyro saw eye to eye. They both recommended an education for the
poor which taught acceptance of their social position and of its attendant duties, and endorsed the Church's National Society as its agency.
'Venables preached a capital sermon on popular Education on behalf
of the National Society', wrote Kilvert.[18] Both men saw democratic
political movements as wicked because they undermined social order.
In one letter, Venables speculated on how labourers would respond
to 'the temptation Chartism holds out'. In another, he pronounced
the Chartist riots 'despicable', while in a third he condemned the
middle-classes for being 'quite as democratic as the mob'.[19]

Neither had any inkling that they would share so much when
Kilvert's candidature for the Clyro curacy was being considered. The
connection that brought him to Clyro was the Clutterbuck family that
had earlier extended its patronage to his father. The Clutterbucks
were related to the Crichton family of Wye Cliff, Clyro, so Kilvert's
name probably came via Wye Cliff to Clyro Vicarage and Venables.
The most important single fact that Venables registered on 10
November 1864, shortly after meeting the candidate for the first time,
was: 'He seems to be a gentleman. I like what I have seen ...it is
evident he is respectable...'.[20] Two months later, in another letter, he
stated: 'I am very glad to have a university man'.[21] One might have
thought that only a university man and a gentleman would have
presented himself for the post, but by this time the Church had
encountered severe problems over recruitment. In the 1850s and
1860s the large number of new churches and the expanded population meant that there was an increased demand for curates. There
were 632 ordinations in 1853 but by the time Kilvert was leaving
Wadham they had slumped to 489.[22] At the same time fewer
gentlemen were choosing to become clergymen. Analysis of the Eton
lists reveal this quite clearly. Whereas 23.3% of boys chose the Church
as a profession in 1811, only 8.1% did in 1850 and 6.7% in 1871.[23] A

decline in belief, exacerbated by the impact of academic philosophy and biblical criticism, low salaries, and inadequate training all helped to make the profession less attractive than it formerly had been. Figures for men leaving Oxbridge and entering the Church between 1841 and 1871 show a steady decline and 'the 1860s were years of particular uncertainty'.[24]

To meet the shortfall and the criticism that the Church provided no real training, a number of theological colleges had been set up.[25] The Church kept quiet about them because their very existence implied criticism of the provision it made for its clergy in unreformed Oxbridge; it was wedded to the idea of a general, non-professional education and resisted the development of separate establishments. The Rev. Meyrick, whose fierce defence of the *status quo* in Oxford was noted earlier, wrote: 'Theological colleges, necessary as they are, are no adequate substitute for our ancient Universities in the formation of the character of our clergy'.[26] Part of the prejudice against them derived from the belief that clergymen should be gentlemen, and part from the fact that some of them admitted non-graduates.

Meyrick argued in favour of gentry clergy on the grounds that it was from them alone that other gentry would accept spiritual guidance. Venables' ministrations to Lord Hereford and Walter Baskerville exemplified this. An element in the satisfaction Venables derived from this role was that he was able to regard the young men who came to him for advice as his sons. For much of his adult life he probably despaired of having a son. None was born of his first wife, who had died the year Kilvert came to Clyro, and he was 58 years old when he married his second wife, Agnes Minna Pearson. When a son, Henry George Lister, was finally born on 27 April 1874, the survival of the Venables' name was, it seemed, assured. Venables pronounced him to be 'a large healthy child'. Early in 1876, however, friends were writing to him to express their sorrow at the death of the boy and no more sons were born.

Venables had, therefore, good reasons for taking an interest in the lives and fortunes of gentry young men in his circle, and it was a role for which he was well known. Henry Dew, who followed him as Rector of Whitney in 1843, wrote to him on 2 March 1873 to say how sorry he was that he was resigning the living of Clyro: 'You have been looked up to as a second Father by all my generation for so many years...'.[27] Lord Hereford, whose father had died when he was only

12, relied on Venables as his father-confessor. His own father had learnt to be idle and dissolute at Christ Church, and he himself, as a young man in 1868, was worried that, without a purpose to which he could devote his life, he might suffer the premature death of 'poor Velters' (Velters Cornewall, who had died that year aged 44; he was the eldest brother of Sir George Cornewall), or of 'Uncle Walter' (Walter De Winton, who died in 1840 aged 31). One of Lord Hereford's problems was lack of money and another was concern for rank. He had difficulty finding his avocation, he said, because he had been reared to be idle, to be conscious of what he called 'his ancient position'. He thought he had left too much of the management of his estate to his agent. His doctor had recommended 'some line of pursuit'. Lord Hereford hoped that Venables would enable him to 'make the best of things' and he warned him on one occasion that he would be visiting him 'to pour out all his griefs'.[28] He steadily became more and more mentally unbalanced as the years went by.

Walter Baskerville, who had also wasted his time at Christ Church but was not so obsessed by rank and could employ himself a little more usefully, made less stringent demands on Venables, whom he addressed as his 'oldest and kindest friend'. He confided to him his growing affection for Bertha Hopton, and when he married her, asked him to perform the ceremony.[29] Lord Hereford and Baskerville would not have accepted guidance from Kilvert. They belonged to the Gentleman-Commoner group to whom he had been considered an inferior at Oxford. Nevertheless, Venables was happy enough with him as his curate. When he expressed satisfaction to his brother that in Kilvert he had secured 'a university man', his concern was that of Bishop Wilberforce, whose view prefaces this chapter: a clergyman of high rank could only work with one of comparable standing. It was a view that would have commanded Kilvert's full support.[30]

To this point the great closeness of Venables and Kilvert has been stressed. That closeness did not, however, exist without its tension. There were, of course, differences of temperament. Venables' tendency towards remoteness and austerity has already been noted. On the basis of a study of his diaries, which contain only the briefest, most prosaic details, Le Quesne made a number of observations of Venables' personality. 'It is entirely characteristic of him', wrote Le Quesne, 'that he gives a brief matter-of-fact account of his second marriage having previously given no indication at all that he was contemplating such a thing and made only one or two passing references to the woman who was about to become his wife...!' Le Quesne looked in vain for description, aesthetic judgement, expressions of opinion, and self-revelation, and concluded that Venables was not a man 'of much imagination or sensibility'.[31] Kilvert noted that Venables' successor had made his study, 'formerly dull, dark and dingy', into a cheerful, pretty room. Though Venables had made his pilgrimage to the home of Sir Walter Scott, there are no references in his letters to reading his novels or to the reading of any imaginative literature. Nor is there any description of scenery or a country house in the romantic vein of Kilvert. There are expressions of opinion but they are not accompanied by critical examination of the issues involved or the arguments that might be deployed on both sides of them. Instead there is dogmatic assertion and a tendency to see political and social questions simply in terms of how they affected the wellbeing of his own class. Kilvert would not have found fault with much of this; he would have expected a man of his age and with his responsibilities to be authoritative and distant.

The basis of the tension that existed between the two men is, in a real sense, reflected in 'The Poacher',[32] the result of Venables' trying his hand at a fictionalised version of rural life. It was probably written when he was a young man and is unfinished, so that it is difficult to be certain about the intentions that lay behind it. In what does exist, however, can be discerned a pattern that complements the vision of rural society Venables expressed in his book about Russia. In the Dingleford of 'The Poacher' we have a village not only idealised in appearance—it was 'pretty' and 'romantic' and situated in 'one of the most fertile counties in England'—but belonging entirely to the world of 'Merrie England'. Its social structure was essentially feudal. Standing like guardians over its 30 houses, 'chiefly cottages' (there was no middle-class in Dingleford), are the twin symbols of traditional power and authority—the Vicarage at one end of the village and the 'ancestral domain' of the Cavendish family at the other. In the name of the gentry home—Dingleford Priory—there is a suggestion of pre-Reformation times. Antiquity is the essence of the place. The Priory had been in the possession of the Cavendishes, so people said, from before the Conquest. (Venables originally wrote 'before the Flood', but rejected that in favour of the historically and socially more suggestive, 'before the Conquest'). The house's history reflected that unattainable dream of all landed families—inheritance through direct descent of father to son, 'for many generations'. Sir Digby Cavendish[33] had not had the good fortune which was Venables' of being the first born son; his eldest brother had, however, been killed by a fall while hunting. He had earlier married Emily, daughter of Sir Edward Scott, 'a baronet of good family and moderate fortune'. Was Venables seeking an echo of the Waverley novels in his choice of 'Scott'?

Strongly 'historical', too, was Dingleford's 'Red Lion', a 'respectable public house', which provided a change of horses for stage coaches. A further mark of the village's traditional nature was its location: it stood at the edge of a common that somehow had remained unenclosed. The church was 'not one of the fanciful erections of the present days, but a venerable edifice with its square, grey tower filling the thoughtful spectator with feelings of awe and veneration for the sacred rites performed therein...'. Venables was overdoing the 'veneration' emphasis, so keen was he to persuade his reader that age itself was worthy of respect. In the figure of the vicar, significantly called Mr. Temple, there was implicit rejection of the ills of Dissent and religious scepticism which had bedevilled the Church of recent times: 'No new doctrine, no enthusiasm could mislead his strong, well-regulated mind'. He was in other respects a traditional clergyman, purveying the Gospel of Christ to the timid, weak and penitent. To the 'profligate and hardened sinner', however, he was stern and severe. To do Christ's work was the sole aim of this 'nearly blameless' man and he was a tireless visitor of the poor, sick and dying. Temple's living was worth £300 - £350 a year (the value of Venables' Clyro living), but additional resources available to him and to his wife provided half as much again, and he lived like a gentleman. His spiritual closeness to the village, however, is underlined by the fact that his Vicarage was separated from it only by his lawn and flower garden.

In his portrayal of Temple, Venables was presenting a version of himself, or of the self he aspired to be: pious, serious, dignified, and unworldly, the fountain of traditional wisdom and authority. There were significant differences between the two men. Temple did not live in the grand way that Venables did. He was not a landowner and his living contributed the greater part of his income, which was not at all the case with Venables. The 'higher inducements that attached a man to his estate' (the phrase was Venables' from his book on Russia) played no part therefore in Temple's life. It seems unlikely that he was a JP or Venables would have mentioned it when he first introduced him. That Temple was an idealised figure in an idealised world is given additional emphasis by the fact that he was neither a landowner nor a JP. In consequence, he would be able to present himself as a simple man of God to the villagers because he did not occupy roles that potentially brought him into conflict with them. Sir Digby Cavendish, by contrast, existed remote from them on the other side of 'the lodges and great gate of Dingleford Priory'. Though Venables possessed the impressive country house of Llysdinam that lay well away from Clyro, until his retirement he lived, as Temple did, in a vicarage in the heart of the community. Perhaps he took comfort from that since he would also be bound to recognise that he was a much less conscientious visitor of parishioners than his fictional cler-gyman. In a letter of June 1869, he assured his brother George that he could always be away from Clyro between Monday and Saturday even when Kilvert was absent.[34] It was perhaps, therefore, a guilty conscience that made him place Temple close to his community.

When Venables chose his curate in late 1864, he made gentleman-liness his main consideration, but there were other things in Kilvert's background: there was his Evangelicalism and his veneration for the kind of clergyman that Charles Kingsley was. In Martineau's view, the theme of all Kingsley's books and sermons was 'noblesse oblige, the true principle of feudalism'[35]—the principle, in fact, which gave meaning and purpose to Venables' life. However, his regard for rank and social eminence and influence prevented him from becoming a Kingsley or a Temple, who were always to be found in the homes of the poor. When Venables expressed sympathy for the sufferings of the poor but urged that they be resigned in the face of them and seek comfort in the consolations of religion, was it simply hypocrisy? When he made close involvement with the lives of his poorest parishioners the outstanding characteristic of Temple, was he making conscious acknowledgement of the gap between his own principles and practice? These questions go to the heart of Kilvert's *Diary* and of Victorian experience. No one can read his *Diary* without feeling some indigna-tion at his acceptance of the social inequality and the suffering he observed every day; it casts a shadow which it is not easy to dispel.

Houghton considered hypocrisy as the Victorians' weakest point when it came to a defence of their culture; they could readily refute other charges against it but not that one. The charge had, he believed, three aspects. First, that they concealed or suppressed their true beliefs and tastes; second, that they professed piety and noble ideals but that their lives revealed quite other concerns; third, that they closed their eyes to anything that was unpleasant or disturbing.[36] Venables and Kilvert demonstrate something which goes against the grain of the 20th century reader: that it was perfectly possible for intelligent and sensitive men to feel some concern at the gross inequalities of Victorian society and at the same time to reject the introduction of democracy, which might be thought to be the sole means of redressing those inequalities. Blocking the path of development of the democratic idea, however, was the aristocratic idea, to which both Venables and Kilvert were devoted. The historian Woodruff expressed the essence of the aristocratic idea in terms of 'breeding': 'we most easily enter into the spirit of the pre-democratic age' when we recognise that breeding, which is essentially a countryman's philosophy, deliberately sets out to produce inequality.[37] Thus, the right to rule is a matter of heredity. From an early point in the 19th century, observers had been noting that the aristocratic principle blocked the flow of sympathy in people. Bulwer Lytton stated in 1833 that the aristocratic doctrine that demanded that all clergymen should be gentlemen ensured that a parson was subject to all the ideas that characterised aristocracy. 'It makes him passionless in the pulpit, but decorous in his habits, and it fits him rather, not to shock the prejudices of the drawing room, than to win the sympathies of the cottage'.[38] That parson might oversee distribution of soup and coal to the poor, but he would not be a frequenter of their homes. This, it will be recalled, was Frederic Harrison's criticism of those Wadham colleagues who elected to become clergymen.

Closeness to an aristocratic code of conduct and lack of closeness to his flock and their needs are central elements in the tension between Venables and Kilvert, and in the 'strange and horrible dream' reflecting it which Kilvert had on the night of 13 October 1872. The dream shows the extent to which his father, his background and home life, his work and his future prospects were inextricably bound up with Venables and values he represented. It is noticeable that the dream occurred shortly after Kilvert had experienced the pain and disruption of leaving Clyro where he had been so happy in many ways, and was back in Langley Burrell, serving his father—a mere curate with preferment and his own home and family still somewhere in the future. It was perhaps anxiety over this state of affairs that triggered the dream, as well as the release of tensions that had had to remain bottled up while he was Clyro's curate. The wording of the *Diary* entry is important and needs full quotation: 'I dreamt that I dreamt that Mr Venables and Mrs Venables tried to murder me. We were all together in a small room and they were both trying to poison me, but I was aware of their intention and baffled them repeatedly. At length, Mr Venables put me off my guard, came round fondling me, and suddenly clapped his hand on my neck behind said, "It's of no use, Mr Kilvert. You're done for". I felt the poison beginning to work and burn in my neck'.[39]

Why should Kilvert have felt that these people, who had been so kind and supportive towards him, wished to destroy him? (Mrs. Venables was part of the plot too. Kilvert had been especially close to her. It was with her, rather than with her husband, that he could discuss his love affairs). And why was their warmth replaced suddenly by the formality of '"It's of no use, Mr Kilvert"'? His response to this confrontation was violent: 'I knew it was all over and started up in fury and despair. I flew at him savagely'. Then comes an abrupt change of scene and the first of several details that links the dream's events closely with Kilvert's home. Suddenly he and the Venables were in the organ loft of Harnish Church. 'Mr Venables, seeing me coming at him, burst out at the door. Close outside the door was standing the Holy Ghost'. Venables knocked the Holy Ghost headlong down the stairs, rushed out and rode off with Kilvert in pursuit. The 'fury and despair' Kilvert felt seems to be occasioned by guilt that he had been found out in some terrible crime or deception. However, some guilt appears to attach to Venables since he assaults the Holy Ghost—a highly significant act performed by a clergyman.

Kilvert determined to murder Venables and again there is the implication that he did so in the conviction that Venables too was a guilty man, even if only for pretending an affection he did not really feel. 'Accordingly', wrote Kilvert, 'I lay in wait for him with a pickaxe on the Vicarage lawn in Clyro, hewed an immense and hideous hole through his head, and kicked his face so that it was so horribly muti-lated... as to be past recognition. Then the spirit of the dream changed. Mrs Venables became her old natural self again'. She reproached Kilvert in gentle terms for being so cruel in mutilating her husband so that she couldn't recognise him. Kilvert's assault on him is both very public and very ungentlemanly. A working man, and not a gentleman, might use a pickaxe to commit murder. And it as though the outwardly kind Mrs. Venables was advancing the view that all genteel society would take of Kilvert's action—that it was unprovoked, unworthy, unnatural, and unjust, the act of an animal and expressive of hideous social disorder. Mr. Bevan,[40] Vicar of Hay, is seen in the dream as Mrs. Venables' ally in evincing the reaction of respectable society: 'Well, you have done it now. You have made a pretty mess of it'.

Again, as though to mitigate Kilvert's guilt and to imply that others, too, might be culpable, comes this emphasis on his devotion to the parish poor (an aspect of the work that Venables left entirely to his curate): '*All this time* I was going about visiting the sick at Clyro...' (my italics; he did add 'and preaching at Clyro Church', but the concern with the sick comes first). However, Kilvert's devotion cannot absolve him from the guilt of the crime of killing Venables. 'I saw that people were beginning to look shy at me and suspect me of the murder...'. Overcome by conscience, he gives himself up to a policeman, is taken to prison, and kept in chains. For the second time the dream is connected to his home, and specifically his father: 'Then the full misery of my position burst upon me and the ruin and disgrace I had brought on my family. "It will kill my father", I cried in an agony of remorse and despair'. Not only is the home of Clyro Vicarage identified in this way, as it was by the earlier reference to Harnish, with the vicarage of his father, but additional reinforcement is given to the idea, also suggested by that reference, that in attacking Venables he was in reality attacking his own father. Thus, the 'inner' dream pictured Kilvert being discovered in some dreadful deception, while in the 'outer' dream he saw himself both attempting to escape the guilt of that while simultaneously bringing retribution too on Venables for his own sin against the Holy Ghost. The close identification of his surrogate with his real father implies that the latter also had that sin on his conscience.

The supremely important thing that follows in the *Diary* entry is that Kilvert emphasises again and again that he 'knew it was no dream'. This, he said, was '*at last...* a reality from which I should never awake. I had awaked from many evil dreams... but this was a reality... It was all true *at last...* Nothing now seems to me so real and

tangible...' (my italics). It seems that the dream was for him the resolution of a long-standing tension, and one is compelled to examine
the immediate circumstances of his life at this time for an explanation of what it was. The fact that he had voluntarily given up the
Clyro curacy a short time earlier and with it the possibility of
becoming vicar there was important. Venables had asked him in
March that year what he would do if the Bishop offered him the
Clyro living and he had said that he would refuse it, upon which
Venables had observed, 'Then you would be mad'. But Kilvert had
insisted (to his *Diary*): 'I don't want the living of Clyro'.[41] He probably felt he couldn't follow Venables in the job and be compared
with him and fail to live up to his reputation as a county administrator, which was formidable. He no doubt realised also that one
would need Venables' background, money and status as a landowner
to fill the position adequately. Mrs. Venables once remarked to
Kilvert that he would not be able to keep the Vicarage in repair. It
seems certain he felt guilty at declining even to be considered for the
job, as well as at resigning the curacy, especially as both fell within
the realm of Venables' influence and he was not accepting a promotion that would justify his leaving. A feeling that he was letting
Venables, his father, and himself down would be an element in this
thinking and appears in his insistence in the dream that he was
bringing 'ruin and disgrace' upon his family. It was probably this
which grew in his mind, especially as the dream coincided with the
time when he was idling his time away in Weymouth where he had
gone to see the Channel Fleet. It is important to notice that the
Diary entry containing his horrible dream also recorded the coincidence that a letter from Venables arrived the morning afterwards
saying that he had recommended Kilvert for the living of Disserth in
Radnorshire, urging him to accept it if offered. Again Kilvert
dithered. 'I hope the question may not arise'. He said he felt settled
in Langley Burrell and yet feared still being a curate in middle age.
But even that thought was in conflict with a desire to be back in
Clyro, his second home, among 'old friends and ...dear old scenes
and memories'.

Anxiety about professional prospects and the achievement of a
proper gentlemanly status was, therefore, part of the dream's
meaning, but the particular way in which his failure manifested itself
reflected a terror that was very real for him and his father. We have

seen that Robert had been haunted from schooldays by a dream he had that the King Edward VI Headmaster, Wilkins, was pursuing him birch in hand in order to flog him before the congregation because he, as Wilkins' curate, had lost the place in the service. Robert also had the memory of his own father's business failure and his terrible anxiety about the family's financial position. His father's mind became ever more troubled about it and obsessed with guilt. Near death 'he had one prevailing idea that his life was forfeited for some capital crime' and he obtained comfort only from the idea that the law would find him guilty and, by punishing him, would redeem him. He died imagining himself on the way to public execution.[42] Kilvert recalled his father talking about these matters,[43] and the end of his dream paralleled these earlier dreams that had dogged his father: Kilvert, too, saw his end in terms of public humiliation and execution. 'The Assizes', I said, 'will come on in March and I shall be hung early in April'. The *Diary* entry ends with his reflections on the family motto, 'We are pilgrims', and the family arms that signified the family honour, which his dream told him he had disgraced, just as his father and grandfather had done by the failure at the centre of their dreams.

On one or two occasions before Kilvert had his 'horrible dream' and with increasing frequency afterwards, he recorded stories in which families suffered dramatic loss of fortune and of status. One of his Clyro parishioners, Hannah Whitney, received particularly regular visits from him and part of her fascination lay in the fact that she had not always known poverty in a tiny cottage, which was her lot in Clyro. She was descended, as he was, from 'a line of squires' and she asserted that 'she had no cause to be ashamed of her family'.[44] On a visit to Liverpool, Kilvert was driven to the station by a cabman who was 'once a man of good estate and county magistrate. He married a woman of family, but he dissipated his fortune and now has sunk to be a common cabman...'.[45] The daughter of a 'litigious farmer' told Kilvert of the death of her husband, the loss of their farm, and her descent into 'comparative poverty'.[46] On another occasion, he was clearly fascinated by the story of a nobleman who had been reduced to being an organ grinder.[47] An old labouring man Kilvert met while visiting Malmesbury, impressed by his clerical status, told him that he (the labourer) had the same great grandfather as the Vicar of Malmesbury, 'but one family had gone up and the other down'.[48]

Kilvert reflected on the shock sustained by a family he knew whose son had been sentenced to 15 years' penal servitude for robbing a Melksham bank.[49] This catalogue of social disasters, which Kilvert made a point of noting, is completed by the case of the Meredith family of Bredwardine which had once owned a hotel and a substantial coaching business. 'Now they have come down to keep a turnpike gate'.[50]

In all these stories, which have clear parallels (some made quite explicit by Kilvert) to his own situation, can be found a mixture of sheer misfortune, sudden death, and personal failure. It appears that all of them had special importance because they reflected his own fear of failure and of public humiliation. They are also a reflection of his family's social position, for the middle-class was no more immune to the vicissitudes of fortune than was the working-class. The business failures that figured in several of the stories of individual 'shipwrecks' Kilvert heard and had been such a significant event in his own background, were an ever-present threat to the middle-class, and when they occurred, it could turn only to the genteel charities and to the patronage that had served the Kilvert family.[51] He declined to link any of these failures directly to the collapse of his grandfather's coach-building business, and it is noticeable that, though he frequently referred in the *Diary* to squire forbears, there is no mention (in what has come down to us) of yeomen ones nor of the tradesman grandfather. Perhaps he was ashamed of being descended from a tradesman, especially a failed one. All his life, Kilvert was afraid that some terrible weakness or mistake of his would culminate in disaster. It is significant that, after a depressing consultation with Mrs. Venables about his doomed courtship of Daisy Thomas (see next chapter), he wrote: 'Alas, who could have believed I could be such a *villain?*'[52]

It has been noted in chapter one that Kilvert's family history included the memory of a humiliating loss of fortune, which drove the Kilvert men to find material success in particularly difficult economic circumstances. His background also left him with a heightened sense of sin, which could perceive business failure as the consequence of irresponsible and immoral behaviour that could verge almost on the criminal. All of this lay behind his steady recording of individual and family disaster. As is often the case with Kilvert, the clearest exposition of his feelings and attitudes may be found in his poems. They abound with references to the 'pilgrimage' that is life, to individual souls seeking their home amid the terror of 'shipwrecks', actual and metaphorical. Thus, in 'Life's Weather', we are told that there are in 'Lightning and thunder, souls in the storm and strife, hearts in the wreck of life riven asunder'. Other poems emphasise the importance of preserving personal honour. 'Honour shines, the guiding star' in 'Noblesse Oblige', while in 'Faithful Unto Death', we are asked 'And what were life with honour gone?' But the lines that best sum up those submerged elements in Kilvert's life that surfaced in his dream of murder and dishonour are to be found in 'Friendship', where he took comfort from the thought of a dear friend who would always be faithful:

> When bowed my face with shame and dread,
> Forsaken in the dust I lie,
> A hand on my dishonoured head
> Is rested, oh how tenderly!

We can grasp the full significance of Kilvert's sense of honour and the way it identifies him with a pre-democratic culture from this statement by an analyst of modern society: 'Honour is ... an aristocratic concept, or at least associated with a hierachical order of society ... such a culture is essentially pre-modern'.[53]

Apart from reflecting the fear of failure that ran like a thread through the Kilvert family, the chief import of Kilvert's dream lies in what it tells us about the regard in which he held Venables and the way he was a second father to him. Kilvert's self-image was, in turn, bound up with the regard Venables and his real father had for him. The terrible 'reality' that his dream forced him to contemplate is concerned centrally with the forfeiture of that regard. It is, however, important to note that his response to Venables' 'It's of no use, Mr Kilvert. You're done for' was not simply 'despair' at being discovered, but 'fury' and a desire for revenge because of the deception Venables and his wife had practised on him. The affection Venables had displayed—'[he] came round fondling me'—had deceived and disarmed Kilvert. Similarly Mrs. Venables had simulated and later recovered a 'natural self' of motherly concern while collaborating in the attempt to poison him. Kilvert was guilty of the savage murder of Venables, but Venables and his wife were also guilty of an attempt to murder him in a manner more 'respectable' but no less cruel. The dream also showed the long-serving, highly respected figure of the

Vicar of Clyro as guilty of the sin against the Holy Ghost. It is in connection with these elements that Kilvert's obsessive harping on the essential 'reality' of what the dream revealed becomes clearer. The mask of piety and respectability that covered the relationships in Clyro Vicarage had slipped. Kilvert's dream was the more terrible because it contained the revelation that Venables, for all his authority, dignity and affection was as much, if not more, of a sham than Kilvert felt himself to be. It was the conflict over the disturbing nature of this reality and the pressure Kilvert had experienced in seeking to suppress it, when honesty demanded otherwise, that lay behind his statement: 'It was all true at last...'. In making Venables' face unrecognisable even to his own wife, Kilvert had literally changed the 'face' that he presented to society, but in rendering it ugly and hideous, had revealed more of its true reality. Venables was akin to the Pharisee in Luke 18.9, the text of the sermon by his father that Kilvert had found especially touching: the Pharisee projected an aura of respectability which cloaked his sinfulness.

What, in Kilvert's relationship with Venables, could possibly have given rise to such a perception? The clue lies in Kilvert's statement that while the attempt to poison him went on, he was, '*all this time*' (and the wording becomes significant), doing his parochial duties—visiting the sick and taking services. (Plomer referred to the way 'the necessary abbreviation' of the *Diary* had prevented 'a just impression being given of Kilvert's constant attention to parochial duties'.)[54] A righteous awareness of his own conscientiousness prompted him to underline that in the account of his dream.

Before going on to examine in more detail the question of Venables' sinfulness and Kilvert's attitude to it, it is appropriate to ask how much of an Evangelical Kilvert was, partly because the terrible dream he had appears to spring from a more than usually strict religious conscience and partly because the precise nature of that conscience has implications for the accounts given in later chapters of his life and attitudes. David Bentley-Taylor has rightly stated that Kilvert 'chose to share his father's faith and to work as he had seen him work', and cited Kilvert's 'incessant' teaching of the Bible as one instance of his Evangelicalism. However, he also observed that it would be wrong to call him an Evangelical because 'he failed to emphasise much that Evangelicals wished to stress and his conduct often fell short of what they would endorse'.[55] Kilvert would have been the first to agree that his own practice often did not live up to his Evangelical principles but an examination of the *Diary* shows that he was continually aware of them. He wasn't the kind to use them as sticks with which to beat others as Esther Maurice and perhaps Mrs. Hare did, but no doubt they manifested themselves in his dealings with parishioners and friends. We have already seen the strong emphasis he laid on sin and repentance in the care of his flock and in his own spiritual progress. Earlier chapters have also shown clear evidence of other Evangelical principles and habits of mind. The absence of pride noted in John Fry of Chieflands, for example, derived from Kilvert's awareness that pride could get in the way of true Christianity. Political conservatism and an acceptance of the existing class structure were Evangelical traits, as were authoritarianism, a distrust of the intellect in favour of the wise heart, and a respect for work and philanthropic endeavour. Kilvert had all of these. His rather austere righteousness, seen in his relish for whipping children and his acceptance of the idea of original sin, echoed Wilberforce's approval of strict parents who worked to overcome 'the perverse and froward dispositions' of their children.[56]

In later chapters, we will find in Kilvert's conduct other Evangelical elements such as condemnation of idleness and luxury among the rich, support of missionary work, and an opposition to field sports. (Evangelicals were committed to the reformation of manners and field sports were Kilvert's chosen area of concern). His concept of manliness was underpinned by Evangelical notions of piety and self-sacrifice. His poem 'Noblesse Oblige' is devoted to the theme of self-sacrifice for the sake of others and one section of it pictures a Christian woman, 'noble in Faith's simplicity', facing the lions in a Roman arena and calling on Christ, who died for her, to help her to meet her own fate. (Finlayson, in his book on Lord Shaftesbury, the Evangelical reformer, highlights as one of the key features of Evangelicalism the way God showed his 'unspeakable love for mankind' in sacrificing His own son).[57] Kilvert shared Wilberforce's deep respect for the English country gentleman and the honest yeoman, while the idea that all ranks of society finally achieve equality in the grave, which we will see Kilvert expressing in chapter 8, was one of Wilberforce's favourites. The most characteristic, as well as the most important, Evangelical belief that Kilvert shared was the notion of the caring heart. Wilberforce had stressed that the particular power of Christianity lay in 'softening the heart',[58] and regretted that one of the effects of wealth was that it hardened it. Kilvert dreaded that the passage of years would harden his own heart and took comfort from the power of children to keep it tender, as chapter 9 shows.

No one could be more respectful of rank and authority than he or more circumspect about what he said in public about those in superior positions, but he was prepared to give vent to those feelings in his *Diary*. Sermons were another means of achieving this as is made clear by the quotation from the *Diary* that prefaces this chapter. He had noticed that though Venables took a reasonable share of the church services, he was away a great deal often in the pursuit of private interests and pleasures, and left all the visiting of the poor and the sick to his curate. The merest implication of criticism comes through the entry for Sunday, 22 October 1871, but it is unmistakably there. 'Single-handed today. Mr Venables being away at Llysdinam'. (Venables was fully involved at this time with his Llysdinam property; large-scale extensions and refurbishments were in hand). The whole of the day's work—and it was a heavy burden—devolved upon Kilvert. 'Taught the first class at morning school. Preached... in the morning and in the afternoon... Read to the children in the afternoon school from two to three o'clock... I expected to have no voice left for the service...'.[59]

Was it coincidence that the text he chose for the morning service was Matthew 5.23-24, which urged that if, 'when you are bringing your gift to the altar, you suddenly remember that your brother has a grievance against you, leave your gift where it is before the altar. First go and make peace with your brother'. Verse 22 cautioned, 'Anyone who nurses anger against his brother must be brought to judgement'. This text must have helped Kilvert through a difficult day and enabled him to make peace in his heart with his brother clergyman.[60] His day was not over when the afternoon service was done: he visited a parishioner, returning at dusk after 'a wet windy walk'. Venables returned from Llysdinam only on 11 November—three weeks later. He was, as has been noted, easy in his mind about his frequent and long absences from the parish. The *Diary* refers to only one visit made by Venables to a parishioner and then, as Kilvert noted, it was because he himself was too ill to go.[61]

References to such visits by any gentry are very rare and stand out when they appear. Thus, we are surprised when we read that Mrs.

Venables was on her way to the Lower House, where Kilvert himself was going. He had just come from one of his regular visits to old Price, the filthy lice-ridden parishioner whom virtually no one, whether gentry or poor, deigned to visit. He had visited Price less than four weeks earlier and found him parched with thirst. Kilvert promptly went home and brought back brandy and water. The Lower House, which was the focus of Mrs. Venables' visit, was a quite different place. Not only was it not the kind of hovel that Price lived in, it was not a poor man's home at all, but that of Richard Williams, a farmer with 300 acres. Kilvert, nevertheless, was quite moved when he encountered Mrs. Venables: 'It was like meeting an angel in the way ...I was much ... cheered and encouraged'. His enthusiasm was perhaps his way of underlining the rarity of the event. However, the remainder of the *Diary* entry concerning his visit heaps extravagant praise on Mrs. Venables—or appears to do: 'Some of the noblest lives are unrecorded upon earth ...But they are recorded in a better place ... in the great and imperishable Book of the Remembrance of God'.[62] If Mrs. Venables' visit was rare, as it appears it was, why the extravagant praise, unless to him it possessed an element of irony, even mockery? He may, in his generous way, have been giving whatever credit he could where it was due. Another, or additional explanation, is that he was indirectly acknowledging his own worth—for, on the occasion when he took the brandy to Price, the old man had said with touching gratitude: 'I hope you will be remembered in heaven'.[63] In his terrible dream, Kilvert had similarly registered the contrast between his own care for parishioners while implying criticism of the Venables'. In his 'tribute' to Mrs. Venables, there is the same gap between appearance and reality that is a characteristic of that dream.

Kilvert steadily recorded Venables' absences, usually without a hint of criticism but on occasion it couldn't be suppressed. He took both services on a dark November day in 1871 and his morning text was Hebrews 2.17-18. He expressed its theme in terms of Christ as the High Priest of Humanity but it is instructive to examine the original wording of those verses and of those immediately preceding, in order to see the general context from which Kilvert's choice was made. Verse 10 states that it was appropriate that God should make Christ, who was to save men from sin, perfect through suffering. 'For a consecrating priest and those whom he consecrates are all of one stock; and that is why the Son does not shrink from calling men his brothers'. Verse 14 declares that 'the children of a family share the same flesh and blood'. The text (verses 17-18) continues: 'It is not angels, mark you, that he takes to himself but the sons of Abraham. And therefore he had to be made like these brothers of his in every way, so that he might be merciful and faithful as their high priest ...'. It is unnecessary to labour the correspondence between this text and the situation of Venables and his parish as Kilvert saw it. It is enough to say that Kilvert thought his vicar was insufficiently close to his parishioners because he was too proud and was unable, in the way Kilvert himself was, to call men his brothers. Kilvert had called Mrs. Venables an 'angel' when he found her visiting a parishioner yet that was expected to be a routine duty for a vicar's wife. The text Kilvert chose for that particular November Sunday emphasised that Christ had no interest in calling angels to him. Kilvert walked to Bettws in 'drizzling rain' for the afternoon service. The subject of his sermon then was citizenship so he had the opportunity once again of developing the theme of the need for men to accept each other as brothers. As was noted in chapter 3, the central place in Kingsley's ministry was occupied by his devoted visiting of the poor in their own homes, his 'delicate, deep respect for them' (his curate's phrase) and this was the example, glimpsed in Kingsley's novels and printed sermons, that Kilvert had before him; the contrast between it and Venables' example was all too plain.

Earlier that year the burden he was left to carry was greater and his anger correspondingly so. He had to take both services on 16 April while suffering from a large boil on his thigh, which made all movement difficult. He had a very painful journey to Bettws chapel for the afternoon service, partly because of the boil but also because he had 'a racking headache'. Again, he had selected his Biblical texts with care to relieve his feelings and to express a point of view that had specific implications for Venables. The morning sermon was from James 5.11 and concerned the need for bearing suffering with patience. However, the immediately preceding verses urge men to be patient and to refrain from judging the rich, who 'have lived on the earth in luxury and in pleasure' while the wages of the labourers who mowed their fields were kept low 'by fraud'. In the afternoon service the text was John 21.15 and there Jesus tests the faith of Simon Peter by telling him that if he loved Jesus as he claimed, he would feed His lambs and tend His sheep.[64]

Kilvert had had the boil for three days when he took the services on the 16th and presumably the Venables were aware of it, since he had accompanied Mrs. Venables the previous day on social visits. It is not clear whether Venables was away that Sunday but he was at the Vicarage the following Wednesday because Kilvert noted that he left there to stay overnight at Llysdinam to check on building work there. Was it guilt that prompted the Venables to make a great fuss of Kilvert when he hobbled to the Vicarage on the Friday? Mrs. Venables had a sofa moved to the lawn and supplied him with books and newspapers while Venables wrapped him in his own Inverness cape. (Kilvert always acknowledged the kindness and generosity in ways such as these, shown him by the Venables.) Mrs. Venables summoned the doctor, who came on Saturday and ordered poultices be put on the boil every four hours. 'He would not hear of my going to church tomorrow', Kilvert wrote, which perhaps carried the implication that *Venables* would have been happy for him to go. Kilvert knew that Venables did not intend to take both services for he added: 'I fear we shall have to shut the church up in the afternoon'. The alterations to Llysdinam were probably coming between Venables and his duties on both Sundays.

Nor was this an isolated incident for we learn that 15 months later, feeling 'wretchedly weak' with face-ache and an abscess in his mouth, he 'crawled' to church and took both services, the morning one being extended by the fact that Holy Communion featured in it, while the afternoon one involved a christening. He read the prayers 'in a thick lisping muffled voice'. He also took the Sunday School. Venables was unavailable to take either of the services, most probably because it was exactly a month before he moved his household to Llysdinam and was occupied with the necessary preparations.[65] Just how many occasions there were when Venables made similar demands on Kilvert, whether well or ill, in the years 1865 to 1872, we shall never know.[66] Even after he left Clyro, he was still being approached by Venables as, for example, in February 1873. Venables wrote from Clyro on the 11th, asking Kilvert to replace Irvine, his successor as curate (whose six months' tenure was coming to an end), from 3 to 22 March. Kilvert agreed readily because he wanted to revisit his beloved Clyro. Venables wanted to spend the time in London, yet a week after writing to Kilvert (i.e. by 19 February), he was already in London. Kilvert stayed with him in

London until the 25th, so Venables was away from his parish for possibly two weeks in February, in addition to the three weeks he intended to be away in March.

In failing to feed adequately the lambs who were his parishioners and in neglecting other basic parochial duties, Venables in Kilvert's eyes was sinning against the Holy Ghost; that was how it manifested itself in his dream. The theological implications of that sin have an importance, with regard to Venables, commensurate with that which attaches to some of the sermons Kilvert preached while he was Venables' curate. He did his best to explain the sin to one of his parishioners in April 1870. To any clergyman it had one central meaning: it was the sin for which there was no forgiveness; all others could be forgiven. 'Whoever blasphemes against the Holy Spirit never has forgiveness', because he is assumed to have 'an unclean spirit'.[67] In Psalm 51.3, it is underlined that the Holy Spirit is the chief power making for the moral purity of the 'clean heart', while in Corinthians 2.6.6 good Christians show their worth by their kindness and their genuine love.

For Kilvert, the most clear example of Venables' 'unclean heart' was his sale of Vicar's Hill to Walter Baskerville in October 1871. In the entry (13 October 1871) that records it, Kilvert's sympathies were clearly with the labourer, James Pitt, who told of the loss this would be to Venables' tenants. 'Now Mr Baskerville has bought the glebe and the Vicar's Hill he said the tenants will not be allowed to cut and sell the fern as they have been doing under Mr Venables'.[68] Baskerville wanted the fern to grow up to provide cover for pheasants. Kilvert had no sympathy whatever for the sport of shooting, as a later chapter shows. The local poor were to suffer too because they relied on fern for bedding. Pitt made it clear that he knew Venables' retirement was imminent and Kilvert shared his view that his selling of Vicar's Hill to the local squire in order to enhance his sporting opportunities constituted a betrayal of lesser folk. It seems that Venables owned the Hill as a result of the exchange made years before by his father of tithes for mountain land.[69] The Rev. J. Williams in his *History of Radnorshire* noted disapprovingly that Dr. Venables, Venables' father, was 'tempted to accept of a barren and unproductive hill in exchange for tithes'.[70]

The tithe map for 25 May 1838 shows that Vicar's Hill consisted of 86 acres and was part of the Clyro glebe lands. The glebe was of course Church property and a conveyance dated 13 June 1872 records its sale to Walter Baskerville, who paid the Church Commissioners £10,000 for it.[71] Its mixture of arable, pasture, woods, waste, a quarry and a few buildings comprised 689 acres, which meant that Baskerville had paid £14.50 per acre for it. It was predominantly pasture but nevertheless he got a bargain. (The average cost per acre of land at this time was about £50; values would be lower in Radnorshire.) It is not known how much Venables received for Vicar's Hill but the value of moorland had gone up since Dr. Venables had bought the so-called 'unproductive' hill. The *Hereford Times* for 8 October 1864 stated that a moor, let at £300 a year two seasons before, had since doubled in value and that a mere hill could currently command a rent of £200 a year. A counterpart to Venables' (and Baskerville's) action could again be found in the Bible and Kilvert would have known the passage. Acts 5.1 relates the story of Ananias and his wife, Sapphira, who, in contrast to the apostles, who inspired local people to give proceeds from the sale of their land to the poor, sold a property but brought only part of its value to the apostles for distribution to those in need. Peter rebuked Ananias and his wife for lying in their hearts to the Holy Spirit, and they dropped down dead. As was shown earlier in this chapter, Venables was in the habit of preaching that wealth was to be used for the benefit of others, but in the matter of Vicar's Hill, the benefits of the land were denied to the poor and given to a man of rank like himself. That it was possible for a large part of the Clyro benefice to be sold by the Church to Baskerville is confirmation of the extent to which it was a rich man's Church at the time.

Trollope recognised the tendency for the kind of parson who stood on equal terms with the squire to experience conflict between various aspects of his personality. In spite of his prejudices, he was, so Trollope maintained, a liberal. 'He has something of bigotry in his heart... but though he is a bigot, he is not a fanatic'. Hypocrisy might seem to be a necessary component of his character yet he always strove to be honest. He always set moral standards higher than those he followed himself. Trollope's insistence that his gentleman-parson was honest in spite of apparent hypocrisy brings us back again to Houghton. He believed that the Victorians were more guilty than people of the 20th century of pretending to be better than they were. He pointed to the fact that since they lived in an age when the highest moral standards were expected, it was that much easier to fall short of them, and to be seen to be doing so. The result in Himmelfarb's opinion was 'an identifiable spirit of Victorianism... an unique ethos', which was a combination of moral fervour and rigid propriety that co-existed with licentiousness and scandal, so that 'even the violations of propriety reinforced the sense of propriety'. One was the mirror image of the other. In such an ethos, it was common to find people paying lip-service to propriety, preaching what they did not practise.[72]

Is it, however, either accurate or fair to accuse them of outright hypocrisy? Was Trollope ducking the question when he claimed that his gentleman-parson was honest in spite of apparent hypocrisy? Trollope, after all, took a tolerant view of the foibles of his clergymen, choosing often to smile rather than to condemn. In his essay, 'Bishops, Old and New', he spoke of the 'sweet flavour of old English corruption'.[73] Houghton, however, confirmed on the basis of his analysis of the social and psychological realities of the period, that Trollope was fundamentally right, because, while accepting the charge of hypocrisy as just, the Victorians would have argued that there were extenuating circumstances and that the motives behind it needed to be taken into account. 'For one thing, hypocrisy might not be conscious or calculated (for the sake of personal gain). It might very well be unconscious or half-conscious, a conforming to the conventions out of sheer habit, or an understandable piece of self-deception. Furthermore, even when the deception was deliberate, it might be practised for disinterested reasons... And, as for evasion, one might refuse to look at certain facts from sheer terror quite as much as from selfish prudence. In short, if we are to charge the Victorians with hypocrisy, the term must not carry its usual connotations of guilt. It should be used as they themselves used it for the most part, as a synonym for insincerity. It should be written "hypocrisy"'.[74] Himmelfarb was even inclined to see 'hypocrisy' in this sense as a positive element, testifying to the power of the moral revolution, the code of propriety, achieved by the Victorians. 'It is a considerable achievement to convert men to the extent that they feel obliged to mask their passions and inclinations. Even if the inner lives of the upper-classes, or the outer lives of the lower, fell short of the ideal, it was a great accomplishment to have converted both to the ideal as such'.[75]

In order to focus more precisely on the case of landowner-parsons, as represented by Venables, it is necessary to ask whether they must not be more guilty of the charge of hypocrisy (without the inverted commas) because, by preaching one thing and practising another, they ensured that they enjoyed wealth and physical comforts bought by the labour of another class, whom they were content to keep in poverty and degradation. Could they honestly believe that poverty and degradation was due entirely to improvidence and not at all to the sheer inadequacy of the wages paid? Could they claim ignorance of the fact, commonly spelt out in parliamentary reports and debates, in the press, and in sermons by such men as Kingsley and Sidney Godolphin Osborne, that a labourer needed a minimum of 14s - 15s a week to provide properly for his family yet was compelled to manage on 8s - 9s? If they were conscious of such things, could it be claimed that they allowed that situation to exist for 'disinterested reasons'? If they were only half-conscious of them, could it be dismissed as 'an understandable piece of self-deception'? Again, Houghton's analysis indicates that even this formulation of the problem is not as simple as it first appears. He cited the example of Kingsley, who was capable of arguing in a sermon that all worldly rewards—wealth, honour, power, luxury—could be granted to men as a result of their living a Christ-like life. 'You shall find', he said, 'that godliness hath the promise of this life, as well as the life which is to come'. Houghton underlined that Kingsley was not, in that statement, advocating the Christian life for unacknowledged worldly reasons: he was being perfectly honest, he sincerely believed that what he was saying was true.[76]

This, finally, becomes the test with regard to hypocrisy: did the man who preached one thing and practised another, nevertheless believe every word he said? In the case of Venables the answer seems to be that he did. He believed sincerely that the amount of money a man possessed was immaterial and that what mattered was the use to which he put it. He believed sincerely that the education of the poor should have enhanced morality and not a better social position as its aim. He believed sincerely that the poor were equal with the rich before the law, and that Chartism was a snare that would lead to bitter hostility between classes and to disorder and misery. He believed devoutly that labourers should and did show 'sincere and voluntary attachment' to their landowner masters. He believed it to be his duty as a landowner and parson to assert these things and that to do so would promote morality. It was, nevertheless, a deception of himself

and of others. It also meant that his labourers endured misery and
want for their entire working lives, and when old age and sickness
brought their toil to an end, their reward for their 'sincere and voluntary attachment' was the workhouse. In the self-deception was an
element of naiveté amounting almost to stupidity for, as Kingsley
observed, 'I am trying... to do good; but what is the use of talking to
hungry paupers about heaven?' He was prepared also to question the
sincerity of the motives of men like Venables: 'I will never believe that
a man has a real love for the good and beautiful except that he attacks
the evil and disgusting the moment he sees it!'[77] Kilvert also was guilty
of self-deception, but though he was too accepting of many social ills
that were evil and disgusting, he had more real love of the good and
beautiful than Venables had. He also had more imagination than
Venables, lack of which compounded the latter's self-deception and
naiveté and prevented him from apprehending what the lives of the
poor were like. If it were true that one could be godly and still enjoy
material success, it should be pointed out that Venables was not all
that godly in the eyes of Kilvert.

There is one further way in which Trollope's words concerning his
gentleman-parson picture Venables' situation with almost uncanny
precision. His home, wrote Trollope, would be one of the pleasantest
in the county, 'just reaching in well-being and abundance that point
at which perfect comfort exists and magnificence has not yet begun
to display itself'.[78] For Venables' friend and neighbour, Tomkyns Dew,
the inclusion of a peach house among other additions at Llysdinam
had overstepped the line into 'magnificence'. Venables noted in a
latter to his brother George that Dew considered it extravagant.[79]
Bulwer Lytton had no doubt that if a clergyman lived in style, it
inevitably separated him from his parishioners, in spite of his having
the best intentions. The more he identified with the aristocracy, the
greater was that separation: 'Charity ceases to be sympathy and
becomes condescension'.[80]

Lytton could see that an aristocratic Church also created problems
for the poor curate of good family. The gap between him and his
parishioners in sheer financial terms might not be spectacularly great;
his difficulty stemmed not from his wealth but from his very poverty,
because, aware of his birth and station, he felt under some obligation
to stand aloof from the poor of his parish from a feeling of pride.
Having 'his very poverty to keep up', he could not easily condescend

to visit the homes of the poor. There is something of relevance to Kilvert in these observations: he did share Venables' aristocratic outlook and was very aware both of his social origins and of his poverty. His concern for his pedigree and for his family's armorial bearings show his desire to play up the one in compensation for the other.

Perhaps it was as well that he was not more Evangelical than he was. Trollope believed that his gentleman-parson would inevitably hate an over-pious young curate; provided he was not of that kind, he would 'manage' him effectively and inspire 'awe and affection' in him, which is exactly what Venables did with regard to Kilvert. However, Venables' curate was enough of an Evangelical, with a strong enough belief in the good heart, to be able to see his vicar's failings as a Christian, though neither his character nor his social status would permit him to point them out publicly. He was conscious of 'nursing anger against his brother' but strove to rise above it and to pay tribute to those things for which Venables was to be commended.[81] In his *Diary*, however, may be found the evidence for his private condemnation of the vicar who so resembled his own father and induced the same mixture of feelings.

Kilvert's Evangelicalism placed him in an intolerable dilemma. On the one hand, it compelled him to recognise Venables' sinfulness, while on the other it made him feel guilty at even daring to doubt the probity and authority of such a pillar of the community. To accept the rule of all lawful authority was a central tenet of the religion in which Kilvert had been raised, but there was another tenet of deeper and more far-reaching importance—the strict watchfulness over one's own spiritual development that was necessary in order to attain grace. In Venables, Kilvert could see a lack of strict watchfulness and a bad example set to parishioners; the situation also compelled Kilvert to search his own conscience in order to decide what his own stance should be. His religion provided guidance. Wilberforce had written of those Christians whose 'life of general activity and usefulness' was commonly mistaken for the very essence of religion and consequently greatly overrated. (It is immaterial whether Kilvert had read the actual passage from Wilberforce's *Practical View* that dealt with this type of Christian, although it is very likely that the book had an honoured place in Kilvert's home and in his education; the dangers for the true believer outlined in it would have been part of any Evangelical's religious awareness).

Because such people are full of 'obliging attentions' and courtesies, and seem kind and 'universally acceptable and popular', it is easy to be impressed by them, but there is many a 'false pretender' among them, who 'gains credit ... which he by no means deserves'. Their supposed high moral qualities are merely assumed, 'a mask which is worn in public only'. Even where their moral qualities are genuine, 'they often deserve the name rather of amiable instincts, than of moral virtues', because they are not the product of 'mental conflict' nor of 'previous discipline', and are 'apt to evaporate in barren sensibilities and transitory sympathies' instead of producing true piety and service. Because their qualities lack 'firmness' they can lead their possessors into conniving at wickedness. 'Thus, their possessors are frequently, in the eye of truth and reason, bad magistrates, bad parents, bad friends'.

These 'irreligious men of useful lives' are a danger, Wilberforce warned, because their example discourages genuine goodness in others. Furthermore, their example induces others into the error of so exaggerating their merits as to see them as some kind of compensation for their lack of the 'supreme love and fear of God'. The effects of this error are 'highly injurious to the cause of religion'. Wilberforce was aware in this passage, as in several others, that he was interpreting the duties of religion in a highly intense and strict manner but he was especially keen to emphasise that these men of 'benevolent tempers' and 'useful lives' were too apt to deceive us, 'to disarm our severer judgments'.

There is no doubt that Kilvert had recognised in Venables the particular pattern of tendencies Wilberforce had outlined in this passage from *Practical View*[82] (whether Kilvert knew the passage or not), and was disposed to apply his 'severer judgment' to it. Venables had, as has been noted, inspired in him 'awe and affection', as the nominal Christian in Wilberforce's account tended to do among those around him and that made Kilvert's position all the harder. Thus, when Venables raised with him in March 1872 the possibility that he might be offered the Clyro living, he knew that, leaving aside the difficulty of not being socially significant enough to follow his vicar, his conscience would never permit him to fill the place of one for whom he felt respect but also resentment and to whom he would be obligated for the promotion, because Venables would be certain to recommend him for it. In addition, he would still have to socialise with Venables, who would be only a few miles away at Llysdinam. The prospect was unthinkable and he did the only thing he could do: he resigned his curacy. Kilvert's feelings were so bound up with the Venables and the degree of confusion he felt as a result was so great that a year before he left Clyro he had another disturbing dream—this time of seeing his own grave among the graves of the Venables, as though he were their child.

Since Venables reminded Kilvert so much of his own father and became a second father to him to such a marked degree, challenging Venables seemed not only tantamount to murder but to that foulest of murders—patricide. And in both of Kilvert's fathers, there resided so much goodness as well as sinfulness. The outcome of so much conflict and so much guilt was Kilvert's dream/nightmare, which was especially horrible because it involved the double murder and the question still nags as to the nature and extent of the hostile feelings he harboured towards the father he had always revered. It could be argued that the dream located Venables in Harnish simply because he resembled Kilvert's father, and further that Kilvert's exclamation, (regarding Venables' murder) 'It will kill my father', records the fear he had that any news of failure of his own would lead to his father's death. It is, however, hard to accept this formulation if we pay attention, as Kilvert did, to the precise details of the dream. Firstly, the initial attempt to murder Venables actually occurs at the Kilvert home. Secondly, the home in question is not Langley Burrell, the current home of the Kilvert family, but Harnish where he was born and raised, which reinforces the identification with Kilvert senior. Thirdly, that identification is made even clearer by the fact that the murder attempt is located, not in the Rectory, but in the building that was pre-eminently Kilvert's father's domain. One could speculate on the added significance that it occurred in the organ-loft—the channel of communication between Harnish's Vicar and his God? If that is too fanciful, it is nevertheless a detail which makes more inescapable the question as to why he could appear to Kilvert guilty with Venables of the sin against the Holy Ghost.

The strong link that the dream makes with Harnish focuses attention on the past, on the home that Kilvert loved, and on shared experiences between him and his father in which Venables played no part. Did Kilvert have disturbing memories of a father who played the tyrant and the bully in the Harnish schoolroom? Had he harboured for many years a deep admiration for another Evangelical, Kingsley, especially for his devotion to his flock, only to hear him steadily denigrated by his father?

Had Robert shared with his son his deep attachment to Psalm 15? Robert was able to read at an early age and even before he started school used to read to his grandmother the Psalms chosen for the day. 'The fifteenth', he recalled, 'made a deep and lifelong impression on me', so much so that he regularly asked if he could read that one in addition to the others that had been selected. He attributed its appeal to the 'grandeur of the imagery',[83] which is decidedly odd because it contains virtually none, most other Psalms have more. Its outstanding feature is its strong sense of what it means to be one of the elect of God. It begins: 'O Lord, who shall sojourn in thy tent? Who shall dwell on thy holy hill?' Evangelicals believed that once a man had recognised his sinfulness and accepted Christ as his saviour, he was 'converted' and became one of the elect.[84] Kingsley shows his hero Alton Locke responding as a child to the austere Evangelical upbringing provided by his mother, who held to Calvinistic principles. She regarded herself as one of the elect and wished her children to become so too. Alton, however, though he admired and respected his mother, rejected this extreme view of redemption, recognising in it a basic conflict: 'What was the use of a child's hearing of "God's great love manifested in the scheme of redemption", when he heard, in the same breath' that only one in a 1,000 were to be saved and the other 999 were condemned to everlasting fire because of their original sin?[85] For Kilvert, who expressed hearty approval of *Alton Locke* when he read it, Evangelicalism always tended to produce conflicts of this kind.[86] Another conflict that it produced was of deep consequence for Kilvert. He appeared to accept the doctrine of original sin yet was convinced too of the essential innocence of children, as was Alton Locke, who suffered a savage beating from his mother because he expressed the view that if his gentle, affectionate sister was made to suffer hell then God must be the Devil. Psalm 15 indicates how conflicts of this kind can arise and shows how a balance can be kept. Good men were not simply those who led moral lives but those 'who fear the Lord'. Wickedness in others had to be acknowledged and good men were those 'in whose eyes a reprobate is despised', but even then they were not to take up a reproach against a neighbour, which brings us back to Kilvert, his father, Venables and the Holy Ghost.

Kilvert was forced to hide his resentment of the way his father left Sunday duties entirely to him exactly in the way Venables did. For one sermon's theme when he had to stand in for his father (18 April 1875), Kilvert took 'Secret Sorrow'. He chose as his text Kings 2. vi. 30, which talks of the king of Israel, disturbed at the sufferings of his starving people, wearing sackcloth under his clothes as a token of his care for them. Kilvert expressed the grief he felt at having to wear a mask (for which he criticised Venables) by quoting Mrs. Browning's poem 'The Mask': 'I have a smiling face, she said / And so you call me gay, she said / Grief taught me this smile, she said / And wrong did teach this jesting bold ... / Face joy's a costly mask to wear; / 'Tis bought with pangs long nourished'. The poem ends with the bitter statement that it was more important to grieve for those who claim a compassion they did not feel than for those who were suffering.

In Kilvert's eyes, his father had got the balance wrong. He was too conscious of his own goodness, his own piety, too content in feeling himself to be one of the elect, and had attached too little importance to the caring, generous heart. It is a notable omission that neither in the *Diary* nor in Emily Kilvert's memoirs do we find any tribute to Robert Kilvert's care of parishioners though we know he did visit them from the entry for 5 January 1874, 'Father came in from his parish rounds', but this is the only reference to *Robert's* visits during the four '*Diary* years' in which Kilvert lived at home. Perhaps Kilvert was more interested in recording his own visits and naturally would not bother with those of his father, who was anyway over 70 by 1874 and inclined to deafness and to taking things more easily. Nevertheless, parochial visiting was an important issue to Kilvert as it was to Wilberforce. According to Wilberforce's reckoning the true Christian as opposed to the nominal one possessed a 'holiness of heart' that made him 'more than commonly gentle and kind' and especially solicitous of the poor and weak.[87] Robert's own *Memoirs* had shown him to be indifferent to the sufferings of the poor and weak labourers who were finally driven in 1830 to rise up and demand bread and higher wages from their employers. In addition, even though the abolition of slavery was one of Wilberforce's prime goals and Robert's close friend and fellow Evangelical, Rev. Hume, was active in the anti-slavery campaign around Melksham, Robert's own compassion was not aroused by the cause. The evidence of Kilvert's *Diary* suggests that he had a holier heart than that of his father.

Was Kilvert forced to recognise that his father, like Venables, was too aloof from the poor and insufficiently benevolent towards them? Lack of kindness and of genuine love for others is the mark of those who sin against the Holy Ghost. It was the absence of that genuine love in Venables' treatment of Kilvert that most offended the latter, and it is underlined in the dream by Venables' 'fondling' of Kilvert the way a real father would do. Though he had great respect for authority himself, Kilvert may have found excessive the authoritarian nature and deference to rank of both men. Later in the book will be found evidence that Kilvert rebelled against attitudes and practices in society that he found abhorrent. In one of them—field sports—both Venables and his father participated: Robert Kilvert shot birds, which Kilvert thought profoundly sinful and had been identified as such in a book to be found in the nursery of the Harnish home. And finally, though it is a matter of no small consequence, Robert showed Evangelical hostility to poetry and on one occasion, as was noted in chapter 1, opposed his son's wish to publish his own, a reflection of the tension which must have existed between the passionate, artistic Kilvert and his inhibited, prosaic father. Contemporary pressure to exclude unpalatable facts from biographies and autobiographies meant that there are the merest hints of these matters in Kilvert's *Diary*. It is clear that suppression of them could give rise to intolerable tensions within individuals.

Thus, though father and son were close, as chapter 1 has shown, Kilvert had a different personality. He used his *Diary* as the outlet for his resentment of social ills and for the expression of his deepest feelings but it is significant that he chose not to share his writing with, nor even to mention it to, his father. He preserved a distance between himself and his father. The distance between the latter and his parishioners was less than that between Venables and his; Venables had much more pride. The words that Bulwer Lytton applied to the aristocratic parson who, because of his excessive pride in his rank, could never hope to meet the needs of his poorer parishioners, might well serve as Venables' epitaph: 'He is a good man, but he is too great a man'.[88] Kilvert was a better man and a better Christian but he was hamstrung by his too great veneration for the country gentleman. Venables represented for him the tradition, order, integrity, history and romance that characterised the institutions of the Church and landed property. Venables' life in most respects legitimated rank and wealth, he was the yardstick by which Kilvert measured success or failure.

When it comes to what Venables felt about Kilvert, the evidence does not suggest that he meant all that much. Details suggesting emotional closeness as the time for Kilvert's leaving Clyro drew near are notable by their absence. They might have disappeared in Plomer's editing but it seems unlikely that a scene of affectionate leave-taking would have been omitted. Perhaps Kilvert's own ambivalent attitude to the Venables led him to suppress what did take place during the days he spent at Llysdinam from 19 to 24 August 1872. Other contact between him and them was inevitably reduced when they moved there from the Vicarage on 6 August. Venables was still Vicar of Clyro at this point but he was contemplating retirement, as Kilvert knew. Venables' letter of resignation from the living was written sometime in early March 1873. Kilvert must have felt that Venables' departure from the Vicarage was a convenient moment for him to bow out of his own curacy. He did not want to be put in the position of having to reject the offer of Venables' job, nor did he want to have to adjust to a new vicar. However, the timing of his departure was also affected by the rejection of his offer of marriage to Daisy Thomas, daughter of Venables' friend and neighbour, Rev. Thomas of Llanthomas, an event which is dealt with in the next chapter. It is possible that Kilvert feared that even more of the duties of the parish would fall on him once Venables moved out of the Vicarage. When Henry Dew, Vicar of Whitney, wrote to Venables expressing his regret at his resignation, he said he recognised that the latter would wish to devote more time to his young family and therefore to be unencumbered by parochial work.[89]

The impression is left of a certain emotional distance between the two Clyro clergymen as the last weeks went by. Kilvert had received a leaving present of a 'magnificent writing desk' from the Venables the day before they moved to Llysdinam. He recorded the sorrow at his going expressed by parishioners: 'What am I that these people should so care for me?'[90] There was a presentation to him at the village school, attended by the 'gentle and simple' and presumably by Venables, who had accompanied him to Clyro that day from Llysdinam. At the morning service at Clyro the following day (Kilvert's penultimate Sunday), Irvine the new curate preached when one might have thought Venables would in order to pay tribute to his curate, but he 'sat in his pew'. Kilvert preached at Bettws in the afternoon, and burst into tears. His last Sunday in Clyro was 1 September and again Venables declined to preach at either service. Irvine took the morning one and Kilvert was left to struggle through the afternoon one and of course broke down. 'I don't know I got through the service', he wrote. Venables had failed him again. Nor was his presence in the church recorded by Kilvert, who left Clyro the next day.

At the time of Kilvert's death, Venables wrote kind things about him to his father (in a letter that unfortunately has not survived). Kilvert's father thanked him for his feelings which, he said, were 'reciprocated most fully' by his son, 'with the addition of sincerest respect and regard'.[91] Venables' tribute has to be set alongside the fact that there is not one reference to Kilvert in the whole of Venables' correspondence, apart from the two letters that concerned his application for the Clyro curacy. Venables made this terribly matter-of-fact entry in his diary when he received the news of Kilvert's death: 'Heard by telegram that Kilvert had died yesterday... He was married only a month ago in August... Kilvert became curate of Clyro at the beginning of January 1865 and he held the curacy till the summer of 1872. He had held the Vicarage of Bredwardine only about two years'.[92] When Venables learnt in 1880 of a letter (which had been mislaid at Llysdinam), offering Kilvert the Bredwardine living, its discovery elicited no fond recollection of him, even though he had died only 18 months before.[93]

'Though freedom was hampered by private reticence and social conformity, enjoyment was restricted by shibboleths, fulfilment was obstructed by convention, confidence was underscored by anxiety and doubt, and rebellion was confronted by stern orthodoxy and authority, the recognition of limits and barriers lent both edge and inner tension to much of the creative writing of the period'.

Asa Briggs, *The Age of Improvement*, p.446

CHAPTER 5
Kilvert and *A Week in a French Country House*

When Kilvert recorded that he had been reading *A Week in a French Country House*, Britain was taken up with the Franco-Prussian War. He left no doubt as to which side he was on. The war declared by France was 'the wickedest, most injust, most unreasonable war that was ever entered into to gratify the ambition of one man'.[1] Like most people in England, Kilvert sided with the Prussians and saw the war as Napoleon III's desperate bid to save himself and his dynasty. The Victorian writer, Belfort Bax remembered that the general sentiment in England was strongly pro-German and that most recognised, as the sole justification for France's aggression, the motive identified by Kilvert. The latter's understanding of the reasons for the war had received some shaping from the stance adopted by *The Times*. 'The "Times",' said Blunt, '... declared that the French Emperor had committed the greatest crime Europe had witnessed for thirty years. The Times had since persisted that the war was one of aggression on the part of France'. He thought feeling in England was evenly balanced between France and Prussia.[2] Charles Kingsley, however, was firmly on the side of the Prussians and Kilvert. Belfort Bax could recognise another significance in the war. It led to the Commune, 'the first organised Government founded in the interests of the working-class...' by men who were 'Socialists by instinct'. He was horrified, as Kilvert was, by the bloodshed but was in despair as he read of the ruthless suppression of the uprising and the 'martyrdom of all that was noblest...in the life of the time'.[3] All Kilvert himself could see in the days of the Commune in March 1871 was 'Another Revolution.....insurgent National Guards.....the beastly cowardly Paris mob', and France as the 'bottomless pit of revolution and anarchy'. The passion in these words indicates the extent to which the shadow of the first French Revolution lay across his consciousness.

The Commune still lay in the future when Kilvert was enjoying Adelaide Sartoris' novel. It had first appeared between January and June 1867 in the *Cornhill Magazine*, and was published as a book later that year. She described it as 'more than a sketch and less than a story'. Like its heroine, Ursula Hamilton, Adelaide Sartoris was a singer, who began her career somewhat uncertainly (because of extreme nervousness) in England before appearing in Germany, Prague and Paris. She also appeared in opera in several Italian cities. Born *c.*1814 into the theatrical Kemble family, she was the younger daughter of Charles Kemble and her aunt was Mrs. Siddons, the great 18th-century actress. After Adelaide's marriage to Edward Sartoris in 1843,[4] she lived for much of the time in Italy. She was doubtless writing of herself when she described Ursula as 'much more like a foreigner than an English woman in all her ways'.[5] The period between 1837 and 1842, brief though it was, in which Mrs. Sartoris was studying and singing in Europe, had a profound effect on her. Her sister described in a letter of 1841 how Adelaide, who had recently returned from abroad, had acquired 'something completely foreign in her tone and accent', and complained of the lack of sunshine and the dullness of social life. Her 'directness of talk and incisiveness' was attributed to her French blood.[6] The novel had its beginning in an English country house, Warnford Park, the Hampshire home of Mrs. Sartoris' husband and several people who regularly met there appear disguised in the book. Warnford was very grand, 'far more impressive and solemn than most French country houses'.[7] The Sartoris family, originally from Savoy, were of Sceaux Park, near Paris, but this was not the 'Marny-les-Monts' of the book. The chateau in question was that of the Marquis de L'Aigle, who had married Mrs. Sartoris' sister-in-law.

Kilvert was reading the novel at the end of September 1870. His thoughts had been filled for the previous two and a half months with news of the Franco-Prussian War. He recorded a number of conversations in which French matters were invariably touched on. Wharry, the Chippenham chemist, had recently been in Normandy and had had an unpleasant time. He complained that a failing of the French was that they demanded total loyalty and support for themselves and for whatever enterprises they undertook. Kilvert's barber had happy memories of Prince Louis Phillippe when he lived in London. John Bryant, an old parishioner, told Kilvert's father he remembered hearing the news of the beheading of the French king during the

Revolution. Kilvert attended on 31 August at the Hay schoolroom a talk on St. Helena, in which Napoleon was spoken of favourably.

Thus, his mind was attuned in the period leading up to the *Diary* entry about the Sartoris book to the 'problem' of France as a neighbour and an old enemy. What he heard was a mixture of positive and negative impressions. It was his own experience of the manners of English country life, however, that produced the vehement declaration of 31 September 1870: 'Read that clever and amusing book "A Week in a French Country House". Dear Ursula. What an elegant ease and simplicity there is about French manners and ways of domestic country life, and how favourably it contrasts with our social life, cumbrous, stiff, vulgarly extravagant, artificial and unnatural'. The entry is notable for reasons other than its vehemence. It is one of the few moments in which the Diarist comes close to advancing an intellectual point of view; he seems eager here to engage with ideas. The passage is brief and inexplicit so that we are not clear about the point he was making. It is, nevertheless, suggestive enough, especially when set alongside other *Diary* entries. Short though it is, there is a considered feel to it: the words are precisely chosen to establish the exact terms of the contrast between English and French manners. What was it in the former that he found 'artificial' and 'unnatural'? What qualities did he have in mind that he designated 'cumbrous' and 'stiff'? Why, precisely, did French manners appear to have an 'elegant ease and simplicity'? He was careful to limit or direct his criticism to 'country life'; he was not at the moment concerned with homes he had visited in London or Bristol. The homes in which he had experienced these failings must have been largely those of his Radnorshire friends.

To see what clues the *Diary* furnishes to explain his statement is one way to penetrate further into his mind on this point. Another is to examine closely the book that sparked off his observations. *A Week in a French Country House* concerns the visit of Bessie, an English music teacher, to the home at Marny-les-Monts of the Comtesse de Caradec (Mme. Olympe), to whom Bessie's mother had been governess years before. Mme. Olympe's mother was English though she herself was born in France and she and her brother are very pro-English. Bessie has Kilvert's intense joy in landscape. On her first morning at Marny she looks out on her surroundings: 'I unfastened those delicious French windows that open from top to bottom, and seem to let all heaven and earth at once into the room, threw back the outer jalousies, and feasted my eyes on the landscape'.[8] Another guest is Ursula Hamilton, the character with whom Kilvert specially identified and to whom he referred as 'Dear Ursula'. Her father had once had wealth but had squandered it, and Ursula was left destitute. Her intention to make a career on the stage scandalised her relatives and friends, but an aunt died and left her a fortune. A distant cousin, Lady Blankeney, who also becomes a member of Mme. Olympe's house party, immediately showed interest in her now she was rich. Mme. Olympe is incredulous in the face of Lady Blankeney's guardedness over who was and who was not worthy of acknowledgement in society, especially when it became clear that she could not bring herself to visit former friends since they had become poor. Ursula was especially disgusted at such behaviour. To Mme. Olympe true *gentilesse* lay in treating all people, not the rich only, with courtesy. It was a quality that Mary Mitford singled out for comment in another Frenchwoman, the 'émigré of distinction', Mlle. Thérèse, in 'Our Village'. She was 'a pleasant Frenchwoman, whose amenity and cheerfulness, her perfect, general politeness, her attention to the old, the poor the stupid and the neglected, are felt to be invaluable in society'.[9] Mme. Olympe has much in common with this lady and it is significant, in terms of the contrast between French and English manners that interested Kilvert that Mitford in the late 1820s and Sartoris in the 1860s were both endorsing these particular French qualities. Mme.Olympe's most important trait was her obliviousness to matters of rank.

Like Ursula, she had a spontaneity of feeling that amounted to a 'grand innocence'. She had refined manners but they were combined with a warmth and candour, qualities which, as will be argued later, were particularly favoured by Kilvert. It is underlined that for most people compassion was a mere 'sentiment'; for Olympe it was a passion. She was entirely free of coquetry and affectation and though beautiful had no vanity. Early in the book, Bessie is surprised to find her dusting her books in a way Bessie thought quite un-English—she dusted the books because the particular servant whose job it was did not do it well; he was more artistic than practical and devoted much time to flower arranging. A large space is created in Olympe's home for the artistic and it is often filled with artists who are also her friends. Ursula arrived with the poor but talented violinist, Dessaix, a ridiculous but entirely lovable man to whom she was devoted. The atmosphere of Olympe's home is made the more informal by the way in which artistic concerns hold pre-eminent place: the talk was often of music, of collaborative singing endeavours, of the best time and the best location at which to paint the river. Social arrangements are always easy and relaxed, emphasis always being placed on ensuring that everyone feels valued and at home and a general urbanity prevails. It is stressed that Olympe's house (unlike that of Mrs. Sartoris' husband in Hampshire) lacks architectural pretensions; it has been planned for comfort and the enjoyment of beautiful views rather than for impressiveness. It is clear that much of the 'elegant ease and simplicity' that Kilvert thought characteristic of French country manners resided in these qualities.

Bessie commented on the more relaxed and much simpler arrangements, as compared with England, that regulated the lives and duties of servants in Olympe's house. The communal existence of servants familiar to Bessie is absent. 'There was nothing like the servants' hall... The menservants remained by themselves, and the women sat entirely in their own rooms (which were) large, airy, with every comfort, and a look of prettiness and elegance... quite unknown with us'.[10] The servants came together for meals but they were informal and eaten quickly. Another factor that made life simpler and easier for servants at Marny was that children did not lead an existence separate from that of adults as they commonly did in English country houses; they ate with adults, kept largely the same hours, and generally shared their lives. It all contributed to produce an existence marked by fewer divisions and social distinctions. Among the impressions recorded by the French critic Taine during his stay in England in the 1860s, was an overwhelming sense of the rigidity of the gentry household, as compared with the typical French one. He attributed its tightness and efficiency to the English sense of duty. Servants had a measure of independence and were self-monitoring with regard to their duties and responsibilities. And just as they exercised authority over themselves and over each other in their own sphere, so the head of the household was a figure of considerable authority both to them and to his family. While this made for order and smooth running, it produced a forbidding atmosphere. Taine disliked the excessive stiffness and deference he witnessed among servants and governesses towards their employers. He referred to the 'humble and subdued respect' of English servants.[11]

Hannah Cullwick, who was a lower servant mainly in Shropshire and London all her working life, which began at the age of eight, told of how she was conditioned into that attitude: 'At the charity school I was taught to curtsy to the ladies and gentlemen, and it seemed to come natural to me to think of them entirely over the lower-class and as if it was our place to bow and be at their bidding, and I've never got out of that feeling somehow'.[12] Awareness of rank was to be found within the servant class itself, where there was a broad distinction between upper and lower servants. They dined separately and lower ones wore uniforms while the upper did not. In addition, there was a highly complex and rigidly observed set of distinctions within the broad bands. Individuals were very conscious of their position and resented any failure by their colleagues to accord them the respect they felt went with their status.[13]

Taine observed a similarly high degree of rigidity and formality even among members of families. He commented particularly on the amount of respect shown by sons to fathers. The inequality in terms of the incomes enjoyed by sons of different ages within families was for him another source of the coldness he found within households. French homes were markedly different in this respect because primogeniture was not observed and there was a feeling of real equality among brothers and sisters. By contrast, the English drew 'lines of demarcation' and both the individual family and the individual person had a highly developed sense of their own separate identity, which was respected by others. The result was a degree of reserve not easily overcome; people were less easy with each other, especially about personal feelings, and knew so much less about each other as individual personalities. As one example of this distance between members of families, he noted that parents did not share in the personal lives of their children. Taine thought that such reserve was the basis of the famed stiff upper lip of the English. He talked of a stoicism and self-restraint even in cases of bereavement, when it would be expected that an individual would control his feelings and keep them to himself. To give in to sorrow was considered unmanly and might interfere with the discharge of one's duties. In summing up his impression of English manners, Taine found two factors stood out. The first he referred to as 'energy' of character, which enabled a man to be master of himself, to be self-sufficient. The second, which he saw as a corollary of the first, was the existence of 'a hierarchy which, even in private life, upholds inequality, subordination, authority and order'. One of its consequences was that it produced 'many tyrants, louts, mutes, down-trodden and eccentric persons'.[14]

Explicit contrasts between English and French manners abound in *A Week in a French Country House*. M. Berthier, another of Olympe's guests, commented on the way English people, crossing the Channel, maintained at all costs a front of decorum and self-control even when their stomachs were churning with sea sickness. Another of Olympe's guests did express approval of some aspects of English manners. M. Berthier, in spite of his attack on English artificiality, is not, however, the mouthpiece for enlightened views. Ursula's qualities are seen at their best in the debate with him on the alleged intellectual inferiority of women to men. His was the typically male Victorian attitude: women were charming, mindless creatures whose function was to create repose for men, who did the business of the world. Ursula angrily rejected such condescension and argued, as George Eliot did, that any differences were the result of the education allowed to women, which lacked the depth and seriousness of men's education. Another male guest stated that he liked a woman to be 'tender and trembling.... looking up to a man as her natural guide and protector'.[15] He could accept Ursula's moral integrity but not her forthrightness, which appeared as 'male energy' and was, therefore, inappropriate in a woman. Because she expressed her opinions and feelings fearlessly, it implied to him the sexual forwardness that was the mark of the whore. Thus, in Ursula, Kilvert had a heroine with the intelligence, spirit and integrity to oppose the codes that sought to impose deadening restraint on natural, spontaneous feeling.

About two years later he read about another young woman in the mould of Ursula Hamilton: this was May Dimsdale in Lady Verney's novel *Fernyhurst Court*. May is intelligent and well educated. She had been tutored alongside her brother, Tom, and was a better Greek and Latin scholar than he. He can see classical plays and poems only as 'grammar' whereas she appreciates the beauty of their poetry.[16] She is also very fond of observing plants and animals. Her father, Squire Dimsdale, who is continually improving his estate, involves her in his plans. Though the youngest, she is 'counsellor' to her brothers and has 'a brave little heart and a sound little head'.[17] Like Ursula, she is frank and open and is regularly found discussing ideas in male circles. In her naturalness and warmth, she forms a contrast with her 'rather fine and cold' sisters. Just as Ursula had a counterweight in Lady Blankney, so has May in the cold, snobbish, narrow-minded

Lady Wilmot. Her son, Lionel Wilmot, wants to invite to dinner the poor curate, Johnson, because he (unlike Kilvert in Clyro) had hardly any other homes he could visit, but Lady Wilmot resents him because of his lowly position and 'liberal' sermons.[18] Johnson eventually obtains a better living and is able to marry, while May marries her brother's friend, who works for the poor in London.

Though it was the spirited, candid Ursula whom Kilvert found most appealing, it is Bessie who is technically the book's heroine and who resembles Kilvert more closely. At first taken aback by Ursula's manners and her bohemian relationship with Dassaix, the violinist, Bessie begins to like her more and more. She recognised the healthiness, reality and mutuality of their relationship. Ursula's strength and decisiveness were a support to the retiring Dessaix, while his devotion and practicality protected her, whose 'impulsiveness, combined with her extreme simplicity of character, tended to put her in the power of designing people'. It is clear that Bessie wished she had Ursula's strength and confidence to express openly what she felt, but she is compounded of 'strong prejudice and a weak mind', a phrase which has some aptness as a description of Kilvert's personality. He too was apprehensive about expressing his views publicly and avoided debate. On one occasion, a parishioner sought his guidance on a theological crux. Kilvert's reaction was 'I am ashamed to say that I knew as little as he did, and cared to know less ...'.[19] On another occasion, he found himself with other clergymen caught in a theological debate that went on until the small hours. He said he found it all pointless because it was inconclusive, and added 'I hate arguing'.[20] His *Diary* was the repository for his strong opinions and prejudices; it was more acceptable and safer that way.

Bessie endorsed Ursula's praise for Italians' 'impulsive candour', which is also Ursula's clearest characteristic. Impulsiveness was an important element in Kilvert's make-up. His impulsiveness, especially where pretty young women were concerned, is illustrated throughout the *Diary*. The most startling example is his encounter with Irish Mary, which he recounted in detail. He met her on a train and was immediately taken with her 'merry saucy' manner, her dazzling smile and lovely eyes, and her unashamed indication that she was drawn to him. Her natural vivacity captivated him totally: '...her swift rich humour, her sudden gravity and sadnesses, her brilliant laughter, a certain intensity ... and richness of life ... gave her a power over me which I could not understand or describe, but the power of a stronger over a weaker will and nature ... A wild reckless feeling came over me. Shall I leave all and follow her? No - Yes - No. At that moment the train moved on. She was left behind ... Shall we meet again? Yes - No- Yes'.[21] Kilvert found the same spontaneity in 'a genuine Cornish Celt', who was 'impulsive, warm-hearted, excitable, demonstrative, imaginative, eloquent'.[22] She and Irish Mary resembled Ursula but Kilvert could not express among his own class the part of his personality that he shared with them; they had, as he saw it, stronger wills and natures. Propriety overcame his 'wild reckless feeling': he left the physical Irish Mary on the platform. But he affirmed her emotional significance for him by ensuring that his final word to her in his *Diary* was 'Yes'.

The fairy-tale ending of Sartoris' novel had some significance for Kilvert. Bessie had been engaged for 11 years to an impoverished curate, who was quite unable to marry until he had obtained some preferment. Ursula was appalled at the waste, as she saw it, of 11 years and she proposed that a living that was in her gift on her Devonshire estate should go to Bessie's fiancé, thus enabling them to marry. A year on from his reading of *A Week in a French Country House*, Kilvert was to experience rejection, because he was a poor curate with no prospects, at the hands of the Reverend William Thomas when he asked for the hand of his daughter, Daisy Thomas. 'Long engagements are dreadful things', remarked the Rev. Thomas. 'I cannot allow you to become engaged but I won't say don't think of it'. He proposed that Kilvert went on visiting the Thomas home of Llanthomas near Clyro but stipulated that he said nothing to Daisy of his love nor in any way let his attentions to her be any more marked than those shown to her sisters. It was a cruel and impossible condition, though the acquiescent, deferential Kilvert accepted it without protest. He was a victim of the kind of inhuman, unnatural code resisted by Ursula Hamilton.

Kilvert simply did not come up to the standard required in a son-in-law by the Rev. Thomas. The business of rank had been of partic- ular importance to the latter since he was a young man. The Thomas family had always shown a strong interest in pedigrees but that of William Thomas was especially 'dedicated' in the opinion of one of his descendants, Richard Thomas.[23] At the age of 26 he had made a detailed study of the family's early history, which featured connec- tions by marriage with the Baskerville and Devereux families. Perhaps his sudden application in 1837 to that study had something to do with the intense activities of John Burke in this field. The latter's first publication, the *Peerage and Baronetage*, was in 1826 and by 1837 it had been through five editions. Three volumes of Burke's *Landed Gentry* appeared in 1833 and 1835. They were re-issued in 1836-7 and a fourth volume was added in 1837. The first three volumes were reprinted several times between 1833 and 1838. Thomas made certain of strengthening the family's lineage by purchasing in 1858 the Llanthomas estate, which had been in the possession of his 16th-century ancestor, and for which he paid £8,000 for its modest 200 acres, though by the time Kilvert was living in Clyro the estate had grown to 878 acres. It was only Thomas' wife's marriage settlement that enabled him to set himself up in the grandeur of Llanthomas. She was Anne Jones, niece of Edmund Burnam Pateshall of Allensmore Court, a Herefordshire family which claimed to be able to trace its ancestry back to pre-Norman times. Inheriting the Pateshall home may have been part of Thomas' long-range planning, according to Richard Thomas.

Daisy Thomas was only 19 years old in autumn 1871, when Kilvert's courtship of her began, though he had known her, or at least had known of her, since she was 13. Even in 1871 she was extremely child-like and unsophisticated, all modesty and tender heart. On the day he decided he had fallen in love with her, he had been particularly touched by her requesting the footman to bring bunches of grapes for him to take to a sick child, one of his parishioners. He was also pleased to learn that parishioners who knew her when she was younger valued the visits she made to them in the company of her sisters, and was always 'a kind friendly humble young lady'. The importance of such gentry charity towards the poor had been impressed on Kilvert through the pages of Grace Aguilar's *Home influence*. His own sisters accompanied him on visits to cottagers' homes and Daisy appealed to him partly because he could readily imagine her as one of them. In the *Diary* entries that deal with the first flowering of his love for her, he was accompanied by one or more of his sisters and on one occasion was delighted at the sight of his sister Dora chatting merrily with Daisy's sisters during a walk near Llanthomas, while he noted how pretty Dora looked. There was a close physical resemblance between Daisy and Dora and Emily Kilvert: they all possessed the same full, round, open face. *Diary* entries frequently show that Kilvert thought of his sisters with the tender affection that a husband would feel for a wife, as, for example, on New Year's Eve 1871, when he relished the closeness of the moment he shared with his sisters Dora and Thersie. Once, when he returned home after midnight and was let in by Dora, he commented: 'I never saw my dear sister look so pretty', and, after they had warmed themselves by the fire, 'a shower of sweet kisses and I sent the dear pretty girl to bed'.[24] From all of his sisters he received the support in his church duties that he could have expected from a wife.

The situation of Daisy Thomas after Kilvert was rebuffed is painful to contemplate. Whether her father had said anything to her on the subject it is not possible to know for certain, but a few days later, Kilvert noted a change in her manner: it was 'more quiet, guarded and reserved'. And a short time after that came a letter from the Rev. Thomas, 'kindly expressed and cordial, but bidding me give up all thoughts and hopes of Daisy'. If Kilvert had been denied access to a member of his own family, it could hardly have been more painful. It was just the kind of situation with which the period's elaborate code of manners was formulated to deal: a message of consummate heart-lessness enfolded in a tissue of cordial formalities. Feel free to visit the princess in my castle, wrote Giant Authority, but abandon any preten-sion of proving worthy of her love. The letter's content and tone strongly suggested that he had had a change of mind regarding Kilvert's hopes, was now determined to extinguish them, and had counselled Daisy against encouraging them.

One of those accidental but revealing juxtapositions of the *Diary* occurs at this point because, just at the time when the course of his own love affair was being taken out of his hands by higher authority, paternalism was demanding that Kilvert exercised his responsibility as clergyman in relation to the Venables' servant, Gibbins. Mrs. Venables had expressed her concern to him about the attention being paid to Gibbins by 'young Lewis' the Hay tailor. He had paid court to Gibbins before, but Mrs. Venables had hoped that Gibbins' interest in him had faded. Now Mrs. Venables wanted some 'reliable information' on Lewis so Kilvert was required to seek it from other authority figures—Evans, the schoolmaster and Mrs. Bevan, wife of the Vicar of Hay. To Kilvert's consternation, he learnt that Mrs. Venables subsequently read aloud to Gibbins the letter containing the information he had collected. He was sure Gibbins would hate him for what he had written but she took his interference as kindly interest. She had learnt the same lesson as Hannah Cullwick and Kilvert was gratified at her compliance: 'I must give her a copy of "Stepping Heavenward", I think it will do her good'.[25] Gibbins later expressed her gratitude for this uplifting volume. What Kilvert learnt of Lewis must have been favourable for he was able to marry Gibbins a short time later. Kilvert and Daisy were less fortunate. They came up against the additional complications which attended the business of marriage for the gentry. As Jack de Baron observed in *Is He Popenjoy?* by Trollope: 'We can't marry like the ploughboy and the milkmaid'.

Gibbins, in addition to having to accept as Hannah Cullwick had, that as a servant she was entirely under the control of her betters, experienced other facets of paternalism and the way it operated in a parish. The episode illustrates the way the reputation, and therefore the future employment prospects, of servants and of other members of the lower-classes, were largely dependent on the approval of the gentry.[26] A grapevine operated among gentry women with regard to servants and along it passed references and other information.[27] Gibbins was watched over as if she were a child and not a woman of marriageable age. That was exactly what the manuals of the period on the management of servants recommended: look on servants as children and take 'a kind interest in their affairs'.[28] Servants in country houses had their lives regulated very much as the lives of children were: 'Both were under the authority of the "parents" of the house, and their routines were separate from that of the "grown ups".'[29] This was the 'demarcation' that Taine had found so prevalent in English gentry households. In spite of it, he paid tribute to the concern and efficiency of English clergymen and landlords, as 'spiritual and temporal guides; on both sides the superior class fulfils its task'.[30] In some landlords, an upbringing that laid great emphasis on 'breeding' in both the animal husbandry and the exclusive education sense, as the main, or indeed, the only determinant of men's destinies, produced a fierce attachment to rank and to the notion of an unbridgeable gulf between masters and men. Rural society for them consisted of 'a small select aristocracy born booted and spurred to ride, and a large dim mass born saddled and bridled to be ridden'.[31] Paternalism's stress on the duties attaching to property, could often mean that the dependants ended up being treated as property, in spite of all the rhetoric about their being part of the family. Owning property gave one the right to interfere in the lives of one's servants and workers. Harrison believed that the gentry's claim to have a deep concern for their servants' lives does not bear scrutiny. 'Perhaps no group was taken more for granted', he wrote, 'less enquired into, and, on rare occasions when it was noticed, treated with condescending humour'.[32]

Servants certainly received short shrift from Kilvert on occasion. He could speak with apparent sympathy for a parishioner's daughter who was being exploited by her London employers, but when the case was closer to home and impinged on him more directly, he had no inclination to take the servant's side. He declined to look into the circumstances of his sister's under-nurse, 'one Fanny from Whitney, professing herself to be unhappy, disappeared and ran away at 7.30... without shawl or bonnet'. Kilvert's mother thought the girl had drowned herself in the river, but she was returned covered in mud by her mother to his sister's home that afternoon. 'The girl was crying and howling like a mad dog and clinging to her mother as if she were crazed'.[33] None of this distress, however, warranted any enquiry as to its cause. That the girl had no entitlement, in Kilvert's opinion, to be unhappy with her place is evident from his dismissive 'professing herself to be unhappy', and he expressed satisfaction that she was sacked.

On another occasion, the servant in question came from Kilvert's own household. Again, it concerned a runaway, Anne Pugh, and his lack of interest in the girl's feelings was total. She had been reproved for some negligence the previous day and failed to reappear after being sent on an errand. 'This morning early John Couzens was sent with the pony carriage to Grittleton to see what was become of Anne Pugh... At noon John returned driving Anne and her mother to our great indignation and the poor pony's distress. I wouldn't have brought them in the carriage. I would have made them walk the whole way. A girl runs away from her place for no reason and the next morning she has a carriage sent for her and drives back with her mother in state... I blamed John for bringing them in the carriage... He said he didn't know what to do... He hoped he should never be sent on such an errand again. The girl he declared ought to have been horsewhipped all the way back and sent to jail'.[34]

As far as Kilvert was concerned, the girl's flight from her position deserved only punishment, not an enquiry into the reason for it. She was guilty of insubordination and that was that. Her offence was the more disturbing because she had secured her place with the backing of the grapevine; she came with the recommendation of Mrs. Boldero of the family that provided Chippenham's MP in the 1830s and 1840s. For Anne Pugh and her mother to be conveyed in the carriage back to the Kilvert home had compounded the insubordination. In the first place, John Couzens' offer to drive them was a grotesque error of judgement. And secondly, by acquiescing to it they had behaved as though they were gentry. They had lost all sense of their place. As members of the lower-class, they were not entitled to be treated as human beings. As people, with legitimate thoughts and feelings, they were invisible; only their status was visible. The indignation felt by the Kilvert family (he did register 'our' indignation in his account of the episode) extended to the 'poor pony's distress', caused presumably by being overloaded with extra passengers, unless its sense of social propriety was also outraged. It is noticeable that his anger had not diminished when he came to write the episode up; he was quite unable to recollect it in tranquillity. Anne Pugh challenged his view of the social order and he felt threatened. The impression of incipient anarchy was deepened by the fact that another servant had had the gall to invite the runaway into the Kilvert carriage. On many occasions in the *Diary* Kilvert showed himself to be acutely conscious of carriages as signs of rank.

A further sickening aspect of the incident is the agony suffered by Couzens as a result of the moral dilemma in which he had been placed by his superiors. He resented being the means of securing the return of his fellow servant to face retribution. In his uncertainty about what to do when he located Anne Pugh in Grittleton, he stood in the street 'like a stunned pig', we are told. He had not the authority, or perhaps the will, to insist that she walked back from there to Langley Burrell, a distance of almost ten miles. Nor had he been given by his superior clear instructions of the course he should take when the runaway was found. Yet he, as the Kilvert gardener, clearly knew it was wrong for a lower servant to be conveyed home in the master's carriage. He had accepted the principle of hierarchy in society as servants had to and it had made him savage to one of his own class, more savage even than Kilvert. His rage drove him beyond all reason: horsewhipping and jail were just punishments for a girl whose only crime was that she was unhappy in her place. Of all the detestable aspects of paternalism that are arraigned in the affair of Anne Pugh, the one which stands out most is the poison it spread throughout society. It is that recognition which goes a long way to explain Couzens' rage towards her. He was bitter and frustrated at a system that could make him the scourge of his own class. The *Diary* established at another point his resentment of that system, his feeling that it would burst apart in consequence of its own unnaturalness and injustice. He was the man who told Kilvert that a revolution was coming in English society. The volcano that had erupted briefly at the time of the Swing riots had become quiescent since but Couzens felt that it was still alive under the gentry's feet. 'I know it's coming', he said, 'as sure as this is a prong in my hand'.[35] (Couzens' bitterness no doubt experienced some development during the years he worked for Mr. Clutterbuck, Robert Kilvert's patron.)

When Kilvert died, one of his parishioners singled out gentle kindness as the quality for which he would be best remembered: 'He was a *good* man - his *preaching* was good, his *living* was good, his *heart* was good, and he was *all* good - good to everybody'.[36] Fanny from Whitney and Anne Pugh would have had other memories. There is no reason, nevertheless, to doubt either the accuracy or the sincerity of Kilvert's parishioner: that Kilvert had all the qualities he attributed to him is patently clear from the *Diary*, which demonstrates various facets of his affectionate heart. The parishioner's tribute is of particular significance, too, because it is one of the few pieces of objective evidence we have about how Kilvert was regarded by those who knew him. It is important to remember that virtually the whole of the picture we have of him is that which he provided himself. Nevertheless, his *Diary* provides material from which it is possible, as has been shown, to determine the Venables' approach to him: they were prepared to exploit his good heart while at the same time treating him with great kindness. Mention will be made later of evidence from alternative sources which suggests that others had a view of him that was at variance with that he projected of himself. To suggest, therefore, that Fanny, Anne Pugh, and perhaps John Couzens too would not have regarded kindness and consideration as Kilvert's foremost qualities, is simply to recognise that other viewpoints could and did exist. It is also an almost inescapable conclusion from the 'evidence' supplied in Kilvert's own accounts of the episodes examined earlier. The attitudes which informed his approach towards dependants were typical of the period. To the master from an Evangelical background, the duty of property owners to rule and guide their inferiors was especially sacred.

Kilvert's background included, as we have seen, sustained exposure to the Evangelical novel, *Home Influence* by Grace Aguilar, which set out to illustrate the nature of piety. Though the education of the heart was its chief aim, it is important to recognise that the Evangelical heart was a somewhat tough organ. The head of the Evangelical household could be harsh and sometimes cruel to both children and servants. However, while it was sometimes necessary for children's transgressions to receive severe chastisement, as *Home Influence* made clear,[37] that novel also taught a lesson in relation to servants which was in sharp contrast to Kilvert's behaviour in the affair of Anne Pugh and John Couzens. The fashionable but worldly and heartless Eleanor in the book had not deigned to bring her children up in the observances of religion and her son, Edward, is bemused by the devotion exhibited in family worship in his aunt's home, especially by the consideration shown to servants, who are included in the ceremony. His mother 'had never shown feeling or kindness to her inferiors' and he had been raised to have the same attitude. On one occasion, when his servant, Robert, had failed to have a clean pair of shoes ready the moment he had wanted them, he had cursed him and thrown the shoes at his head. His pride had been hurt even more when Robert protested at the way he was treated.

His aunt, Mrs. Hamilton, rebuked Edward for his behaviour and told him that Robert had shown himself superior to Edward in their contretemps. She asked him what had prevented Robert from acting in the same manner he had. 'Do you think he has no feelings?' she asked, 'that he is incapable of such emotions as pain or anger?' And when Edward stated that the fact that he was a gentlemen and of higher rank gave him the right to behave as he had, he was asked whether he had behaved in a gentlemanly way.[38] In his handling of the Anne Pugh affair, Kilvert was, by this token, guilty of ungentlemanly behaviour. He had failed to show that degree of consideration for servants which Mrs. Hamilton inculcated in her children; indeed his attitude was indistinguishable from that of Edward, her nephew. He had behaved as though servants were without feelings. Intuitive sympathy for others was the quality that chiefly distinguished all really kind and civilised people, in the opinion of Grace Aguilar.[39]

Domestic relations were, as *Home Influence* demonstrated, intended to replicate their divine models—God the Father, Christ the husband of the Church, and all men and women the children of that union. It was, significantly, Kilvert's mother who read that book aloud to her family : '...to be religious, especially for a woman, we must do good in those simple everyday relations and duties of the family...'.[40] In the

Kilvert home, as in many others, the family included the servants, and when the crisis of Anne Pugh's defection occurred, all the accumulated weight of these moral considerations lay behind the stern authority that bore down upon her. In the Evangelical emphasis on the central importance of the individual soul, lay the seed of political conflict within a family because it recognised that, in the eyes of their Maker, servants were the equal of their masters. The Evangelical preacher, William Jay, once preached a funeral sermon for a female servant in which he noted that there were two things which caused religious servants to be generally disliked. The first was their fondness for religious gossiping, which caused them to neglect their duties. The second was 'their aptness to carry their equality as Christians into their secular stations, and to use an unbecoming familiarity, instead of a dutiful respect, to their masters and mistresses'.[41] Both faults are found in the garrulous, sanctimonious Joseph in *Wuthering Heights*, and make him obnoxious to his social superiors; Anne Pugh was guilty of the second and had to pay for it.

Kilvert's position, in the matter of his courtship of Daisy Thomas at least, bore some similarity to that of John Couzens. He, too, had been humiliated and made to respect the power of authority. He had to smart in the knowledge that he had been compelled to recognise his place, to feel that he belonged to an inferior rank. That inferiority denied to him, as it denied to Couzens, the right to feel. 'Give up all thoughts and hopes of Daisy', the Rev. Thomas' letter had said, in words 'kindly expressed and cordial'. The good manners of the letter stood in the sharpest contrast to its brutality, a fact that would have been recognised and condemned by Mme. Olympe, Ursula Hamilton and Mrs. Sartoris. Kilvert reeled under the shock of it. 'The sun seemed to have gone out of the sky', he wrote. To his credit, his reply did voice some sort of protest. He stated that, though he accepted Mr. Thomas' decision, he nevertheless reserved the right to continue to feel because no worthy love could be extinguished by 'the first breath of difficulty'.

Thomas' implacable opposition and perhaps the very fact that he erected no barrier to Kilvert's meeting with Daisy, allowed a kind of poison to seep steadily into the relations between the lovers as surely as it had seeped into Couzens' relations with the Kilverts and with his fellow servants. After Thomas' letter, the lovers met in ever deepening pain and confusion, feelings of guilt grew and some degree of resentment, until finally a numbing sense of loss ensued.

It was six weeks before Kilvert saw Daisy again, when he visited Llanthomas. In his *Diary* he commented on the cordiality with which Mrs. Thomas received him. He was invited to join the entire family on a walk to Hay. Ironically, nature seemed to encourage his hopes, for, though it was November, the Llanthomas gardens were full of roses in bloom. 'There is no last rose of summer at Llanthomas', Kilvert noted optimistically and he fancied he could see Daisy's love burning clearly in her eyes. However, she gently rebuked him for not visiting her for a long time, adding, 'I suppose you have been busy'. Kilvert replied that he would have liked to visit but must not. Later that month he saw her again and she seemed 'shy and reserved and... troubled' and appeared to avoid him. When he visited her home the next day, the scene reflected the realities of a gentry household: its head sat reading the paper while his wife attended to the Clothing Club accounts.[42] Daisy was very warm towards Kilvert and he hoped that she would attend George Venables' lecture at Hay, the following Tuesday but he looked for her there in vain. He next heard of her coming out at the Hereford Hunt Ball, a social occasion he would not have chosen to attend but which anyway was probably beyond him socially. A month and a half after he had last seen Daisy, he attended the Wye Cliff ball where there were nine members of the Thomas family—but not Daisy. He was feeling more and more excluded from her. 'Oh Daisy dear, my own dear love', he confided to his *Diary*, 'it's a long weary while since I have seen you'. That was January 1872.

When Kilvert saw Daisy again it was on 13 February and it was almost three months since their last meeting. Hearing her enthuse, on his next visit to Llanthomas, about a walk she was to go on with her father and sisters, Kilvert mused: 'Rest, happy child, guileless and unspoilt'; he had already given her up. He spoke intimately to her at the Clifford Priory ball in early April and then felt guilty that he had done so and his immediate reaction after the ball was gloomy: 'All the old feelings of last September have revived again as keenly, as vividly, as ever. The old wounds are all open... I can rest nowhere in my misery'.[43] Later that day, Mrs. Venables urged him to speak again to the Rev. Thomas about Daisy but he said he was reluctant to humiliate himself a second time, and in any case, his prospects were no better.

What faced him here was another situation for which his Evangelical upbringing provided quite explicit guidance and this time he followed it. The parallel between his predicament and that of Arthur Myrvin in Aguilar's novel *A Mother's Recompense*, which Kilvert's mother had read to him when he was about 13, is so uncannily close that he must have been reminded of it. Myrvin, a penniless curate and son of a humble clergyman, aspired to the hand of Emmeline Hamilton, who moved in aristocratic circles. He was 'a poor curate of a country parish with no resources but his own salary' and could expect no financial aid from his father.[44] He decided to do what Kilvert did when forced to recognise that he had no hope of marrying the girl he loved: 'He would withdraw from her sight ... break the spell that bound him near her ... he would resign his curacy'.[45] Emmeline recognised that the real reason for his departure was his honourable acknowledgement that further courtship was futile, and Daisy probably had the same awareness with regard to Kilvert. Myrvin was more able to reconcile himself to abandoning his suit because he felt the 'glow of approving conscience', but was not, however, able to leave without making a passionate declaration of his love. Kilvert's own highly emotional and impulsive nature should have prompted him to do the same but something held him back and again, the reason for his restraint may have originated in another lesson learnt from Aguilar's bracing pages. In *Home Influence*, the virtue of 'strict watchfulness' over one's moral self is enjoined. Self-control is everything: 'just as you have learnt the necessity of control in emotions of sorrow', her mother tells Emmeline, 'so [you must] practise control even in the pleasant inspirations of poetry and joy'.[46] The docility with which Kilvert accepted the Rev. Thomas' injunction to cease his courtship of Daisy may therefore be traced to this Evangelical training.

That training affected *how* he would go but the explanation as to *why* he chose to go had, it seems, more to do with the unease he felt in his post as curate of Clyro. He had already decided as early as November 1871 that he would leave Clyro because on the 11th of that month his friend Morrell was asking him if it were true that he was going to go and Kilvert told him that he was 'not at liberty to say', so it is clear that rumours were already beginning to circulate. However, only five days before, Kilvert was still entertaining hopes that his courtship of Daisy Thomas would succeed finally, because he was not only enthusing in his *Diary* about the strength of his affection for her, but also noting: 'I wonder if Daisy and I will ever read these pages together. I think we shall'. Even if that entry indicates only that he was struggling to keep his spirits up, the fact that he had dropped hints of his departure from Clyro six months before he had finally reconciled himself to losing her, proves that another force was driving him away. It will be recalled that on 17 March 1872, Venables suggested to Kilvert that on his retirement the Clyro living might well be offered to him but Kilvert stated flatly that he would refuse it. If Kilvert had become Vicar of Clyro, with all that that meant in terms of enhanced salary and status, probably all of the Rev. Thomas' objections to him as a son-in-law would have been removed, yet he was not prepared even to entertain the idea. Thus he must have had a reason for leaving Clyro that overrode the question of whether he won Daisy or not.

A few days after the ball came the full realisation of what it would mean to leave Clyro and the parish into which he had poured so much love and effort: 'I shall see no more the beloved scenes which have been so familiar to me for so many years. In the prospect of their loss how doubly precious...'.[47] Such was his despair at his rejection by the Rev. Thomas, that he told Mrs. Venables that he thought he would never marry if he could not marry Daisy. She was connected more closely than anyone with his experiences of the physical beauty of the region. He recalled a picnic to the top of the hill Wen Allt he had shared with her in August 1869. As though deliberately mocking him and the bitterness of his departure, the local scenery had never seemed so beautiful to him in the spring weather. The next three *Diary* entries following the one in which he declared his intention of leaving all testify to it. In one visit to a poor parishioner, he described how the mountains 'flushed red and purple, then faded into dark cold clear blue', as evening came on. When he went to bed, the sky had changed again. 'The crescent was setting in brilliant splendour up the dingle and all the stars were standing still in their courses, to watch the sight. They seemed like handmaidens waiting on their mistress as she retired to rest'. The next night, which was Saturday 13 April, he saw another sky 'too magnificent to be described. There was not a cloud in the sky. Night was still in the dark West, but all the Eastern horizon was brilliant with light and colour—crimson, orange and yellow bands gradually shading into each other and melting into the splendid blue'. On Sunday he saw Clyro village as he came down a hill: 'The brilliant golden poplar spires shone in the evening light like flames against the dark hill side of the Old Forest and the blossoming fruit trees, the torch trees of Paradise blazed with a transparent green and white lustre up the dingle in the setting sunlight. The village is in a blaze of fruit blossom. Clyro is at its loveliest. What more can be said?'

The beauty of Clyro was, of course, also the beauty of the human spirit. Just before he said his final farewell in August he wrote of the kindness that the people (he had farmers and their families particularly in mind) had shown to 'the stranger'. When he wrote that, he must have recalled the family motto he had invented about all men being strangers and pilgrims on earth. He had probably considered it unlikely that any area other than Wiltshire could offer him so much generosity of spirit, could provide a home that came so close to rivalling his own. The pain of being shut out from it equalled in intensity that which he would have felt if he had in truth been shut out from Harnish Vicarage. With the fading of the hope of marrying Daisy there faded also his hope of attaining the dream of marital bliss which he believed was his parents' dearest possession.

When the moment of leaving drew near on 12 July, Daisy gave him one of Llanthomas' roses. Revisiting Clyro in March of the following year, 1873, he visited Llanthomas and saw Daisy. A year later, he met her on Brecon station and noted 'a half sweet, half sad look, a little reproachful' in her beautiful eyes. As they parted on another occasion, tears came into her eyes and she turned her face from him. 'I saw the anguish of her soul', Kilvert observed. 'What could I do?' That July he was recording that he thought continually of 'sweet loving patient faithful Daisy'. The *Diary* mentions only one other meeting with her, in April 1876 and by then they were able to chat about old times without anguish always ready to well up and engulf them. Daisy was left to reflect on her anguish, confusion and disappointment for the next 52 years.

A similar fate was to overtake two of Daisy's sisters. Local tradition had it that the hand of Charlotte Thomas was sought by Morgan, curate of Glasbury, but he also was rejected by the Rev. Thomas because he was socially below par. Mr. Edward West, devoted Kilvert scholar, who spent part of each summer in the Thomas household between 1932 and 1949, recounts a story passed on to him by the niece of Daisy Thomas about Daisy's sister, Grace. After the suitor of Grace was dismissed by her father, her health broke down completely and she was despatched to a private asylum. Her name does not appear on any of the headstones in the nearby Llanigon churchyard. A darker and even more disturbing element in the story West heard was that the dowries of Thomas' daughters were commandeered by him and used to pay for substantial additions he made to Llanthomas. A contributor to a Kilvert Society newsletter confirmed that the occupants of the house lived in style. His son's wife was housekeeper there during the last part of Daisy Thomas' life and she told of the luxuriousness of the house, the sumptuous meals, and the many servants.[48] The outdoor clothes of Daisy and her sisters were, however, very plain and austere. There was an Evangelical strain in Daisy evidently because she founded a Temperance Society and was instrumental in closing the Swan public house owned by the Llanthomas estate. In spite of that, she was remembered by her nephew as 'great fun' to be with and was an amateur painter. She lived with her sisters at Llanthomas after her father died in 1886.

The 1870s were years of affluence and power for the entire Thomas family. The eldest son, Colonel William Thomas, who commanded the 3rd Battalion of the South Wales Borderers, succeeded to the estate on his father's death. When he died in 1909, it passed into the control of his three surviving sisters although Mrs. Sandys Thomas, widow of one of their brothers, acted as mistress of the house for some years. Daisy died in 1928. The estate was bought in 1949 by a local farmer but was bought back the following year by a member of the Thomas family. She was forced to sell up in 1956 and the house was demolished, and its influence as a property was at an end. A terrible price was paid for that influence by Daisy and her sisters: they all lived out their lives lonely and unmarried.

The quotation from Asa Briggs which prefaces this chapter draws attention to the conflicts experienced within Victorian society and together they provide a fair summary of 'Victorianism' itself. Kilvert's impassioned statement about the 'cumbrous, stiff, vulgarly extravagant, artificial and unnatural' qualities of English domestic country life, in contrast to the 'elegant ease and simplicity' of French, was simultaneously an attack on Victorianism and an indication of how much he was a Victorian. The sudden eruption of his inner conflicts in the otherwise serene surface of the *Diary* is part of its fascination, and provides one spur to its exploration. It underlines again what an enigmatic figure Kilvert was and how, in spite of all that is revealed of him in its pages, much more remains hidden below the surface.

The conflicts resulted from the fact that the Victorian age was one of transition; the Victorians themselves knew it and regularly commented on it. 'This is the basic and almost universal conception of the period', Houghton wrote, and explained that though all ages can be described as transitional, 'never before had men thought of their own time as an era of change *from* the past *to* the future'.[49] Earlier chapters have shown how it was the pressure to jettison old institutions and ways of thinking in favour of new ones as yet half formed, that caused so much hostility, conflict and bitterness. The transition that had to be endured was specially brutal because the past that had to be left behind was not the century that had just gone but the Middle Ages. Houghton identified the central strands of this medieval tradition: '...Christian orthodoxy under the rule of the church and civil government under the rule of king and nobility; the social structure of fixed classes, each with its recognised rights and duties; and the economic organisation of village agriculture and town guilds'.[50] It was these institutions which claimed the allegiance of Kilvert and his father and provided their sense of social stability. Had Kilvert lived, as he very easily might have done, till 1914, he would have experienced the transition from the old to the new world in its completeness; as it was, he died when it was almost three quarters over and was spared more pain. Nevertheless, he left behind in his *Diary*, one of the greatest and most moving testimonies to what the experience of change meant to a mid-Victorian.

Kilvert did eventually marry but it was almost eight years after he had been told to give up all hopes of Daisy. In those years there were, of course, other lovers; he did not spend them pining for Daisy, though evidence suggests he never got over the pain of his disappointment. In the years following his departure from Clyro, he had two love affairs, both of which came to nothing and increased his bitterness. In his typically impetuous way, he 'fell in love at first sight' with Kathleen Heanley on 11 August 1874, when he met her at the wedding of his cousin, Adelaide Cholmeley. Katharine had the qualities that he liked to find in most of the women whom he considered as potential lovers and wives: she was 'simple, kind, unaffected and self-unconscious'.[51] Their relationship flourished during the remainder of that year, largely encouraged by Adelaide, or Addie, as Kilvert called her. Katharine Heanley was the daughter of a prosperous farmer, whose home was at Croft in Lincolnshire, and letters from her to Kilvert had to reach him via Addie after December 1874 when she was forbidden by her parents to write to him.

After that their romance petered out and by September 1875, he had begun another with Ettie Meredith Brown. He was much taken with her sensuous appearance: 'Ettie Meredith Brown is one of the most striking looking and handsomest girls whom I have seen for a long time. She was admirably dressed in light grey with a close-fitting crimson body which set off her exquisite figure and suited to perfection her black hair and her dark Spanish brunette complexion with its rich glow of health which gave her cheeks the dusky bloom and flush of a ripe pomegranate'.[52] There is every indication that their relationship was passionate and intimate, as it induced in Kilvert feelings of guilt for the way he had led her on: 'I have been, alas, very very wrong ... I will not make my darling sorrowful or cause her to shed one unnecessary tear, or tempt her to do wrong'. (This decision replicates that made by Myrvin and Emmeline in *A Mother's Recompense*. Emmeline's sense of duty led her to encourage Myrvin to leave the district, thereby ceasing to be a temptation to her. The lovers part, conscious they are submitting to a trial of their moral integrity imposed by God.) Kilvert received a letter of farewell from Ettie and another rejection, this time in the form of 'a kind friendly little note from young Mrs. Meredith Brown' (Ettie's sister-in-law) saying that he and Ettie were to have no further communication.[53] This was in April 1876.

Ettie had been conveniently located close to Langley Burrell and it was easy for Kilvert's affair with her to flourish, whereas he was compelled to maintain contact with Katharine Heanley by letter and managed meetings with her mainly when she visited Addie's home in Bristol. Their romance revived in the summer of 1876, however, and they became engaged sometime during the next 12 months. Little is known of their relationship because Kilvert's widow removed a number of references to her from the *Diary*. There is a gap in it from June 1876 to December 1877, covering Kilvert's entire period in the living of St. Harmon. It is possible that Kathleen visited him when he was Vicar there. It was a very remote, sparsely populated parish on the very fringe of Radnorshire, north of Rhayader. Kilvert actually lived in Rhayader and not in the vicarage of St. Harmon. Perhaps Kathleen disliked its isolation and its lack of social opportunities and that was one reason for breaking off their engagement, or perhaps she became aware of the relationship he had had with Ettie. Kilvert was deeply disappointed at the breaking off of the engagement. The degree of hurt he experienced was probably greater than was the case with Daisy and Ettie because in this instance his hopes of marriage were dashed by the woman herself whom he had sought as his partner. St. Harmon would not have been a place which he would have chosen to set up a home with a new wife and his references to it after he had left are uneasy and tinged with guilt. He had stayed there little more than a year and ten months later no one had followed in his place. In early 1878 he was writing to several of his former parishioners there and received from one a letter which said, 'We have lost our shepherd ...'. He made a point of revisiting the parish three times in 1878.[54] His departure to take up the Bredwardine living in November 1877 may have been an attempt to free himself from the sad associations St. Harmon held, and Venables may have had a hand in facilitating that move because he was one of the trustees who controlled the right to the living. He had presumably recommended Kilvert for the post because the body of trustees sent a letter to Venables on 18 October 1877 to ask him to inform Kilvert that they would agree to nominate him.[55] All of Kilvert's failed love affairs left him a sadder and more embittered man as the dream of a happy home with a loving wife and children retreated before him.

The price that Kilvert paid when he was rejected by the Rev. Thomas was a particularly heavy one. He was denied the comforts of a wife and his own home until 1879 and within a month of his marriage in that year, he was dead. The children he had so much wanted and of whom he might have had the joy, for some years at least, were unborn. In 1842 Charles Kingsley, one of Kilvert's heroes, was blocked in his courtship of Frances Grenfell in identical circumstances: she was of the wealthy and powerful Grenfell family, which, three generations later, was to produce the World War I poet, Julian Grenfell. Kingsley, too, was an impecunious curate and was disliked for that reason and for his radical Christian views by her well-connected relatives. However, her determination to marry no one but Kingsley eventually broke down family resistance, and her brother-in-law, Sidney Godolphin Osborne, was able through his influence to secure Kingsley a rich living of sufficient status to satisfy her family. It was the same fairy-tale solution that had solved Bessie's problem in *A Week in a French Country House*. Kilvert unfortunately never benefited from such patronage.

'As I went down the garden path today I saw some forget-me-nots in the children's little gardens. The children's eyes seemed to look at me through the blue beautiful flowers, and I almost heard their voices saying "Forget me not". It almost overcame me. "No, dear children, I will never forget you"'.

Kilvert's Diary 6 June 1878

'The most common reaction of clergymen to rural poverty and ignorance was to establish a school'.

G.E. Mingay, Rural Life In Victorian England, p.158

'To deal out education to the poor only on the terms of religious conformity is, in my opinion, a species of persecution...'

Sir Thomas Bernard. Report of the Society for Bettering the Condition of the Poor with particular reference to education,1809

'...any attempt to keep children of the labouring class under intellectual culture after the very earliest age at which they could earn their living, would be as arbitrary and improper as it would be to keep the boys at Eton and Harrow at spade labour'.

Adderley, vice-president of the Committee of Council for Education

'The School Board was the assertion of independence against the dominance of squire and clergyman'.

M. Sturt, The Education of the People, p.313

CHAPTER 6
Kilvert and the Village School

It was generally assumed throughout the 19th century that clergymen would be involved in education. They regarded the poor as their special responsibility and often made great sacrifices of time, energy, and money in the establishment and maintenance of schools. By the time Kilvert arrived in Clyro, they had already set up 19,500 schools in which 1.5m children were educated.[1] A mixture of motives lay behind their efforts. They believed that children, by knowing their Bible and basic Church doctrine would lead happier and more moral lives. Society, too, would benefit from having a deferential populace that accepted its lot of poverty and labour because the existing social order could more easily be maintained for the benefit of the ruling class. This attitude was especially strong in the countryside, where the Church was dominated by the landowning class. Early in the century, Bulwer Lytton had paid tribute to clergymen's work in popular education: 'No men have been more honestly zealous in their endeavours to educate the poor'.[2] However, he also underlined that they had been unwilling to educate working men as opposed to children and to encourage secular learning because they were intent on control of the poor. Kilvert accepted his place in this tradition naturally and easily. He not only loved children and could communicate effortlessly with them, but their beauty and innocence were for him closely bound up with his deepest Christian beliefs. He also believed in the village school as a source of beneficent influence in the community. In all the places where he served as a clergyman, he was to be found actively involved in the local school. His *Diary* indicates that when he was Vicar of Bredwardine, for example, he would sometimes be in the school every day of the week.[3] He had also been a schoolmaster for a year, teaching the sons of gentlemen, at a prep school at St. Leonards-on-Sea, most probably before going up to Wadham in 1859.[4]

When Kilvert became curate in Clyro in 1865, the notion still held firm that the education of the lower-classes was matter of basic literacy and the truths of religion. That situation represented some advance on that which had pertained at the start of the century, when there was no suggestion that universal literacy was either possible or desirable. 'A traditional culture, a craftsman's skill, a dogmatic religion provided all that was necessary for the greater part of the nation'.[5] Nor was education considered necessary for individual advancement, a view supported by the economic facts. In a still mainly unmechanised society, a large body of people were needed for the heavy work so that life functioned smoothly. To encourage such people to move out of their class, to have ideas above their station, was inconceivable. The education given to the poor was, therefore, designed to preserve the *status quo*, to ensure that they accepted their position and performed dutifully in it.

This requirement was reinforced by the way in which the poor appeared to their superiors as a separate species, whose harsh working conditions, bad housing, and bad health produced stunted minds and sensibilities as well as bodies. The Rev. Skinner, who worked in a parish near Bath in the first third of the 19th century, was convinced that this was part of the divine plan. Visiting the home of a tenant family, the mother of which had just died, he observed that her children's grief would initially be great but would soon wear off because of the happy circumstance that 'people in the lower ranks of life are not possessed of the same sensibility as their superiors...'.[6] Their limited share of life's pleasures was balanced by their limited capacity to feel sorrow. He had his doubts, therefore, of the value of teaching them anything beyond reading, and the Bible provided all the material that was necessary. Skinner shared the fear of many that literacy opened the way for subversive literature.

Subordination was instilled into the labouring poor in a variety of ways, most of which deepened the sense of them as a separate species. Their dependence on charity in times of unemployment and in old age was a mark of shame. They were made to sit at the back of the church behind their betters. Frederick Meyrick recalled approvingly that in his father's Wiltshire church in the first 40 years of the century there were two galleries set aside for male and female labourers.[7] The Church had been criticised for the way in which 'some memento of [labourers'] inferiority' was thrust upon them and the pew system was cited as one of the main reasons for their dislike of church services.

A further cause of the poor's alienation from church was their feeling that clergy and 'professional Christians' were indifferent to their poverty and ignorance.[8]

The quiescence of the poor in the face of these humiliations was the result of several factors. Since for centuries there had been no possibility of social mobility, it was virtually impossible to imagine oneself experiencing the life enjoyed by one's superiors, a situation reinforced by the limited horizons of the local community in which most lived and died. The poor were also resigned to their poverty, as they were encouraged to be. The deep social divisions were sanctioned by a variety of agencies including schools and, particularly, the Church. Each parish priest had the duty of teaching his parishioners' children the Catechism. This is what it consisted of:

> My duty towards my neighbour is to love him as myself, and to do to all men as I would they should do unto me; to love, honour and succour my father and mother; to submit myself to all my governors, teachers, spiritual pastors and masters; to order myself lowly and reverently to all my betters; to hurt nobody by word nor deed: to be true and just in all my dealings; to bear no malice nor hatred in my heart: to keep my hands from picking and stealing, and my tongue from evil-speaking, lying and slandering: to keep my body in temperance, soberness and chastity: not to covet nor desire other men's goods: but to learn and labour truly to get my own living, and to do my duty in that state of life unto which it shall please God to call me.

Children had to learn the Catechism by heart partly because they were largely unable to read but importantly because it had to be repeated at Confirmation to the Bishop. The injunction of obedience in it derived its force from the commandment 'Honour thy Father and they Mother'; children were expected to recognise that failure to show obedience to anyone in authority was akin to disobeying parents. The doctrine was reinforced by the notion that disobedient children were destined to die young. On obedience and the showing of proper respect depended opportunities for employment. Thus, the pattern of authority in the rural community had a familial basis to it. To challenge an authority that was so overlaid with spiritual and economic sanctions required a very brave or a very desperate individual.[9] Kilvert was reinforcing this message in January 1878: 'Gave the upper standards at the school questions on paper on the

Catechism'. The next sentence of this *Diary* entry indicates the quite different message that was conveyed to gentlemen (or to those who aspired to be): 'Promised Mr. Bates the schoolmaster to read the first book of the "Iliad" with his son Henry to help him in his Greek. He is at the Cathedral School, Hereford'.[10]

Kilvert accepted, as did most Victorians, that different kinds of education were required for different classes. The Clyro National School illustrated clearly the tradition of elementary learning that had grown up for the poor since the latter part of the 18th century when Charity Schools and Sunday Schools were conditioning them to accept their position in society. A short time after his new mansion was completed in 1843, the squire of Clyro, Thomas Baskerville, had established in a cottage on his estate his own school, which typified his paternalistic outlook. An HMI reported on it in 1846. He recorded that Mrs. Baskerville supervised an 'entirely private', small day school for girls, who were taught sewing and household duties, and were supplied with some of their clothes. Its educational standards were poor. 'Seven or eight only read well in the Scriptures... but they were deficient in spelling, and knew next to nothing of arithmetic... They wrote indifferently'. They had been well grounded, however, in the Church Catechism, but they were unable to explain 'the moral duties enforced by the Parables'. The inspector summed up witheringly: 'I am informed that the family at Clyro Court are desirous only of giving the children a plain education, suited to their station; if so, their school fails in accomplishing their object'. It is not hard to imagine Baskerville's fury at this report from an interfering government official.

The other school in the parish was that run by the Rev. Venables for 36 children, who were also taught religion, though not very well in the inspector's view, and their station in life. His school was run at a loss, which he made up out of his own pocket. Though Baskerville's school operated without any superintendence from Venables, it was the kind of voluntary initiative which the Church encouraged. In the battle for control of the education of the poor, which was at its height in the 1840s, between the Church's National Society and the non-conformist British and Foreign School Society, the two main problems were shortages of schools and of teachers. The Church was keen to establish its own schools, in which its teaching was paramount. The non-conformists were content to retain only a grounding of

Christianity, to avoid sectarian teaching, and to promote secular education. Venables had explained in a sermon that the work of education could be shared by high and low; the role of the high was to provide the necessary schools, while the actual task of teaching was undertaken by others who, by implication, were the low. The responsibility that masters and employers had for giving time and opportunity for education to the young under their control was a sacred trust, Venables said. The 'sound and religious' education that he was recommending for the poor in this sermon of 1847 was to be accompanied by a stress upon 'the duties attendant on [their] position'.[11]

From the 1840s, a steady element in the growing state involvement with education was a concern for and a fear of the poor. 'The condition of the people' became an issue, especially since hunger, unemployment, and the Chartist movement made revolution seem a real possibility. One government response in 1846 was an effort to improve the supply and quality of teachers.[12] The state and the Church were collaborating in a system designed explicitly for the poor; it had a separate ideology and was quite distinct from other school systems.[13] The shortage of schools continued to be a problem, however, and two types of district—the very poor rural parish and the equally poor, crowded district of the industrial town—always missed out on schools because both lacked sources of private charity.

Radnorshire was an example of the former. There were almost no great landowners, or great employers, or substantial citizens of any sort. The HMI who visited the schools of Baskerville and Venables was critical of the way voluntary effort was dissipated. In most parts of Radnorshire, the problem was not competing charitable efforts but the entire lack of them. A few examples from locations Kilvert knew will illustrate the position 20 years before he came to the county. (They are taken from the Report of the 1847 Commission on education in Wales.) Mr. Phillips, landowner of Abbey Cwmhir, had provided for an 'active school' in a 'species of hay loft', reported the HMI who had visited Clyro, and in the loft were 39 children reading their lessons simultaneously. The master claimed he was able to listen to and correct them, but the Inspector thought otherwise and was generally critical of the young man in charge. The Phillips ladies helped out at the school when they were in residence. At the equally remote Aberedw, no school at all existed to serve its two parishes, though one had functioned earlier behind a partition at one end of the church. If Kilvert had taken up the post he once considered at Bettws Disserth, he would have found no permanent school. The Inspector found a school had existed there the previous winter, run by a farmer; the Sunday School had closed for lack of teachers. At Boughrood, there was 'an inferior day school, kept by an elderly person in a cottage'. At Bryngwyn, considered by the Inspector 'a fair specimen' of the moral condition of the Radnorshire hill districts, a 'private adventure' school was held in a cottage by the roadside with no furniture apart from two tables and some benches, a floor that was 'half-earthen', with holes in the door and windows. The children were deeply ignorant of the simplest things.[14]

The father of Kilvert's vicar, Archdeacon Venables of Carmarthen, and other clergy and gentry submitted to the Commission evidence which endorsed the Inspector's findings. 'There is a most lamentable want of proper schools for the working-classes', the Archdeacon wrote. 'Nothing can be expected from the private subscriptions, and the poor people are certainly not able to support schools... There is a desire for better education among the people'. He expressed the anti-Welsh prejudices, especially on the morality of the locals, that characterised many of the reports from clergy and gentry.[15] 'The bulk of the poorer classes are excessively cunning', observed the Archdeacon, 'and their morals are at a very low ebb'. His son referred to their 'great ignorance, both intellectual and moral', and pointed to the widespread 'unchastity' among women, the prevalence of poultry stealing, sheep stealing and drunkenness. Part of the problem, he thought, was the remoteness of their cottages because the people were 'little under the eye of their superiors'. And in cottages which he knew to be primitive, he criticised the lack of neatness and cleanliness. Improved education would counteract the people's immorality, though they valued only the 3 Rs and had 'no idea of the essential part of education - religious and moral training'. Edward Thomas JP (of the Welfield branch of the Thomas family who lived at Llanthomas) also thought education would improve the people's morals, and that they needed much exposure to the English language to break down their 'hostility to the settlement of English [people] amongst them'. His view was echoed by other clergymen, one of whom recommended: 'Teach English, and bigotry will be banished'.

The Rev. Bevan thought the Radnorshire parishes 'disgracefully neglected', a situation he attributed to the clergy. In his own area of

Hay and its four neighbouring parishes, he believed there were enough gentry to provide schools, but the gentry 'do not have such liberal ideas on education as the gentry in England'. His own school was highly praised by the HMI: '...among the best I have seen in Wales... of those belonging to the National Society'. Pupils were well taught in the Catechism and were generally less ignorant than most Welsh children. Part of the reason was Bevan's support and part the well-trained schoolmaster, who was also paid (by Bevan) 'a very liberal salary of £80 - perfectly unexampled' in the area. (Archdeacon Venables thought £40 - £50 more than enough).[16]

The reaction of Welsh bishops to the 1847 Report further under-lined the problems. Bishop Copleston of Llandaff was more than a touch complacent in asserting that 'a prodigious improvement' had taken place in his diocese.[17] He himself did contribute generously to the education of the poor and had, the year before, expressed disgust at the parsimony of landowners.[18] He believed that parsimony and neglect were even greater in the diocese of St. David's. Bishop Thirlwall of that diocese thought that if the extent of the immorality and ignorance of the poor had been exaggerated by the Commissioners, it was because they wished to draw attention to the need for a better education system. If the system was poor, it was the fault, not of the people, but of the ruling class. It was noticeable, he said, that the most vehement attacks on the Commissioners had come from that class, which suggested that they were prompted by guilt and a desire to draw attention away from deficiencies in the system.[19]

There was much in what Thirlwall said because, as the reports have shown, there was mutual recrimination among the ruling class, with landowners blaming clergy, clergy blaming landowners, clergy blaming other clergy, and Bishops blaming landowners. The better system of education proposed by Thirlwall was to be permeated totally by religious principles. That what he was advocating was in essence social control was evident from the qualities he singled out as characteristic of 'the well-managed school': 'the habits of reverence, or order, of decency, of self-control'. A decade of Chartist agitation for political rights, the campaign to abolish the Corn Laws, and wide-spread revolution in Europe in 1848 made those habits particularly desirable. His prime concern was to resist the call that some were making to institute a completely secular education system as a means of removing the obstacle of sectarian differences. He deplored those differences because they deprived thousands of children of their education. Nevertheless, secular education should never be divorced from religious. Thus, no matter how much the education of the poor was disrupted or denied because of sectarian conflict, he as a Bishop was not prepared to give an inch on the issue of religious instruction. Education for the poor had to remain religious in character, which meant that the Church had to control it, which meant the retention of the voluntary principle.

The voluntary initiatives of Baskerville and Venables continued to compete with each other during the next decade. However, the latter was informing his brother, George, in late 1857 that Baskerville intended to build a school in Clyro at his own expense, but not that year. The parish was already indebted to its squire for the re-building of Clyro Church in 1852, towards which he had contributed £200, more than one third of all the subscriptions.[20] The new Clyro School in which Kilvert was to spend much of his time as curate, was opened on 17 April 1861 and was marked by an entertainment given by Mrs. Baskerville to all the school age children of the parish. 'Nearly 150 tickets were issued, and shortly after 3 o'clock, the boys and girls arrived in a long procession carrying flags... The proceedings were commenced with a short prayer and the singing of a psalm, followed by a short address from the esteemed vicar of the parish'. The children were then regaled with tea and plum cake, after which they paraded with their flags and then moved to Clyro Court where the rest of the afternoon was spent 'with much merriment in races and other games on the lawn'.[21] As an event it epitomised paternalism and voluntaryism in action and thus indicated that the values which Thomas Baskerville had become an MP to defend 20 years before still flourished.

However, though there was a new school to welcome teacher and pupils in 1861, the Revised Code, which followed the report of the Newcastle Commission[22] of that year, was destined to sour the atmosphere of elementary education. The Code, introduced in 1862, was the brain-child of Robert Lowe of the Education Department and it made school grants conditional on pupils' proficiency in tests conducted by HMIs. Each child over six earned 4s for a stipulated minimum number of attendances throughout the year, and 8s as a result of successful examination. Of the latter, 2s 8d was forfeited for failure to satisfy the inspector in reading, and the same amount for failure in the other 2 Rs. Efficient teaching of the 3 Rs was seen as a matter of supply and demand: teachers would make a better job of it if the grants payable to their schools and the salaries payable to themselves depended on it. The Code caused great controversy and resentment and its side-effects were damaging to the Clyro School Kilvert knew, as they were to all the nation's elementary schools as shall be indicated below.

Kilvert took a keen interest in the inspections demanded by the Code, putting in considerable extra efforts before them in order to maximise children's success and therefore the grant the school received. He recorded that before the inspection in July 1871 'we are working double tides to push the children on and I am going to the school three times every day'.[23] When the inspection came, whether as the result of the extra work or the accident of having 'a pleasant kindly fair examiner', the result was a relief for one and all. 'We presented 35 for examination out of an average attendance of 51, while Hay school... presented only 42 out of an average attendance of 105'.[24] The entry shows the extent to which the Revised Code had produced an obsession with attendance as well as with pupils' ability on the day to produce answers that would guarantee success in the all-important tests. At an inspection the year before, Kilvert was less satisfied about the inspector's approach to the tests. The older pupils had been examined on their special subject of geography, and the inspector was not happy about the standard reached and said that the grant would be withheld for that part of the examination. Kilvert, however, thought that the inspector's questions were unfair, 'more catch and cram than practical questions'.[25] Nevertheless, the overall results were regarded as good, Evans, the schoolmaster, considering them better than in any previous examination since he had been in charge. It may have been the strain of this system that had turned Mr. Fancroft, master at St. Harmon's School in Radnorshire, into a 'soured, disappointed' man, complaining to Kilvert of the 'managers, the people, the school, the schoolhouse, everything'.[26] Under the Code, teachers' salaries were no longer paid directly to them but to school managers, who had the power of deciding what sums they received. Fancroft told Kilvert that he was seeking another appointment in Northamptonshire, where presumably he hoped to get a better deal. Not being a headmaster or full-time teacher, Kilvert would have understood only some of the stresses that men like Fancroft had to endure at this time and could find scant sympathy for him.

The Code had reduced teachers' freedom as professionals in a variety of ways. One HMI stated that it had made their work 'in some degree lifeless, inelastic, and mechanical'.[27] Because the pupil tests loomed so large, teachers taught as little as possible to ensure that what was taught (the minimum needed for the tests) was well known. Inspectors, too, could concentrate only on the tests and not on getting an impression of whole classes and schools' general ethos. Pupils' knowledge was reduced to nominal, testable snippets of information and the emphasis was on rote learning: '...you did almost nothing except reading, writing, arithmetic... Reading was worst; sums you did at least write on your slate, whereas you might wait the whole half-hour of a reading lesson while boys and girls who could not read stuck on every word'. At exam time, 'the master's anxiety was deep, for his earnings depended on the children's work. One year the atmosphere of anxiety so affected the lower standards that... the boys howled and the girls whimpered'.[28] Hatred of education, rather than a desire for it, was the result of such a system. Under it, 'proficiency is sought ...by cramming the pupils to bursting point with definitions, dates, and figures, all of which ...are wholly uninteresting and practically useless...'.[29] The pressures of the Code drove many teachers out of the profession and Miss Coleburn, mistress at Clyro School from February 1864 until the summer of 1866, may have been one of them. No explanation for her going is provided by the School log book.[30]

The Code had been introduced partly to offset weaknesses in the teaching of the 3 Rs caused by poor attendance, though the obsession with attendance was the result not simply of the desire for pupils' consistent schooling, but of the National Society's perennial need, under the voluntary system, for pupils' fees. A significant part of the Society's income from the time of the first grants to schools in the 1830s came from fees paid by 'poor' parents. It was, therefore, inappropriate to regard elementary education as a charitable gift and schools began to emphasise their efficiency as a result of the competition between the two School Societies. One effect of the Revised Code was to increase secular education because of the stress on the 3 Rs and the reduced importance of religious instruction. The Church, however, continued to demand both a religion-based education and a subordinate position for the poor. As time went on the Church could ignore less easily the right of the working-class to have a voice in what their children were taught.[31]

Sheer lack of schools continued to deprive Radnorshire children of schooling in the more remote parishes. Thirlwall reported in his Charge of 1866 that 120 of the county's parishes still lacked any school for the poor, and he was forced to conclude that this lack could never be remedied while a voluntary system of provision existed; more public aid was needed. The 1870 Education Act brought an end to this shortage and a publicly funded state system of education a significant step nearer. It also brought nearer the end of the closed parochial world of Baskerville and Venables and Kilvert. The Act was the inevitable result of the 1867 Reform Bill because, as Robert Lowe had told the Commons that year: 'You have placed the government in the hands of the masses, and you must therefore give them education'.[32] In Kilvert's *Diary*, the very first reference to elementary education is concerned with the new Act: 'Evans the schoolmaster very concerned about the Education Bill'. Kilvert did not mention any anxiety of his own but it will be evident from the foregoing account, that as a clergyman he would have been troubled by the increase of government control and of secularisation. Of course, Evans had the task of implementing any changes that came about in the school. Josiah Evans had taken over the school in autumn 1866, at the age of 30, replacing Miss Coleburn. An inspector's report following her appointment noted that she had found the school 'in a poor state', which probably referred both to pupils' standards and their attendance.

Poor attendance was criticised in an HMI report of November 1865 and Venables had stated that the school was 'very badly attended' in the summer just before Evans arrived.[33] The need for local children to add the few pence of their earnings to the family budget was largely responsible for their erratic school attendance, as is evident from the Clyro School log book. A series of entries for 1866/7 tells of boys being absent to help with cider-making, planting potatoes, and other jobs. On the Radnorshire hill farms, which employed few labourers, the labour of children was a necessity. Many began work at the age of eight. Their parents, whose money was 'hardly earned', were unwilling to spend much of it on schooling, and though they thought that 'every child should know how to read and write, they do not think it necessary he should know much more'.[34] It was a great temptation, therefore, to keep children at home. Pupils of Clyro School were also very frequently absent because they were employed as beaters for shooting parties on the Baskerville estate.

The 1870 Education Act set out to increase the amount of pupil attendance, not by making it compulsory, but by providing more schools. It laid down that where there were enough schools deemed to be efficient, they would be allowed to continue; where gaps in provision existed, the voluntary bodies had 12 months to remedy deficiencies; if schools could not be provided where they were needed, School Boards were to be set up and they would levy rates to build them. In schools supported by rates, no religious teaching was to be given that was characteristic of any denomination, and a conscience clause enabled parents to withdraw their children from religious instruction. The ever-perceptive, political intelligence of Thirlwall had recognised what the effects of Lowe's Revised Code would be: it encouraged, said the Bishop, the cause of those who wanted to see the voluntary, Church-dominated system replaced by a national, secular, state one.[35]

To the clergymen around Clyro, the 1870 Act constituted another onslaught on their control and their status, and their reaction was similar to that of the Wiltshire landowners at the time of the Swing riots who offered to raise labourers' wages only when their property was threatened—they banded together to provide schools for the poor so that no School Board would be established in their district. They were led by Rev. Henry De Winton and were dedicated to the denunciation of the Act and the raising of money for more voluntary schools. Kilvert recorded a meeting at which their strategy was agreed: 'Yesterday Sir Gilbert [Lewis] and Mr Venables went to an Education meeting in Brecon'.[36] The previous day Kilvert had dined with Sir Gilbert at Clyro Vicarage and had enjoyed his stories of the visit of Louis Napoleon to England. It must be assumed that over dinner the purpose of the education meeting had been mentioned but Kilvert does not refer to it. This is consistent with the lack of any developed political or theological point of view in the *Diary*, though it is evident he took some interest in such issues and details of the meeting may have been omitted by Plomer. He recorded, for example, the fear that the Bishop of Bath and Wells had of the disestablishment of the Church.[37] He also noted in April 1870 that Rev. Henry De Winton was deeply opposed to the threat that faced clergymen that year: 'Henry De Winton of Boughrood... made some good remarks about the undesirability of separating education from religion...'.[38]

Venables gave full details in two letters of what went on at the Brecon education meeting. In the first he noted that the clergy led by Rev. De Winton, had raised over £2,000 for schools in the Archdeaconry and that he himself stood alone in refusing to contribute to the fund. The explanation for his refusal was connected with the way De Winton used every meeting to declare that the government was attacking the clergy and religion. Venables believed that clergymen should not publicly denounce the law.[39] It was a typical Venables response: the law was the law, authority—even wrong-headed authority—had to be shown respect. He was not a Chairman of Quarter Sessions for nothing. The second letter stated that a committee had been set up to administer the fund, which then stood at £2,300, and that the landowner, Middleton Evans,[40] had put forward Venables' name to be a member of it, but Venables declined because he had not contributed to the fund. Sir Gilbert Lewis told him he had better contribute and consent to be one of the committee. Venables thought that 'to hold aloof' after this sort of pressure was 'undesirable' so he acquiesced. The committee was made up half of squires and half of clergy, and, he noted, 'may do some good'. Lord Tredegar, Viscount Hereford, and Sir Joseph Bailey were on it.[41]

Kilvert's humble position excluded him from these proceedings. His role was to teach in the school, to catechise the children,[42] and to liaise with its headmaster, Josiah Evans. The exact nature of the relationship between the two men is one of the intriguing aspects of the *Diary* and of the relationship between Anglican clergy and local people. Born in Pembrey, Carmarthen, in 1835, Evans was 34 years old when he was expressing anxiety about the 1870 Act. He was clearly a religious man, as was appropriate for the headmaster of a National School. He and his wife were great servants of Clyro Church and were always to be found dressing it at Easter, Harvest Festival, and Christmas. He had a strong sense of humour, according to Kilvert, roaring with delight at the misprint in the newspaper account of the Harvest Festival, which stated that 'the *widows* were decorated with Latin and St. Andrew's crosses...'.[43] His sense of humour did not apparently extend to his own violin playing. He was a beginner but took it very seriously, though had to perform on an instrument that

was inferior and in poor condition. 'It had a broken string, and...
something wrong with all the rest', and the noise it made, said Kilvert,
'"fairly raked my bowels" as old Cord used to say at Wadham of
Headeach's violoncello. The schoolmaster however did not appear to
notice that anything was wrong'. He sawed away at the broken strings
'loudly and cheerfully', all the while singing 'Glory be to Jesus'. It was,
Kilvert said, 'the most ludicrous thing'.[44]

Though Kilvert came close to laughing out loud at Evans' perfor-
mance, there is no real humour in this account; the feeling is much
closer to contempt. Kilvert was not ready to be amused that Sunday
evening because, as a result of Venables' absence from the parish, he
had had to undertake all its duties himself and was still angry about
it. Of Evans' professional abilities, he had some respect. He was happy
to record that a Painscastle farmer praised Evans 'to the skies'
because of his son's progress at his school. In addition, Kilvert had,
with others, produced a testimonial to the schoolmaster, an action
which earned the disapproval of Mrs. Morrell. (She came into the
school regularly to inspect the girls' needlework). Her disapproval
and Kilvert's contempt for Evans' violin-playing may well have had the
same origin. It is likely, given Kilvert's attitudes to class, that he
regarded it as an inappropriate aspiration for one of his station.
When Kilvert received a notice about a meeting to discuss a proposed
'Club and Reading Room in Hay, where members can... have
luncheon, mutton chops', his reaction was to snort, 'Great nonsense.
I did not go...'.[45] His denigration of the proposal noticeably ignored
the educational and political aims behind the reading room movement. It was a reaction against the Mechanics Institute, which the
working-class felt catered for lower middle-class folk under upper
middle-class patronage.[46] While anxiety about the potential subversive nature of a Hay reading room was one element in Kilvert's reaction, another seems to have been that he saw it as a club for would-be
gentlemen. He similarly could not endorse Evans' violin-playing
because he was not a gentleman, for a gentleman would have known
that in 'the noise, the heartrending, bowel-raking uproar... there was
something... utterly incongruous'. The student at Wadham made a
similar noise but would not have been oblivious to the effect of it,
which is the point that Kilvert was inclined to labour. The reference
to Wadham underlines his awareness of the gap between a
gentleman's education and that of Evans.

The educational level of schoolmasters had been controversial since the 1846 Special Minute of the Committee of Council for Education, which was aimed at augmenting their numbers, quality, and status. It proposed to select the best scholars for training as pupil-teachers and then pass them on to a training college and certification. The Church welcomed this development but extreme non-conformists declared 'it was undesirable to improve the position of the schoolmaster because he would have gone up in the world sufficiently to consort with the clergyman'.[47] Social inferiority was built into the training system of teachers. Those at Battersea Training College, which became the model for other institutions, received an education whose limited nature indicated the role they were to occupy. In a course of only one or two years, they were examined weekly in Scripture knowledge and Church doctrine. The 'ultimate aim was to produce... lay priests to the poor, "moved by Christian charity"'.[48] Inevitably, only a man of low calibre would 'doom himself to the worst paid labour and almost the least appreciated office to be met with in the country', wrote one of the Commissioners of Enquiry into the State of Education in Wales in 1847.[49] The Clyro School log book records that Evans was 'certified in the 3rd class, 3rd division'. It is possible he had not even attended a training college: 'The majority of country headteachers had never been to a training college, having acquired certificates only by external exam...'.[50] Teachers with the lowest standard of certification served mainly in rural schools. Teachers everywhere continually complained in their journals of their low social status and their salary level continued to be poor. A Berkshire clergyman was saying in 1861 that £45 - £50 a year was common for teachers and, in his view, too much.[51] Miss Coleburn at Clyro School received £45 and a furnished house in 1866. The mistress at Boughrood in the same year had a salary of £51, of which £13—more than a quarter—had been contributed by poor parents. At Llowes, the salary was a miserable £35 in 1866, which had risen to £45 by 1869. Evans, on £60 a year, plus 'half the Government grant' (according to Venables) and a furnished house, was the aristocrat among local colleagues.

As compared with Kilvert, however, Evans occupied a much lower position in the social hierarchy and this may be the key to the ambiguous relationship that existed between the two men. Kilvert liked to think that he was on very friendly terms with the schoolmaster. After he left Clyro, he heard from Evans: 'This evening I had a letter from Josiah Evans, my friend the Clyro schoolmaster...',[52] and on one of his return visits to Clyro, he made a point of calling on Evans and his family. Evans' youngest daughter, Amy, was deputed to present to Kilvert a gold pencil case, saved up for by the school children, to mark his going, and he was so overcome with emotion, he could not thank them. He had made a special pet of Amy. When she was five in April 1872, he made a 'love-token' (his phrase) for her out of a threepenny bit dated 1867, the year she was born. He was also very fond of her older sister Boosie, whom he was in the habit of kissing; he called her his 'darling'. By arranging a special party to mark her birthday, he underlined not only his need for children of his own, but the special place that Evans' children had in his heart. He had a party for children every year he was in Clyro. The one for Boosie was held on 12 February 1872. It is noticeable that the eight children who attended were all girls and were drawn from the most respectable families among the local folk.[53] He amused them with games and stories and felt entirely at ease. He was very sad when 'all the bright faces trooped out into the dark night ... and left me alone in my silent room'. In personal terms, the Evans family could hardly have been more important to Kilvert.

One would have expected that evidence of a close relationship, certainly on the professional level, would be found in the Clyro School log book. The mystery of the log book's complete silence on this relationship has been appropriately underlined: 'Neither Miss Coleburn nor Mr Evans, whose tenures of office more or less coincided with Kilvert's sojourn at Clyro, make a single reference to him, despite his regular attendance at the school. This is all the more surprising in view of the friendly relationship between Kilvert and Evans. Even when Kilvert leaves Clyro for good, amidst great lamentation and ceremony, there is no reference to him'.[54] It has been remarked earlier in these pages that our picture of Kilvert badly lacks the perspective supplied by people who knew him. Venables' letters and diaries fail to provide one. Kilvert appears from his *Diary* to have been very close to Rev. Bevan's daughter, Mary, but when her diary came to light in 1977, it was found to contain only two references to him in its 64 pages, covering three years, and they were of the most matter-of-fact kind. Grice noted, too, that where the two diaries report the same events, Kilvert mentioned Mary but she did not mention him.[55] So once again, where we might confidently have relied upon finding in the Clyro School log book a full picture of the Diarist in his relationship with the school, we meet another blank.

For a National School log book to contain little reference to the local clergyman would be very unusual; for it to make none at all over a period of seven and a half years suggests a deliberate policy on the part of the teacher who had control of it. The Revised Code laid down that it was a teacher's duty to make a daily entry 'which will suffice to specify ordinary progress or whatever fact concerning the School... may require to be referred to at a future time...'. Confidence was expressed in the capacity of the 'zealous and intelligent' teacher to recognise other 'worthwhile experiences' encountered during the year, beyond ordinary progress, appropriate for recording. Examples of 'entries of importance' were the visits of the school managers to examine classes, reports on progress, and observations on particular subjects and teaching methods. The teacher was warned that 'no reflections or opinions of a general character are to be entered...'. It is noticeable that reporting on religious instruction or on the intervention of clergymen is not mentioned, which is probably attributable to the Education Department's policy of emphasising secular teaching and of playing down religion.[56] Teachers in National Schools, nevertheless, habitually reported the visits of clergymen and the teaching they contributed. This was done partly out of deference, and partly because, as an examination of log books makes clear, teachers, under pressure to make some sort of daily entry, would turn to recording clergymen's visits, even when routine, for lack of anything else. Sometimes the entry reads: 'Nothing of special importance to report today'. Thus, teachers were pleased to be able to say that their clergyman had taken a Scripture lesson or a religious service, or had examined children.

In the Clyro School log book, for example, Miss Coleburn noted that in April 1865 and in May 1866 the pupils were examined by the Rev. Bevan. Evans, too, regularly recorded Bevan's visits of that kind (he was the Diocesan inspector), as well as inspections by an HMI, the Rev. Heinaman. On 26 March 1872, the state of Religious Knowledge was examined by a Rev. E. Thomas. Venables also figures in the school record. His routine visits are mentioned, as well as the occasion on 1 August 1867 when the entire school attended a tea party at Clyro Court to celebrate his marriage. Of Kilvert, there is no mention whatsoever, nor of his predecessor, Lee, though the man who replaced Kilvert as Venables' curate is acknowledged: 'The School [was] kept today by the Rev. H.R. Irvine... who kindly relieved the master'.[57] Throughout Kilvert's period as Vicar of St. Harmon, the teacher noted all his visits, which were very frequent. The pattern is the same in the Bredwardine School log book, except that Kilvert was prevented from visiting by increasing bouts of illness.

It was, therefore, virtually automatic for teachers to mention clergymen's visits and if they did not, it can only be construed as intentional. Schoolmasters like Evans had to win the approval of a variety of clergymen—the local one, the Diocesan inspector, the HMI, and others. Furthermore, a National School's board of managers would often be dominated by clergymen. It was inevitable, therefore, that schoolmasters had to defer excessively to clergymen and were made to feel that everything they did had to receive their sanction.[58] The sensitivity of the former to their lack of gentlemanly status was, as has been noted, considerable. The Association of Schoolmasters was designed to enhance their status and some clergymen around Clyro attended the meetings of its local branch. One quarterly meeting took place in the Hay schoolroom on Saturday 12 May 1866. Further proof of schoolmasters' low status is evident in the fact that while the *Hereford Times* does list the names of clergymen in attendance, it omits those of schoolmasters; if Evans was there, Kilvert certainly was not. His *Diary* makes no mention of these meetings. His absence from the Hay one is remarkable because it was hosted by Rev. Bevan and attended by another close friend, Rev. Tom Williams, plus two other clergymen, all giving support to the teachers in their schools. Furthermore, Rev. Bevan gave a talk on 'The significance of place names', a topic close to Kilvert's interest in dialect words. Kilvert disapproved of most kinds of organisations for the lower classes. It has already been shown that he rejected the proposed Hay Club and Reading Room and he was equally dismissive of the suggestion by Bridges, a Clyro friend, of an archery club for the neighbourhood: 'I don't think it desirable or practicable'. The activities of trade unions provoked in him a fury that has been described as 'almost vindictive'.[59]

The entire voluntary system of education had about it 'a faint odour of charity and social inferiority', which clung to elementary teachers, some of whom were condescended to by clergymen.[60] One HMI, after years of visiting schools, could hardly recall an instance, outside London, of a clergyman shaking hands with, or even talking in a familiar way with, a parochial schoolmaster.[61] Schoolmasters had to get used to reading pieces such as that which appeared in the *Hereford Times* of 15 June 1861. It reported a court case in Dublin where a Mr. Hutchinson was described as a gentleman, but it was proved he was a schoolmaster, a writing clerk, and a collector of parish taxes. The judge commented that he might be all of those things and a gentleman, but Mr. Heaton, QC, replied: 'I submit not, my Lord', and quoted precedents to the contrary.

It seems unlikely that Kilvert deliberately showed this sort of condescension to Evans but it is equally unlikely that, being the man he was, it would not make itself felt in their relationship. Was Kilvert's stance towards him inevitably affected by the lingering memory that he too had spent a year as a lowly schoolmaster? In the episode of Evan's violin-playing, Kilvert had remarked: 'I never was so hard put to it not to laugh out loud'. He had a strong tendency to laugh in inappropriate situations as, for example, in Clyro Church when the clerk was attempting to pull down a blind to keep out strong sunlight. Kilvert watched the man make several vain attempts until a very violent tug smashed the blind, which 'hung in ruins'. 'It was almost too much. I was nearly choked',[62] Kilvert observed, and he tried to resist 'inextinguishable laughter'. One suspects that his attempts to conceal laughter failed to be completely successful on that occasion as they did on the occasion involving Evans. Kilvert did admit then: 'I smiled. I could not help it'. Given his fondness for passing on a good story, it is quite conceivable, also, that word of his amused contempt came to Evans' ears.

Evans may have maintained relations with the curate that were friendly on the surface while simultaneously resenting his superior social status, connections, and attitude. Perhaps he, like M.K. Ashby's grandmother, 'hated the demand for servile manners'.[63] Perhaps, also, the fact that Evans was Welsh played a part in his attitude to Kilvert, who, in spite of his avowed love of all things Welsh, was as fully representative of all things English and Tory as it was possible to be. This factor had not, however, prevented Evans from mentioning other clergymen in his school log book. Was Kilvert one of the Oxford clergymen deemed by Frederic Harrison to be unlikely to win the confidence of the poor? Whatever it was that caused him to maintain a steady silence about Kilvert was personal in nature and it was a silence he was not prepared to break even when Kilvert left Clyro. It is relevant to mention in this connection, that when Kilvert's friend, Andrew Pope, left Cusop, a parish near Hay in 1873, he had, in the words of the *Hereford Times*, 'won the esteem of all classes', and there were 350 people at his farewell service, though the parish contained only 208 residents. The ceremony marking his going was, it seems, a more significant affair than that marking Kilvert's. And when, later, Pope left another parish (that of Diddlebury, near Hereford), where he had been notably active in the school as Kilvert had been at Clyro, the log book paid him a very full tribute.[64]

For the son of the agricultural labourer, whose schooling was in the care of such as Evans and Kilvert, the problem was that whatever knowledge was acquired would soon have to be forgotten when the time came for him to begin his working life, and if he had developed a real taste for learning, he would be unable to indulge it and would be frustrated and discontented. Perhaps it was fortunate that for most children their education would rarely foster intellectual curiosity because it dealt in 'simple items of knowledge which... were too scrappy and too few to begin running together into an understanding of the larger aspects of life. A few rules of arithmetic, a little of the geography of the British Isles, a selection of anecdotes from the annals of the ancient Jews, no English history, no fairytales or romance, ...but merely a few "pieces" of poetry, and a few haphazard observations... about familiar things - "the cat", "the cow", "the parsnip", "the rainbow"... - this was the jumble of stuff offered to the child's mind...'.[65]

Kilvert's teaching seems to have consisted of this 'jumble of stuff', which, in its incoherence resembled the educational fare that he, with other Harnish pupils, had been offered by Kilvert senior. Kilvert told children at Clyro about different areas of the country. His imminent departure from the School prompted Mrs. Harris' son to observe: 'There'll be no one to come and teach us now. Mr Kilvert do come and tell us about all parts'.[66] There were 'pieces' of poetry, as at Langley Burrell School where he read the verse 'Consider the ravens' and encouraged pupils to recount their own experiences of ravens. He regularly taught the Scripture lessons that were the staple of the local clergyman's contribution, favouring the 'dear old Bible stories' which, he told Mrs. Venables, he would teach his own children. He once taught the higher standards at Bredwardine the story of Hezekiah's illness, and this provides an illuminating example of his approach and purposes. Hezekiah was king of Judah and known for his trust in God and his faithful observance of His commandments. In recognition of his loyalty, God ensured he was successful in everything he undertook. Eventually, however, Hezekiah became mortally ill and God told him to prepare for death. Hezekiah in his prayers reminded God that he had always been faithful and wept bitterly. Isaiah told him that God would heal him and add 15 years to his life, but Hezekiah wanted a sign as proof of God's intention. Accordingly, God made the shadow on the sun dial move backwards ten degrees. Thus, the sons and daughters of the Bredwardine labouring poor had set before them the example of a servant of the Lord specially singled out for divine benevolence for a lifetime's faithfulness and humility. It was the message of the Catechism all over again.[67]

Some clergymen objected strongly to using the Bible for this kind of moralising. To John Clay, for example, the mark of the poorly educated Sunday School teacher was the 'desecration' of the Bible by turning it into 'repulsive lesson-books', and the 'cramming of the Catechism, seldom explained, and soon forgotten'. Moral duties, thought Clay, should be taught by 'interesting narratives, real histories, and an occasional... reference to Him who loved children, and specially taught the poor'.[68] There is no doubt that Kilvert loved children and believed in his work with the poor. He also made attempts to explore with them aspects of the Catechism. He was, in fact, the kind of clergyman Mozley wanted to see in village schools, rather than the professional lay teachers, who put children through the Catechism and commented on the Bible without proper reverence or understanding. Mozley sympathised with clergymen who had lost control of village schools after the 1870 Act. 'Be the clergy ever so weak, ever so wrong-headed..., I could not bear to see the education of the poor passing out of their hands'.[69]

Kilvert in his well-meaning but wrong-headed way compounded the problems of a curriculum made up of scraps of information sustained by no organising principle. 'I asked the children... what an embalmed Egyptian body was called. "A life preserver", said one. "A muffin", said another. "What is a muffin?" I asked. "A bird", said a child'.[70] He risked similar idiocies when he set his class the task of explaining in writing 'What makes a true Sacrament?' However, on this occasion he was well pleased when several pupils gave him sensible answers.[71] He was afforded a glimpse of better educational experiences when he took some pupils to the Temperance Hall in

Chippenham to see the 'Panorama of the African travels of Dr. Livingstone'. 'What pleasure these few pence have given to twenty-one young hearts', he commented.[72] Kilvert's background had not encouraged in him a belief in intellectual enquiry and he was not likely to consider it an appropriate educational objective for the working-classes. In the view of one HMI, the elementary school was permeated by the bleak Protestant ethos in which Kilvert had been reared. There was a heavy emphasis on original sin, on rules and laws rather than on ideals and values, on obedience to authority, and on the measurable in behaviour. The individual growth of the child was stifled, and the 'good' child aimed at by the system was that amalgam of 'stupidity, patience, and submissiveness' favoured by the upper-classes when they took thought for the welfare of the poor.[73]

Kilvert accepted the split between a utilitarian education for the lower-classes and a liberal one for gentlemen along with most of his contemporaries. This, for the historian Kitson Clark, was one of the two major differences between the way Victorians thought on these issues and the way we do today. The other was that 'to nearly all clergymen, and indeed to most laymen, the dogmas of religion would seem more important than they would seem to most people today... It would seem to be all-important for a boy or girl to be correctly taught what they should believe'.[74] This, Clark acknowledged, was the cause of much stupid teaching. He also acknowledged that teaching the poor to be obedient and keep their place was a very convenient philosophy for the ruling class, but he insisted that it was not the sole, or even the primary aim of Church education. Clergymen believed that it was their religious duty to do so in order to help the poor to save their souls; they were not simply seeking to control the poor, because, if that had been their only objective, they would not have been so keen for them to become literate.[75] However, this argument is weakened by the fact that literacy was advocated primarily so that the poor could read their Bibles and secular education was resisted. To Joseph Arch, leader of the Agricultural Labourers' Union, elementary education was appallingly bad because the gentry sought to limit it to a very basic literacy; knowledge of 'the right sort is a dangerous thing'. He added that gentry did not want the labourer's child to *know*, 'they only wanted him to work'.[76]

For most of the century, the education of the poor was inconceivable to the Church without a religious purpose. Yet it had been told by its own clergymen that that purpose was fatally undermined by poverty itself. It was utterly futile, in the opinion of the Rev. Sidney Godolphin Osborne to teach 'truth, purity, honesty, industry, religion to children who return each day to homes in which life itself—human life—is almost a lie...'.[77] Another clergyman, as a young curate, recalled being told by an elderly colleague, who had worked all his life in poor parishes, that 'starvation was a soil on which piety will not grow'.[78] As long as the landowning class repudiated the legitimate claim that their labourers had on them to ameliorate their living conditions, the specious morality directed at labourers and their children would be rejected. It was not only the poverty that came from inadequate wages but, as the account of Radnorshire schools has shown, the poverty of educational provision that denied a proper life to the poor. Selfishness was one barrier to landowners' and clergymen's ability to see the poor as human beings like themselves. Fear of the poor was another. All that was then required to make impassable the gulf between them and the poor, was their public school education and their pride in their rank.

It was the deliberate policy of those who controlled elementary education to perpetuate those barriers. Those in Parliament and in the Church who framed the policy were public school products almost to a man.[79] By inculcating deference and acceptance of menial work, the ruling class was determined to retain the past and its own traditional power. It preferred to ignore the link between education and the economy, which from Kilvert's day increasingly demanded more skilled and more adaptable workers, who had a broad education as well as vocational skills. Accordingly, it blocked moves towards a modern, state education system, and tried to keep working people as subordinate, unenfranchised children.[80] The 1870 Act was a compromise: schools were still religious in character after it, but were based on a joint effort of voluntary bodies and the state. The Church responded to the challenge to establish more of its own schools by applying for hundreds of building grants.[81] After 1870, more and more schools came under state control and it became evident to many people that the voluntary system had reached the end of its development. With the establishment of Board Schools in numbers, the continued influence of the Church was going to depend on whether clergymen were going to be welcome in them. The answer in many cases was that they were not. Richard Jefferies was noting in a book, largely based on Wiltshire experience and published a year after Kilvert died, that after the 1870 Act 'the parish seemed to have quite left the Church, and the parson was outside the real modern life of the village'.[82] The Act did nothing to solve the problem of attendance, and the Education Act of 1876, which tried to make it compulsory, was only partially successful.[83] Clergymen's influence on those who did attend was, however, steadily diminishing.

By the last quarter of the century, the Church did not possess a moral authority that the nation as a whole recognised. 'However devoted were many of its ministers, however valuable their service, it was inescapably a rich man's Church'.[84] As a result of placing so much emphasis on difference of rank, the Church was reaping what it had sown. It had always prided itself that it flourished most strongly in the hearts of the rural poor; now they too rejected it. Its tradition of parochial care had been a positive force but it was based on inequality and was indefensible. Communication across the gulf created by landowners and Church leaders was always going to be difficult for parish clergymen, even for those like Kilvert who were especially warm-hearted. In the Welsh border country, where an English ruling class was imposed on an indigenous Welsh population, the gulf was that bit deeper. 'It was a gulf that Kilvert was aware of and in his natural way he bridged it', wrote Lockwood. 'It was partly because, though he occupied a place in higher society, he remained poor, but mostly because he was so very approachable [and] was humble in the truest sense of the word'.[85] This is a judgement which, in the light of the exploration undertaken in this chapter, requires much qualification. Kilvert's awareness of the gulf between the English ruling class and the Welsh people was limited. His love affair with Clyro and its community, in which his romantic and paternalist attitude played a large part, tended to blind him to the realities lying just below the surface, which he under-estimated because they did not fit his view of himself and his class as the focus of respect and affection and the source of benevolence.[86] Kilvert actively sought to bathe Clyro in the golden glow of Chieflands.

He blinded himself to the realities that lay behind the Jarvis Charity in Bredwardine that is dealt within chapter 8. An HMI's report on its school, copied by Kilvert into the school log book on 21 November 1877, contains the statement: 'Considering the very great advantages given by the rich Jarvis Charity, the attendance might in many cases have been much better'. He added that out of 31 infants only 11 qualified themselves for grant by their attendance. It was no doubt Kilvert who had encouraged the inspector to believe that the poor attendance was the fault of parents who showed no gratitude or responsibility as beneficiaries of a charity, which *was* rich, but which signally failed to give the poor their due because of the determination of landowners and clergy to increase their control of elementary education. When criticism of its gentry administrators was voiced by representatives of other classes of the community, Kilvert was quite unable to do any 'bridging' that might reconcile the conflicting interests; he immediately closed ranks with the gentry. When he talked of the 'kindly Welsh', he had largely in mind the farming families of Clyro who received the bulk of his visits and in whose company he felt particularly at home. It was also they who were most regretful at his leaving.[87] He was no more able to bridge the gulf between himself and labourers and their families than he was that between himself and Josiah Evans. Though Kilvert was poor, his poverty was of a different order from that of his poor parishioners because he was a gentleman. And if being humble 'in the truest sense of the word' means that he acknowledged, as he did, his own worthlessness when compared with the perfection of his God, it is nevertheless true that Kilvert's personality also craved social recognition. He was never able to forget his own rank, his background that gave him the right to armorial bearings, his gentlemanly Oxford education, and the deference that he enjoyed from lower-class parishioners.

Edward Carpenter, writing a little after Kilvert's death, loathed deference because it meant that the people would never speak their minds or commit themselves to anything not sanctioned by authority. Unable to speak his true mind either face-to-face or in his school log book, Josiah Evans, it appears, preferred to say nothing at all, unless it was in private and to his own. Carpenter blamed landlord and parson for their 'paralysing influence' on the lower-classes, and it did not matter whether their concern was prompted by kindness or repression, the result was the same. And he welcomed the way in which bicycles and cars, newspapers and telephones and 'torrents of tourists' were stimulating people into independent life.[88] That was exactly what Kilvert dreaded because it disrupted traditional rural society and the social harmony which he was desperate to believe was its distinguishing feature.

'Mr Phillips [was] an Eton and Christ Church man and a great sportsman'.

Kilvert's *Diary*, Vol. 1, p.113

'Hunting was the gentlemanly activity par excellence'.

J.F.C. Harrison, *Late Victorian Britain*, p.39

'If hunger made a man go into the woods to get a pheasant, he would get fourteen years'.

James Hawker, *A Victorian Poacher*, p.2

'I hear the wakening birds
At their sweet laud;
So let my rising heart
Sing praise to GOD'.

Francis Kilvert, 'Advent'

'India was given to us, and will be kept, by men who, in the high mission of her mastery and redemption, are cautious in counsel without dullness, and swift in action without rashness'.

Lord Dalhousie, Governor-General of India from 1848 until just before the Indian Mutiny. Quoted in Edwin Arnold, *Dalhousie's Administration*, p.103

'... the urgent sense of a mission to civilise - that is to say, Christianize - unenlightened heathen tribes overseas or the unwashed heathen poor at home ... had tangled emotional roots ... They could serve as a cloak for imperialistic military or commercial designs, but Victorians were also driven by personal devils to be exorcised by self-destructive ventures abroad, by unimpeachable benevolence, by active feelings of guilt over one's privileged position - or by a mixture of them all'.

Peter Gay, *The Cultivation of Hatred*, p.69

Robert Francis Kilvert. (The National Library of Wales, Aberystwyth)

Chieflands farmhouse. (John Toman)

Robert Kilvert
Left: Aged 37 in the year that Francis was born, 1840, as depicted in a
pastel drawing by his brother Edward. (By kind permission of
Miss Muriel Kilvert). Right: In his 70s. (The National Library of Wales,
Aberystwyth)

Hardenhuish Rectory. (John Toman)

Hardenhuish House, home of Squire Clutterbuck, Robert Kilvert's patron. (John Toman)

Langley Burrell Rectory. (The National Library of Wales, Aberystwyth)

Moccas Deer Park with a large oak tree, an etching by Benjamin Pouncy after the watercolour by Thomas Hearne

Wadham College front, photograph by John Freeman. (By permission of the Warden and Fellows of Wadham College)

The Fellows' Garden, Wadham College, watercolour by C. Wild, 1819. (By permission of the Warden and Fellows of Wadham College)

Ashbrook House, Kilvert's lodgings in Clyro.
(Courtesy of the Kilvert Society)

Rev. Richard Lister Venables and his wife, Mrs. Venables.
(The National Library of Wales, Aberystwyth)

Lysdinam Hall, Newbridge-on-Wye

Rev. Richard Lister Venables and Daisy Thomas.
(The National Library of Wales, Aberystwyth)

Llanthomas

Ettie Meredith Brown (left) and Katharine Heanley (right).
(The National Library of Wales, Aberystwyth)

Clyro School, watercolour by Thermuthis Kilvert (sister of Francis Kilvert). (The National Library of Wales, Aberystwyth)

School Feast near Bredwardine, 1869.
(Courtesy of the Kilvert Society)

Left: Charles Kingsley by William S. Hunt aftre a photo by an unknown photographer. Right: Sir Bartle Frere by Sir George Reid, oil on canvas, 1881. (Both reproduced by permission of the National Portrait Gallery)

Officers of the 1st battalion, 24th Regiment with Sir Bartle Frere (the central seated figure), Kingswilliam's Town, South Africa, 1877

John Brinkworth, qho worked as a hedger and ditcher in Kings Stanley.
(Rural History Centre, University of Reading)

Workhouse inmates, 1911

Blenheim Cottage, Brighthampton, an example of a farm labourer's cottage (Oxfordshire County Council Photographic Archive)

'The Rivals' (a Punch *cartoon)*

A farmworker and his family being evicted from their tied cottage, Cherhill, Wiltshire, February 1876. The family were obviously supporters of the NALU, as the placard in the hedge exhorts onlookers to 'read Joseph Arch'. (Cole Collection, by permission of the Warden and Fellows of Nuffield College, Oxford)

Maesllwch Castle, home of the De Wintons

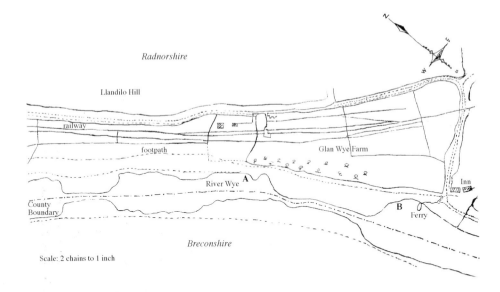

Radnorshire

Llandilo Hill

railway

footpath

Glan Wye Farm

River Wye A

Inn

County
Boundary

B

Ferry

Breconshire

Scale: 2 chains to 1 inch

The Glangwye fishery. The disputed section lay between points A and B

Tichborne House,
from a lithograph
by G.F. Prosser, 1833

Arthur Orton,
The Tichborne Claimant

Clyro Court. (Courtesy of the Kilvert Society)

*'View of Moccas in Herefordshire the seat of Sir George Cornewall Bart
taken from Brobury Scar 1788'
painted by Herefordshire artist James Wathen*

Mrs. Francis Kilvert (née Rowland). (The National Library of Wales, Aberystwyth)

Sir George Cornewall. (*From* Herefordshire Portraits)

Bredwardine Vicarage, Kilvert's first and only home. (Logaston Press)

CHAPTER 7
Kilvert and Manliness

A significant element in the Kilvert family's ambivalent attitude to aristocracy and country house values was field sports. The Kilverts were country people and field sports were part of their heritage. Robert Kilvert stated that one amusement of which has father was 'extremely fond' was the field. 'He was a keen sportsman and an excellent shot... Of course it was the greatest possible treat for any of us... to go with him either partridge or woodcock shooting...'.[1] Fishing was an equal passion for all the sons of the family. Robert recalled the excitement of an early sporting experience. He was roaming one day on land belonging to a cousin. It was a hot day and he found inviting the shade of a plantation bordering the river. 'I had scarcely stepped within when up jumped a fine hare... My gun was at my shoulder in a moment; the next, the hare was rolling on the ground. This was bad enough, for I had not either game licence or private permission to do more than shoot rabbits'. He quickly and guiltily retreated but was confronted by his host, who had heard the report of his gun. If he had been a labourer's son, his punishment would have been three months' hard labour. His host merely commented on the 'very fine hare' he had shot.[2] It was the kind of story that would have gone down well with the gentlemen-commoners of Oriel College, but it is very doubtful whether he would have been given the chance to share it.

The date of this episode was 1820 and Robert was 16. It was the period of the 19th century when the cult of the sportsman had reached its first zenith. Lady Louisa Stuart was observing in 1802 how absurdly punctilious men had become about 'shooting exactly in the English manner', as if 'the business itself was one of importance instead of a diversion'.[3] She had misunderstood what was happening:

all field sports, but particularly shooting and fox-hunting, had acquired almost mystical significance as activities for gentlemen by this time. Mere diversion they certainly were not. Fox-hunting began to grow in importance about 1780, reaching a peak in the 1820s and 1830s. But while these sports had flourished so had opposition to them from among the very social group to which the Kilvert family belonged, so that Robert's passion for shooting represented something of a betrayal of the values his family espoused, at least as far as their religion was concerned. By the 1830s, concern over cruelty to foxes was openly expressed in newspapers and journals. The winner of the prize for the best essay on the subject of cruelty to animals was a clergyman, the Rev. John Styles, who, in 1839, accused huntsmen of deriving their pleasures from the tormenting and destroying of 'unoffending and happy creatures'.

By this time Evangelicalism had found wide support among clergy of all denominations and one of its objectives was the raising of standards in personal and social morality. Anglican clergy were especially anxious to dissociate themselves from the 18th-century sporting parson who participated in the hunting and shooting activities of the gentry. There was a campaign, too, to reform working-class social pastimes, especially blood sports. The very first Act to protect animals from cruelty was passed in 1822, two years before the establishment of the Society for the Prevention of Cruelty to Animals. Cruelty to animals was part of the coarser manners of those days and many otherwise good people were capable of mistreating animals. Sportsmen commonly beat their dogs for small acts of disobedience. Kilvert's sister, Emily, recalled the occasion when the family's spaniel was beaten for some misdemeanour, on the orders of her mother. Horse-racing was a favourite target of reformers, as it was for that friend of the Kilvert family, the Rev. Moule, but since this sport attracted aristocrats as well as working people, it resisted attacks. Another sport—boxing—which was also a focus of criticism, prevailed because it too attracted aristocratic patronage and a case could be made that it, like horse-racing, fostered manly qualities which were the basis of the national character. However, refined people looked down on it, associating it with everything 'blackguardly and disgusting'.[4]

In the post-Waterloo years when many country gentlemen were looking back nostalgically to a pre-industrial, pre-revolutionary past, it was natural that they would make heroes out of sporting figures who best seemed to represent traditional rural values. The most famous was Assheton-Smith, Etonian and Master of the Quorn Hunt. His biographer included this list of the virtues of fox-hunting in his account of Assheton-Smith's life: 'Its pursuit gives hardihood, and nerve, and intrepidity to our youth, while it confirms... the strength and vigour of our manhood... it serves to retain the moral influence of the higher over the lower-classes of society'.[5] Another Etonian, Sir John Shelley, was less famous but no less convinced that field sports were responsible for the 'manly qualities of the higher orders of the people', and that if the right of shooting game were extended, the country would become the contemptible 'nation of shopkeepers' which Napoleon had declared it was.[6] His fanatical defence of the law which stated that only those owning land worth £100 a year were 'qualified' to shoot game, provides a clear insight into the passions and traditions surrounding the issue of game. It was the licence possessed only by the 'qualified' that Robert Kilvert lacked when he killed his hare in his cousin's plantation. Though he respected the law, there is a suggestion that he resented his 'unqualified' situation, just as he resented, along with the rest of the Kilvert family, the change in fortune from the 'palmy times' when his paternal grandfather lived 'a simple patriarchal life' on his own property in Shropshire, to the 'straightened circumstances' of his own youth.[7]

His feeling that the right to shoot was part of his rural heritage received some support from his religion, which deplored the way in which landowners had arrogantly declared certain fowls of the air and beasts of the field to be aristocrats like themselves and had forbidden lesser men to shoot them. Wilberforce thought the Game Laws excessively severe particularly because most people were unable to see the taking of game by unqualified persons as a crime. The property qualification that gave some people the right had been established in 1389 but it was the Game Act of 1671 that stipulated the need to own land worth £100 a year. From that time onwards it was illegal for the unqualified to take game, though a statute of James I had first prohibited its sale. How exclusive the privilege of shooting game was can be seen from the fact that in Wiltshire in 1785 only 0.5% of the population were qualified. Inevitably, making game rare encouraged the growth of a black market in it, which was supplied partly by poachers and partly by the qualified themselves. An attempt to undermine that market was made in 1821 by proposing that the qualified be allowed to sell their game, but it was rejected because it would devalue the game franchise. A further attempt to legalise the sale of game was blocked in 1823 when Viscount Cranborne's bill to allow the qualified to sell it was rejected. On that occasion, Sir John Shelley told the House that to legalise it would be to 'disturb the good old habits of the country', and he talked of the ignominy of exchanging game 'for a paltry consideration of money'. This was another expression of that particular version of a gentleman's honour which held that all commercial transactions for profit were unworthy.

Kilvert would have felt much sympathy for a concept of honour which venerated 'good old habits of the country'. However, he believed that there were limits to the assertion of rank, even though rank was central to his vision of social order. Its edges had to be softened and it was both the duty and particular talent of a true gentleman to know when and how that was to be managed. The following *Diary* passage indicates one way in which the line was to be drawn between legitimate and illegitimate assertion of rank: 'Miss Mewburn went to the Agricultural Meeting at the Town Hall at Chippenham yesterday and came away furious at the patronizing manner in which the labourers were preached at and the way in which poor old people were kept standing during the whole meeting, while "*their betters*" (?) were comfortably seated in cushioned chairs... I very heartily sympathize with her feelings'.[8] Over-stepping the boundaries of rank, or insensitivity to the effect on others of its assertion, disturbed the all-important sense of community which was a main theme of the Chieflands passage. There, the emphasis was on the duties, the natural ties, which bound landowner and tenant together, and the breaches which resulted if they were neglected. A good landlord, it was made clear, such as Kilvert's grandfather had been, would not scruple to help out his tenant in hard times.

Many who saw themselves as good landlords were fond of drawing attention to the harmony of the rural community but any harmony that existed was severely undermined by the Game Laws, the harshness and injustice of which were widely criticised. One Wiltshire landowner of traditional outlook told a government enquiry into them that 'most of the offences of the country might be considered as results of the severity of the Game Laws'. When asked whether any shame attached to poaching in the eyes of labourers, he replied, 'Not the slightest'. The 'notorious poachers' to be found in most villages were often 'among their most intelligent, respectable and hard-working characters'.[9] The war between them and gamekeepers, who were employed by game-preserving landowners in increasing numbers to protect their privilege, continued throughout the century. Between 1860 and 1890 there was a 60% increase in the number of gamekeepers and deaths among their ranks and among poachers were frequent. Kilvert was recording in his *Diary* in October 1871: 'There was a murderous affray with poachers at the Moor last night. Two keepers beaten fearfully about the head with bludgeons and one poacher, Cartwright, a Hay sawyer, stabbed and his life despaired of'.[10] The fact that Cartwright was one of the better paid and more respectable of agricultural workers tells its own story about attitudes to poaching, and about Kilvert's attitude to game-preserving: there is an implication that too high a price was being paid for one class's pride.

It was during Kilvert's years as a country clergyman that field sports experienced their second flowering. De Broke noted that fox-hunting flourished in the golden years of the squirearchy between 1850 and 1880, a period in which there was a 40% national increase in the number of foxhound packs. Fox-hunting was, he asserted, the 'distinguishing characteristic of the country gentlemen of England', and he developed a vision of rural society, symbolised by the country house, in which all classes were united by the sport's traditional rela-tions.[11] Democratic as well as traditional values were claimed for it by the Master of the Old Berkshire Hunt in 1851: 'No other country but England knows anything of a sport which allows a chimney-sweep or the lowest man of the community to ride by the side of a duke'.[12] Bromley-Davenport, the Cheshire landowner, also underlined its patriotic and political values:

> Yet here all are equal - no class legislation,
> No privilege hinders, no family pride:
> In the "image of war" show the pluck of a nation;
> Ride, ancient patrician! democracy, ride![13]

The idea that the fox-hunting field was open to all had some truth in it. Foxes as vermin were not protected by any game law so that there was no problem over who was 'qualified' to kill them. In addition, since it was accepted that hunts could cross any property boundaries, they were seen as based on agreement and co-operation. However, farmers often objected to having their fields invaded, and the social contact allowed by hunts was very limited and confined to specific situations. Individuals from various social classes could make conversation at the meet of the hounds but on the basis of condescension, not of equality. Contact while the hunt was on was impossible and was restricted away from it. 'At the social events associated with hunting, such as balls, dinners and races, the social differences were maintained all the more sharply'.[14] Membership of hunt clubs was for gentry; farmers had separate social occasions.

De Broke claimed for field sports in general a mode of contact between men closer and deeper than any known among those who lived in cities. Men in cities could not know each other as could those who had 'hunted and fished and killed rats together'.[15] It is at this point that the fox-hunting ethic leaves the realm of rationality and becomes semi-mystical. In company with many hunting men, De Broke made much of the 'honour' involved in the sport. For him it was inappropriate to use the word 'sport' to dignify almost any competitive activity; it was one of the many aspects of the modern world he deplored. It was properly associated only with field sports, the pursuit of wild animals. The true sportsman had 'honour', and though that could be attained in realms other than field sports, it was in those sports, and particularly in fox-hunting, that that virtue had supreme significance. It derived from the experience of taking risks at speed on horseback and from the manly grappling with dangers.

Kilvert was compelled, especially during the period 1865-1872, when he was in Clyro, to rub shoulders with country gentlemen for whom field sports were their *raison d'être*. The fox-hunt in particular should, in theory, have found favour with him because of the way in which, like the friendly society parade, the school feast, or the birth of an heir in the big house, it brought together landlord, farmer, clergy, and tradesmen, in shared activity and pleasure. (Labourers, too, often followed the hunt on foot). Kilvert was, however, deeply opposed to fox-hunting and almost all field sports (he did occasionally fish). They were disapproved of by the religion he had inherited, and Wilberforce had specifically drawn attention, in his *Practical View*, to the anomaly of man destroying creatures for his pleasure whilst remaining totally incapable of understanding the simplest living thing. It is clear that in this respect as in so many others, another major influence was Wordsworth, from whom he had learnt a reverence for all creation and the importance of a sensitive response to it:

> Thanks to the human heart by which we live
> Thanks to its tenderness, its joys and fears,
> To me the meanest flower that blows can give
> Thoughts that do often lie too deep for tears.

The poet had also urged that we ought

> Never to blend our pleasure or our pride
> With sorrow of the meanest thing that lives.

These last two lines had been quoted in an article in the *Saturday Review* on 'The Morality of Field Sports', the title of an earlier article in the *Fortnightly Review* by the historian, Professor E.A. Freeman. His article, which appeared on 1 October 1869, aroused a nationwide controversy of which Kilvert must have been aware. Not only was he vitally interested in the issue, as the following examination of *Diary* entries will show, but, since he was in the habit of reading both the *Saturday Review* and the *Daily Telegraph* (in which the ensuing debate was also carried on), it seems certain that he was closely acquainted with the controversy. Freeman's name would also have been familiar to Kilvert from his days at Wadham, where he studied history. Freeman had hoped to be appointed as Oxford's Professor of Modern History in 1858, but Goldwin Smith was chosen. Just prior to Kilvert's arrival at Oxford in 1859, Freeman was an examiner for Kilvert's course, so it is quite probable he heard his name mentioned. Kilvert would certainly have known that he was a candidate, again unsuccessful, for the professorship of ancient history in 1861, and for modern history in 1862.

Opposition to field sports had gained ground in the 1860s. The issue of fox-hunting had blazed up in *The Field* for two months in 1862. Blood sports as an issue kept on surfacing in most of the periodicals during the 1870s, following the confrontation between Freeman and Trollope. *The Times* discussed the morality of shooting birds in a leader on 1 August 1870, and the topic was discussed in the

Cornhill Magazine in February 1874. In the *Hereford Times*, Kilvert's local newspaper, both before and after he came to the district, there was a steady stream of articles and letters expressing disquiet about various aspects of field sports. Some dealt with the over-preservation of game, like the article in the edition of 19 May 1860, which noted a paper that had been read before the Central Farmers' Club. Its author had stated that the rearing of vast numbers of birds for the 'battue', a shoot at which hundreds were slaughtered, was deplorable and reduced squires to poulterers. The system was also grossly unfair to farmers: 'The landlord has all the pleasure of the shooting and all the profits of selling the game; the farmer's share is the simple satisfaction of keeping it. And dearly does he pay for the satisfaction, not only in the havoc of his crops, but in the keep of poachers in prison... for every shilling the squire gains the farmer loses twenty'. A letter of 11 May 1865 complained that in the interests of game preservation, gamekeepers were constantly snooping around tenants' farms to ensure they did not interfere with the game that destroyed their crops. The field sports issue was, therefore, a sensitive one locally in the 1860s, but it was Freeman's article and the reply that it provoked from Trollope, also in the *Fortnightly Review* (on 1 December 1869), which began the national debate that lasted throughout 1870 and even into 1871, partly as a result of Freeman's second article on 1 December 1870.

Kilvert's *Diary* contains many references to field sports but it is very noticeable that the great majority of them occur within, or only a short time after, the period of controversy that followed Freeman's original article. Later entries are neither as numerous nor as sharply critical in tone. Together they provide the fullest possible insight into the Diarist's reaction to a variety of field sports—shooting, harecoursing, hunting, and fishing. Some of the earlier entries are brief and matter-of-fact. Many others, however, especially those concerning shooting, are much fuller and leave no doubt as to his view of the morality of the sport. In one episode, he was visiting the Dew family at Whitney Rectory and then 'walked down to Whitney Court with Jack Dew and young Elwes who both had their guns... Elwes shot at a starling flying and... at a sandpiper... Happily however he missed it'.[16] A few weeks later, on a walk to Aberedw with his brother, he was captivated by the sight of newly hatched partridges, 'too young and inexperienced to be afraid... beautiful little creatures'.[17] An entry later that month presents a contrasting gentry interest in young game birds: Walter Baskerville and another gentleman were visiting a country house to see the 'quality' of the young pheasants. In another entry, Kilvert's pleasure in the sound of a woodpecker's tapping is juxtaposed with the comment, 'partridge shooting on all round'.

Kilvert would have had to endure many gentry dinner parties at which sporting achievements and prospects were an important feature of the conversation, as on the occasion when he 'dined at the Vicarage with Lord and Lady Hereford who came today and stay till Saturday for the shooting at Clyro Court'. It pelted rain all the next day, and he was pleased when he heard that the Clyro Court party were denied their shooting, and had to be content to play 'battledore and shuttlecock in the hall, gentlemen and ladies'.[19] Some shooting did, however, take place later because Kilvert received a brace of pheasants from his squire within days of the Vicarage dinner party. An American girl visiting England in 1851, was amazed at the obsession of gentry with field sports and poaching: 'Conversation at dinner dwelt interminably on poaching, the shooting of game, and the hunting of foxes'.[20] This was very probably the case at the Clyro Court luncheon Kilvert attended in May 1871 with a group of sportsmen that included Walter Baskerville, some of his Mynors relatives, Morrell, Trevellyn, and Blisset.[21] They had spent the morning rook shooting and invited Kilvert to join them for another bout after the meal. 'I went but I did not like it and soon came away... Trevellyn shot the best. He is a capital shot. He shot a rabbit with his beautiful little rook-rifle like a long saloon pistol. The old rooks were all scared away, sailing round at an immense height in the blue sky, and it was pitiable to see the young rooks bewildered, wheeling and fluttering helplessly from tree to tree, and perching, only to be tumbled bleeding with a dull thud into the deep nettle beds below, by the ceaseless and relentless crack crack of the beautiful cruel little rifles, or to see them stagger after the shot, hold on as long as possible and then, weak from loss of blood, stumble from their perch, and flutter down, catching at every bough, and perhaps run along the ground terrified and bewildered, in the agonies of a broken wing. It may not be cruel, but I don't think I could ever be a sportsman. It seemed dreadful to bring death and misery into such a sunny lovely scene, among the helpless innocent unsuspecting birds, when everything else was glad and rejoicing, merely for the sake of sport'.[22]

It is one of the fullest statements of his position in relation to field sports, and is remarkable partly for its evocation of the horror he felt at the remorseless slaughter and suffering of the birds, and partly for the care he took to condemn the sport without condemning the sportsmen. It was a distinction Freeman had made: 'I have nothing to do with persons, but only with condemning things'. Kilvert admitted the skill involved but thought it misused, if not abused, when applied to such weak, defenceless creatures. Freeman was far more ready to condemn the cruelty of fox-hunting. 'Cruelty is an essential element in the sport', he had stated. Kilvert had said that the shooting he witnessed 'may not be cruel', but he clearly thought it was. Freeman had taken his stand against field sports because they involved need-less suffering, which was also the basis of Kilvert's case against what Baskerville and his friends were doing when they brought death and misery to the rooks, 'merely for the sake of sport'. For Freeman, too, death should never be a matter of sport, and his assertion that 'to take a direct pleasure in slaughter as slaughter would surely show a hard heart' is essentially what Kilvert was getting at when he said, 'I don't think I could ever be a sportsman'.

For Kilvert all creation was holy and birds particularly so because they represented the essential goodness of God, who advocated a reli-gion of peace and mercy. In this attitude, too, he was following Kingsley, whose working-class hero, Alton Locke, remarked: 'I loved and blessed the birds which flitted past me'.[23] Bird song in spring was a powerful symbol of this religion as Kilvert made clear in an entry about Langley Burrell churchyard. 'Everything was still ... and the only sound was the singing of birds. The place was all in a charm of singing, full of peace and quiet sunshine. It seemed to be given up to the birds and their morning hymns'.[24] When he found a blackbird dead with its legs caught in a trap, he was overwhelmed by a sense of sadness and guilt: 'I felt sick and sorrowful as I went on. "The whole creation groaneth and travaileth in pain together until now". Somehow the suffering creature reminded me of the Saviour on the Cross. I felt as if some sin of mine had brought him there'.[25]

A factor in his reluctance to condemn the rook shooters was deference, which played a prominent part in all field sports. He knew it was not his place to criticise the squire who invited him to lunch and to rook-shootings, and who regularly made him gifts of game. Such gifts had a clear place in the hierarchy of classes. 'A gift of game was a benison bestowed. If bestowed upon an equal the manner of the bestowal saluted and cemented the mutuality of their order; if upon an inferior it compelled and consolidated deference in the most effortless manner'.[26] Kilvert was, therefore, forced to acknowledge, 'people are very kind in sending me game', but probably experienced some guilt over accepting the gifts.[27] His reverence for living creatures was accompanied by a resentment of the idea that they could become the property solely of the rich and denied to the common man. Sir William Blackstone, whose laws of property Kilvert had studied at Oxford, had declared the notion of 'permanent property in wild creatures' to be 'unreasonable' and the laws based on it as 'tyranny'.

Kilvert took the opportunity, during the period 1870 to early 1871, to record his general disapproval of other field sports in which wanton, unsporting cruelty featured. He had no sympathy for hare-coursing, the 'sport' in which greyhounds tore living hares to pieces. It was widely practised around Clyro, having been founded in the neighbourhood, probably in the 1850s, by Captain De Winton of Maesllwch Castle, which explains why the Rev. Venables had been compelled in January 1847 to walk all the way to Bredwardine to enjoy the sport. 'There were some beautiful courses and hares found every minute', he recorded, in one of the rare bursts of feeling to be found in his letters.[28] Venables was providing coursing meetings for his tenant farmers on his Llysdinam estate in the late 1860s and early 1870s, another circumstance which made Kilvert's position on field sports awkward. Walter Baskerville was patron of the Clyro Coursing Club, which met regularly on his land during the time that Kilvert was curate in the village. At a meeting of the Club in November 1862, there was a dinner to round off the day's sport and one of the toasts drunk was to Walter, 'a devoted lover of field sports'.[29] The newspaper reporter remarked that the newly founded Club could hardly fail to be a success under such patronage. He also noted that there had been no breaking down of fences such as often displeased farmers when they allowed coursing on their land. The Clyro Club's meetings took place on the estate's home farm, the tenant of which was Mr. Partridge, who knew what deference was due from him to his landlord.[30] At a Club meeting in 1863, he stated 'with considerable feeling that he lived under one of the kindest and best landlords in England', in the words of the *Hereford Times* reporter. Shortly after his 21st birthday, Walter Baskerville had donated a silver cup worth £5 for the owner of the best greyhound.

When Kilvert saw 'a stout brown hare... [with] the sun shining on her clean red brown fur', his delight in the moment was overshadowed by the thought of what its fate would be if men like the kindest landlord in England had his way. His feeling for such creatures was all bound up with his feeling for young children. The wild, innocent, spontaneous joy in living which they had in common is a strong element in the *Diary* entry that deals with the visit he made in April 1870 to Mouse Castle, a motte near Hay. The party of pubescent girls engaged in giddy rompings he saw as semi-magical beings, who 'seemed to have come from nowhere... but just to have fallen from the sky' for the sole purpose of amusing themselves. They had the freedom of young animals in their natural surroundings and are described as 'young wild goats', 'wild as hawks', with movements 'as quick, graceful and active as young antelopes or as fawns'.[31] That night Kilvert had a vivid dream in which he imagined that he was 'out coursing with two greyhounds each of which had only one eye. They started a hare apiece... but each greyhound could only see the hare that the other was coursing. The consequence was that both hares escaped...'. Kilvert had a particular reverence for St. Anselm, who was noted for kindness to animals, having on one occasion saved a hare from its pursuers. On a visit to St. David's Cathedral in October 1871 Kilvert referred to the tombs of two former bishops, one of whom was St. Anselm. It seems likely that it was Anselm who wore the 'sweet and peaceful smile' noted by the diarist.[32]

Fishing was the only field sport Kilvert allowed himself, which constituted a weakness in his front on the issue of cruelty to animals, just as shooting did for his father. (E.A. Freeman, who was born in 1823, was brought up to believe that it was 'unbecoming in a clergyman to hunt, but that there was no objection to his shooting').[33] Handley Moule, son of Robert Kilvert's friend, the Rev. Moule, had two brothers who were skilled fly-fishermen, but Handley himself declined even to fish because he could find no pleasure in any kind of killing.[34] Kilvert had his worries about fishing, too, which emerge in two entries he felt compelled to make in the 1870-1 period when he was particularly sensitised to the issue of cruelty. The first was in the summer of 1870 and concerned a very large eel that was 'fearfully torn and mangled about the head and neck and ripped open a good way down the side'. He was told the eel had caused this itself by its struggles to break free from the line but he knew that its injuries were the result of men removing it.[35]

Walter Baskerville and his fraternity of sporting gentlemen were involved in the second episode, the netting of the Wye for salmon. Kilvert described the operation: 'The net is dropped in a semi-circle... There is a double wall of netting, corked and leaded, the inner wall fine mesh and the other wall larger mesh. Within the semi-circle the water is beaten with poles to... drive [the fish] into the net. When a fish "strikes", i.e. rushes into the net he bolts through the large mesh of the outer net carrying with him a bag... of the inner fine net which he cannot get through and there he hangs helpless'.[36] Baskerville did go in for the more skilful rod and line method of catching salmon but seems to have favoured the blunt instrument of 'netting', as Kilvert recorded another occasion a month earlier when Baskerville netted the pool below Hay Church. The famous Victorian poacher, James Hawker, distinguished between true sportsmen and poachers. The former were those who, when out shooting, were content to bring down one bird with each shot; that gave birds a sporting chance and ensured more sport. The latter were those who wanted as much prey as they could get—and that category included gentlemen as well as working men. To ensure a large catch of fish, Hawker recommended the double-walled net that Baskerville used.[37] This made Baskerville as much a poacher as he was, and was another way of illustrating the truth that the only difference between the gentleman and the poacher was that the former made the laws which gave him the right to all forms of game, and denied them to the lower-classes. Of course, Kilvert would never had accused gentlemen of being poachers, but an important part of his case against the so-called 'sports' of the field was that no sportsmanship was involved when animals were slaughtered wholesale.

Fox-hunting did not entail large-scale killing but was marked by other cruelties and illogicalities. Sportsmen were always ready to cast the fox in the role of the villain of the countryside, but Kilvert indicated that he was not at all inclined to see it as a vicious pest. He described one tame fox cub he saw as 'a pretty, merry, good-tempered beast... very full of fun and not at all savage'.[38] At the same time, he could recognise that farmers had reason to see foxes as pests and habitually killed them. He was, therefore, able to see how absurd it was for the Master of Foxhounds of the Radnorshire and West Herefordshire pack to express 'disgust' when he came across several dead foxes strung up on trees. 'Of course the farmers having no interest in preserving foxes, killed all they could find', Kilvert noted.[39] It was a point on which Freeman had laid much emphasis in his first article on field sports. There was no intention on the part of fox-hunters of ridding the countryside of a pest, he insisted. On the contrary, 'the breed is artificially preserved [and]... it is held as a point of morality that the life of the fox is sacred except when his death is accompanied with the prescribed amount of wanton fright and suffering'. It was both illogical and unjust that farmers had to accept the damage done by foxes (as they had that done by game to their crops) and were forbidden by their landlords to kill them. A further illogicality was that gamekeepers were also required to preserve foxes, even though they were the biggest destroyer of game birds. Thus, in April 1864, we find the landowner, Sir Velters Cornewall, thanking the gamekeepers of the Herefordshire Hunt district, at a dinner given in their honour, for their efforts in preserving foxes.[40] The gentlemanly sports of shooting and fox-hunting were, therefore, in conflict over the problem of foxes, and it was only a gentleman's agreement that provided a part solution to it. But in order to ensure that gentlemen had their sport, farmers and gamekeepers were required to neglect their interests.

Kilvert took much pleasure in a story told him by Venables' coachman about a 'bag fox', one that was kept in a bag prior to a hunt to ensure that on the day a quarry was guaranteed. 'The bag fox had been kept in a dark cellar so long that he was dazed and half blind, when he was turned out...'. The day before the hunt little Rosie Hodgson 'let the fox out of the bag' to one of the guests. 'Papa has got a fox in a bag down in the cellar', said the child inno-cently.[41] Kilvert also enjoyed the coachman's account of a hunt in which one of its lower-class followers, a local tailor, so offended the Master of Foxhounds by charging along on his old pony with the hounds, that he actually rode at the tailor and unseated him. The tailor was nevertheless in at the death before almost all the gentleman followers of the hunt. Discovering that lower-class hunt followers beat the riders on the fine hunters was as frequent a source of satisfaction for Kilvert as hearing that foxes or hares got away from their pursuers.[42]

226

In some *Diary* entries can be found a contrast between the pride and self-importance of sportsmen and the reality of their sports, which they cloaked in all sorts of romantic, mystical nonsense, some evidence of which was given earlier in this chapter. Freeman drew attention to the way in which sportsmen sought to disguise the true nature of their activities. Pretending that they were serious about destroying vermin was one of the disguises of fox-hunting, another was exalting it as a source of healthy fresh air and exercise. Some devotees made much of the smart hunting clothes, the well-bred hunters, and the huntsmen's skills. Lord De Broke not only regarded fox-hunting as the sport most expressive of the honour of a gentleman, but even attributed a sense of honour to the fox. He was particularly taken with these words that were used of Peter Beckford, the famous Dorsetshire squire and huntsman: 'Never had a fox or a hare the honour of being hunted by so accomplished a huntsman'.[43] Kilvert encountered another of De Broke's stamp who cherished a similar notion. Again, Kilvert was the guest of a country house, 'the hospitable Manor House of Great Durnford, the seat of Mr John Pinckney', in south Wiltshire. Another guest was Major Fisher, 'the Champion Archer of England'. As suited a champion archer, the Major had a purely medieval view of field sports. On this occasion, however, nature's creatures were not co-operating with the Major in his efforts to display his medieval skills. As Kilvert drily remarked: 'Major Fisher was not shooting like the Champion Archer of England and kept on dropping his arrows into the green'. The reason for his poor aim seems to have been that he was angry with the wood pigeons, which were diverting his falcons from their game. The Major assured Kilvert that 'a falcon is a true gentleman... He never eats a bird alive, but always breaks his neck first'.[44]

Kilvert was obviously not impressed by this proof of the falcon's 'honour' nor by the efforts commonly made by sportsmen to present the deaths of hunted animals in a favourable light. He was haunted by the story of a deer which had been pursued all night by hounds and men armed with rifles. The creature had finally taken refuge in a stable. 'Mrs Jenkins said she went into the stable... and saw by the hoof marks and the mud which the deer had brought in with it that the poor hunted creature in its frantic terror and attempts to escape and hide itself had climbed up into the manger and tried to scramble into the rack'.[45]

To Kilvert it was a matter of shame that suffering of this kind should have a place in what Freeman had sarcastically called 'the manly and gallant sports of high-minded... English gentlemen'. Trollope, in the article he had written to counter Freeman's, had tried to convict objectors to field sports of squeamishness. He said that non-sporting men were like old ladies who had no idea what was involved in fox-hunting and imagined huntsmen up to their elbows in blood. Since, according to divine law, all animals hunted and were hunted, life inevitably involved pain and death, and objections to fox-hunting were a brand of 'mawkish sentimentality', unworthy of real men. (It was Sydney Smith who had quipped that there were three sexes: men, women, and curates). In spite of Trollope's reference to divine law, the case he made out on behalf of fox-hunting was an extremely weak one, chiefly because it lacked any true religious or moral dimension. Also missing was an imaginative apprehension of the suffering involved, which was an important part of Kilvert's antipathy. The manliness Trollope advocated was a matter largely of physicality. The sport fostered, he said, the manly qualities of 'ambition, courage, and persistency', and promoted a spirit of community. The suffering of the fox was necessary, he assured readers, so that a 'large number of men may enjoy a sport which is thought by them to be salutary, noble, and beneficial'. It was important for Trollope to be found in the majority of manly men; it was relatively unimportant for Kilvert. Trollope had known what it was to be the fox. He was marked for life by his desperately unhappy existence at Harrow and Winchester where he was ostracised and bullied because of his family's poverty. In his *Autobiography*, he recorded his 'strong wish to be popular' with his fellow pupils, and in his novels there is a reiterated theme of social isolation.

Kilvert's father had experienced that isolation at Oriel. Kilvert himself had never been to a public school, and Oxford in the early 1860s was a much more civilised place than it had been in the 1820s. Nevertheless, his situation in Clyro in the years 1865-1872 was a very difficult one. There was, as has been shown, a tension between himself and Venables, his host and patron, and he registered his deep unease with the life he encountered in the English country house. When he castigated that life for its 'unnatural' quality, the 'manliness' of its men must have formed a significant part of his general case. When he experienced this full exposure to country house society and its dominant masculine ethos, it was at a particularly critical time of his life. He was just 24 years old when he accepted the Clyro curacy and until that point the only substantial male company he had known was the student body of Oxford. The small numbers of pupils who attended the Harnish and Claverton Down schools can hardly have appeared threatening because they were encountered in family settings where he would be conscious of having a secure place. Out walking with his brother Edward and Morrell, one of his Clyro friends, he recorded feeling an outsider because he had not been to a public school: 'Morrell and Perch got up on the subject of Marlborough ... and I came on alone'.[46] Since Oxford, he had served as curate to his father, a position which had not yielded contact with gentry society on anything like the scale that was his in Clyro. For his entrée into that society, especially into its higher reaches, he had Venables to thank, another complicating factor in his situation. He had no professional role vis-a-vis these gentry families: he did not read the Bible in their households as he did in those of his humbler parishioners, nor did he act as their spiritual advisor, a role filled, as we have seen, by Venables.

There was, on the evidence of the *Diary*, no common interest in literature between the gentry men and Kilvert, and Morrell was the only one who joined him in his country walks. Kilvert took no part in the tasks of local administration that would have provided him with a shared experience. Nor did he have any interest in politics. So that only left sport, which was both the major activity of the local gentlemen and, in a real sense, one of the principal premises on which country house society was based. In the 18th century, the poet Shenstone had said that '...the world may be divided into people that read, people that write, people that think, and fox hunters'. Sportsmen's manners had improved since then and it was possible in 1888 to claim that, while country gentlemen had retained the 'more simple and masculine habits' of their forefathers, they also exhibited equal development of 'physical and intellectual faculties'.[47] The evidence we have suggests that the balance among Clyro gentlemen was decidedly in favour of the simple masculine habits.

Kilvert's participation in sports was limited to croquet and archery. The presence of Major Fisher at the south Wiltshire archery meeting demonstrated that some men did go in for the sport, but it was associated mainly with women in Kilvert's day because they were not expected to indulge in sports any more vigorous than it and croquet. Tennis, which Kilvert did occasionally play (though he objected that it was far too violent to be a summer game) was just beginning to make an impact in the 1870s and women were participating in it a decade later. It was in 1870, when his mind was particularly exercised by the problem of field sports, that Kilvert recorded he was considering taking up archery because friends were urging that it was 'prettier and more pleasant than croquet'.[48] His comment indicates the gap that existed between his attitude to sport and that of the gentlemen of Clyro. To be unable to participate in their more manly sports was a serious matter for Kilvert as far as country house society was concerned; it came near to nullifying him socially. In psychological terms, it meant that as a young man he had nothing to express, no valid experience to contribute to the common pool. The experience he did have—of visiting the poor, teaching in the village school—would have appeared contemptible to the aggressive sporting males, many of whom were also military men, of Clyro Court, Llanthomas, and Maesllwch Castle. To those of other country houses it would have seemed at best insignificant. Kilvert was a great walker to whom 25 miles in a day over relatively rough terrain was nothing and his stamina attracted comment and perhaps qualified him as 'manly' to a degree.

It seems very likely that Kilvert would have been included with the unsporting men, known, according to Lady Warwick, as 'darlings', men of 'witty and amusing conversation [who] were always asked as extras everywhere to help to entertain the women'.[49] This information helps us to see him more clearly in the country house milieu, to which the patronage of the Venables gave him access. It is doubtful whether Kilvert had either the confidence or the personality to be significantly witty or amusing. His awareness that he preferred solitude to 'gaiety and noise' has been noted in chapter 2. We do not hear of him telling jokes or funny stories and he was not in the habit of singing songs in company as many men did. On one occasion when he was in Clyro he surprised himself by singing at a choir supper. 'To my great astonishment I sang three songs, "The Vicar of Bray", "When Good King Arthur", and "The Blue Bells of Scotland"'.[50] He seemed to distance himself from those men who relished being noisy and hearty. While holidaying in Cornwall with the Hockins, Kilvert went on an excursion in a waggonette driven by an Edward Noy. 'Capt. Parker was the life and soul of the party and kept the waggonette in a roar.... Presently we stopped to have sherry all round. When we were ready to go on Capt. Parker said to Mrs H., "If we wanted a donkey to go on what would you say?" Then he added instantly in a loud voice, "Proceed, Edward". There was a roar from the waggonette, everyone was convulsed...'. It seems clear that Kilvert was not, and that he had some sympathy for the unfortunate waggonette driver who 'looked somewhat red and foolish'.[51] Ill at ease himself, he was sensitive about the feelings of others who became the butt of the company as a result of the 'manly' behaviour of a Capt. Parker. He himself felt foolish on the occasion when he spoke 'most awkwardly' as he proposed the health of a bride and bridegroom, even though it was among people he knew very well.[52] When Mrs. De Winton of Maesllwch Castle 'begged' the Venables to bring Kilvert to her 'great picnic', he was fulfilling the 'darling' role as capably as he could.[53]

Kilvert was quite certain that he had to reject the concept of manliness which was such a force in the lives of women as well as men of country house society. He did have, however, to put in its place, his own concept, in which physicality played an important part, and much of it derived ironically from Charles Kingsley, who was such a firm believer in fox-hunting that he actually recommended it as an occupation for clergymen because it both enabled them to mix with all classes of the rural community and to win their respect. He felt people would pay more attention to sermons if their author showed himself to be a 'manly' man. Nevertheless, his hero Lancelot (in *Yeast*), who is sensitive to natural beauty, feels some shame when he is out fox-hunting, and in spite of his love of it, recognises there is a 'ghastly discord in it' because its noisy, frantic, trivial quality (though not, apparently, its brutality) is at odds with the eternal peace of Nature. Kilvert had the simple faith of Kingsley, whose wife remarked that 'no explanation was so complete as the one which one had learnt at one's mother's knee',[54] which recalls Kilvert's delight in 'the dear old Bible stories', which, he said, he would ensure he told his own children. In *Alton Locke,* the ideal clergyman is pictured as having a deep personal faith and a 'delight in God'. That delight is seen more plainly in both men's relationship to the natural world. Kilvert had derived from Grace Aguilar and from Wordsworth some of his capacity to recognise God in natural forms. Kingsley, too, was convinced that a way into people's hearts that was easily overlooked because of the customary emphasis on the rational/intellectual, was through the senses. 'Never lose an opportunity of seeing anything beautiful', he wrote. 'Beauty is God's handwriting'.[55]

Kilvert's *Diary* is filled with this awareness and it gives rise to such passages as: 'A beautiful sunny afternoon and the cuckoo calling everywhere. Perhaps the cuckoo is the angel of the spring to remind us of the Resurrection'.[56] When Kingsley's pupil, John Martineau, wrote of his master: 'Earth, air, and water, as well as farm-house and cottage, seemed full of his familiar friends... he drank in Nature... he caught and noted every breath, every sound, every sign', he might have been talking of Kilvert. Did Kilvert learn from Kingsley something about the importance of precision in describing natural forms? He wrote about the effort he had made for some time 'to find the right word for the shimmering glancing twinkling movement of the poplar leaves in the wind. This afternoon I saw the word written on the poplar leaves. It was "dazzle". The dazzle of the poplars'.[57] Kingsley's *Yeast* provides a close verbal echo in Lancelot's observation: 'What a delicious shiver is creeping over [the lime trees]'.[58] For Kingsley, the natural world existed for man to admire and understand, which is the impulse lying behind such utterance of Kilvert's as: 'To be alone out of doors on a still soft clear night is to me one of the greatest pleasures that this world can give'.[59]

The contrast of city and country produced a parallel reaction in both men. Kingsley's hero, Alton Locke, expressed his joy at escaping from London and its 'ceaseless roar of the human sea, casting up mire and dirt' into 'the blessed silence' of the country and the 'capability of clear, bright meditation'.[60] After one visit to the capital, Kilvert declared: 'I do loathe London. How delicious to get into the country again, the sweet damp air and the smell of the beanfields'.[61] This refreshment of spirit at its best produced the 'quiet eye and the contented mind' of his Chieflands visit. In *Alton Locke*, the Dean remarks that mountains tell no lies as men do, that 'there is no lie in Nature', and that Nature's laws are 'the only true democrats'.[62] When Kilvert observed that it was difficult for a man alone on a mountain to be either a beast or a fool, he was reaching out for the same understanding.

Kingsley made out a passionate case for the worth of ordinary working men in *Alton Locke*. Their superiors were inclined to lump them all together as 'the swinish multitude', but he knew that they were not 'all by nature dolts and idiots'. Kilvert shared Kingsley's love and admiration for ordinary people but, unlike Kingsley, held back from political involvement. However, though Kingsley backed the Chartist movement for political rights, he always counselled moderation, and encouraged working people to aspire to be better human beings rather than demand radical social changes, as we have seen. His radicalism was basically conservative, stemming from 'a moralised vision of the past and from a reappraisal of existing structures...'.[63] This was the essence of Kilvert's political position. Kingsley tried to establish a clear connection between Christ's teaching and the living, working experience of ordinary men. Kilvert was unhappy, in a way Kingsley would not have been, with Holman Hunt's portrayal of Christ as a working man in his painting, 'The Shadow of Death'; it was both too radical and too secular for Kilvert. However, he did discover heroic, manly qualities in lower-class men he met in his parochial work.

Often his appreciation took the form, as it did for Kingsley, of admiring their robust, physical strength, health, and beauty. 'The finest of us are animals', Kingsley had observed in *Yeast*, and he believed that God too found those qualities attractive and valuable. Wherever Kilvert found them in working people, he commented on them. One *Diary* entry reads: '...met a young man coming down from Craswall where he had been hedging... His face was very handsome... eyes fine and black...'.[64] Another tells of 'a handsome young man... fine open face and dressed as a miller'.[65] He found he warmed naturally to 'a comely wholesome girl... washing at a tub'.[66] On a train, he encountered 'a young handsome intelligent gentlemanly farmer... with a ruddy face, light brown hair, merry blue eyes...'.[67] Strong, healthy farm labourers were the exception rather than the rule, which is probably the reason for Kilvert's commenting on them. (Cf. picture of John Brinkworth, who was more typical). It was to be expected that a man who urged the moral value of 'honest work' should comment on examples of it whenever he met with them. He noted Clyro's 'industrious blacksmith [who] chinks away at his forge night and morning ...'.[68] On those rare occasions when gentlemen did physical work, Kilvert found it equally satisfying. Once at Llanthomas, he found Henry Thomas chopping up the branches of a fallen apple tree 'in his shirt sleeves ... quite in a workmanlike way'.[69]

Herriman, the Langley Burrell railway porter, exemplifies the moral manliness that Kilvert perceived in working men. He once saw Herriman coming home from his night shift at the station: 'I could not help thinking of the difference between my lot and his... How differently we both spent last night, but how much better he spent it than I did. He was doing extra night duty that a fellow porter might enjoy a holiday... Herriman has only three days' holiday during the whole year, while to me every day is a holiday...'.[70] Utilising one's gifts and one's natural affections towards the service of others in this way was a salient feature of Kingsley's piety and of his Christian manliness. He had set the example in his Hampshire parish of Eversley, where he worked ceaselessly for the poor. It was the example Kilvert, too, admired in the Rev. Moule, and he made his own effort, especially in Clyro, to emulate it.

The ideal means of demonstrating physical strength, healthiness, enjoyment of nature, and manliness, was, for Kingsley, fox-hunting. These qualities come together in the character of Col. Bracebridge in *Yeast*. He is immensely superior to the naive, youthful Lancelot, the novel's hero, though the latter is 'immeasurably beyond Bracebridge in intellect and heart'.[71] Lancelot is at first contemptuous of Bracebridge because he wastes so much time on fox-hunting, but he defends the sports against the attacks made on it by his curate cousin. He claims it developed 'freedom, activity, foresight, daring, independent self-determination', and links, in a characteristically Kingsley way, the physical with the moral: 'the cleverest and noblest fellows are sure to be the best riders in the long run'. And he claims that men like his cousin 'make piety a synonym for unmanliness'.[72]

The curate of Clyro, though quite unlike the ascetic, unworldly curate of *Yeast*, was unable to agree with Kingsley that the hunting field was the training ground of manliness. The battlefield was a different matter; for soldiers, especially veterans, his admiration was unbounded. Morgan, the old soldier of Clyro, is the subject of many entries which pay tribute to his bravery and hardihood in the Peninsular War. 'I found the old veteran sunning himself in the garden', Kilvert wrote on one occasion. 'He crawled in by dint of crutches very slowly...'.[73] Sometimes Kilvert was pleased to help the old man as he attempted to do his gardening on crutches. Among Kilvert's Langley Burrell parishioners were two soldiers who won his admiration. He described Frank Vincent, son of the village policeman, as a 'fine handsome fellow' and in another passage makes clear the connection between his attractive looks and his moral worth: 'He is a noble young soldier and singularly attractive and lovable'.[73] Then there was John Gough, a veteran of 21 years' service, whose breathing gave him continual pain, and whose stories of privations and horrors, especially from the Crimean War, won Kilvert's respect. The war provoked fierce patriotism and was very popular with all classes and the Kilvert family were no exception. Kilvert's sister Emily recalled that it was the first war she remembered anything about, partly because after so many years of peace 'it made all the greater impression upon my young mind'. The impression made on her brother's mind would have been greater because he was 13 when the war began in March 1854, whereas she was only 11. Mrs. Kilvert collected warm clothing for soldiers such as Gough. 'No one but themselves who went through it', Gough said, 'will ever know what our soldiers endured in the winter of 1854-1855. No firewood but what they cut down or the roots grubbed up under the fire of the enemy's guns... When they came in from the trenches or night fatigue duty, no fire, no straw to lie down on, only a blanket and greatcoat and the mud ankle-deep'.[75] Much of the suffering was due to the 'shameful mismanagement' of the aristocratic high command, as Kilvert underlined here and in other entries. The general attack on the aristocracy that followed the war contributed to the distrust he felt towards the nation's élite.

Kilvert gave his full backing to the Volunteer Rifle Movement in which worthy members of the lower-classes could find the opportunity to express their manliness through military skills under the control of caring officers. The Hay Rifle Volunteers were formed in spring 1860, and the *Hereford Times* noted that since the equally new Hay Cricket Club was largely composed of Volunteers, 'who are all men of great strength and activity', there was a reasonable certainty of their having a first-rate team.[76] Kilvert was congratulated by Venables' groom on the 'lovely sermon' he had preached to this manly group of part-time soldiers in April 1871. He also made a habit of attending their band concerts, as did others of the local gentry and he even went up to Rhayader to see that town's Volunteers drilling. It is not hard to see why he should give such enthusiastic support to the Movement. It was founded when he was an impressionable young under-graduate at Oxford with the patriotic aim of establishing a body of trained citizens which could resist a French invasion, at the time a distinct threat.[77] A further aim was to channel working-class energy into disciplined constructive activity and thereby divert it from subversion. Lord Monson saw it as a means of resisting 'red republicanism'.[78] Carlyle praised it because it brought working-class men under discipline, which did them more good than Christian Socialist lectures or art classes.[79] Recruits to the Movement were, in fact, generally from the middle-class, while its officers were upper middleclass—professional or business men—and not the more aristocratic types who commanded county yeomanry units.[80] In the countryside especially the existence of a force made up of 'reliable' men under gentry officers was a source of comfort and security. All of this helps to explain Kilvert's involvement with the Movement. His support would be further consolidated by the knowledge that Kingsley too was a supporter.[81]

For Kilvert the supreme focus of the values of patriotism and stability was the Prince of Wales. He was one of many who loved the Prince because he seemed to be the incarnation of 'that simple and kindly jollity which was one of [the nation's] most lovable characteristics'.[82] Lord Redesdale denied that the heir to the throne was a mere playboy and argued that his strict royal upbringing had cut him off from many normal pleasures, including the stirring adventure stories of Sir Walter Scott, but Redesdale still found him manly enough. He also praised his deep love of England.[83] While one aspect of the Prince's appeal to the nation was his intense patriotism, another was that reverence for family which was also a strong element in Kilvert's adulation. The biographers of A.P. Stanley recorded the impact made on the country by the Prince's illness of 1871-2. 'On the issue of that battle with death the whole nation hung with expectation ... gathered round one hearth with a renewed sense of the nobility and sanctity of family affection'. Stanley was a personal friend of the Prince and his concern was all the deeper as a result, but also because of his sense of 'the beneficent influence that the heir to a noble inheritance might exercise over the community'.[84] It is evident that Kilvert's reaction contained these elements. His fear that 'a noble inheritance' might be severed was the reverse image of the joy he experienced at the birth of Venables' son and heir, which signified that an inheritance was secured. The royal home stood as the supreme example of domestic affections.

Kilvert's soldier friend, Gough, had volunteered, immediately after the Crimea, to go to India and he gave Kilvert an account in January 1873 of the ghastly atrocities inflicted by the mutineers on the British. They showed no mercy and deserved none, in Gough's view. Kilvert, too, was moved to horror and indignation in which Christian mercy had no part: the mutineers had confirmed that they were savages whose conduct revealed the extent to which they stood in need of white man's civilisation and white man's religion.[85] Later that year, Kilvert attended the Church Congress in Bath and heard one of the leading colonial administrators, Sir Bartle Frere, give a paper on the form that missionary work should take in the Empire. Kilvert had been brought up to believe in the importance of spreading God's word to what he called 'heathen' peoples and had regularly heard at home accounts of missionary work. He made sure, when he was master of Bredwardine parish, that missionary work was supported with regular meetings and went himself to hear lectures by workers in the field.[86] Frere's life and work had touched the Kilvert family at several points before this. The Freres lived in Bath at Widcombe Cottage and so were neighbours of the Kilverts and Bartle had attended King Edward VI School from 1827 to 1832. He proceeded to Haileybury, the East India Company college, and afterwards to India. Some interests there argued for and some against the spread of Christianity. The East India Company opposed it and the British government thought the wisest course was to avoid interference with Indian institutions. Things began to change, however, at the beginning of the 19th century, when Evangelical influence was very strong, and pressure grew, from such leading Evangelical figures as Wilberforce, to send missionaries. He thought that their exclusion from India was 'by far the greatest of our national sins'.[87] This approach gained strength during Frere's time in India and there was an increasing effort to anglicise the country and to introduce social reforms. Those who advocated them, such as Lord Dalhousie whose view forms part of the preface to this chapter, saw a parallel between the spiritual transformation of the individual through grace and the transformation of an entire nation through civilisation. Evangelical missionaries carried with them not only the Christian religion, but a firm belief in the superiority of the culture based on it and in the duty of bringing both to India.

Frere had initially believed that government education and missionary work should be kept separate;[86] he had come round to a different view by the time Kilvert heard him. He told his audience that Church Missionary Societies had habitually sent only clergymen to parts of the Empire to preach religion and had urged them to avoid interference with the 'temporal affairs of converts'. He, however, was advocating that in the more 'uncivilised' parts of the Empire 'instruction in the rudimentary arts of civilised life should be part of the ordinary... system of missionary work'. What he had in mind was a body of doctors, nurses, agricultural experts, teachers, and printers to accompany missionaries. They would encourage the development of a 'civil society', which every native could join, 'on his renouncing the errors of his own religion'.[89] Kilvert recorded in his *Diary* that he thought Frere spoke 'admirably'. Frere had expressed similar unbounded confidence in Christianity in an earlier lecture. On that occasion he stated it was a religion 'perfectly adapted' to most races, from the lowest to the highest in terms of stage of civilisation reached. It was, he said, the central element of the civilisation Britain had brought to India, and it had brought 'a civilising and humanising influence tending to make the believer in Christianity a better man and a better subject'.[90]

Kilvert had assimilated this Evangelical attitude to Empire since childhood. It was, in fact, one of the major causes of the Indian Mutiny since Indians resented the contempt shown for their institutions, habits, and feelings, and feared that it was the ultimate goal of the British to impose Christianity.[91] Kilvert was imbued with the vindictiveness and aggressiveness that came to characterise British post-Mutiny policy, which was based on military repression and racial conquest. Contact first with Church Missionary Societies and then the marriage of his sister Emily to Lt. Col. Wyndowe, a surgeon in the Indian Army, made India a permanent element in his consciousness, and Indians to him were subject peoples so that when they resisted British rule as they did in 1857, they were 'rebels'. For him, the men who undertook the civilising mission envisaged by Frere and others were doubly heroes because their manliness had a moral dimension, as well as a physical one. India and Africa, like the Crimea, became natural arenas for highlighting heroic examples of Christian manliness.

The appeal of Empire for Kilvert, as for many Victorians of his time, lay partly in its religiosity and partly in its stern sense of duty and mission. It was a humanitarian impulse as well as an image of glory, self-sacrifice and courage. While he was himself a humble and unassuming man, he responded to the notion that the British were called on to raise the cultural level of native peoples just as clergymen of his class had the task of showing the rural poor how to live a better life. Certain imperial leaders were heroes to him because they were Christians who remained loyal to their divine mission amid all the privations and dangers of life in India or Africa. The essential rightness of the Empire was demonstrated by the fact that so many of its leaders were imbued with a missionary purpose. As Morris succinctly put it: 'Anglicanism was generally accepted as the outward form of [Empire's] inner grace'.[92] Dr. Livingstone had a profound appeal for Kilvert as he had for most mid-Victorians. He included the funeral of Dr. Livingstone among his topics for evening lectures during the winter of 1874 and took a party of Langley Burrell children to an illustrated lecture of the great explorer's travels in December of that year.

The precise way in which such a gentle creature as Kilvert was able to accept the aggressiveness, cruelty, and injustice of Empire is perfectly demonstrated by his approval of the actions of Sir Garnet Wolseley in the West African kingdom of Ashanti.[93] Kilvert recorded his exploits in this *Diary* entry: 'Today the paper brought us good news from Cape Coast Castle. Sir Garnet Wolseley was within a march of Coomassie. The King of Ashantee has sent in his submission and agreed to pay the £200,000 demanded by Sir Garnet'.[94] The Ashanti war was a representative example of what Empire had come to mean by this time; Kilvert accepted it wholeheartedly. To Wolseley the expedition was a divine mission and he and his officers were convinced of its rightness. They believed that the Ashanti people in their arrogant, superstitious faith in their own power, thought that they could resist the steady expansion of the British Empire. The natives had besieged the British base of Cape Coast Castle and had to be taught a sharp lesson. Wolseley stated that he was determined to inflict 'such a heavy punishment upon King Koffee, to show him [and] his people that no extent of deadly forest could protect them from the British Army'.[95] An ultimatum was issued to the Ashanti king, demanding submission and an absurdly high figure for compensation.

Kilvert's *Diary* entry appears to have been made after news had come through of the decisive battle of Ejinasi when the native army was destroyed by the artillery, Gatling guns, and superior rifle power of 4,000 regular British troops. Kilvert rejoiced with the rest of the public at what was portrayed as the triumph of order, authority, and civilisation over ignorance and savagery. The expedition's punitive aspect appealed to the authoritarian side of his nature, as did the fact that Wolseley represented the traditional aristocratic leadership to which he generally gave his support. Kilvert was far less blood-thirsty than most Britishers who believed in the empire's inestimable benefit to what Sir Bartle Frere had called, in the talk Kilvert had heard him give in Bath, 'uncivilised populations'. If Kilvert had witnessed the slaughter of the Ashanti or of Indians after the Mutiny, his faith in the Empire's divine mission might have been severely undermined. But to him, as to most Victorians, the locations of colonial wars were remote and colonial peoples could be too easily stereotyped as 'niggers' or 'savages'. He could, therefore, remain a warm-hearted clergyman with deep prejudices, a love of military show, and an admiration of military figures who displayed dash and courage.

A particularly striking example of this type was John Hanning Speke, the African explorer who was very probably another of Kilvert's physical/moral heroes, and when he died in tragic circumstances in 1864 when Kilvert was just a young man, the effect on him must have been considerable. The Speke family receives only one mention in his *Diary* but the entry reveals that he knew a good deal about it. Speke the explorer would probably have first crossed Kilvert's horizon during the latter's time at Wadham. His articles about his second African trip in the company of Richard Burton were published in *Blackwood's Magazine* in autumn 1859 and summer 1860 and caused something of a stir, chiefly because of Speke's claim that he had discovered the source of the Nile. Part of Kilvert's interest in him would turn on the fact that he was a local celebrity and of a landowning family. This son of the soil would have been a heroic figure to Kilvert not only because he had been a soldier in India and in the Crimea, but because of the implications of his discovery of the source of the Nile for Christianity and for Empire. He had 'an urgent desire to expose the natives of Central Africa to the Christian faith',[96] which was the motive behind the Missionary Working parties in the years of Kilvert's youth in Harnish.

Both at home in Wiltshire and in Clyro, Kilvert was surrounded by young men whose experience of the authoritarian regimes of public schools, in which subordination and sporting manliness were the prime goals, fitted them perfectly for their role as administrators and soldiers of Empire. All the major gentry families of the *Diary*—the Awdrys, Moneys, Venables, Baskervilles, Thomases, Cornewalls, and De Wintons—had colonial connections. They were also closely linked to upper middle-class families who derived their income from business, but business only superficially connected to the rest of the commercial world. They were old-established merchants, East and West Indian traders, bankers, brewers, and even some manufacturers. In life-style and attitudes they were, however, almost indistinguishable from landowners, and some were landowners as well as businessmen. Examples from the *Diary* are the Cornewall family, which had intermarried with the Amyands, who were merchants and owned a sugar plantation in Grenada, the De Wintons, East India merchants and bankers, Andrew Pope, whose family had for generations been sugar refiners in Bristol, Morrell, whose family was in brewing, and the Penoyre and Oswald families, who had Jamaican business connections.[97] Kilvert blended perfectly easily into this group, which supported, as he did, the landed interest, whereas a large part of the middle-class, especially the commercial and urban sector of it, were hostile. It was natural for landowners to see native peoples of the Empire in the same light as their dependants at home. When Frere talked of Indians becoming, as a result of Christianity, 'more temperate and chaste, more cleanly, more honest, and more industrious', he might have been referring to English agricultural labourers. This, too, was the way Kilvert regarded the rural poor.

When Frere's influence touched Kilvert's life on a further occasion, Kilvert was probably aware of the role he played because the newspapers were full of it, and it suddenly brought home to him and others the reality of events that took place in remote colonial territories. He first heard of a military disaster in South Africa on 11 February 1879, when revisiting Clyro. He had gone from Bredwardine on the 10th, stayed overnight with the Crichtons, dined at the Bevans, and when the news came through was at the Volunteer concert at Hay Drill Hall. Frere at the time was Governor of the Cape and Commissioner for Native Affairs. Lord Carnarvon, the Colonial Secretary, had a plan to unite the South African colonies in a confederation, and had dangled before Frere the carrot of his becoming the first Governor-General of it with a salary of £10,000 a year.

Frere became obsessed with the idea that the Zulus under Cetewayo planned to invade Natal and issued an ultimatum to the Zulu king, which was in effect a declaration of war. To Frere, Cetewayo was 'an ignorant and bloodthirsty despot' and he was determined to 'put an end to Zulu pretensions'.[98] He objected particularly to the Zulu king's practice of killing his subjects unjustly and arbitrarily. Cetewayo asserted that it was his and his people's business, and that his people would not be amenable unless the right to kill them was maintained. Frere was determined that the Zulus capitulated to superior European morality and military power. He ordered the invasion of Zululand with an inadequate British and native force, whose vulnerability was increased by being divided into three columns. Lord Chelmsford, C-in-C of the army, was in charge of one column and left a camp of 1,600 men in his rear at Isandlwana, while he pushed on looking for a Zulu army to defeat. He had nothing but contempt for Zulus' fighting qualities and strategy. The camp should have been protected the way the Boers protected theirs by a tight circle of wagons, and Chelmsford had been advised to do this but gave no orders for it. It had been further weakened by the sending out of a mounted force on patrol and by spreading its defensive line too thinly. A force of 20,000 Zulus had gathered in the surrounding hills and swooped down on the camp, killing most of its inhabitants.

'News came today of the terrible disaster inflicted by the Zulus on the 24th Regiment at Rorke's Drift, S. Africa. Col. Thomas much affected by the news and obliged to leave the concert room', Kilvert wrote in his *Diary*.[99] Though he took an interest in colonial affairs, his interest, like that of most Victorians, was a casual one, as is shown by the fact that he made a mistake over the location of the disaster. Rorke's Drift was in fact the place where a small garrison heroically defended themselves against a much superior Zulu force.[100] Col. Thomas' distress was occasioned by the fact that he had known the officers of the 24th Regiment when they were in Brecon, their depot since 1873.

Inevitably in a situation where almost every gentry family had colonial connections, war brought tragedy, and this was the case with the Zulu War. One of its casualties was Walter Baskerville's cousin, Arthur Baskerville Mynors, and the tribute paid to him shows very clearly the mood of late Victorian imperialism in which Kilvert was caught up. To one of his religious background and romantic nature, the mood had powerful appeal. To many who had ceased to be religious by this period, the poetry and idealism that had formerly found expression in religion, had been channelled into a romantic patriotism, which permeated the attitude even of Matthew Arnold, who was so deeply affected by the death of Arthur Mynors that he wrote an article about him. The young man's letters and diaries had come into his hands. After Eton, Mynors had joined the Oxford Militia, and later became a lieutenant in the 60th Rifles. He went to South Africa in 1878, and having first thought that 'the Zulus or niggers are scarcely human beings', came to the view, once he had seen them fight, that they were 'the bravest fellows I ever saw'. He contracted dysentery and died in April 1879. His nature, said Arnold, was 'fresh, wholesome, gay; an English boy with... a keen love of sport, with a genuine love for the country... full of natural affection... bred in the habits of religion...'.[101]

Kilvert would not have tolerated the criticism made of Frere after the Isandlwana débacle; he would continue to be a hero in spite of newspaper attacks. The *Daily News* said he had 'allied himself with the worst passions and sinister motives of the colonists - their fear and hate of a savage race... their desire for conquest and spoil, [their goal] of annexing their territory...', and it accused him of wrapping up his policy in 'phrases of religion and pretences of superior morality'. The Cabinet wanted to recall him but the Prime Minister and Disraeli supported him with the result that he was simply censured. A terrible revenge was exacted by the British army for Isandlwana, with at least 3,000 Zulus being slaughtered after the battle of Khambula alone. When the war was over, Zulu leaders stated that they never had any intention of invading Natal. After all Zulu resistance was crushed, Zululand was split into many small chiefdoms, with the inevitable consequence of civil war, which erupted as soon as British troops left. The country became 'a large pool of cheap migrant labour'.[102] There was no question of blacks owning land and they were allowed in Boer territories only as labourers and servants.[103] In essence, the Zulu wars were a struggle for land and between the fate of the Zulus and that of English farm labourers there were several close parallels.

The cult of manliness, of which Kingsley's was one version, derived much of its force from the contrasting ideal of womanliness. In the preface to *Yeast*, he referred to the benign influence of a man's 'mother, his sister, the maid whom he may love'. The joy Kilvert felt at being within the circle of his own family has already been underlined. Some of the appeal of Mme. Olympe's home for him derived from his perception that the friends who met there created the sense of warm family relationships that Taine had found to be lacking in many gentry houses. A later chapter provides further evidence of the intensity with which he kept an image of married life before him and sought it in social relations more akin to those of his own home than in those he found in the country house. It was an above average intensity, just as Kingsley's exaltation of the family went well beyond the conventional middle-class valuation.[104] Kingsley taught that the emotional ties of the home and of married love were one of the prime ways by which a man could establish the proper values of life and please his Maker. Marriage was a source of spiritual ennoblement, which resulted from the breaking down of purely selfish concerns and from the development of a sense of responsibility for wife and family. In *Alton Locke* we hear of 'the music of loving voices, the sacred names of child and father, mother...'.

After seven and half years in Clyro, Kilvert was still without a wife and family, and his own home. When he resumed work as his father's curate in September 1872, he became increasingly aware of his need for them. *Diary* entries tend to dwell more and more on his past in Harnish and Langley Burrell, and while contemplation of his beloved home and its close family relations always gave him comfort, it also reminded him of how much time had gone. He was always in danger, therefore, when meeting people from his past of facing the response he encountered in old John Eatwell, one of his Harnish cottager friends, in March 1876: 'I suppose you are married'. Kilvert wasn't and was approaching his 36th birthday. The tone of melancholy in the later *Diary* entries and the succession of minor illnesses they record, bear witness to the strain he felt at being without a partner and without a home.

Kilvert's religious background was one source of his antipathy to blood sports. Concern for their victims was the kind of 'healthy moral feeling approved of by Evangelicals'.[105] To show it, however, incurred the risk of appearing unmanly, though it was more acceptable in a clergyman because it could appear as a natural part of his general spiritual and moral outlook. It was reasonable to expect a clergyman would attach more importance than others to the 'divine virtues of mercy and pity', even in relation to dumb creatures, which, according to Freeman, hearty sportsmen deliberately stifled. When Kilvert said he could never be a sportsman, he meant that he as a clergyman and as a man was incapable of stifling those virtues. Lancelot, in Kingsley's *Yeast*, distinguishes between man and woman by stressing woman's capacity for feeling. Her 'mission', he says, was 'to look at the heart and have mercy', by which he meant she was able to win men away from materialism, immorality, and callousness, and point them towards 'purity and innocence'. This simplistic contrast was an inevitable consequence of the differing Victorian concepts of 'manliness' and 'womanliness', which Kilvert in fact generally accepted. For him the most important part of woman was her tenderness of feeling, as we have seen. However, while he was very much a Victorian, he was also, like Kingsley, a poet, and was unique in the quality of his sensibility. It manifested itself, as Kingsley's did, in the way he treated all classes with a genial courtesy. It showed up mainly in the more feminine side of his nature, which gave rise to the quality for which he is most remembered as a man and a writer. Again, some words applied to Kingsley by Martineau, best sum up its essence: '...for all his man's strength there was a deep vein of woman in him, a nervous sensitiveness, an intensity of sympathy, ...which gave him power to understand and reach the heart'.[106]

Martineau's judgment was based on his knowledge of Kingsley in the middle years of the century when Kilvert himself grew to adulthood, a period of increasing differentiation between the sexes, which resulted largely from the growing commercialism and materialism of society and the worship of power—technological, political, military, colonial. These new gods accentuated reason, seen as a predominantly masculine trait, in opposition to feeling and imagination in which women excelled.[107] These latter qualities were perceived to be characteristic of the 'feminine' side of another writer, Charles Dickens, by mid-century commentators. One of his friends said it was discernible in Dickens' quest for the most apt word in his writing. Quickness and delicacy of perception were seen by another friend as a particularly 'feminine' quality of his. Another commentator noted that Dickens' imaginative faculty generally overcame his reasoning faculty.[108] A later chapter will suggest that Kilvert felt just as defensive about his 'feminine' side, among gentry circles, as Dickens did about his, with the result, in the case of the former, that he turned inward upon himself and upon his *Diary*.

One hundred and fifty years later, it is possible to reject the notion that a woman has greater capacity for feeling than a man, as well as the notion that, even if it were true, it constitutes a weakness. Out walking one day, Kilvert heard the sound of an animal facing death. 'I dread the sound, the terrible cry that animals utter when the sanctuary of life is forcibly violated'.[109] His sensitivity to such moments lay at the bottom of his determination to oppose those sports which multiplied the number of occasions when that sanctuary was unnecessarily violated simply to provide sport for gentlemen. Whenever that happened, it was an evil and, as Freeman wrote, 'evil exists in order that we may grapple with it, pain exists in order that we may relieve it. Every act of charity and kindness that has ever been done to man or beast goes on this principle'. (One of the virtues of John Fry of Chieflands was that 'he was very fond of all his pets and dumb creatures').[110] In the light of this principle, wanton cruelty was a sin, and Freeman and Kilvert were unable to see it any other way. It was a lesson that had been instilled in Kilvert in the nursery and drawing room of harnish Rectory. He also found sinful the way which some men expressed their enjoyment of nature in the wanton killing of natural creatures. On one occasion when he saw Walter Baskerville ride by with a shooting party, he wrote: '"What a fine day it is. Let us go out and kill something". The old reproach against the English'.[111] (In his first *Fortnightly Review* article on field sports, E.A. Freeman had attacked the claim that the passion for 'killing something' was an eternal one in human nature.) Kilvert's response to a fine day was to celebrate its beauty and to thank God for it; sinfulness lay in the unnaturalness that celebrated beauty by killing.

Because of their innocence and vulnerability animals and children occupied a pre-eminent place in Kilvert's moral universe. The case of Indian or African natives was different. Uncivilised they undoubtedly were, but innocent they were not. Their savage behaviour was proof, especially to one with Kilvert's religious upbringing, that they were marked by original sin, and to find charity and kindness in his heart for them would have been to condone their sinfulness. The psychological and emotional complexity of Victorian sensibility in relation to these issues is illustrated by the fact that E.A. Freeman possessed not only Kilvert's deep compassion for suffering animals but also his harsh and aggressive attitude toward subject peoples.[112] The strength of Kilvert's antipathy to field sports was due to the way in which his religious and artistic sensibility came together to reinforce it. Almost all the major moral and literary influences upon him since childhood further strengthened his position. The exception was Kingsley, but he was likely to have been the source of the moral manliness Kilvert endorsed, traces of which can be found in so many facets of his moral outlook that an inability to see eye-to-eye with Kingsley on the subject of fox-hunting was an irrelevance. He could still retain Kingsley as one of his heroes, just as he could the Prince of Wales, who was the sportsman *par excellence*. Kilvert's moral position on field sports was crystallised by the groundswell of opposition to aristocratic values that had been boosted by public disquiet over the management of the Crimean War, and by the political and religious confidence of a middle-class that was in process of 'redefining the qualifications of a gentleman more in terms of conduct than heredity'.[113] The conduct of Frere and Wolseley was acceptable because theirs was a good cause. Being brought up next to landed gentry, being dependent on them for patronage, and being partly descended from squires, left the Kilvert family with a more than average regard for the importance of heredity.

Kilvert's stand against field sports, for all that it was a private one, is the more impressive because it brought him into conflict with this powerful strand in his own background and with the class whom he otherwise accepted as the rightful rulers of the society he loved. His opposition can be seen, therefore, not as a demonstration of 'feminine' weakness, but rather of a moral strength, of which anyone might be proud. The cruelty, suffering, and the self-deceiving notion of 'honour' involved in field sports were deeply offensive to Kilvert, both as an artist and a moralist.

'We owe to the poor of our land a mighty debt. We call them improvident and immoral, and many of them are so: but that improvidence and immorality are the results, in a great measure, of our neglect, and not a little of our example.'

Lord Shaftesbury, quoted in Canon Charles Smyth,
'The Evangelical Discipline', in
Ideals and Beliefs of the Victorians, p.100

'The same vulgar, shallow, aristocratic error runs through all [approaches to charity]. Everyone thinks of relieving, no one of removing, the mischief. The prevailing idea.....is.....to give benefits to an inferior, not to do justice to a fellow man'.

W.R. Greg, *Westminster Review*, June 1845

'What a luxury it is to be hungry and thirsty and to be able to satisfy your hunger and thirst.'

Francis Kilvert, *Diary*, Vol. 3. p.267

'I would have a man do a fair day's work for a fair day's wage... I believe that every man who is willing to toil for his bread is entitled to sufficient to feed, clothe and educate his family, and to lay by something to keep him in his old age, so that he shall not need to work after sixty or sixty-five years of age.'

Robert Applegarth, trade union leader, quoted in A. Briggs,
Victorian People, p.195

'The agricultural worker's position is an anomaly in the nineteenth century; it is a relic of feudalism minus all its advantages.'

Richard Heath, *The Victorian Peasant*, p.72

CHAPTER 8
Kilvert and the Poor

The traditional poverty of the rural poor had always presented a challenge to the Church, however, by the 1830s a change had occurred in its attitude—from an obligation to help through charitable giving to a judgmental stance that assumed almost automatically that poverty was the result of idleness and improvidence.[1] Cobbett witnessed the change and tried unavailingly in his writings to convince the Church that its real enemies were not the poor or those who tried to imbue them with radical ideas, but those in power who used the Church to repress the people.[2]

Kilvert inherited the attitude that was adopted generally in the 1830s, following the economic theories that produced the New Poor Law of 1834, that if idleness and improvidence were eradicated, poverty also would disappear. It was an attitude that dominated manuals on pastoral care between 1830-1870.[3] The New Poor Law (NPL) emerged out of a conviction that the existing system of poor relief was inefficient and wasteful. A good flavour of the period appears in this passage written in 1828 by a clergyman, keen to recommend an efficient workhouse: '...before we can enforce discipline, so as to control the vicious and refractory, we must provide a place of refuge as well as restraint'. The workhouse was to be subdivided into wards 'according to the conduct and character of the pauper'. Kindness was to be shown to 'the infirm, the aged and the guiltless', while 'wholesome restraint' was to be imposed on 'the idle, profligate and refractory'. The chief objective was to keep paupers out of the workhouse and the means was the steady shaming of them, and the exalting of 'that independence ... earned by ... honest industry'.[4] The NPL enunciated the view, which would persist throughout the century, that if the labourer would work harder and live decently, he would be rewarded with higher wages and more secure employment. Relief was to be available in the workhouse on the basis of the 'less eligibility' test, whereby its conditions were to be markedly grimmer, and therefore 'less eligible', than those obtaining outside. The food inside might be better in quantity or quality than that normally enjoyed by labourers, but the monotony of the diet, the strict workhouse discipline, the shame, and the breaking up of the family, were designed to supply the necessary moral corrective.[5] Although the workhouse test existed to deter the able-bodied, it was not they who were most found there, but the physically and mentally sick, the aged and the orphan.[6] The harsh conditions designed to shock the idle into industrious independence were, however, applied to these last three categories, which was regarded as unfortunate but necessary if the workhouse was to be a deterrent.

Central to workhouse philosophy was the notion of the deserving and the undeserving poor. It was assumed that it was easy to differentiate between the industrious and the idle, those who made a moral effort and those who did not. Thus it emphasised character and conduct and played down social conditions. If a man wanted to work and remain in work, he could be independent and happy; the fact that for virtually all labourers in England's southern counties wages were insufficient was irrelevant. The *Diary* entry that deals with the case of Henry Estcourt Ferris gives the clearest indication of the extent to which Kilvert had absorbed this view. Kilvert met him one night walking the Wiltshire lanes. He was an 18 year-old, had walked a long way and was weary and dispirited. Kilvert let him tell his own story: 'My father is a labouring man working in Wales... He ran away from my Mother and forsook her six months before I was born'. Kilvert's response in his *Diary* was judgmental. 'Alas, the old, old story. Trust misplaced, promises broken, temptation, sin and sorrow, and the sins of the parents visited on the children'.[7] Ferris himself was guiltless but inevitably he had to suffer for his parents' sin. The whole episode might have come from a Victorian book of moral tales or from a novel by Grace Aguilar. In Kilvert's treatment of Ferris, however, it was kindness that predominated. He showed sympathy for the young man's plight and for his tears, walked with him a good way, and tried to obtain a night's lodging for him. As he left him, however, he could not refrain from giving him some 'good advice'.

Kilvert brought a judgmental rather than a sympathetic stance to a case he encountered in Clyro. In May 1870, he was so scandalised by the cohabitation that existed in a cottage let by James Allen, a young farmer, to the labourer, Edward Morgan, at Cwmpelved Green, that he asked an older and particularly well-to-do farmer, William Wall, to put pressure on Allen to eject his 'immoral tenants'.[8] Kilvert was very friendly with Wall whose respectability and wealth enabled him to provide separate bedrooms, with an interconnecting door that could be locked, for the male and female servants in his new farm-house.[9] In less wealthy farmhouses, and of course in most labourers' cottages, the inhabitants lived in much more cramped conditions. Like many clergymen of the period, Kilvert was over-ready to detect cohabitation and bastard children everywhere rather than to speak out against the appalling living conditions which made immorality almost inevitable: '...one great source of demoralisation ... arose from the overcrowded dwellings of the poor. In too many instances the common decencies of life were disregarded...'.[10] When, a few months later, Edward Morgan was accused before Clyro magistrates, one of whom was presumably Venables, of being the father of Emily Evans' bastard son, Kilvert was pleased to see the claim fail. Mrs. Evans had been, in his view, 'shameless enough to let the young man sit up at night with Emily after she and her husband had gone to bed. Mrs. Venables most properly reprimanded her publicly and turned her out of the Club'.[11] Kilvert knew that Morgan was already living with a woman whom Kilvert called his 'concubine' when Emily Evans was in a late stage of her pregnancy and perhaps that encouraged him to believe that he was not guilty of seducing Emily as well. What secured Kilvert's approval, however, was the fact that Morgan married his 'concubine' in Clyro church (before Kilvert it seems). The labourer had not only done the decent thing, had not fathered any illegitimate children, but his bride was, Kilvert was pleased to note, 'rather nice looking and seemed quiet and modest'.[12] The achievement of total respectability was confirmed two weeks later when Kilvert visited Morgan's home, which Kilvert had always assumed was 'comfortless and miserable', and found it to be 'exquisitely clean and neat, with a bright blue cheerful paper and almost prettily furnished... I could have eaten my dinner off every stone of the floor'.[13]

Kilvert's morality induced him to see in the cases of Henry Ferris and of Emily Evans and Edward Morgan the 'old story' of sin and shame. Another clergyman, the Rev. James Fraser, was a moralist with a different outlook: '...the most malign aspect of poverty is its power to generate the loss of natural affection. Poverty is emphatically hardening - at any rate, in its influence on the natural man'.[14] Warmth of affection was what Kilvert valued most in people, hardening of the heart the condition he most dreaded in others and especially in himself. The former, he believed, was to be found pre-eminently in families. In the privacy of his *Diary*, he praised Venables when he showed it and criticised him when he did not. Edward Morgan's situation was an unusual and a fortunate one: his affection and that of his 'concubine' had triumphed over poverty. If he *had* sought solace with Emily Evans because his cottage was 'comfortless and miserable', it was only what might have been expected. Most labourers and their wives found it impossible to create the loving home that was so important to Kilvert. The handsome and healthy labourers he admired were as much the exception as were those who achieved happy cottage homes.

The pastoral care exercised by Kilvert in his various parishes repeated the pattern evident in these cases, which was one advocated by the Archbishop of Canterbury in 1844: the preaching of the gospel and the relief of distress. Matthew Chapter 25 and Deuteronomy 11.15 formed the basis of the programme enjoined upon clergy at this time. The latter accepted the situation that 'the poor shall never cease throughout the land' and the former urged the remedy, which was that the hungry be fed, the naked clothed, the sick visited. No change in the poor's condition was, therefore, envisaged; the clergyman's visits were designed, among other things, to reconcile them to their lot. The only reform in which the clergy were generally interested was that of the individual soul. It was not Evangelical clergy alone who urged quiescence on the poor and the virtue of independence won through honest labour. The misery of poverty was widely seen as the means of developing the patience that led to salvation, which compensated for the ills of this world. These doctrines encouraged an indifference to social abuses[15] which was attributable, even among humane clergymen such as Kilvert, to two main factors: their loyalty to the upper-classes and the recognition that reform movements were often atheistical in tone. Kilvert's approach to charity had much in common with that of his mentor, Wordsworth. To both men, it was one of the 'primal duties'

(Wordsworth's phrase—the passage is quoted in full in chapter 2) of clergymen. In Wordsworth's poems Kilvert could find clearly set out the qualities of the pastor. Though he was 'meek and patient' and had 'gentleness in his heart', he also rebuked sternly the waywardness of his flock.[16] He knelt beside the afflicted and enabled the 'true penitent' to find God's pardon.[17]

The social conscience of Kilvert expressed itself through charitable work of various kinds. While a curate in Clyro, he visited the Hay workhouse on a regular basis. His visit on Good Friday 1870 found him in sole charge because the master was on holiday. 'I had the poor people to myself', he observed, 'and went through the events of the day with them', which couldn't have been a rich experience either for them or him. That in no way denies the essential kindness of his actions, which emerges in the way he referred to these unfortunate members of his flock as 'my own dear lambs'.[18] One of his motives was plainly religious, recognising the Christian duty of spreading the gospel to the poor, and ministering to their spiritual and physical needs. He also understood that the man who extended kindness received a spiritual benefit himself, as was instilled into him as a child in the example of Emma Hamilton in Aguilar's *Home Influence*. She was brought up to believe that whenever she was kind and good to the poor, God was pleased with her.[19] A similar point is clearly put in his poem 'We Wear Our Rue With A Difference':

> Let it be mine to seek relief
> In comforting another's moan,
> To wear the rue for others' grief
> As well as for mine own.

He was in the habit of using the word 'lamb' with its conventional overtone of Christ as the 'lamb of God', to convey the tenderness and gratitude he felt particularly towards anyone of the lower-classes who enabled him to feel he was walking in the footsteps of his Master. He once saw a little, barefoot girl in a Bristol street who fulfilled for him precisely that function. She had a roguish, eager face, which looked at him with 'a beseeching smile'. Kilvert being Kilvert, her attraction lay also in her bare 'shapely limbs' and her 'beautiful eyes'. But it was what looked at him through those eyes that had special significance: 'Christ seemed to be looking at me through [her] beautiful wistful imploring eyes... Poor lamb.'[20] She had helped to sustain his capacity to feel, to reassure him he had the compassionate heart of the good man and the true Christian. Another of his younger 'lambs' was Esther Hyde, who lived in a cottage near Bredwardine. She had none of the sensuousness of the Bristol waif. When he visited her in April 1878 she was pale and ill, but he valued her spiritual gift to him: 'Poor little girl, my faithful companion and loving fellow pilgrim on many a dark winter's night walk to Crafta Webb...'.[21] Again, Kilvert felt a better person because he could love her, just as he felt the Bristol child had enabled him to be more worthy of Christ. In these poor children and in the adult poor, whom he also viewed as children, he was able to find some compensation for the real children he lacked.

The full extent of his Christian compassion can be seen clearly in relation to the death of poor children and especially in the case of 'Little Davie', the young son of a shepherd of Bredwardine. His death, on Christmas Eve in a time of bitterly cold, snowy weather, deeply affected Kilvert, and he identified himself wholly with the family's sorrow. 'I never saw death look so beautiful before', he wrote. 'The pretty innocent child face looked as peaceful and natural as if the child were asleep ... the poor mother knelt with me by the little bedside while I prayed for them all'. He seemed particularly sorry for Davie's father who was 'crying bitterly for the loss of his little lamb'.[22] Kilvert was expressing a sincere belief when he wrote in his poem 'In loving Remembrance of Little Davie' that 'safe forever Davie rests in that Better Land, for now no one can pluck the child from out his Father's hand'. Davie had come home. Knowing Davie, and experiencing his death and his family's sorrow, had enriched Kilvert.

It was, therefore, the case that he felt that in his charitable work it was his own character as a giver that was experiencing benefit. Belief in the importance of improving one's character was strong in Victorian times and it represents a marked difference between the Victorian and the modern mind. Kilvert was a member of a Mutual Improvement Society and took it seriously. One of its members was his lover Katharine Heanley and the 'questions and answers' she produced for him he valued greatly. 'Her sweet pure thoughts came to me at a time when I sorely needed them', he wrote.[23] Some moral benefit was thought by Victorians to be desirable in both the donor and the recipient of charity, and for some donors this meant a rejection of paternalism. In the relationship between rich and poor fostered by paternalism, the poor were generally unable to give anything of themselves except their deference. Paternalists consistently claimed a high degree of reciprocity was involved and exalted the relationship because it belonged to a pre-industrial and allegedly kindlier age and was an 'antidote' to socialism.[24] It gave Kilvert, for example, pleasure to reflect that Draycot House, home of the Long family, 'was always very hospitable in the olden time. The poor used to come away... loaded with bread and broken meat'.[25]

The pattern of Kilvert's visits to the homes of his Clyro flock is an interesting one. The 1871 Census shows that there was a total of 178 households. In 68 there were labourers' families, of whom Kilvert visited only 20; ten housed old men, some no longer working; five were decidedly 'respectable' (one was married to Venables' cook, one was his gardener, another boasted to Kilvert that he had never been drunk, and a fourth, though listed as a labourer, was referred to by Kilvert as a 'little clerk', the fifth was Morrell's gamekeeper). Kilvert had contact with only two labourers under 50 years of age. Most of his visits were during the working week, which meant that he dealt mainly with women and children. This was as inevitable as it was that he would target women as objects of charity because they were the housekeepers. Of 12 labourers' widows, he visited eight. It was women, especially older ones (as well as older men), who were the targets of Bible readings. It seems likely that he did not choose to visit 48 of the labourers' families because he was uncertain of his reception. He may have deemed some of them insufficiently respectable; nearly one third of them were under 35 and less likely to show deference or the gratitude, often expressed by older men, that times were not as hard as they used to be. Kilvert certainly visited fewer labourers than farmers or tradesmen: only 29% of labourers received visits, as compared with 50% in the last two groups. Kilvert did not read the Bible to farmers and tradesmen. (It is of some relevance to note that the only reference in the *Diary* to a parochial visit made by Kilvert's father concerns the Grimshaw family who owned a farm at Langley Burrell).

'Cottage lectures' were also occasions for Bible readings to the poor. We don't hear of these in Clyro; perhaps Venables disapproved or perhaps Kilvert decided to institute them at Bredwardine where he was vicar in sole charge. They were a recognised strategy of parish evangelism and had been recommended as an approach to the poor as early as 1829. They were especially favoured in the 1850s and 1860s.[26] In the Crafta Webb cottages near Bredwardine were to be found some of Kilvert's poorest and oldest parishioners, and in his readings to them can be discerned an effort to reconcile them to their poverty and their death. In early January 1878, he spoke of entering upon the New Year as Abraham entered 'the strange and Promised Land'. (Hebrews 11, verses 8, 9, and 10.) The theme of the passage concerns the importance of faith in a heavenly country, which is superior to an earthly one. He followed it up two weeks later with a talk on 'Wist ye not that I must be about my Father's business', another injunction to ignore the business of this world. Later his theme was 'the Lord whom ye seek shall suddenly come to the temple'. In February he spoke on the parable of the Good Shepherd. In his work of visiting the worst cases of elderly paupers, those living alone, ill, hungry and filthy in remote cottages, Kilvert was truly one of those 'blessed angels' who, in the words of Richard Heath, might be found in various parts of the country 'restraining these poor devils, binding up their wounds, sitting at their bedsides, filling their minds with a hidden hope ...So you may enter these hovels, and find a resignation, a peace of mind, a trust in God absolutely sublime. It is the spirit of Jesus Christ which we have driven to dwell in the nethermost hells of English society...'.[27] Behind Kilvert's efforts lay a conception of religious faith that largely disappeared with the 19th century. In his day it was tacitly assumed that faith would make a considerable difference to how a person lived his life, and there was a serious commitment to the life that succeeded the earthly one.

When Kilvert came away from homes of his poorest parishioners, he had often left gifts behind him, sometimes out of his own pocket but usually notes for the supply of blankets, food, or coal from the charities of which he was the agent. This was the result of his goodwill, energy and persistence. Clyro retained a memory of his enthusiastic pastoral care a hundred years after he had left. Villagers Le Quesne talked to understood from their forbears that women were especially grateful for his charitable work and responded to his warm nature. As to whether he was generally popular, 'The village today has its doubts'; it was felt that he was too fond of the women.[28] He took hot cross buns to outlying parishioners and helped with the clothing club. He persuaded local women to attend to the needs of old men lying in squalor in remote mountain hovels. About to leave Clyro, he was unable to think of anything but 'what the poor people will do... what with the dear coal and bread and meat...'.[29]

It is noticeable that, whereas his *Diary* contains many instances of charitable giving, his father's *Memoirs* do not, a contrast that partly reflects the difference between the two men and partly the difference between the early and late Victorian period. The former was heavily marked by the fear of the labouring masses and by a fierce determination to promote self-reliance and to discourage idleness and immorality. In the latter, the fear of the masses had declined considerably, especially among the urban middle-class who had benefited from the Reform Bills of 1832 and 1867. The growth of a more confident and articulate middle-class tended to spell the end of paternalism. Legislation had ameliorated factory conditions and trade unionism was more acceptable, so that conflict between masters and men was less overt. The prospect of democracy was viewed with greater equanimity. The public who had property and were anxious for it, liked to believe that the 'respectable' working man would not, when given the vote, go in for excesses and would exert influence against the rougher elements who might. Their faith was largely justified. The working-class was not in a militant mood in the 1860s. The main reason for its quiescence was that by this time bourgeois values had taken a strong hold on working-class culture. 'The economic values and ideals mid-Victorian workmen inclined to accept were largely those of economic individualism, the social ones, those of independence and respectability'.[30] Among trends making for respectability was the huge growth of friendly societies and savings banks in the 1850-1875 period. That Kilvert officiated regularly at the Hay Savings Bank is indicative of his support for this development. Other elements promoting social cohesion were shared religious and educational interests, patriotism, xenophobia, and the Royal Family.

Though all these factors were felt in the remote parishes where Kilvert worked, other, longer established factors continued to exert powerful influence, and his attitudes to the poor received more shaping from them than from the more recent ones, many of which he opposed. When it came to extensions of democracy, trade-unionism, increased educational opportunities for the masses, he was stubbornly conservative. It was far easier for him to be a traditionalist in the country. As Cannadine observed: 'The Reform measures of 1832 and 1867 had simply altered and adapted the old rural oligarchies and proprietary system'.[31] Britain was still dominated by a patrician class in the last quarter of the century. Only one third of all adult males had the vote, the vote was still attached to property, and landowners were still a powerful force. Kilvert's parochial work was permeated by the values of rural paternalism and followed closely the recommendations laid down by Church authorities. Two handbooks were particularly influential: R.W. Evans' *The Bishopric of Souls* (1841) and J.J. Blunt's *The Duties of a Parish Priest* (1856). Both writers had spent long years in country parishes and assumed their readers would too; handbooks later in the century did not assume this. Evans and Blunt assumed clergymen whose university education would make them by far the most learned in the parish. Evans referred to the clergyman's 'superior education and status in society', and to his role in supplying information about parishioners to the 'ruling powers'.[32]

For Evangelicals a key Biblical text was 'the powers that are ordained by God' and Kilvert accepted as a matter of course that there were, and ought to be, 'ruling powers'. He had accepted Venables and Walter Baskerville as his natural leaders and as leaders of the community when he was in Clyro. When he became Vicar of Bredwardine, his deference to Miss Newton, his immediate social superior, is very noticeable. In all *Diary* references to judgments made by her, his approval is implicit. He was deeply gratified by the offer she frequently made of rides in her carriage and he was pleased when she bought a new brougham—'a very nice carriage, dark blue picked out with red, a great improvement on the last'.[33] He paid tribute when she showed generosity to his two churches as, for example, when she provided a text for Bredwardine at Christmas and a banner for Brobury. After the Christmas Day service in 1878, he and sister Dora went to her home to eat their dinner 'by Miss Newton's special desire', he noted proudly. When traditional courtesy was extended to himself by the poor, he was pleased and flattered: 'Some of the old-fashioned folks still call me "your honour" and "your reverence"'.[34] The tradition of doling out soup to the poor in hard times was maintained by Miss Newton and she and Kilvert were irritated when the poor declined to collect their allowance of it from her house. He reacted by taking 'a pitcher full of the despised soup' to some parishioners, so determined was he that gentry charity should be accepted.[35] To refuse even to collect it showed a disturbing want of gratitude and humility.

It is not clear what had produced this mild protest at condescension but Kilvert was always very resentful when he thought that the alleged good relations between classes was poisoned by the interference of troublemakers. Thus, he cast dissenting preachers in the same role as trade union leaders because, as he saw it, they fomented disaffection among the ignorant poor at supposed injustices. While visiting Wales, he was told of a Liberal MP bringing dissenting voters into Merthyr 'in cartloads ... before they went to the poll [and] they were driven like sheep to the chapels and preached to for half an hour'. They were told, Kilvert's informant claimed, that they would go to hell if they didn't vote for the Liberal MP. 'Talk of being priest-ridden, 'tis nothing to being ridden by political dissenting preachers', Kilvert fumed.[36] As is shown in the next chapter, he was encouraged in such attitudes by bishops of the Church of England. He always believed that dissenters were at best misguided and when he was Vicar of St. Harmon, where the majority of parishioners were dissenters, he was apparently kindly disposed towards the prominent ones at least.[37] However, in his *Diary*, he wrote of dissenting preachers as though they were agents of the devil, especially when they encouraged destruction of the social system by turning class against class. Their lack of respect for authority made them sinful in his eyes.

They threatened the loving family which, at its best, was society and the Church of England, and because of the pain and terror he felt at this threat, Kilvert was quite unable to see how the situation could appear from a poor man's perspective, as is clear from the entry for 11 May 1876 when he attended a lecture by a dissenting speaker at the local 'Liberation Society'. 'First came out the smooth velvet cat's paw with the claws carefully ... hidden. The Liberation Society, it seemed, were so anxious for the well-being of the dear old Church of England and merely desired to free the Church from State control and tyranny. But by degrees the cloven hoof peeped out and we heard more of the rights of the Nation ... the intolerable monopoly of the Church, the social disadvantages of Dissenters, the arrogance of the Church and clergy, and the usual rigmarole'.[38] His detestation of dissenters had an historical and aesthetic aspect as well as the politico/moral one. Once, when he was in Cornwall, he visited the British Church at Gwythian, 'this most interesting relic of the earliest British Christianity', and was incensed that 'it had got into the hands of a dissenting farmer who keeps the place for a cattle yard ... what more need be said'.[39] On another occasion, he similarly identified dissenters with barbarians in a way that reflected his fear of working-class ignorance: 'Some barbarian - a dissenter no doubt - probably a Baptist, has cut down the beautiful silver birches on the Little Mountain ...'.[40]

Nothing illustrates more tellingly the importance of a clergyman's superior education and status than the *Diary* entries that concern Kilvert's Langley Burrell parishioner, John Hatherell. They also neatly encapsulate Kilvert's attitude to the poor and the workings of paternalism. His classic statement of rural harmony, his own 'elegy in a country churchyard' of April 1876, includes a reference to Hatherell. Kilvert was walking alone around the churchyard and visited the graves of his 'sleeping friends', one of whom was Hatherell: 'There they lay, the squire and the peasant, the landlord and the labourer ... the infant of days beside the patriarch of nearly five score years, sister, brother, by the same mother, all in her breast their heads did lay and crumble to their common clay... There they lay all sleeping well and peacefully after life's fitful fevers...'.[41] All classes found, finally, equality in the dust, as William Wilberforce was keen to emphasise. Hatherell, born in 1800, was a sawyer and lived on Langley Common, not far from Kilvert's home, in one of the dwellings called the Pound Cottages. The *Diary* references to him begin in late November 1872, after Kilvert had returned to Langley Burrell to resume duty as his father's curate.

It is very noticeable that from the moment he left Clyro at the end of August 1872, his *Diary* contains an enormous body of reminiscence, and the recollection of his 'sleeping friends' in the passage above is central to it. In one sense it is to be expected because once back amongst family, old friends, old parishioners and scenes familiar from his youth, his thoughts would inevitably turn to the past. However, the sheer quantity of reminiscence suggests that he was discovering much satisfaction from a deliberate contemplation of it.[42] The past always had, of course, a special appeal to Kilvert and there were special reasons during this Langley Burrell period why he would find the rural past more comforting than the rural present and what the latter presaged for the rural future. In February 1872 had occurred an event of momentous significance: Joseph Arch had set up a labourers' trade union in Warwickshire, which grew some months later into the National Agricultural Labourers' Union. One consequence of this was 'the strike and lock-out in the Eastern Counties' that Kilvert was recording in June 1874. The 'squire and peasant, landlord and labourer' who were sleeping peacefully in Langley Burrell churchyard exhibited a sharp contrast to their living counterparts in Suffolk and elsewhere.

In John Hatherell, Kilvert had a farm worker for whom revolt against his master was unthinkable. When Kilvert visited him in February 1874, he was an old man: 'I fear his strength is failing him', he wrote, 'he is nearly 75'. The astonishing thing was that he was still working. Kilvert noted that he began 'sawing for the Manor' in 1823, and 'has been at the call of the Manor ever since'. He had worked hard all his life, endured many hardships, including working often up to his knees in water and going to bed hungry so that his children might have bread. Like most farm workers used to labouring in all weathers, he suffered from rheumatism and by April 1875 he was hardly able to walk to church. He had been visited earlier by his master, Squire Ashe, who had reminded him of the nights they had patrolled the roads seeking to apprehend machine-breakers and incendiaries during the Swing troubles. His special kind of loyalty had included resisting the claims of his fellow labourers for higher wages.

Labourers of Hatherell's kind belonged to the 'official' as opposed to the 'dark village', as identified by Hobsbawm and Rudé: 'Each village ... hid two villages: the official parish [of] ... landowners, resident gentry, farmers, publicans etc. - and the dark village ...'.[43] The 'official' village gave recognition to men like Hatherell because their example bolstered the gentry's image of the harmonious community. In the 'dark village' were to be found poachers and politically aware persons who resisted gentry rule. Kilvert glimpsed the 'dark village' when he met shrewd, articulate, and literate shoemakers, who, he recognised, were involved in activities that alienated them from the 'official' village.[44] In his childhood, Kilvert had learnt from Aguilar's *Home Influence* that such patriarchs as Hatherell were worthy of all respect. That novel singled out an ancient family servant called Morris for special praise because he had shown refined feelings and devotion to his master's 'house'. Kilvert was gratified on one visit to Hatherell to hear of his desire (in 'a waking dream') to kiss 'sweet Jesus'. A few days later his health was 'in a precarious state ...one lung quite gone'. Later that month he was dead, and the cause of death was given as chronic bronchitis and old age.

Kilvert's support of the old man in his last years is testimony to the love and admiration he felt for him. When he visited on St. Swithin's Day 1874, he was troubled by a problem of his own concerning the singing in Langley Burrell Church. The voice of the lead singer, George Jefferies, was giving way because of old age and Kilvert and his father favoured the introduction of a harmonium to make up the deficiency. However, this was opposed by Squire Ashe. The Biblical passage Kilvert chose to read to Hatherell on this occasion was Ecclesiastes ten, and in verse four Kilvert came upon some advice helpful in the confrontation with the Squire: 'If the Spirit of the ruler rise up against thee, leave not thy place; for yielding pacifieth great offences'. Kilvert found these words 'came in season to warn, soothe and comfort me'. He decided to yield to higher rank. The text that had by chance comforted him had, however, been chosen specifically for Hatherell, who was not only Kilvert's favourite patriarch, but stood in special relationship to the Squire, whose authority overshadowed them both. Choosing a reading for this man required particular care, so it is worthwhile to examine the text to try to discern factors that may have influenced Kilvert's choice.

The verse that follows the one he found comforting refers to 'an error which proceedeth from the ruler', that had created a disturbance in the order of society: the ruler had allowed a man to occupy a high position who was unfitted for it. Verse six of the passage states: 'Folly is set in great dignity, and the rich sit in a low place'. In Hatherell's limited world there was only one person 'set in great dignity' and that was the Squire. Hatherell was also to understand that Kilvert regarded him as one of 'the rich set in a low place'. Though not 'rich' in any material sense, he had in Kilvert's eyes 'riches' of another kind. It was his practice to distribute to his poor parishioners his poem, 'Honest Work', which aimed to reconcile them to their humble position:

> Envy not the rich, the great,
> Wealthier in your low estate,

Nobler through your workful days,
Happier in your simple ways.[45]

Kilvert tried to help John Hatherell, near the end of his life and with his days now workless, to find riches in the contemplation of a life of honest work. People who did hard manual work attracted the Diarist's sympathy, if they stuck at it and remained independent of the parish, they also won his respect. He regarded Hatherell as a notable example of strength and integrity.[46] His love of such patriarchs was an integral element of his conservatism and they figure prominently in these Langley Burrell parts of the *Diary* and provided comfort for Kilvert when change seemed especially threatening for they represented a simplicity and a strength, a form of manliness, of moral maturity. They had been through hardships, had maintained dignity and independence, and the present and the future seemed to lack their wholesomeness.[47] Their wholesomeness and simplicity enabled Kilvert to see them more like children. Where he encountered them wearing smocks, a practice still maintained by some older men, he commented approvingly.[48]

Ecclesiastes ten was, in some sort, a confirmation of their worth. Verses 16 and 17 of the passage consider the question of when and why a land is happy. 'Woe to thee, O land, when thy king is a child... Blessed are thou, O land, when thy king is the son of nobles, and the princes eat... for strength and not for drunkenness'. (The New English Bible clarifies the sense of the last words by rendering them as: 'and the princes feast... with self control and not as drunkards'.) Mere wealth, then, was not a sufficient qualification for a position of authority. The stress upon the king being the son of nobles indicates that breeding was assumed to play its part in the development of moral worth. Freedom from self-indulgence was an important aspect of worthiness to rule for paternalists. Drunkenness was seen as the besetting sin of the working-class and the chief cause of pauperism. With all classes it led to a loss of dignity but in the case of a man in a position of authority, it risked losing the respect of the poor.

When Kilvert was curate in Clyro, he encountered one of the poor whose respect for his betters had been squeezed out by sheer volume of drink. Kilvert described how he had met Ben Lloyd 'reeling up the steep fields' carrying 'a horse collar and a butter tub'. The passage continues: '...When I said how his wife would be vexed and grieved to see him rolling home, I found I had touched a tender point. He became savage at once... Then he began to roar after me... cursing parsons and shouting what he would do if he were younger...'.[49] Ben Lloyd's disrespect to the village curate was injudicious, almost as injudicious as Kilvert's decision to moralise at this juncture (he was quite mistaken in attributing Lloyd's abuse to guilt; its real cause was his own priggishness). Lloyd's loss of dignity hardly mattered since he was one of the lower-classes. However, the failure of an authority figure to set a good example in such matters was particularly deplorable.[50] For the humble man, faced with self-indulgence or irresponsibility in high places, the advice of Ecclesiastes 10.20, was, nevertheless, forbearance and circumspection: 'Even in your thought, do not curse the king, nor in your bedchamber curse the rich; for a bird of the air will carry your voice, or some winged creature tell the matter'.

Kilvert also intended to take that advice; opposing Squire Ashe over the harmonium was not worth the effort. Though he thought his behaviour was extremely overbearing, Kilvert felt he had to follow a course of deference and discretion. Moreover, he and his father had a responsibility to ensure that harmony was preserved for the good of the congregation. They also had before them the good example of George Jefferies himself: 'George Jefferies is as good as gold, no jealousy or spite or resentment at the summary way in which he has been treated or dismissed from his post as chief singer'.[51] George was a supremely good-hearted man and a good servant of Langley Burrell Church. In addition to being chief singer, he was parish clerk from 1849-1863. Over a period of 30 years, he did plastering and other repair work in the church and at the age of 69, in the year of his death, he was replacing tiles on its roof. In 1874, when he was summarily dismissed from the choir, he whitewashed the church, a huge undertaking that required many hours, as is indicated by the fact that he was paid £5 7s 11d for the job, seven or eight weeks' wages. He also saw to the provision of communion bread, candles and the washing of surplices.[52]

His devotion, like John Hatherell's 50 years' service to Squire Ashe, was emblematic of a traditional way of life that was deeply significant for Kilvert and he wished to see endure. Service of that kind reinforced the structure of society. An equally deep sense of justice in Kilvert, however, cried out against the master who was unworthy of his position, who ruled tyrannically and in other ways betrayed the trust he had been given. Kilvert had a natural sympathy for the down-trodden but it did not lead him to adopt liberal political principles, and he could not countenance political movements which, in seeking to raise the down-trodden, advocated structural changes in society. The conflict with Squire Ashe over the harmonium was a trivial matter and Kilvert recognised it as such. However, as it dragged on, the affair took on darker overtones.

Kilvert's sister had approached the great man to head the subscription list for the instrument, but he had rebuffed her with the declaration that neither he nor any of his family would donate a farthing. On discussing this turn of events with Sarah Hicks, one of his parishioners, whose 'beautiful large dark eyes' rendered her moral indignation all the more appealing to Kilvert, she burst out: 'oh, it's a comfort to know that there's a time coming when no one will be able to reign over us and when we shall be as good as those who are so high and proud over us now'. To which hope Kilvert added: 'Patience, dear Sarah, patience a little while longer. And then -'.[53] He was urging patience in the short-term—until the moment the harmonium subscription list was full and it could be bought in spite of the Squire's opposition (as it soon was). Her words suggest an objective that was both more long-term and of more profound consequence: the end of the autocratic power of the landed gentry. Kilvert didn't see or didn't want to see, the implications of her statement.[54] His background and instincts disposed him to accept the Bible's counsel of patience and submission. For one in subordinate position to do otherwise constituted a threat to the entire social structure. 'Leave not thy place', advised Ecclesiastes ten, and 'place' in that sense was not a geographical but a social entity. Leaving one's place was a form of rebellion.[55] Acceptance of one's place produced the ideal rural harmony exemplified that year for Kilvert by the Whitney Harvest Festival: 'after service the whole parish came up to the Rectory and dined and had tea under the spreading oak on the lawn like one great family. It was very pretty and pleasant'.[56] (Kilvert was aware, as has been shown, of the symbolic overtones of oak trees, so his reference to one here was not casual).

Kilvert did not share the egalitarian view of Sarah Hicks. His advice to her and to John Hatherell was to defer to the Squire because he was a social superior. Evangelicals often urged that the poverty of working people should be relieved but the strong backing which they gave to authority appeared to condone the actions of uncaring governments and employers. His admiration for Hatherell carried with it a full endorsement of existing social relations. The patriarch had managed to remain independent of the workhouse by existing, year upon year, as thousands of other labourers had, on starvation wages. In 1837, wages in Wiltshire were 8s. a week. They were at that level in 1850 but were reduced in parts of the county to 7s. and even 6s. In 1867 some men earned 10s., though others would have considered themselves to be lucky to be on that rate. The average wage for agricultural labourers in England in 1870 was only 12s. 4d.[57] As a sawyer, Hatherell might have earned a little more. Lauding the achievements of men like him implied that frugality, temperance and loyalty produced rewards in terms of happy, healthy, fulfilled living, whereas the reality was essentially otherwise. To praise the long service of the 'good' labourer suggested that the system was a good one and the gentry deserved praise for administering it. If a man achieved the long honourable service of a Hatherell, credit was not due to the system, firstly because it was not acknowledged what dreadful conditions had to be endured simply to survive, and secondly, no blame attached to the gentry responsible for the deplorable conditions in which the system's 'failures' lived and worked. Thus, it was the most shameful hypocrisy for gentry to preach morality at those whose grim lives were the result of their greed and inertia. To praise those who rose above the conditions, which lay in the gentry's power to change, was adding insult to injury.

When Kilvert met with the appalling case of one old man who was put on the parish when he became old and ill, he accepted the inevitability of it, and, as in his account of Hatherell, he merely underlined the theme of 'honest work' and independence from charity. 'He was a very good faithful servant and a man of sturdy independent character who could not bear the idea of not being able any longer to maintain himself and hated to be supported by the parish'. One day he went missing and hours later, he was found in a barn, as Kilvert's farmer friend, Mr. Wall, recounted. 'He had then taken out a razor, unsheathed it, putting the sheath back in his pocket. He was lying on the floor on his face when we saw him. [We] turned him over. Heaven send I never see such a sight again. His head was nearly cut off, both arteries were cut through, the tongue was unrooted and, (perhaps in his agony), he had put his hand into the wound and torn his "keck" and everything out'.[58] There is no doubt that Kilvert was shocked by the physical horror of the old man's suicide (Kilvert said the story stayed in his head for days), but there is no suggestion that he found the event socially and morally intolerable. For him, it was immensely sad that such a thing could happen, but it was not an horrific indictment of the social system as it would have been for other clergymen whose views are recorded in this chapter.

Perhaps the gentry's greatest sin was the way they accused of moral deficiency those who succumbed to conditions which required almost superhuman qualities to survive unsullied. The Rev. Sidney Godolphin Osborne (SGO) knew that in country parishes the clergyman was expected to condemn the immorality of labourers: 'You are expected to work at those *poor* poor; to preach down drunkenness, poaching, stealing of all kinds... You know full well that these *poor* poor have been starved on low wages, that they are dependent on the poor rate for every interruption to their normal starving state; you know that they are so housed that all ordinary rule for the protection of modesty is a farce; that drunkenness to them is a dearly-bought forgetfulness, for a time, of the wretched monotony of a struggling life... You know that their condition can truly be traced to the door of some of the other classes to whom you have to preach; that they, owners and occupiers, do reap the benefit of keeping these poor as they are. Now, dare one clergyman in a hundred - could he get a bishop to do it for him? - preach Bible-truth as plainly about the duty of employer and landowner to their poor as they expect him to preach to the poor the virtues which heaven demands from them, and which will make them better earthly servants?'[59]

SGO was one of the very few clergymen in a hundred (his brother-in-law Charles Kingsley was another) who was prepared to speak out in this way against the injustice and cruelty that disgraced rural society. He was invoking the ethic that stood at its very centre: 'noblesse oblige', the hierarchy of rights and duties. Kilvert accepted that ethic wholeheartedly and therefore the passage has particular relevance for him and the issues highlighted in this chapter. He knew the housing conditions as well as SGO; he knew labourers' wages were inadequate; he knew that if there was any interruption of them, they would be thrown on the parish; he preached down their drunkenness and immorality.[60] Of course, Kilvert lacked the social position of SGO and his confidence.[61] As to the question of whether he saw SGO's letters, the answer seems inescapable that he must have. They had appeared, virtually since Kilvert was born, in *The Times*, which he regularly read, caused considerable controversy, and continued up to 1888. Neither Kilvert, nor hundreds of other country clergymen, were fired by them to preach at the vices of landowners as they were expected to preach at the vices of the poor.[62]

This chapter has shown that Kilvert was very selective in the use he made of the Bible. He declined to preach 'Bible truth' in the way advocated by SGO, contenting himself with the occasional oblique reproof of gentry who were neglectful of their duty. He drew attention to failure to repair cottages, and the destruction of trees to pay debts. However, he did not face, as SGO did, the reasons why labourers lived in squalor. A few months after Kilvert became Clyro's curate, SGO was expressing in one of his *Times* letters, his weariness of the oft-repeated, 'wretched, selfish argument, "We don't build cottages because they do not pay; the rent won't cover the outlay and repairs"'. That argument was conveniently forgotten when it came to the housing of the gentry's hounds, horses, bullocks and other livestock. In his 30 years' experience of the countryside, SGO had, he declared, heard agents of estates admit that the charges on estates, the private expenditure of the owners, the necessary repairs on the house, the 'increased luxury in which owners live', left no money to spend on the homes of estate workers. Owners were 'over-housed and over-domesticed' and undertook high costs in preserving parks and gardens largely for the admiration of others, and they were determined, for the same reason, to extend their estates.[63] The wealth of estates was not used to ensure that servants like John Hatherell did not, after a life-time of devoted service, become paupers.[64] 'What is a pauper?' asked SGO. 'They are sick, aged, ...powerless human beings, bred in our cottages, worked out on our farms, perhaps maimed in our service'. And he pointed out that the gentry too had their paupers: the squire's aged mother, 'poor old thing, born a lady, bred a lady', yet she didn't end on relief in a squalid hovel, but was 'pensioned to live a lady, [a] great estate pauper'.[65]

Labourers ended as paupers because it was quite impossible to save for their old age out of their wages. For gentry to praise the diligent, frugal labourer was, in SGO's view, not only hypocrisy but a specious confidence trick. He wanted to know 'why is it that we have no society to reward other servants than farm servants? Is [it] ...an admission that long service is proof of more than ordinary endurance ...indicative of a belief... that neither the wages we pay, nor attachment to our service... will, unaided, call forth the full exercise of that skill?'[66] SGO was noting around the time Kilvert began his visits to Hatherell that the great bulk of labourers were living like animals. The landed gentry, on the other hand had enjoyed, during the previous 30 years, unparalleled prosperity. Agricultural rents rose by an average of 30% between 1842 and 1878, and the average price of land rose from £38 an acre in 1857-61 to £54 an acre between 1873 and 1877.[67] The praise of the long-serving labourer was, in other words, an admission of guilt; it was, like the estate cottage, part of the show put on by landowners to assert the harmony and benevolence of the system.

Friendly societies were another part of the show. They had come out of the working-class movement to encourage self-help late in the 17th century. Later they were used as fronts for trade unions when the law declared them illegal. They expanded rapidly from 1760 onwards and total membership exceeded 900,000 by 1815 and four million by 1872.[68] They were encouraged by the upper-classes because they were seen to develop independence and respectability among the working population, who were in favour of them because they provided for hard times and were an alternative to the workhouse. They also supplied fellowship and solidarity against employers.

Kilvert gave his support to a local one that met at Monkton, Wiltshire, in July 1875. Captain De Winton sponsored the 'Friendship Lodge of Oddfellows', which met at the Maesllwch Arms.[69] One large entry of the *Diary* is devoted to the parade of Foresters which took place at Oakfield, the home near Clyro of the elderly landowner and JP, Henry Allen, in July 1870. He made a speech to the Foresters, who afterwards paraded past him and saluted by doffing their caps. His acceptance of their deference acknowledged the observance in the community of strict hierarchy. The very existence of friendly societies signified a labouring class which was unable to manage on the wages employers paid. Four shillings a quarter, or 4d. a week, was the fee commonly charged.[70] By 1870, improved wages had enabled many more than formerly to share the benefits. The Foresters' green and white banners that Kilvert saw summed up what friendly societies meant for labourers: they pictured relief being brought to distressed families. He had much affection for country people but was probably not alone among the gentry present in finding the parade ridiculous. Two Foresters were dressed in green tunics to represent Robin Hood and Little John, and 'they rode and rolled about on their carty horses looking very foolish and uncomfortable... Then in straddled the Rifle Corps band blasting with their trumpets, and blowing out their cheeks till their eyes started, and the rear was brought up by the lurching banners'. The parade filed past with the Foresters all out of step, at which point 'they took themselves off'. It was one of those occasions when the ways of labouring folk seemed alien and contemptible to Kilvert, as had the violin playing of Evans, the Clyro schoolmaster. One can almost feel the relief of the 'ladies and gentlemen of the neighbourhood', grouped on the side lawn, 'more or less in the shade', as the rustics trooped away. Kilvert joined them for a chat before they repaired indoors to a cold luncheon: 'salmon, chicken salad etc and everything very nice'.[71]

The Rev. Venables made an amusing impromptu speech and proposed a toast to Henry Allen, their host. Mozley, Venables' Charterhouse friend and Robert Kilvert's Oriel contemporary, in his essay on castes in society, had written of the way a clergyman inevitably allied himself with those of the same background and class as himself and was powerless to avoid deepening social divisions within a community. He divided 'antagonistic and dissociable elements', and, as the Oakfield parade graphically demonstrated, he allocated 'the families comprised in his sphere in their fitting quarters'.[72] For all the appearance of social harmony, the Foresters did not sit down to luncheon with the gentry. Rarely, if ever, would they or their families, taste the viands of which it was composed. Some of the gentlemen, such as Walter Baskerville and Crichton, had declined to attend the parade; they preferred a shooting party from which labourers were excluded. In one sense, the parade might be seen as a triumph over social divisions because the Foresters were living proof of the extent to which the middle-class values of independence and respectability had permeated the working-class. The gentry frequently deplored the drinking that accompanied parades and feasts as wasteful indulgence. However, Canon Girdlestone wrote in 1873 of the 'innumerable, bankrupt village clubs patted on the back by owners and occupiers of land and by some publicans, where the poor man's small and hard-earned savings are wasted in bands... flags and feasting.'[73] The parade could be seen less as a sign of social harmony than of social control.

Cobbett, 40 years earlier had pointed out that friendly societies served the interests of the landowning class. He said that landowners had invented the scheme in order to induce labourers to give up part of their pitiful earnings so that they themselves would pay less in poor rates.[74] The virtues of independence and respectability functioned as 'fences erected by a superior social class to mark itself off from, and to protect itself against, an inferior culture'.[75] A strong sense of an inferior culture and of condescension to it marks the *Diary* account of the Oakfield parade.[76] Ashby's description of a Foresters' parade also noted its comic absurdity but she could see meaning and dignity in it too, which are absent from the *Diary* one. There were, she said, 'some fine, thoughtful faces [that] gave tone to the group'.[77] Unlike Kilvert, she respected the labourers' values and experience because she shared them. He was, nevertheless, much more able than many of his class to draw close to poor people and there is no doubt he won the respect of many. It was typical of him that shortly after the end of the Oakfield parade, he went visiting some who were sick.

The Oakfield parade occurred early in Kilvert's career when he was still a curate. Towards the end of his life, when he was in full charge of a parish, he was involved in a large scale charity—the George Jarvis charity. Its workings are illustrative not only of his approach to the poor but that of several other clergymen. An old parishioner, Priscilla Price, warned him of the charity's troubled history when he had been only a few weeks in his job as Vicar of Bredwardine. 'God sent you to overturn the tables of the money-changers', she told him. 'I mean the tables of sin in this place... This Charity interferes with people, and does them harm. Those who get it are discontented and those who don't get it are discontented'.[78] His brother-in-law, the Rev. William Smith, had become Vicar of Monnington, a parish near Bredwardine, in 1874 and had written to Kilvert's mother about a clerical meeting he had attended at the home of the Rev. Phillott, Rector of Staunton-on-Wye. He had returned from it 'not very deeply impressed by the brilliancy of some of the Herefordshire Clergy'. Kilvert's mother had capped the story with the case of the Rev. Ormerod of Presteigne, who was a good example of a money-changing clergyman. Ormerod, she said, 'has a living of over a £1000 a year but ... is ... always head over heels in debt'. This worthy man regularly put his pocket knife into his church's collection plate with the excuse that he had no change. After services he took back his knife but declined to redeem it with any money.[79]

Unsurprisingly, Kilvert found 'tedious' the first meeting he attended of the Charity's Trustees, of whom he automatically became one on his appointment as Vicar of Bredwardine. Committee work was not for him, and he would have preferred to be visiting the people who were the objects of the Charity. He was nevertheless dismissive of their 'rooted and ineradicable belief' that Trustees were paid £100 a year out of its funds for their services and that was why the local poor were denied relief.[80] He clearly found their suspicion of their social superiors presumptuous and insulting. His first meeting of the Trustees had, however, acquainted him with the disturbing fact that the funds of the Charity were over-drawn and that 'the poor people who came for relief were sent empty away'.[81] In consequence, the efficiency and even the probity of the Trustees, most of whom were local clergymen, had been called into question. That this could even happen was an indication that times were changing. There is no doubt that there was deep-seated disaffection in the parish of Bredwardine and Kilvert received a further warning from Mrs. William Newton, who told him 'it had become a difficult parish to manage and would require much care and judgment and tact'.[82]

The Charity had been set up in the name of George Jarvis, who was born in the parish of Staunton-on-Wye in 1704, though he spent his boyhood in Bredwardine.[83] He made a fortune out of his hide and leather business in London and lived a gentleman's life. Disaffection within his family seems to have caused him to disinherit his one surviving daughter and her children, and, on his death in 1793, he left his fortune of £76,000[84] in a charitable trust for the poor of the parishes of Staunton, Bredwardine, and Letton. By 1878, when Kilvert became part of the Charity's history, its account showed a debt of £4 and was unable to furnish relief to the poor Jarvis had so favoured. The Charity was to provide food, clothing, coal and medicine, and he had made a particular stipulation that no funds were to be used to erect buildings. The early years of the Charity were marked by controversy. Disquiet was expressed almost from the outset about the encouragement given by it to idleness and improvidence among the poor. Then in 1841 its medical officer and schoolmaster were charged with indecency with patients and pupils, drunkenness and misappropriation of funds. Two local landowners, Sir John Geers Cotterell and Sir George Cornewall, had provided schools early in the century and it was the attempt later to improve these that was to bedevil the Charity. Its Trustees proposed to erect larger schools, a store-room, a surgery and an office, using surplus investment income. When this scheme was put forward in 1852, the Charity's income was £3,000 a year and exceeded the demand for poor relief. The Jarvis Charity Act of that year granted permission to build in Staunton-on-Wye an infant school and a boarding school for 30 older boys and 30 older girls, chosen from the children of poor parents eligible for relief in the three parishes. The boarding school, known locally as 'The White Elephant', was never properly established because there were never sufficient funds for its administration.

This was the situation facing the Trustees when Kilvert joined them in January 1878. He referred to Mr. Phillott and Mr. Haigh Allen setting out 'a new and amended scheme' for the working of the Charity. The former had been a Trustee since 1852 and had been responsible with other Trustees (among whom were the Bishop of Hereford, Sir Velters Cornewall, and Tomkyns Dew[85]) for the setting up of the boarding school. The 'new scheme' proposed that all school premises be provided for out of the Charity's income, and that the boarding school should in future function as an elementary and industrial school for girls, teaching domestic economy, cookery, needlework, as well as the 3 Rs. Phillott, Haigh Allen, the Rev. Davenport, and Sir George Cornewall recommended these 'sweeping changes', Kilvert recorded, while he, Rev. Whitley, and Freeman Blisset[86] 'formed the Conservative element' and opposed them.[87] Behind Kilvert's opposition lay commonsense, a distrust of grandiose schemes for the benefit of the poor (he had regarded a mere reading room in Hay as a waste of money), and a desire to limit charity to its traditional form: bread, meat, and clothing. No doubt compassion was an element, too, because he thought it wrong that claimants desperate for relief should be denied it. Was he, in allying himself with the faction representing humbler local people, displaying the tact and judgment which, he had been told, were essential in the new Vicar of Bredwardine? Perhaps it is always easier to vote for the *status quo* but Kilvert was learning that by doing so he was not going to please everyone. It also took some courage to oppose not only senior clergymen of the district, but also his squire (Sir George Cornewall) and Haigh Allen, who had been for years part of his Clyro social circle.

Kilvert last attended a meeting of Trustees on 8 July 1879. Further meetings would have confronted him with more developments he would have found disturbing. A room in the boarding school became a Parish Reading Room and Library in 1881. A year later the allowance for medicine for the poor was reduced, and the Rev. Phillott proposed that £300 be used for teaching cookery. In 1885, the Charity's original purpose was further threatened by the proposal of the Charity Commissioners to allow children from outside the three parishes to become pupils at the Staunton school. Dissatisfaction with the distribution of funds had reached such a peak that in March 1888 there was a public inquiry. During it, Sir George Cornewall admitted that applications for relief had had to be refused because of shortage of funds, but underlined the great difficulties under which the Trustees worked. Many local people, including some of the poor, attended the inquiry and a counsel represented their views. He pressed Sir George to explain why the Trustees had not been prepared to appoint as Trustees local men (he had in mind some of lower standing than Sir George and his colleagues) who knew the needs of the poor. Sir George replied that if, for example, local farmers were appointed, they might obtain tenancies elsewhere and so need to be replaced. The counsel pointed out that this objection related also to clergymen. This had happened in the case of the Rev. Davenport (one of the backers of the 'new scheme' for the Charity), who left Herefordshire in 1881 and took up a post in Leicestershire. Sir George thought him 'a very proper person' to serve as a Trustee and wanted him reappointed since he had returned to the district, even though, as the counsel pointed out, he had attended only nine meetings out of 37.

Rev. Phillott (by then a Canon of Hereford Cathedral) stated that no parish could have a better representative than a clergyman, whose knowledge of the poor was considerable. To demonstrate that knowledge, he declared that 'the want and misery that prevailed amongst the poor' was the result of 'ignorance about cookery'.[88] The testimony of some of the poor that came later in the inquiry showed the fatuity as well as the injustice of this statement. Phillott did say, however, that there should be some body in each parish with the power of electing Trustees. Had that been the situation, it would have prevented his appointment of Major Palmer, a landowner of Eardisley (not one of the three Charity parishes) as his successor. One of Kilvert's parishioners, the farmer Frank Evans, was very critical of this appointment, implying that Trustees saw to it that only members of the gentry class were appointed. Haigh Allen of Clifford Priory qualified for this reason, as did Colonel Bridgford; both lived outside the three parishes. The latter actually lived in Manchester and had attended only seven out of 37 meetings. He 'did not know much of the details' of the Charity's working, he admitted, but 'was conversant with what was going on to a certain extent'. It went without saying amongst the Phillotts, the Palmers, the Haigh Allens, and the Bridgfords that they alone were the 'proper persons' to administer the Charity. Major Palmer told the inquiry that this was so because landed gentry 'lived in the midst of the people, and no one knew better than they the wants of the people'.

This was the Rev. Venables' conviction, as has been shown earlier. The conflict adumbrated in Venables' story, 'The Poacher', between the clergyman as simple man-of-God and as paternalist landowner and JP, was implicit, and often explicit, in the 1888 Jarvis Charity inquiry. It was a body of Trustees, virtually all of whom were landowners and/or clergymen, who had drawn up the Charity's 'General Rules' in 1860. No one was entitled to food relief who had not continually resided in a parish for five years. Anyone convicted of a criminal offence was excluded from all benefits of the Charity 'during the pleasure of the Trustees'. No one who had received parish relief within the last 12 months, nor anyone who took in a lodger without the sanction of the Trustees, nor anyone who had an unemployed son or daughter, not attending school, residing at home, nor any single woman who was the mother of an illegitimate child, could receive benefits. In a letter written to the *Hereford Times* after the inquiry, a local man stated that he could hardly believe that such rules had been framed by men calling themselves Christians, some of whom preached 'Sunday after Sunday about doing unto others as you would they should do unto you'. He was particularly horrified by rule seven, which stated that no one under the age of 70 could receive a weekly allowance of meat except where sanctioned by a medical officer. The correspondent knew that very few among the working-class lived to the age of 70.

The inquiry revealed that the 'wretched pittance' (the newspaper correspondent's phrase) doled out to the poor weekly was 11d. (1s. 11d. for those entitled to the meat allowance). People received more if they applied to the workhouse, but that would mean they lost their Charity money. As far as we know, Kilvert did not feel inclined or able to protest against the un-Christian rules of the Charity but did try to ensure that his parishioners claimed what they could from it. He helped one, Mary Jackson, to apply for Charity relief. He found her 'ill with a bad cold and very poor and destitute and lonely... she told me of the death of her young daughter by consumption and her husband's agonizing ...death from internal cancer, the result of... a log of timber having fallen on his back... where he was an under-sawyer...'.[89] She was granted the full allowance of 1s. 11d. a week and was one of the lucky ones.[90]

Relief for the poor was inadequate, it was stated at the inquiry, because only one third of the Charity's total income was devoted to it; the remainder went towards the administration and maintenance of the schools. Asked by counsel whether he thought it right that relief money went towards the costs of the boarding school, the Bishop of Hereford refused to answer. The school offered nothing to the local poor, who could neither afford the fees it charged for board and lodging nor to be without the wages which their daughters would have earned in employment. Sir George Cornewall expressed his confidence in the school because it proposed to train girls as 'good domestic servants - a want that was very much felt nowadays'. Kilvert's brother-in-law, the Rev. Smith, also expressed faith in it because technical education was then in great demand—a revealing comment.[91] Critics of the school stated that the Trustees had 'higher education on the brain'. The school was symptomatic of the determination of local clergy to remain influential in the field of education and its planning coincided with the agitation over the efficiency of elementary education. The Newcastle Commission of 1861 was set up to enquire into it, and most clergymen who testified to it favoured a curriculum that went beyond the 3 Rs. They were also concerned to keep control of education in their hands, largely in order to promote Christian belief and to keep churches as full as possible. Frank Evans, the local farmer, believed that the administration of the Charity had in fact caused church attendance to drop in the three parishes. The school scheme was rejected by the House of Commons in 1895 and this was seen as a defeat for the Charity Commission, as well as of the local gentry, who had together tried to override local wishes.[92] The school was an utter failure; it was only used properly for ten years of its 60-year history.

Kilvert's successor, Rev. H. Trevor Williamson, declared ingenuously at the inquiry that the Trustees had always done their best for the people of the community, and this applied also to the boarding school, which he recognised they thought to be a 'fad' of the local clergy. He complained that Trustees had been presented as guilty of a crime but insisted that he did not feel at all like a criminal. The Jarvis Charity epitomised the Church's predicament in the 19th century. The remedies it sought to apply to the massive needs were always inadequate. Its social welfare was inadequate; its education was inadequate; its vision of England was inadequate. It fostered a relationship in which people were unable to grow and become responsible for themselves; it preached independence yet kept people dependent. It presumed to know the needs of the people yet persisted in regarding them as not fully human. Individual clergymen performed valuable service but 'though the power to understand was there', there was not 'the will to listen... the control of Church affairs continued to be in the hands of a class... which was little conversant with the special necessities of the new order'.[93] Williamson's attitude was shared by his clerical and gentry Trustee colleagues and their predecessors; none of them felt they had done anything wrong. Perhaps their gravest weakness was their failure to listen to the people for whose benefit they existed. Kilvert, as we have seen, would not tolerate criticism of the Trustees, even though he had heard that the Herefordshire clergy, from whom they were drawn, lacked 'brilliancy'.[94] His brother-in-law, the source of that observation, denied at the inquiry that there was widespread dissatisfaction locally with the administration of the Charity; Kilvert knew there was.[95]

The gentry class to which so many rural clergymen belonged favoured the closed parish where patronage ruled and where 'a bird of the air' might tell any matter to the superior powers. It could be said that such gentry as those of Kilvert's *Diary* and of the Jarvis Charity created both the John Hatherells and the 'undeserving' poor by creating closed and open parishes.[96] Kilvert's vision of rural harmony presupposed a parish in which squire and dependents lived in close relationship.[97] Both Kilvert and Hatherell suffered for their loyalty to that relationship. In his poem, 'Honest Work', Kilvert wrote of how loyal servants with 'the kindly heart and busy hand' of Hatherell proved themselves 'the sons to be/ Of Heaven descended Charity', and how they would finally achieve 'a sure but all unsought reward' in Heaven. Its price, however, was a life-time of toil and penury.[98] The price for Kilvert was that outlined by SGO: '...there is many a pure heart which feels itself choked in utterance because, forsooth, the higher order are not to be offended'.[99] Kilvert was such a 'pure heart' and his reverence for authority and his romantic attachment to the notion of rank choked him. He wholeheartedly accepted the tradition of charity embedded in paternalist society. Like SGO he saw any move towards a modern social welfare policy as a retrograde one, based (in the former's words) on 'mere mechanical charity'. In his view of labourers' 'parochialism', SGO was also close to Kilvert. SGO defined labourers' 'parochialism' as their 'patriotism', while recognising that some would scorn such a view as backward looking, the deliberate limiting of mental horizons to the parish and the 'records of the churchyard'.[100] He did not, therefore, lack the love of traditional ways expressed by Kilvert in his 'sleeping friends' entry. He almost idolised, he said, the parish as the 'parent of ties which connected to their mutual benefit the rich and poor'.[101] Unlike Kilvert, he could respect the parish while simultaneously recognising its limitations. His respect was never automatic as Kilvert's was. John Hatherell belonged to the 'official' parish; SGO recognised the existence of the 'dark' parish, which Kilvert preferred to ignore.

Kilvert loved the 'dear lambs' who were his faithful, humble poor and was grateful for the opportunity they gave him 'to bind up broken hearts' and 'help to bear the Cross a little way'.[102] But his love could not include a desire to see them grow into bigger, happier, more confident human beings. His benevolence was vitiated to a degree by a sentimentality, focused on children and worthy patriarchs, that was part of his romantic attachment to the rural past. Ashby, in her account of Warwickshire rural society, stated that the great house depressed the manhood and culture of villagers and that its gifts might be ropes 'to tie you down'. At the time of the controversy over the Farm Labourers' Union and their wages, *The Times* wrote (June 1873): 'We cannot think that the question before us is simply one of labour and wages. It is rather the real and complete elevation of the agricultural labourer to a higher and larger share of our common, and perhaps we may add, our Christian humanity. He is to be made more independent, more self-governing, more rational, more a social personage - in a word, more of a man...'.

'Not land, but land in the possession of families, was the essence of the landed interest'.

N. Gash, *Reaction and Reconstruction In English Politics 1832-1852*, p.137

'At the heart of [middle-class] hostility [to landowners] lay the denial of the economic necessity of the landowning class. Brought up on the gospel of work and the horror of waste common to the Evangelical and the Benthamite, they could not separate unearned luxury from the idea of sin. It was the idleness rather than the wealth of the "lounging class" that offended them'.

H.J. Perkin, *Land Reform And Class Conflict In Victorian Britain*, p.183

'...the ground-swell of rural grievance came back always to access to the land'.

E.P. Thompson, *The Making of the English Working Class*, p.253

'An acre of land was not particularly important to a marquis who had thousands more, except that he would not part with it too easily for how else had his family acquired such a large estate if not by extending it when the opportunity arose?'

D.R. Mills, *Lord and Peasant in Nineteenth Century Britain*, p.53

'The landowners of our country are, in general, cruel, unreasonable, unfeeling, and unpitying men'.

The Dissenting newspaper, the *Banner*, writing in 1887 of landowners in Wales

'We do not ...live—and I trust it will never be the fate of this country to live—under a democracy'.

Disraeli introducing the Second Reform Bill in the House of Commons on 18 March 1867

CHAPTER 9
Kilvert and Property and Politics

One of this book's themes is the growth and preservation, in an age characterised so much by class conflict, capitalist entrepreneurship, *laissez-faire*, obsession with rank and property, of a humanitarian spirit. It has been presented in various aspects as a matter of 'heart', the capacity of an individual to feel sympathy for his suffering neighbour. The conventional picture of the 19th century, while it gives full representation to the horrific social ills that beset it, also lays heavy emphasis on the remedial measures pioneered, against determined opposition, by a host of philanthropists. Jennifer Hart has questioned the view advanced by several historians that the century was genuinely humanitarian, and she attempted to discern the extent of humanitarian feeling. Her conclusions were bleak. Most managers of factories and mines were, she declared, indifferent to the deaths and injuries suffered in employment by their workers. While it may be true that in theory the Poor Law was not in itself cruel, 'the fact remains that its administration caused hardship'.[1] The preceding chapter has shown this hardship and charitable efforts to relieve it in Kilvert's Bredwardine parish. The so-called 'philanthropic' motive behind Evangelicalism had its origin more in a revulsion at laziness, drunkenness, and sensuality than in genuine sympathy for the suffering poor. The silence that Robert Kilvert preserved in his *Memoirs* on the condition of his poorest parishioners has been attributed to this fact and to one closely allied to it—that 'many Christians were not interested in social or political problems at all'.[2] Similarly, his son devoted little space in his *Diary* (at least in the part that has survived) to the founding of the NALU and its members' struggle against poverty and injustice. Such *Diary* clergymen as Venables, Bevan, and Thomas minimised suffering and played up instead the immorality of labourers who lived in squalor.[3] The concern was, as Hart argues, with 'saving souls, not bodies', and the influence of religion finally was that it retarded, rather than promoted, social progress.

'The possession of a quarter of an acre of garden ground... will make to the labourer... all the difference between want and sufficiency, between privation and comfort'.[4] This was the major theme of the 1867 Report on agriculture, and it concluded that allotments had not been provided over the years because of the prejudice, selfishness, and inertia of landowners. That the business of land ownership was a key issue in 1867 may be seen from the fact that this Report chose to give a full account of the 'gradual alienation of... labourers from the soil'. As will be argued later in this chapter, the singling out of this issue was intimately connected with the movement that culminated in the Second Reform Bill. In the run up to it, all kinds of fundamental questions of rights and injustices could more readily be focused and many people sensed that the day of reckoning for the landed gentry could not be long delayed.

There was no one to whom the landed estate mattered more than to Kilvert but his vision of rural society included a concern for the small man. Enclosure of common lands, on which the poor exercised rights, has a long, complex history and it will not be fully opened up here. There were 4,000 parliamentary acts of enclosure between 1761 and 1841. Landowners were fond of holding up to the rural poor the values of industriousness and thrift yet it was the opportunity afforded by the possession of a little land to develop these qualities that was lost with enclosure. Small pieces of land acted as an incentive to the most hard-working. Above all, they gave hope to people— as Lord Ernle indicated: 'They formed the lowest rung in the social ladder, by which the successful cottager might hope to climb to the occupation of a holding suited to his capital. Now the commons were gone, and the farms which replaced them were too large to be attainable'.[5] Kilvert expressed regret at this loss of opportunity in almost identical terms: 'What a pity that these ancient humble farms should be destroyed and thrown into the great farms, thereby taking away all the poor man's prizes and the chance of his rising in the world'.[6] Kilvert had had the example of the industrious, independent cottager held up to him in his childhood in the person of Collins in Aguilar's *Home Influence*.[7] Perhaps Kilvert's father had been the source of other examples of aggregation of farms in Wiltshire earlier in the century. When Kilvert wrote of the loss of small farms, it is clear he was thinking of the recent past. The period in which they disappeared most rapidly was between 1813 and 1835,[8] the time of Kilvert senior's school and university days and first curacies at Keevil, Melksham and Alton Barnes. He recorded that the Keevil district was made up of small farms and spoke of humble people who, 'by regular industry under Divine blessing', had prospered.

The possibility that the good and industrious labourer could end up owning his own small farm was part of Kilvert's vision of a perfect rural society. The Fry family of Chieflands, though only tenants, epitomised for him wholesome and morally beneficent independence. He made a point of expressing his admiration for Meredith, 'the poor honest earnest... struggling farmer', who tried to make a go of a small farm near Clyro.[9] Kilvert encountered the dream of independence for the labourer in the poems of William Barnes. In 'Eclogue: Two Farms in Woone', Barnes gave an account of the merging of small farms, while in 'Eclogue: The Common A-Took In', agrarian capitalism stands accused of taking away from the poor man even what little he had. It was Barnes' quality of caring that endeared him so much to Kilvert. We are told that 'a beautiful benevolent loving look shone in his eyes' and that, in Barnes' view, 'in all which he himself had written there was not a line which was not inspired by love and kindly sympathy...'.[10] It might appear that in Kilvert's championing of the labourer's right to aspire to own a small farm there was a democratic element essentially at variance with the spirit of paternalism. Both, however, were reconciled in the romantic and Evangelical traditions which he inherited. Stokes underlined that the ideal of peasant ownership figured in the political outlook of poets of nature, especially of Wordsworth: 'To take the peasant in all simplicity, to secure him in the possession of his land, to rule him with a paternal and simple government... these political aims spring directly from the Romantic movement'.[11] Nevertheless in the momentous year of 1867, the latent conflict between peasant ownership and the landed estate emerged for Kilvert in a challenging local event.

While it will always be a matter of regret that Kilvert did not begin keeping his *Diary* from the moment he arrived in Clyro in January 1865, instead of January 1870, the fact that we have no record of his reactions to events, both local and national, in 1867, represents a particularly important gap in our understanding of him. The local event that would have been the talk of all the villages around Clyro was the court case of Vaughan v. De Winton, that came on at the Radnorshire Spring Assizes that year. The judge at the outset remarked that the case would be 'of very little interest to the public' because it concerned merely the right to a small strip of land beside the Wye. It was a remark that exhibited the lack of percipience and sensitivity commonly found in utterances of circuit judges. Ownership of land had always been an issue. Kilvert almost came to blows with Mr. Latimer Jones over it. The eagerness with which he would have devoured the account of the De Winton case in the *Hereford Times* (which he read regularly) can easily be imagined.

He had a particular interest in the De Winton family and entries early in the *Diary* reveal quite unequivocally that he had conceived an antipathy to it by the time he started to record his life in Clyro. The very first De Winton entry, for 13 April 1870, is marked by that awareness of the power of the Maesllwch estate which typifies several others: 'A cavalcade of horses seven in number has just passed through the village... with four horsemen. They belong to Maesllwch'.[12] Later, he noted that 'at Maesllwch Castle last week four guns killed 700 rabbits in one afternoon'. He was aware, as locals were, of the price that De Winton's tenants paid for the abundance of rabbits that provided an afternoon's 'sport' for gentlemen. One tenant told Kilvert how De Winton was insulted during the 1874 election by men kicking round him a football made of a rabbit skin stuffed with bran, 'in allusion to his propensity for ruining his tenants by keeping vast hordes of rabbits on his estate'.[13] Indifference to his tenants was a charge Kilvert advanced against De Winton in other entries. One tenant complained her farm 'was going all to pieces' and Kilvert commented, 'no repairs to house or buildings, the usual fate of the Maesllwch farms'.[14] De Winton's failure to be a good steward of his property is specifically linked by Kilvert to his self-indulgence, as is seen clearly in the entry concerning a De Winton picnic, to which Kilvert had been invited. During lunch, De Winton told one of his guests—a Thomas from Llanthomas—that he would be sick because he ate too much. When some tipsy cake was handed round later, the Thomas accused of greediness retaliated by saying 'viciously': '"We call this tipsy squire". "That'll do for you then", retorted the host. "No", said the guest meaningly, "I never get drunk"'.[15] Local gossip also brought to Kilvert's ears another aspect of De Winton's irresponsibility that pained the Diarist deeply. 'The whole of the Cwmganon woods are to be felled... the cottagers say... to pay for De Winton's gambling debts'.[16]

Resentment of this kind of aristocratic irresponsibility was something Kilvert had learnt in his Evangelical childhood. The depth of Kilvert's anger towards De Winton may be grasped from the *Diary* entry concerning the resident baboon of Maesllwch Castle, which, according to local gossip, sought an opportunity to take the young heir of the family to the top of one of its towers and drop him off, as it was accustomed to do with the Castle's cats. Normally, the mere thought of an inheritance being lost as the result of such a grotesque accident would have horrified Kilvert, but in the case of the De Winton family it filled him with malicious glee. Kilvert was brought up honouring his grandfather, Squire Coleman, as the model landlord of Chieflands, in contrast to the neglectful Sir John Neeld who succeeded him. Aguilar's *A Mother's Recompense* cited examples of estates ruined by self-indulgent owners. It was the arrogant pride of landowners and farmers that, in Kilvert's view, partly fuelled their demand for the aggregation of farms. And finally, the fact that he referred to rows of elms chopped down, 'so as to devastate the pretty village' nearby,[17] by the Lord Malmesbury, who, as James Harris, was the arrogant contemporary of Robert Kilvert at Oriel, raises the possibility that Kilvert had heard his father mention that gentleman.

The Vaughan v. De Winton case in March 1867 may well have been the event which ignited Kilvert's hostility to the lord of Maesllwch.[18] In some ways it was the classic border story. It had a David and Goliath aspect to it—small farmer challenging the might of the landed estate—and the David in question stood for Welshness, while De Winton, in spite of his Welsh heritage, was identifiable with an English or Anglo-Norman tradition. The small farmer was James Williams Vaughan, and he had brought a case against De Winton over a strip of land bordering the Wye, and adjoining the Vaughan's farm of Glangwye near the village of Llandeilo Graban.[19] Though the principle of who owned the land was important, the crucial factor in the case was the right to fish the Wye, and both parties knew it.[20] Thus, the shadow of the Game Laws fell across it. It would be of the utmost concern to Kilvert because he violently opposed field sports and staunchly upheld the cause of the yeoman proprietor.

It was alleged that the defendant (De Winton) had repeatedly entered the strip and had cut down fences and a 'no-trespassing' notice-board belonging to Vaughan. Vaughan's lawyer, James, rejected De Winton's claim that it was common land, because it was entirely surrounded by freehold property; to be common it would have to have had open access. If it was held to be freehold, then its fishery belonged to the owner of that freehold. The defendant freely admitted that similar strips and their fisheries in the vicinity were the property of freeholders. Since the decision had been made to bring the dispute to court, De Winton had cut down the wood adjoining the strip so that it now appeared that the area occupied by the wood was part of the common land. Mr. James thought this regrettable.[21]

A previous owner of the Glangwye farm, Jenkins, gave evidence of various acts of ownership he had performed which proved his right to the strip. De Winton's lawyer claimed that prior to Jenkins' tenure, it was common land, which had been encroached upon by Mr. Jones, Jenkins' uncle, who had paid rent for it to the Maesllwch estate. When Jenkins became tenant of the neighbouring De Winton farm of Cwmgivir, he also became tenant of the disputed strip and paid rent for it. That his encroachment had taken place was not challenged by Vaughan's lawyer. It was entirely typical of the pattern of resistance to Anglo-Welsh gentry rule practised at this time (and earlier) by farmers. Upland areas such as the Radnorshire hills were in the control of Liberal-Radical, Welsh-speaking non-conformists, who opposed, with increasing confidence in the 1860s, the dominance of the (usually) Tory, English and Anglican landlords, whose traditional areas of power were the low-lying parts of the Welsh-English border-land and the coastal strips. The kind of encroachment that Vaughan wished to defend was 'widely practised in the upland Wales as population pressures drove people on to marginal land'.[22] Kilvert himself recorded an example of it. The Mayor of Painscastle told him he had enlarged one of his fields at De Winton's expense, 'because the Lord had not land enough before'.[23] Confrontations over gaming rights on both land and rivers and over enclosures were also frequent in upland Wales in the 19th century.[24]

As time went on, it became clear that Jenkins was laying claim to the disputed strip and he was told he must give up the claim or lose the tenancy of Cwmgivir, the De Winton property. It was Major Charles Stretton, guardian of Captain De Winton when he was a child, who took this uncompromising stand, and Jenkins left Cwmgivir. Vaughan had bought the Glangwye farm in 1860, but, as De Winton's lawyer pointed out, had no documents proving his right to the adjoining strip. Stretton appears to have played a rather dubious role in the saga of the Glangwye fishery that was entirely in accordance with the impression he gave of himself as an adventurer and opportunist in his autobiography. His sojourn at Harrow, and particularly its system of allowing boys to run up debts, had, he said, engendered in him 'a degree of misplaced independence of character and action'.[25] There had begun his descent down 'error's ladder'. He became a trustee of the Maesllwch estate, in which role he approached one of Vaughan's witnesses before the trial and was alleged to have said, 'What do you mean by coming against us?' In court he denied this, though he did not deny using the Cwmgivir tenancy as a means of bullying Jenkins to give up his claim to the Glangwye strip.[26] In summing up, the judge noted the conflicting evidence regarding ownership but was confident that those jurymen who knew the disputed strip, would be able to decide the issue. After a retirement of only a few minutes, the verdict was awarded to Vaughan.

There were factors in the social and political climate that gave Vaughan the confidence to take on the might of Maesllwch just when he did. Support for Dissent, which was strong in his community, had grown considerably in Wales generally from 1815 to 1870, so that by the 1880s, non-conformists outnumbered Anglicans by three to one.[27] Non-conformity was the ideal vehicle for social protest because of the Church's solidarity over many centuries with the landed gentry, and non-conformists were in the habit of referring to 'Church landlordism'.[28] It was common for Englishmen such as Copleston and Thirlwall to hold Welsh bishoprics and to favour the appointment of English gentry clergy, and this was a source of resentment.[29] Another was the English domination of the magistracy. In addition to these factors, there was the relatively classless structure of Welsh upland areas, which resulted from the fact that farms were small and not very profitable, employed few labourers, and exhibited less of an economic distance between farmers and existing labourers. Where the landed interest evinced the clear divisions of landlord, tenant, and labourer, as was the case in most

English and lowland areas of Wales, it was easier to extort deference. Vaughan's stand may have been a manifestation of that, as well as of the tendency for Dissenters to seek opportunities to assert their independence of Anglican gentry.[30] To these regional factors must be added the national movement towards electoral reform, which had been growing through the 1860s. Disraeli had introduced the Second Reform Bill in the Commons on 18 March 1867, a matter of days before the Glangwye case came to court. More will be said later of the Bill's significance.

De Winton's defeat at Presteigne can only have increased his anger and dismay. His reaction was immediately to prepare for a second encounter. By 15 June 1867, he had a local lawyer, Banks of Kington, prepare an affidavit describing the opposition of the commoners of Radnorshire to manorial rights of lords of manors like himself. The affidavit declared that there was 'great hostility' to these rights and Banks had lost cases he had fought for lords of manors because of it. On occasion, he had requested second trials in Herefordshire because Radnorshire jurors were largely commoners, exercising rights over the county's unenclosed land. Vaughan's lawyer, Humfrys, believed there were enough Special Jurors (they were gentlemen and more substantial property owners) in Radnorshire to hear the action between his client and De Winton. The latter, however, was prepared to be openly insulting about local Special Jurors: 'the Special Jurors were an inferior class of persons', he said, and there was little difference if any in terms of their intelligence and prejudice between them and Common Jurors.[31] He was clearly shocked that the normal pattern of authority and deference had not guaranteed him the verdict at Presteigne.[32] His blood was now up. He insisted on the second trial being staged in remote Chester to increase the possibility that the jury would consist of gentlemen more favourable to his case. The other motive behind this move was to prevent a jury having the knowledge of the disputed strip and of its background that local men would have.

The issue should not have been the battleground for claims and counterclaims but this was the countryside, this was the 1860s, and this was the heyday of field sports. 'Of course the object of the litigation was to obtain possession of the fishery...', acknowledged the Chester court. The dispute over it had a 60-year history by the time it came to court.[33]

The Presteigne jury had found in favour of Vaughan. Perhaps they thought, not unreasonably, that a man who already held huge estates could afford to regard a strip of land a few hundred yards long as indeed 'waste', and to relinquish it to one who had so much less. It would be an opportunity for the lord of the manor to show that generosity of spirit for which ancient families had some reputation. As an undeniably 'superior' person, confirmed in that identity by his Eton schooling, Captain De Winton saw the case differently. If jurors believed he could relinquish the strip it would be the proof of the stupidity that rendered them unfit to pass judgement on his case and prevented them from becoming great landowners like himself. They had presumed to show their prejudice against him; he knew the proper role for prejudice: one had to show it in favour of oneself, steadily and at all times. That certainly was the tradition that he had inherited. Three-quarters of a century before, his great-grandfather had shown in no uncertain terms how the family had won and had retained its land. He wrote in 1792 to his solicitor that he was 'in agitation' over a piece of land in the parish of Llowes, sold a few months earlier by a Mr. Howarth of Llandovery to 'a little cottager of mine by name of Thomas Griffiths. He might with equal propriety... have sold part of my demesne'. It is not clear how Mr. Howarth, recently deceased, had been able to sell land that apparently was Wilkins' (ie. De Winton's—the family regained its Norman name in 1839), but Wilkins was very clear what action should be taken with Thomas Griffiths: 'I should be much obliged by your serving Thomas Griffiths with a notice of ejectment to bring him to a sense of his error in the purchase he made to convince him that Mr Howarth had no title in the property he pretended to convey to him'.[34]

The fact that one jury had thrown out the Captain's claim did not deter him. Clearly the lord of the manor intended to win; losing the first case merely increased the need to win. Nationwide there had been from the 1860s onwards a steady consolidation of landowners' power with regard to field sports. Against poachers of all kinds the war intensified. There was an increase of 60% in the number of game-keepers employed between the 1860s and the 1890s. In 1862, the Poaching Prevention Act had been introduced. This Act, sponsored in Parliament by landed gentry, aimed to cut off the poachers' retreat by allowing rural police to search both persons and carts on the highway merely on suspicion that they were involved in poaching. It was the source of a huge wave of fresh bitterness in rural communities. A letter to the *Hereford Times*, for example, for 31 May 1862, urged the country to 'do away with the Game Laws, which are a curse to cottagers, a curse to farmers, a curse to ratepayers...'. The New Year had begun at Clyro Petty Sessions with an old tale: two labourers were summoned by De Winton's gamekeeper for trespassing in pursuit of game on Bryngwyn Hill, 'over which Captain De Winton has exclusive right of shooting'.[35] The year ended with De Winton buying seven out of nine lots of common land locally. No wonder he felt that the law was on his side.

During the Chester trial, which took place in August 1867, some facts emerged that had remained hidden (or not reported) at Presteigne. First, Stretton had steadily sought to increase Maesllwch's fisheries over several years; it seems that Maesllwch had to have Vaughan's 300 yards of river, even though it already controlled four and a half miles of it in the area. Secondly, during the period of Jenkins' tenure of Glangwye, Stretton set up a board very near the disputed strip, laying claim to it. The report of the Chester proceedings indicates once again what a strong case Vaughan had. On the second day, however, even before the double-barrel of the Captain's two QCs could be discharged,[36] events out of court began to turn the case against the small farmer. The previous day, Thursday, had seen the presentation of his case; Friday would have been taken up with that of the lord of Maesllwch. However, before the court opened, the leading counsel were 'for some time' in the judge's rooms. There was a rumour in court that he was urging a compromise on both parties. An intervention at this stage would have meant that only one side of the case had been heard. Was he so impressed by the strength of Vaughan's case that he considered the hearing of De Winton's could only be disadvantageous to the lord of the manor? It seems inconceivable that the judge would deny him the right to be heard otherwise. On Friday morning the judge felt compelled to intervene again, this time in open court. He said he felt it his duty to urge on both parties the propriety of compromise. He carefully avoided commenting on the case but recommended both parties showed an example of 'peace and amity'. De Winton's counsel said his client was prepared to settle; Vaughan's said his client would prefer to take the verdict of the court. If De Winton was prepared to settle at this point, it seems certain that it was not he who had rejected the compromise a little earlier. Thus Vaughan had twice rejected an out of court settlement and here could only be one reason—he was sure of winning. Conversely, what else would dispose the determined Captain to settle except the certain knowledge that he would lose?

No details were given of how the third attempt to stop the trial was engineered. The report says only that some time after compromise was rejected for the second time, the parties' lawyers again left court. When Vaughan's counsel returned, he told the judge that his client felt he could not resist his lordship's appeal that 'peace and amity' should be restored, and had consented to terms by which each party took half the fishery and paid his own costs. Was Vaughan, in accepting this monstrous compromise, bowing to pressure from the judge and perhaps from his own counsel? Did he fear the further litigation over the strip that the judge saw as a future possibility? If he was prompted by genuine magnanimity, why did the prompting not make itself felt at the time of the judge's second intervention? Certainly the offer to pay his own costs looks like nothing other than magnanimity; he could still have agreed to the compromise but allowed De Winton to pay them. He had won the first case in Radnorshire. Why was he now comprising over a right which his own people said was his alone?

The Captain must have returned home generally well pleased. True, he had not won outright, but he had stared a second and more humiliating defeat in the face yet had come away with half the fishery. The cause that drove De Winton on to the second trial, with all its additional trouble, risk, and expense—the two trials cost De Winton £2,576, or at least £50,000 in present day values—was, it needs to be emphasised, field sports. Inferior persons could not be allowed to participate in an activity which the gentry had decreed was theirs alone. In opting for the second trial, De Winton ran the risk of losing face not only in the eyes of fellow gentry, neighbours, and tenants, but in eyes much closer in every sense to home. Less than two months earlier, he had married, and clearly would not relish the thought of returning to his new bride with the story of a second defeat at the hands of inferior persons. He had married Frances Jessie, youngest daughter of the Rev. Hon. Arthur Talbot,[37] on 19 June.

De Winton had particular significance for Kilvert among the landowners, real and fictional, he encountered. For De Winton property was the source of pride and pleasure and power and when he neglected his responsibilities, he descended into debt and shame. His case was set against that of Squire Coleman and Squire Clutterbuck, whose property benefited entire communities. Sir John Neeld and Sir George Cornewall also took insufficient care of their tenant farmers. Kilvert made no criticism of Walter Baskerville except to record that sometimes he felled trees on a scale that was worrying. Apart from selling Vicar's Hill to Baskerville, Venables had no faults in Kilvert's eyes as a landowner. Kilvert praised his willingness to let out land to tenant farmers, rather than 'add house to house and field to field'. This last phrase was taken from Kingsley's description in *Alton Locke* of Lord Ellerton, who had 'a deep sense of the high duties of a landlord', and gave small owners a share of his estates.[38]

Perhaps the most satisfying example of the dutiful landlord that Kilvert found in the pages of a novel was Squire Dimsdale in Lady Verney's *Fernyhurst Court*. (The similarity between May Dimsdale and Ursula in *A Week in a French Country House* has already been noted.) It is clear for a number of reasons that Kilvert found much to enjoy in the novels of Lady Verney. Firstly, he read more novels by her than by any other writer, on the evidence of the *Diary*. Secondly, of the novels he read of hers, two were tackled in quick succession as though he could not get enough of them, and relatively soon after they appeared. The first, *Lettice Lisle*, published in 1870, he was reading on 18 May 1872; only six weeks later, on 1 July 1872, he was into *Fernyhurst Court*, published in 1871; *Llanally Reefs* had appeared in 1873 and Kilvert read it in April 1875. Thirdly, the timing of his involvement with these novels is crucial. The two he read close together played a part in comforting him in his last few months in Clyro (he left on 2 September 1872), as the *Diary* makes clear. He was regretting the loss of Daisy and the ruin of his 'plans and prospects' and seeking a 'haven of rest'.[39] The hill of Penllan offered it in part: 'I climbed Penllan again with that charming book "Lettice Lisle".' He made sure that he would be undisturbed, the better to dwell on his reading and the location.[40]

Penllan, about six miles from Clyro, was a particularly favourite walk of Kilvert's and he visited it often to enjoy the fine views from its top. Its significance, however, went much deeper. At the nearby farmhouse lived the comely girl whose 'half-uncovered bosom' was the subject of his erotic musings. On his birthday in December 1871, he had received from Mrs. Venables a water-colour sketch of Clyro seen from the hill. And when, in March 1874, he revisited Clyro, Penllan was symbolic of the 'thousand sweet and sad memories' of his time there. With *Fernyhurst Court*, he made absolutely plain the link for him between the experience it offered and his situation. One lovely summer evening, he sat on his favourite ancient tomb in Clyro Church reading the novel and 'musing and mourning over the thought of my departure from Clyro... All the familiar sights and sounds of the dear old village were going on around me'.[41] The reading of *Fernyhurst Court* was in some sense another effort to turn the clock back.

What specifically was in these novels for him that simultaneously complemented his mood of melancholy and nostalgia and eased his sense of loss? One obvious fact is that they both looked backward in time. This is especially so with *Fernyhurst Court*, which is set in 'the time before the railways'. Lady Verney grew to adulthood in this period. She was Frances Parthenope Nightingale (known as 'Parthe'), born 1819, elder sister of Florence. Their father lived the life of a country gentleman in Hampshire. Politically, he was a Liberal and briefly, like Squire Dimsdale, an MP. Parthe had a good education at his hands. Initially horrified at her sister's desire to nurse, she rejoiced in her success in the Crimea and enjoyed the reflected glory.[42] Sir Harry Verney, impressed by Florence's achievement, sought her friendship in 1857 and soon proposed but she declined him. He married Parthe a year later and she became Lady Verney of Claydon Hall, Bucks. It is probable that Kilvert first heard of her in the aftermath of the Crimean War when he was a schoolboy and public acclamation of Florence Nightingale was at its height. Sir Harry was also a well-known public figure as an MP and supporter of Lord Shaftesbury's reforms. He was a staunch Evangelical. That Lady Verney was a novelist may have come to Kilvert's attention from the *Cornhill Magazine*, which published her first novel, *Stone Edge*, in 1868.

In the first scene of *Fernyhurst Court*, Squire Dimsdale is visiting one of his tenants and noting his needs, much as Kilvert's grandfather squire might have done. Dimsdale performed all the usual duties of a landowner: he was a JP, was involved in Poor Law administration, in the local hunt and other county business. In contrast to his wife, who sought fashionable London society, he hated London. He hated party politics too; his concern was with the local community, where he was revered. His wife was much less approachable, villagers considering her 'haughty'. Dimsdale's pride was the legitimate kind which Kilvert had identified in Squire Coleman: Dimsdale was 'an honourable gentleman who did his duty to both man and beast'.[43] He was content to be (as his name suggests) 'a great man in a small way'. Instead of running an estate into debt, which was De Winton's way, he had saved his by careful economy; Sir Harry Verney, on whom Dimsdale's character is based, had done the same.[44]

Lettice Lisle also features strands of Kilvert's origins, but this time the yeoman instead of the squire element. Chapter one, entitled 'A Yeoman's Estate', recalls Chieflands: 'All was neglected and dilapidated: the fences ... were badly mended ... the gates were all half broken, and there was a sad poverty-stricken look about everything'. There was 'a curious old timbered house, its gables and many mullioned windows showing that it had once been a place of much greater pretension than as belonging to the poor yeoman its present possessor'.[45] Amyas, the book's yeoman hero, in name and character recalling Amyas Leigh in Kingsley's *Westward Ho!*, struggles to keep his head above water in hard times. The yeoman class, once prosperous and useful, in Lady Verney's view, 'can not keep pace with the farmers of other men's land ... and are gradually dying out'.[46] Like John Fry, he is in thrall to a master who cares only for profit (in Amyas' case a moneylender who is eager to foreclose on his mortgage.) Amyas is honest, industrious, kind and quite learned. Though he was forced to sell some timber to meet his debts, like Kilvert, he lamented the destruction of every tree 'as if it had been a living thing'.[47] He also allows anyone to enjoy the fishing rights on his land. His farmhouse is old fashioned but homely and he was manly in the way that Kilvert admired.

Lettice, the book's heroine, would have appealed greatly to Kilvert. She loves the natural world, learns easily and eagerly, and is perennially happy and thoughtful of others. In her natural, unaffected grace, she resembles all the farmhouse women that Kilvert preferred to gentry women (see next chapter), and even has something in common with Ursula Hamilton. Throughout the novel, she brings harmony and kindness out of bitterness.

The account of De Winton v. Vaughan has thus far emphasised personal and regional factors, but it was noted earlier that 1867 heralded momentous political changes on the national level that also played their part. The most powerful opposition to extension of the suffrage was voiced by Robert Lowe, who emerged as spokesman for landed opponents of reform in 1866. He was MP for Calne, Wiltshire, very much a local MP therefore for Kilvert, and some of his electors protested against his attack on the venality, drunkenness, and ignorance of the working-class. Kilvert was very close to Lowe in the latter's fear and dislike of the 'mob'. For Kilvert the trade union was the most objectionable manifestation of the 'mob' tendency, and *Diary* entries on the subject of miners' strikes reflect his extreme views. Finding an old parishioner without coal, Kilvert fulminated against the 'baneful tyrannical influence of that cursed Union',[48] and hoped that one good result of it would be that it would 'sicken England of trade unions'.[49] It was the advent of the National Agricultural Labourers' Union (NALU) in 1872 that compelled clergymen to take an interest in industrial disputes. The Church declined to comment on them until the Leeds Church Congress of that year. On that occasion, the Bishop of Manchester observed that working men's representatives should be on the platform and bishops in the body of the hall listening to them.[50] Things had begun to change.

It is significant that Kilvert made no mention of attending a Congress until 1873, when it was conveniently located in Bath.[51] The main theme of it was the Church's attitude to strikes and labour, and Kilvert said he heard some 'good papers'. That of the Bishop of Oxford[52] was the key one. He stated that the Church should be impartial and leave agricultural wages to the law of supply and demand, even though this might smack of indifference in the face of the undoubted poverty they suffered. It was absurd, he said, to expect farmers to pay wages higher than those they were compelled to pay. The role of the Church was to make the labourer '...a better, braver, ...more civilised, more tender-hearted man' via education. The Bishop did not make it clear how this moral and educational improvement could be achieved while labourers' subsistence wages made civilised life impossible. Moments before he had acknowledged that their homes were 'destitute of the endowments which gave grace to human life'. He rebuked labourers' leaders for preaching materialism and a vision of a society of hostile classes.[53] He did not seem to realise that it was precisely the *laissez-faire* system, which he was

295

content should determine wages, that gave rise to the dog-eat-dog society he purported to deplore. He had admitted that farmers would pay as little as they could. The average wage in 1872 was 12s. Northern labourers earned 15s, while in Kilvert's Wiltshire they received 10s 6d—almost a third less.[54] Nor was this the whole truth about wages: '...in adjacent villages, wages could differ by two shillings a week, that is, by nearly twenty per cent, without any difference in demand or supply; in villages further apart... there could be a difference of four or even five shillings - almost fifty per cent'.[55] It was commonly nothing but sheer meanness that determined what labourers were paid.

It is evident from the 1873 Congress that the Church's attitude to agricultural labourers had not changed all that much. It acknowledged the NALU but only with deep reluctance, and showed the same lack of understanding of and sympathy for it that Rev. Venables had shown towards Chartism. Yet there was one clergyman at Bath who did not utter the paternalist cant about labourers raising themselves by industry and thrift, about supply and demand, and about the Church's benevolence. This was Canon Girdlestone, whose paper Kilvert included in those he thought 'good'. Girdlestone thought 'the clergy of the rural districts command from the labouring classes an amount of affection ...impossible... to describe'.[56] To Kingsley, however, nothing signified more clearly that Church Toryism constituted a dying system than when it boasted that its stronghold was still in the hearts of the rural poor. Girdlestone actually gave a much warmer welcome to the NALU than Kingsley did, declaring at Bath that it 'has done more to raise the condition of the labourer... than all the Royal Commissions...'. The wise course was for clergymen to accept it and to seek, by their local influence, to control it. That influence could have been strong if they had, from the beginning, spoken out fearlessly from their pulpits on social questions and put pressure on landowners and farmers to improve the lot of the labourer.

He had done so himself in an article in 1868—the year the Second Reform Bill became operable. He was able then to raise the significant possibility that the franchise would inevitably be extended to the agricultural labourer as it had been to the artisan of the towns: 'who dare define how long it will be ...before the franchise is bestowed on the agricultural labourer?'[57] However, while landowners as a class had experienced some enlargement of their attitudes and sympathies, many, especially in the west of England, were still benighted. 'Such men deem of the land as that which furnishes their income, breeds foxes, hares, pheasants, ...and alas rabbits also, and entitles them to a certain ...social privilege and rank, but not as entailing a corresponding amount of responsibility'. To such men, the idea of agricultural labourers receiving the vote was unthinkable. 'Not a single landowner so far in the west of England has come forward publicly to support any movement for the improvement of the... labourer; many have thrown all possible obstacles in the way of such movements'.

In August 1868 Kilvert, as Chaplain to Walter Baskerville, High Sheriff that year of Radnorshire, had preached the sermon before the Summer Assizes. It would have been too much to ask of him, especially on that occasion, to speak out as Girdlestone had about the plight of labourers, yet in the text he had chosen there was a message for landowners had they been able to apply it to themselves, instead of to the poor who regularly appeared before the bench. The text was, 'For there is nothing covered that shall not be revealed'. The *Hereford Times* indicated how Kilvert developed this theme. 'Dwelling upon our Lord's warning to His disciples against... hypocrisy, the preacher said God required truth before all things... a silent avenger dogs the footsteps of the criminal... Sometimes the avenger... travels in the guilty heart... And the guilty one may go to the grave unsuspected, even respected and honoured'.[58] If Kilvert had a landowner in mind when he uttered these words, it was more likely to have been Venables than De Winton. The latter's dereliction of duty was widely recognised and his reputation in the local community had suffered in consequence. Venables, on the other hand, was a man universally honoured and in Kilvert's mind was more open to the charge of hypocrisy, as has been suggested in an earlier chapter.

Local newspapers were testifying to events and opinions in 1868 that indicated a groundswell of opposition to landowners of the kind that Vaughan had advanced to De Winton the previous year. In September appeared a letter pointing out that the tenant farmers of a Monmouthshire landowner were still in the condition of serfs in that they were compelled to vote as he directed or they would lose their farms. Another letter attacked rich landowners' monopoly of fishing in all the local rivers.[59] Such *Diary* figures as Walter

Baskerville, Walter De Winton, Rev. Jones Thomas, Rev. Blisset, and Tomkyns Dew, formed the board of the Association for the Preservation of the Wye. It had little ecological function and existed largely to 'preserve' their own rights of fishing. Its annual report for 1865 recorded 20 cases of 'illegal fishing', that is, fishing by inferior persons. But what, except a change of political climate, could account for the almost incredible revelation in the *Hereford Times* for 31 August 1867 (the same month in which the second De Winton v. Vaughan court case was heard) that Thomas Baskerville had been summoned by the water bailiff of the Wye preservation body for illegal fishing? 'The case', said the newspaper, 'appeared to excite some interest... in the neighbourhood'. Indeed it would. No details of it were given and it was probably a matter of technicalities and it was adjourned.[60] De Winton tried to appease Rev. Thomas and the other JPs by assuring them that Sir Velters Cornewall, president of the Wye Association, had written to Thomas Baskerville about it; it could safely be left in the hands of gentlemen. If you were not a gentleman, the case was different.

Land and property and politics were key issues in another trial, which also had its origins in the highly charged atmosphere of 1867, and had an enormously powerful, even hypnotic, effect on the public. We are fortunate in having this reaction of Kilvert to one phase of it: 'The Tichborne case has collapsed and that detestable villain, scoundrel, impostor and liar is I am happy to say safely lodged in Newgate to take his trial for perjury. I am filled with a sort of fury whenever I think of that carcase'.[61] A good deal of that fury was still near the surface when he encountered, just two months later, Mr. Latimer Jones, with whom he almost came to blows over property rights. It is quite possible, too, that the Tichborne case figured in the argument. Kilvert, in company with the public at large, would have followed the case from its beginning in 1867 until the final verdict on 28 February 1874.

Gossip and rumour had begun to circulate in 1867 about a missing heir of the ancient Tichborne family returning to claim his inheritance. Roger Tichborne had left England in 1853 for South America and it was assumed he had drowned at sea in 1854, but it appeared he had been rescued and had spent ten years in the Australian bush. His mother had never believed he was dead and had always kept his room ready for his return. The family, who were Catholics, had lived near Alresford, Hants, since before the Conquest and owned vast estates, the annual rent role of which was reputedly £30,000 to £40,000.[62] A man claiming to be Roger Tichborne appeared in England on Christmas Day 1866 and began collecting affidavits from people who had known him years before. He would have been the 11th baronet. His father had married the illegitimate daughter of Mr. Henry Seymour of Knoyle, Wiltshire.[63] She was christened Henriette Félicité and had brought Roger up in Paris. She so hated the thought of Roger's relatives having anything to do with him that she developed a violent aversion to them. Spoilt in her youth, she was an extremely possessive mother of uncertain temper and kept Roger in a frock until he was 12. He first went to school in Paris but his father insisted he be sent eventually to Stoneyhurst, the Catholic public school in Lancashire. Though very thin and short, he did join in games but was an indifferent scholar. As a result of the influence of highly placed family friends, a commission was obtained for him in the 6th Dragoon Guards.[64]

These circumstances alone gave the Tichborne case considerable public interest, but to history, tradition, and scandal was added legend and prophecy. It was, therefore, a story with particular attraction for Kilvert. From the time of Henry II there had existed the Tichborne Dole, a charity for the poor about which had grown up the story that if it were ever discontinued, a curse would fall on the family in the form of the extinction of the male line of succession. Local JPs, alarmed at the number of vagrants flocking to Alresford in the hard years of the Napoleonic War and fearing unrest, persuaded the head of the family to let the charity lapse. When Roger was lost at sea, there were those who saw in it the operation of the ancient curse. Romance enters the story with Roger falling in love with his cousin, Katharine Doughty, when he was 20 and she 15.[65] The Tichborne Claimant was to declare later that he had seduced her and her honour became a crucial issue in the court case and supplied the society of the day with more sensational reading. Her father objected to the marriage and persuaded Roger to delay it. After some years in the army, Roger decided to go abroad. When he was presumed drowned, his younger brother became heir to the estates, becoming the 11th baronet in 1862 on his father's death.

The claim to the Tichborne and Doughty estates grew then out of a colourful and dramatic background that would have seized the imagination of people in any age. However, for the Victorian public the issue of property was of special importance. For many of them it was a dream to possess the kind of property that had descended to the Tichbornes like a blessing. As we have seen, Kilvert had a deep imaginative attachment to such properties as Chieflands, Yaverland, Bowood, and Hardenhuish House, home of the Clutterbucks. He favoured, of course, the organic mode of acquiring property—inheritance. For other Victorians, the realisation of the dream came through worldly success, entrepreneurship, a blessing dispensed by what Ruskin called 'The Goddess of Getting-on'. He envisaged the mansion that would be the home of the successful: 'In this mansion are to live the favoured votaries of the Goddess; the English gentleman with his gracious wife, and his beautiful family'.[66] Kilvert regularly expressed his deep pleasure at encountering such domestic bliss in the homes of the Crichtons, the Phillips of Abbey Cwmhir, and the Mayhews. Property not only signified the sacred institutions of home and family, but also respectability, security, the means of demonstrating one's position in society. On it rested crucially one's right to vote. It enabled one to improve one's position because it facilitated advantageous marriages and Kilvert had discovered that the lack of it could destroy hopes of marriage. However, its virtues transcended the merely material. Woodruff, in his book on the Tichborne case,[67] indicated the way in which property became part of myth in the Victorian age. He noted that the plot in which the long-lost heir mysteriously reappeared to claim his possessions was a favourite one for a society devoted to private theatricals. He pointed out, too, that almost all the Gilbert and Sullivan operas, the first of which came into being in 1878, involve the discovery of the rightful heir to some property.

The struggles of the Tichborne Claimant to regain his estates, which brought the myth to life for Victorian society, began early in 1867. Roger's mother had regularly put advertisements in newspapers, seeking news of him. She had also seen an advertisement of an agency in Sydney that offered to trace missing relatives in Australia and she contacted it and spoke of a reward. It featured her advertisement in Australian papers. A small town lawyer's wife saw it and suggested to her husband that a bankrupt butcher who was his client might be the missing heir; he had referred to owning property in England. The lawyer glimpsed the possibility of claiming the reward.

A series of letters passed between Roger's mother and the butcher Claimant during 1865-6, and although his considerable illiteracy plus the descriptions supplied to her of his appearance suggested a man much different from the Roger who had sailed to Chile in 1853, Lady Tichborne was determined to see him.[68] She was greatly reassured by the fact that he had been recognised in Sydney by two former Tichborne servants. When he arrived in England, he visited Alresford, where again he was recognised by people who had known Roger, and then Paris where he passed his first major test: he was recognised by Lady Tichborne. Grief and loneliness (her husband and other son were dead) may have pressed her to accept him; another motive may have been a desire to prove she was right in refusing to believe in his death.

For seven years the English public had the opportunity to specu-late on the supreme mystery of the case: was the Claimant really Roger Tichborne? If not, who was he? Kilvert no doubt asked himself the same questions and discussed possibilities with a parishioner: '...had some talk with Dyke on the Tichborne case. He instanced the loss and return of Charles James Phillips of Wye Cliff who was believed to be dead and buried in Australia. His family sent out an agent to make enquiries. The agent was satisfied of [his] death. Yet the young man returned in rags and accosted his aunt in Hereford... She disowned him. Yet he proved his identity...'.[69] The Tichborne Claimant rapidly began to consolidate his position in 1867. Servants and tenants of the estate, as well as the family doctor and solicitor, recognised him. Dozens of private soldiers from Roger's regiment swore he was their old comrade. Lady Tichborne was, however, the only family member who supported him and his solicitor was very ready to point out that his client was recognised by everyone who did not have a financial reason for declining to do so. It might have been thought that with her death in March 1868, the Claimant's case would collapse, but by that time 200 people were ready to swear that he was Roger Tichborne. However, the family was determined to prove he was someone else. A detective hired by them to watch him unearthed a lady who was prepared to swear that he was her ex-sweetheart— Arthur Orton, a butcher originally from Wapping.

The story began with the Claimant laying claim to his estates on 27 June 1867 and finished on 28 February 1874 when he was convicted of perjury. In the view of Maugham,[70] one of the main reasons for the case taking so much time was money: both sides were prepared to contest the issue for so long because the Tichborne estates were of such value. The case began on 10 May 1871 in which the Claimant asserted his rights to his estates, and Maugham laid some of the blame for its interminable length on the legal figures involved. The worst offender was Coleridge, counsel for the Tichborne family. John Duke Coleridge was a great nephew of the poet. He had won classical prizes at Eton and Balliol. He was fond of making dramatic speeches but was not noted for the skills of cross-examination. Originally appointed as subordinate to Henry Hawkins QC, he was put in charge after being made Solicitor-General. Hawkins was free of the harshness and arrogance that vitiated Coleridge's approach to the Claimant. In an exchange with Ballantine, the Claimant's counsel, who was concerned about his client's health under searching questioning, Coleridge remarked that he would be as disagreeable as he could. The transcript of the trial shows that there is 'a sort of fury' in the Solicitor-General's manner, of the kind Kilvert recognised in himself when he thought of the Claimant, that is not explained solely by his failure to pin his witness down. He was obsessed with the need to demonstrate that he could not have been at Stoneyhurst because he was so obviously not a gentleman, and had none of the gentlemanly knowledge he would have acquired there.

The aggressiveness shown by Coleridge is indicative of the extent to which emotion and prejudice had come to dominate the case. To seek to 'prove' that the Claimant was not a gentleman was, from a strictly legal standpoint, neither a relevant nor a rational endeavour. It suggests a lack of self-control reprehensible in an eminent lawyer. Of course, the Claimant was aware that he was the subject of personal attack marked by vindictiveness and self-indulgence. He complained that the reiterated questions were only intended to insult him and that he was continually harried and bullied. At one point, he observed to the judge: 'I think the Solicitor-General's conduct is very insolent, my Lord'. Upon which Coleridge replied, 'I mean it to be'.

The Solicitor-General had to question dozens of witnesses but it was the 'slippery scoundrel' (his own description of the Claimant) that he found especially taxing. Confirmation that the cross-examination of the Claimant provoked a personal crisis for Coleridge is forthcoming from his personal diary that he kept during the trial. The Claimant was in the witness box from 30 May to 7 July 1871. On 30 May Coleridge was recording: 'He was worse than I expected in vulgarity and ignorance, with a sort of veneer of manner especially odious'. It was that vulgarity and ignorance that Coleridge was intent on exposing.

Amid the 19th century anxiety about who was and who was not a gentleman, there was some engagement with the problem of those who masqueraded beneath a 'veneer of manner'. Reliance was placed on circumstances producing the test in which the qualities of the true gentleman would appear and the impostor would be exposed. Among writers who tackled the problem was Mrs. Braddon. George Nugent Bankes was a schoolboy at Eton in the 1870s when he was thrilled and disturbed by Mrs. Braddon's novel, *Henry Dunbar*, in which a lowly clerk in an aristocratic banking house murders its head and assumes his identity.[71] Trollope's *Is He Popenjoy?*, which Kilvert made a point of reading the year it came out (1878), was actually inspired by the Tichborne case, though the issue of the identity of the child in it is not a close parallel to it because it turns out to be an irrelevance. Nevertheless, the Popenjoy child and the Tichborne Claimant challenged the order of society by aspiring to a place in it for which they were not fitted.

It was this which so angered Coleridge, who found the Claimant's answers such an exasperating mixture of ignorance and knowledge. His manner in court, for all that Coleridge found it 'odious', was, in contrast to his own, calm and controlled. Some of Coleridge's frustration stemmed from his daily experience that the Claimant was evading his questioning and was tending to appear as the superior gentleman, and it was a fearful drain on his resources. On 12 June his diary notes: 'Another hard day... Went into the [Sessions] House and stayed there working till past 12, when I went home. Then went to bed, but not to sleep...'. On 15 June: '...another long day. I am getting very tired and knocked up. But the ruffian's ignorance is something ...astonishing'. The following day he notes: 'Not quite so good a day... I heard, but hardly believe, ...that a juror had said he would never find against the claimant, because Bovill [the Judge] and I had been hard on him. I doubt this, but it is awkward'. Coleridge was recording on 23 June that he was 'Very unwell... with aches and pains all over me', and on 27 June, 'another long and hard day at claimant. He will kill me before I do him. I am seriously wearing out and getting ill'.[72]

These diary entries show not only that Coleridge was haunted by the feeling that he was locked in some personal combat with the Claimant, but also that he had developed a deep loathing for him that recalls that felt by Kilvert. The Claimant's challenge provoked feelings of profound personal insecurity in the two men that was connected with the case's social and political implications but went far beyond them. Both sought to give expression to their anxiety and loathing through the use of terms that are of the same order of abusiveness. The Claimant to both men was a 'ruffian' and a 'scoundrel'; to Coleridge he was also a 'wretch' and a 'rascal', while Kilvert gained further relief for his feelings by referring to him as a 'detestable villain', an 'impostor', a 'liar', a 'malefactor' and a 'miscreant'. In following the case closely in the newspapers, which Kilvert appears to have done, he had perhaps grown close to the Solicitor-General by accompanying him on his *via dolorosa* through the trial, and had suffered with him, especially at the end of long days spent trying to pin down the slippery, vulgar Claimant. The remark in the entry for 16 June about the juror who stated he would never find against the Claimant because of Coleridge's bullying tactics, is revealing for the light it casts upon why the Tichborne case so completely polarised English society. The juror had already sat through over two weeks of the Claimant's idiotic explanations of some facts and blank rebuttals of others, of his repeated declarations that he had no recollection of crucial events, and he had heard his brazen admission that he had seduced his own cousin. In spite of all that, he maintained a belief in the Claimant because the Solicitor-General of England had bullied him in court.

It was understandable that Coleridge feared that the largely uneducated and gullible public would side with the Claimant. However, the jury at the civil trial, in which the Claimant tried to secure the Tichborne estates, was made up of army and navy officers and landowners,[73] who might have been expected to be so repelled by the Wapping butcher that their verdict would be a foregone conclusion. But Coleridge did not feel able to rely on them either. His despair was shared by *The Times*, which viewed with 'despondency and almost terror' the prospect of the criminal trial of the Claimant that now threatened. Since the Claimant was 'a common-place type', he should be tried in the Old Bailey before a Common Jury rather than, as was proposed, in the Queen's Bench before a Special Jury. Ballantine QC noted that the prosecution would demand a Special one (just as Captain De Winton had) but it did not have its way. At the criminal trial in which the Claimant stood accused of perjury, the jury was made up of solid middle-class people, most of them West End tradesmen.[74] They were deliberately not drawn from the gentry lest it appear that they had been chosen from the class most hostile to the Claimant. His supporters, nevertheless, thought the jurors would vote the way their betters wanted them to.

Coleridge was as aware as anyone of the class factors in the case, and one of the reasons for his hysteria in court and near breakdown may have been his extreme ambivalence towards them. His father, Sir John Coleridge, was a brilliant man, very interested in literature and a friend of Wordsworth, Dr. Arnold, and Newman. Arnold had told him in 1838 that aristocracy had been 'the greatest source of evil throughout the world' and was if anything worse than democracy.[75] He himself published in 1860 his lecture on 'Public School Education', which was an attack on the corruption and inefficiency of Eton.[76] His son had been to Eton and had developed either there or later a hatred of aristocracy. He told his father in a letter of 1855, 'I have no mind to force myself into a set of indolent, corrupt aristocrats whom as a class (forgive me) I hate and despise with my whole soul'. And in a letter years later to Sir William Heathcote he attacked their snobbishness, exclusiveness, selfishness, insolence, and contempt for others.[77] Resentment of aristocratic idleness and self-indulgence had been, as earlier chapters have shown, part of Kilvert's inheritance. He inevitably backed a fellow clergyman who complained that 'indecent efforts and influence had been brought to bear' to have the aristocratic Mr. Bouverie, third son of the fourth Earl of Radnor, appointed to the living of Malmesbury.[78]

Coleridge had become an MP on the Liberal side in 1865 and backed the 1867 Reform Bill.[79] All of this might have led him to be kind to Arthur Orton, especially since his nature was 'receptive and sympathetic to an unusual degree'.[80] The daily spectacle of him in the witness box—evasive, foolish, blustering, corpulent—may have induced in Coleridge a terrible doubt about the wisdom of enfranchising some of the working-class. *The Times* of 15 April 1867 had, after all, noted that 'of the poorer voters even Liberals have begun to be afraid'. Part of Coleridge's panic when confronting the Claimant is explicable in terms of this fear. In other ways Coleridge's situation in the Tichborne civil trial is a complex one. He, as a hater of aristocracy, was being paid by an important county family with strong aristocratic connections to defend their property against the insolent and shameless claim of Orton. Here was Coleridge defending the very principles—primogeniture and hereditary property—that were the life blood of the aristocracy. Such a man, sensitive as he was and passionate about great causes, could not but feel the ignominy of his situation. He, the Solicitor-General, had become subservient to the interests of the Tichbornes. It is highly conceivable, therefore, that the Claimant came in for a larger share of Coleridge's fury than was his due because Coleridge was powerless to direct it at the target he most dearly wanted to hit—the aristocracy. There existed also the disturbing possibility that Arthur Orton really *was* Roger Tichborne and thus his social superior.

There is no doubt that the fact that the Tichborne case had begun in 1867 and had continued through the post-Reform Bill years heightened the social class and property issues that were its essence. What it represented was nothing less than the assertion by the masses that they were as good as any in the land. Woodruff underlined the significance of the treatment meted out to Orton: 'because his speech and bearing were asserted to be those of a common man, the poor were quick to detect an insult, as though a man of rank who came down to their level thereby forfeited his rights as a man and a citizen'.[81] It was after the Reform Bill of 1867 that Robert Lowe made his famous pronouncement, 'we must educate our masters', referring to the newly enfranchised working-class. *The Times* laid heavy emphasis on the Claimant's lack of education: '[he] is a low-born, illiterate, vulgar scoundrel without a trace of education...'.[82] Society's deepest fear of working-class anarchy that would threaten property had been aroused.

A month before the verdict on Orton was pronounced, Kilvert was registering his alarm when a mob of radical supporters, many of them miners, rioted at the Chippenham election and smashed the windows of the Tory committee room.[83] Throughout both trials, a significant part of the Claimant's support came from working-class people.[84] No doubt it was newspaper reports of working-class meetings that kept Kilvert's feelings on the boil between the trials. He was also incensed by the Claimant's counsel, Dr. Kenealy. If Kilvert's moral indignation was aroused by Kenealy's attack on the respectable Tichborne family, it was as nothing compared with that he would experience at the impugning of the honour of a lady. The claim made by Orton in open court that he had seduced his cousin, Katharine Doughty, profoundly offended both his supporters and his opponents. It was the last straw to people like Kilvert, who found him repellent on moral, social and physical grounds. Orton's physical appearance was an important factor. He was 16st when he arrived in England and grew to 27st before the civil trial. Kilvert twice called him a 'carcase'. Coleridge's reference to him as 'an enormous mass of flesh' produced a more, rather than less, favourable response to him from ordinary people, who found him endearing partly because of his size and partly because of his sporting tastes and liking for drink and cigars.[85]

Though Kenealy made absurd charges, which showed a profound lack of judgement, he was nevertheless right when he advanced the view that the Crown's case was marked by a vindictiveness unworthy of it. It ought to have been content to establish facts, instead of which it sought to attack the personality of the defendant. That there was some truth in this view may be seen from the sentence imposed on Orton: he was found guilty on two charges of perjury— that he falsely claimed to be Roger Tichborne and to have seduced Katharine Doughty. Though the court could have given him a sentence covering both charges, it chose to award seven years for each, to run consecutively. Some lawyers of the day thought the sentence actually illegal and certainly contrary to Parliament's intention in fixing the maximum for perjury as seven years. An appeal against Orton's sentence was rejected by the government. Kilvert's reaction to the sentence was in this general spirit of vindictiveness: 'I am only sorry that the Judges could not inflict... penal servitude for life. But it is to be hoped that it will come to the same thing. That carcass can hardly cumber the earth for 14 years more'.[86] He also wanted Kenealy imprisoned. Kilvert's Bishop, Thirlwall, didn't go that far but he had been equally disturbed and shared his sense of relief when it was all over: 'I have taken an almost painful interest in the Tichborne trial, and long for the time when Kenealy will... have said his last'.[87]

Arthur Orton served most of his sentence in Dartmoor, where his weight went down to 10st. It is ironic that if he had been sentenced to only seven years, remission would have enabled him to be free before Kilvert died. He did earn maximum remission and was freed on 11 October 1884. He spent some time immediately afterwards talking about his case in travelling circuses and music halls. A more humiliating fate awaited him, however. Poverty compelled him to accept an offer from *The People* to write, under the name Arthur Orton, a confession of his plot to secure the Tichborne estates.[88]

The essential mystery of the Tichborne case still remains: how was an uneducated butcher able to pass himself off as the heir to the estates of a semi-aristocratic family? A number of observations can be made on this issue. First, even though the Claimant was always bigger than Roger Tichborne, a study of photographs of the two men does indicate that if the extra poundage were stripped away, their features bore a close similarity. This may have been a common perception among all those who 'recognised' the Claimant. Second, the more educated among them were perhaps prepared to attribute his coarseness to years spent in the Australian bush, while the working-class ones unconsciously willed themselves into believing that he could once have been a gentleman (and that they themselves might be). Thirdly, the uneducated character that the claimant so clearly demonstrates in court and in his letters could be attributed, in the view of Ballantine, his counsel, to Roger Tichborne's poor showing as a scholar at Stoneyhurst. Ballantine also remarked on the 'great likeness' between the Claimant and members of the Tichborne family and his lack of coarse features.[89] It was also alleged that Kenealy was convinced his client was 'a gentleman born and bred; lost, half-degraded, but nevertheless, a gentleman...'.[90] Another similarity that the degraded and the real gentleman had in common was a love of drink.

It was shared, too, by De Winton and eventually caused his death at the age of 45. Advanced cirrhosis of the liver made him look 'fearfully ill and shrunken and feeble' when Kilvert met him on a station in September 1874. 'It went to my heart as he said in a mournful voice, "I can't shoot, and I can't fish, and I can't do anything now"'.[91] Without those activities, it appeared he had nothing to live for. Part of Kilvert's resentment of De Winton derived from the fact that the object for which he was prepared to assert so much arrogance and to expend so much effort was nothing more noble than field sports. To the Evangelical mind field sports were, as has been shown earlier, sinful in a number of ways: they represented gratuitous cruelty, they were a gross anomaly in God's benign universe, and were the fruits of idleness. (Compare the quote from Perkin that prefaces this chapter.) Kilvert had a deep reverence for landed estates, especially for the way in which they could create a family ethos within a district. However, when he saw an estate's power being used to divide a community and to tyrannise its weakest members, his sense of injustice, of the betrayal of a God-given trust, was very great. Though he backed the cause of a small farmer such as Vaughan, the Tichborne Claimant was a different proposition altogether. The honour of a noble family had been threatened by an imposter and Kilvert could not tolerate it. The concept of honour was, as has been noted, as sacred to him as to Robert Lowe, who said in April 1866 that aristocracy existed on the basis of honour and that democracy threatened to destroy honour. For Kilvert, the Tichborne case appeared as nothing less than the claim by the masses that they were the equal of gentlefolk and demanded the same rights, and that undermined the relations that governed his ideal community.

De Winton's conduct also undermined that community but when Kilvert beheld him, desperately ill and shorn of all spirit and confidence, he could feel only sympathy for him as a human being, even though he condemned his physical, social and moral degradation. His was a fate that had haunted Kilvert all his life and had emerged, unbidden and terrifying, in the dream in which he had killed Venables in the most savage, ungentlemanly manner. In an obscure way, he feared that his own lack of social success, of social integration, might mean that he had latent within him, a capacity for social anarchy symbolised by Arthur Orton in all his coarseness and duplicity. In the novel that Trollope based on the Tichborne case, he showed in the figure of Lord George Germain what happened when a man isolated himself from society by aberrant conduct. Trollope's novels document a society in flux and he was constantly seeking a set of values that would stand firm in the midst of it. For him, as for Kilvert, the country gentleman was the embodiment of those values, largely because he had a clearly defined place in the social order and his social integration was synonymous with moral integration. 'Morality consists in knowing one's proper place in the social order, and in conforming to society's demands'.[92] Evil is, therefore, social and moral isolation.

Kilvert could see it very clearly in Arthur Orton's crime. But what precisely was that crime? Success for the Victorians was 'the wish to be other than one was'.[93] Could Orton's claim be considered to be an extreme case of that urge? Hardly, since he was not seeking to rise in society by effort, initiative, education, or self-improvement. A man who was not a gentleman by birth might seek to become one, but he needed to be a gentleman 'at heart', which Orton clearly was not. Rising in society was, like everything else, governed by rules, all of which the Claimant had outrageously violated. Kilvert, as we have seen, approved of the industrious labourer aspiring to own a small farm, and to own landed property was of enormous importance to Victorians. Burn suggested that the prestige of the eminent landowner was so great that it tempted men like Orton to make desperate bids to attain the position by fraud. There had been a similar case 20 years earlier when a man called Provis was sentenced to 20 years' transportation for perjury and forgery in his attempt to obtain the estates of the Smyth family of Ashton Court in Bristol.[94]

If society was to continue to accept in the 1870s the social and political eminence of landowners, they had to prove their worth. Kingsley declared that they had to make themselves 'morally necessary' if they were not to become 'politically unnecessary'.[95] This was the view also of John Duke Coleridge. *The Times*, somewhat optimistically, was advancing a contrary view while the Tichborne case was proceeding. 'The common people tolerate and even admire a social aristocracy... because they see real merits in it... it is a practical guarantee for more charitable... gentlemanlike conduct than can be produced by the mere play of self-interest'. It noted, however, the case of the Duke of Newcastle, who had ruined himself by gambling on horses.[96] De Winton's case paralleled that of the Duke, and Kilvert was critical of it. However, he always harboured a respect for the tradition, romance, and social order aristocracy represented. Like Kingsley, he was unable to accept the House of Commons as the only national, legislative body. The Commons, said Kingsley, could only represent 'the temporary wants and opinions of the many', and the many might include Arthur Ortons. It lacked the moral significance and socially cohesive force of the House of Lords, which represented 'all heritable property... all heritable products of moral civilisation'.[97] Kingsley's vision of the inter-dependence of classes was akin to that of the Bishop of Oxford, whose approach to property and organised labour had pleased Kilvert. He was prepared, as Kilvert was, to criticise the education of the landed gentry for being deficient 'in that very important part... which makes [them] humble and... considerate and kind'.[98] The Bishop's answer to the problem of the estrangement of classes was not more justice for the lower orders but more charity. Thus, he made no reference to the enfranchisement of agricultural labourers even though that had been one of the original demands of the NALU.[99] There is no reference to it in Kilvert's *Diary* either, probably because the thought of it was too disturbing; when it happened it would mean the end of rural society as he knew it. An equally potent threat to it was the aberrant behaviour of De Winton and Arthur Orton.

'The history of modern civilisation down to the early twentieth century was one of growing distance from unmediated feelings and spontaneous conduct'.

Peter Gay, *The Cultivation of Hatred*, p.495

'The mid-Victorian impulse was to construct personality through the control and moderation of the desires... The freedom to feel different almost invariably came over as a disruption of the social norms'.

Andrew St. George, *The Descent of Manners. Etiquette, Rules and the Victorians*, p.46

'[The Englishman] is too awkward and ashamed to do as he pleases, for fear it should be odd or vulgar... those who individually are often among the prime of their species, are often socially the most imbecile and incapable of men'.

John Sterling, *English Society*, p.39

'Oh that I too had a child to love and to love me, a daughter with such fair limbs and blue eyes archly dancing, and bright clustering curls blown wild and golden in the sunshine and sea air'.

Kilvert's *Diary*, Vol. 3, p.206

'In her most perfect form the lady combined total sexual innocence, conspicuous consumption, and the worship of the family hearth'.

Martha Vicinus, 'The Perfect Victorian Lady', in *Suffer and Be Still*, p.ix

'A society that sets up to be polite and ignores Arts and Letters, I hold to be a snobbish society'.

William Makepeace Thackeray, *The Book of Snobs*, p.161

CHAPTER 10
Kilvert and the English Country House

Relentless adherence to the notion of rank had as effectively blighted the hopes of Daisy Thomas and Kilvert as it had poisoned the life of John Couzens and led to the dismissal of Anne Pugh. In *A Week in a French Country House*, it was Lady Blankeney who represented this English concern. Ursula's appeal to Kilvert lay chiefly in her uncompromising integrity and freedom from the life-destroying preoccupation with rank. Her stance was not one he could hope to emulate for a variety of reasons. In the first place she was a woman; different things were expected of a man; he was an English country clergyman for whom status in the parish was all important. The French priest in the book is described as 'entirely different' from his English counterpart. He was 'very hard-working and exemplary but in quite a different way, and altogether simpler and more homely'.[1] He would readily assist in manual labour and work in the fields with his neighbour getting in the hay. Kilvert too helped in haymaking, though only on occasion and, perhaps significantly, in his home district of Langley Burrell. It was not a thing English clergymen were regularly found doing. Ursula's successful life as an artist allowed her to stand apart from society and from some, at least, of its conventions,[2] though the position of women artists was, of course, a difficult one at the time and their reputation was always suspect. Artistic sensibility permeates *A Week in a French Country House* and no doubt the artist in Kilvert responded to it. The free-wheeling talk at Mme. Olympe's of art and ideas, of which Ursula is the centre, was, one feels, conspicuously lacking in the drawing rooms of Llanthomas, Clyro Court, and Clifford Priory. Lord Redesdale stated that her dinner parties at her London home were 'perfection', partly because of her own wit, charm and brilliant conversation, and partly because the guests, an intimate group of eight or ten and no more, were drawn from the most distinguished in the worlds of literature, art and music.[3]

The urbanity and humanity of Mme. Olympe's home were the fruits of a society that essentially valued people for what they were and not for who they were. This chapter undertakes further exploration of the implications for Kilvert of the English country house ethos which he was provoked into criticising as a result of reading Adelaide Sartoris' novel. She consistently used her stories to oppose the English tendency to value rank, money, and the authority based on them, above all things. In her novel, *Judith*, the character of Augusta St. John is another English woman in the mould of Lady Blankeney. She is a representative of English country house society and is characterised as 'vain, hard, unloving and unlovable'. The novel's heroine, Judith, has much in common with Ursula. She too is devoted to art and to discovering the integrity and the life-enhancing quality of individuals. Her faith in these things results in a lack of worldliness that produces the impulsiveness and vulnerability to unscrupulous people which endangered Ursula. Judith had become the protégée of an English country gentleman whose natural warmth and spontaneity responded to her own. He had 'a heart overflowing with affection, and a morbid degree of romantic feeling; people in England did not quite understand or like it...'.[4] He took her to Brankleigh Manor, home of his rich but shallow brother, whose wife was the cold, snobbish Augusta, and demanded that she be looked after while she built a stage career. Unsurprisingly, it is left to a German lady, visiting Brankleigh Manor, to observe: '...it is not life among these icy English hearts! I am sick of their pretensions and their pride! Their moral superiority with which they are puffed up...'.[5]

Kilvert's affectionate heart, warmth, impulsiveness, and romantic feelings were similarly repelled by the qualities of English country house society. Its end result was the 'starving of the heart' for which Edward Carpenter blamed Victorian society.[6] Kilvert had glimpsed the possibilities of a quite different social ethos in *A Week in a French Country House*. He could see that one of his temperament had more chance of nourishment in the home of Mme. Olympe, and part of him responded passionately to it. It was not the part that reported on Gibbins, hounded Anne Pugh, and divided the loyalties of John Couzens. Nor was it the part that meekly accepted the prohibition imposed on his love for Daisy by her father. It was that part of him

that responded to the beauty and vitality of children, to the sensuousness of women and of natural landscape, and to the sufferings of
the poor.

It was the naturalness and directness of experiences such as these
that were usually missing from the English country house as far as
Kilvert was concerned, and his capacity for responding to them is
perhaps the most outstanding feature of his personality. It is very
evident in the Chieflands passage and appears again when he visited
another yeoman farmer, Mr. Hill of Upper Noyadd farm, Clyro. 'I felt
at home at once in this dear family circle. There was an air of delicate
courtesy, refinement and high breeding which I have looked for in
vain in many grander homes. All were simple, natural, and at their
ease.'[7] What we have here is a re-statement of the contrast Kilvert
drew between English and French domestic manners, except that the
alternative to English gentry manners is not Mme. Olympe's elegant
home, but a farmhouse up a Radnorshire hillside. Kilvert's gentry
friends around Clyro would have resented, and rejected, the attribu-
tion of 'high breeding' to the Hill family and he knew it. That it was
of special importance for him to find in social situations something
approximating to the relationships of the 'dear family circle' he had
encountered at Upper Noyadd farm and in his own home, is made
more clear from his comments on the party he attended at the
Clifford Priory home of Mr. Haigh Allen: 'everyone about here is so
pleasant and friendly that we meet almost like brothers and sisters'.[8]
It is significant that the company to which he referred comprised the
district's lesser gentry, not those from 'grander homes'.[9] Kilvert's
emphasis on family relations is characteristically Evangelical. It is true
that the celebration of home and family is a general Victorian one but
it was largely Evangelical influence that developed the idea of home
as a source of spiritual values and of stability in reaction to 18th
century immorality.[10]

Kilvert made his own, very full tribute to home as a place of kindly
and sensitive relationships in a series of *Diary* entries that it is worthwhile to consider together. In them he explored the tension he felt
existed between easy and artificial social manners. Often they involve
visits he made to the homes of humble people like the Hills; all of
them can be seen within the frame of English domestic country life.
They are taken not in chronological order but in an order in which
a significant structure of feeling can be discerned, as well as the role

of *A Week in a French Country House* in crystallising the ideas common to them all.

The first concerns Miss Lyne, who was staying in the Clyro area with her brother Clavering.[11] When Kilvert had first seen the couple he had remarked in his *Diary* that 'they seem to be very odd people' and he had been present at a discussion among some friends about whether Clavering was a gentleman or not because he wore strange clothes. Kilvert found him to be something of a 'buffoon' and was irritated by the way he kept taking his hat off very artificially every time he spoke to women at a croquet party. However, Kilvert thought that his sister was 'a nice sensible unaffected girl' and he accompanied her on a shopping trip in Hay. Two days later, he was hurt and disappointed when, after 'becoming so friendly and cordial', she left without saying goodbye.

To have found a girl of his own class free from shyness or reserve, or worse, the affectation of them, only to see her exit abruptly from his life, filled him with anguish. Some of his anguish derived from his feeling that such girls were rare. He longed to kiss her beautiful white hand, 'even at the imminent risk that it would instantly administer a stinging slap on the face of its admirer'.[12] That couldn't be risked because of the social outrage involved. And yet it is clear that he didn't feel ashamed of the erotic impulse that might have driven him to such a breach of etiquette. It is that fact which provokes the anger that is central to the episode for, in addition to some anger at her departure, there is anger directed at the social rules which demanded that she must administer the fearful rebuke, even if, freed from their tyranny, she might enjoy such a spontaneous show of affection. It was a situation that typified Kilvert's position in society: he was keen to be married, Miss Lyne was of his own class and could therefore be suitable as a marriage partner; her naturalness attracted him; he longed to draw closer to her but was held in check by the code of manners and by his own morbid fear of breaching the code.

A passage bearing very similar features to that of his painful farewell to Miss Lyne occurred three and a half years later. This time the young woman was Julia Awdry and the episode is strongly marked by the social unease and baffled rage that characterised the earlier episode. On 29 December 1873, Kilvert had gone to a dance given by the Rookes (neighbours in Langley Burrell), whose drawing room had been turned into a ballroom. The 'fine old oaken floor' is one of only two positive elements in the experience for him. At the start of the entry he noted that he went alone to the function. Whether he danced more than the Lancers and the Quadrille he mentioned is unclear, but for once his ebullient spirit deserted him: 'I felt like a fish out of water all the evening for I don't like round dances and don't understand the figures of the square dances so I spoil other people's fun'. That is virtually the whole of the entry. His ineptitude at dancing seems to provide enough explanation for the typically forthright expression of anger that closes it: 'I don't think I shall go to a dance again'. It nevertheless seems a very extreme reaction if his unease stemmed only from certain kinds of dances, all of which would be familiar. However, his comment on Julia Awdry, his partner in the Lancers, offers another clue to its cause: 'Julia is a singularly nice simple unaffected girl and she looked very pretty tonight'.[13] There is a strong hint here that the real cause of his anger was a stiffness and unnaturalness about the proceedings which contrasted with, and was only relieved by, Julia Awdry's natural charm. This seems the more likely explanation, especially when seen as part of a pattern. She stood out because her manner combined the directness and naturalness that Kilvert craved with the social grace to be expected of the class to which they both belonged. He can be found recording this combination in entry after entry.[14] So important does it seem that one can imagine his regarding it as a *sine qua non* in any woman he might choose as his wife. It was, of course, present in Daisy Thomas. There was just one snag, or perhaps two: first, it seemed to be rarely found, and, second, Kilvert's lack of eligibility made it unlikely that he would be able to exercise his choice just where and when he liked.

Carrie Gore might have been flattered to be considered as Kilvert's wife, but she didn't belong to his social class.[15] She is the focal point of an entry dated 26 October 1870. Her playing of hymn tunes, in response to Kilvert's request, was not particularly accomplished, but he was much taken with her manner: '...what I admired most was her good nature, good breeding and perfect manners in just sitting down to play directly... without any false shame... or false modesty...'. He found it remarkable that such lack of affectation, allied to social grace, was to be found in such an ordinary home. It was something that 'many young ladies might copy with advantage'. He noted, too, that her sister possessed 'the manners, bearing and address of a lady'.[16] The entry closes with the Diarist emphasising in phrase after phrase how utterly at ease he felt in the Gore household because of this combination of warm affection and intuitive social grace. The importance for Kilvert of 'home' as a physical and symbolic place has been examined in an earlier chapter; more will be said later in this one of the importance of his 'feeling at home' in relation to the kind of society he found congenial.

A girl's capacity for playing and singing without false modesty had been remarked by Kilvert before his visit to Whitty's Mill.[17] He had walked to the village of Llowes near Clyro one evening the previous May to attend a concert in the school hall there. The hall was crowded and in between items in the programme, he chatted to a child he knew. His 'pretty little friend' was not part of the programme but in order to fill a gap in it caused by a performer's non-appearance, she was asked to sing. 'With the most perfect breeding in the world, she... cheerfully and gracefully consented...'. The situation was an almost exact parallel to the Carrie Gore episode, as is confirmed by the very similar phrasing. Carrie showed 'good breeding', while the child showed 'the most perfect breeding', Carrie's behaviour was 'cheerful', the child 'cheerfully consented'; Carrie is praised for being 'good-natured', the child for being 'as good as gold'; Carrie performed 'without false... modesty', and the child agreed 'without waiting to be pressed'. Kilvert, powerfully affected by the grateful glances he received from the child's 'grave watchful eyes', in return for the attention he gives her (he escorted her into the supper that followed the concert and ensured she had the best bits of chicken and plenty of jelly), commented, 'I fell immediately deeply in love with her'. One motive for these services was 'that she might not feel strange or lonely or think herself neglected for people... of higher rank or greater consequence'.[18] Kilvert was, in other words, ensuring that she felt 'at home', just as he would wish to feel, in a situation where observance of rank and formality might make her feel uncomfortable.[19] She came and left in a carriage, so it is evident that socially she was at least the equal of the others present but Kilvert was solicitous of her because she was a child. This is another link to the Carrie Gore episode because Kilvert's 'bewitching' friend represented as she did the possibility of encountering perfect breeding outside the class of the higher gentry.

In the entry concerning Miss Lyne, there was only an implied contrast between her naturalness and the affectations of other daughters of the gentry. With regard to Carrie Gore, Kilvert moved towards a contrast in manners between girls who were not gentry, with girls who were. What she possessed for him was infinitely superior to manners that had been deliberately cultivated, which produced more often than not the stiffness and artificiality from which Miss Lyne and Julia Awdry were miraculously free, and which made at least some of those around them feel less, rather that more, at ease. The higher one went up the social scale, the more that artificiality was in evidence for Kilvert. The girl at the Llowes concert either belonged to the lower gentry or was too young to have been trained in artificial manners. Far more acceptable was that natural good breeding, that intuitive understanding of what made for sensitive and considerate communication, which Kilvert had recognised in humble folk and which transcended social class. When one bears in mind Kilvert's social status at this time, one can understand why he was driven to such reflections. He was, by virtue of education and background, gentry class yet not fully of it; he was not wealthy or influential, and his job as a curate placed him near the bottom of county society;[20] he could offer no hospitality in return for what he received. His marital prospects in the Clyro gentry circle were, therefore, extremely limited, as the affair with Daisy Thomas painfully demonstrated. His overwhelming desire to be married with a family was never absent from his mind and implicit in all his contacts with women, therefore, was the question: were they marriageable?[21] And a complicating factor was his need to find one who was natural and unaffected. The theme is taken up so repeatedly in the *Diary* that it begins to appear obsessive.

Mrs. Jones of the Harbour farm[22] was not a possible wife for Kilvert but was another of nature's aristocrats. Hospitality was the need that Kilvert and his father had one June day of pouring rain in 1872. They had set out to fish the Arrow and had hoped the rain would ease off on the six mile journey from Clyro, but they were not to be lucky, and were glad to see, below them through the rain, the Harbour—'a haven of refuge'. Mrs. Jones appeared at the door: 'And now here is a fine specimen of Radnorshire manners. She was in her working dress... but quite unconscious of her dress she simply and naturally came forward at once and welcomed us... with her grand courteous manner as if she had been a queen in disguise'. Like the women in the passages already examined, she combined naturalness with social elegance, and was the equal, if not the superior, of gentry: she had 'all the natural grace... of a woman in the best society'.[23]

The remainder of this *Diary* entry emphasises the Harbour's hospitality. Kilvert had praised the hospitality of Clifford Priory, which manifested itself not only in iced claret cup and enormous strawberries, but in the warmth and social ease of a group that related to each other 'almost like brothers and sisters'. The Gores and the Jones were no less his brothers and sisters, though they were socially lower. However, in spite of this continuity across class differences, there is clearly a conflict going on in Kilvert that appears in these repeated contrasts between real gentry and the natural aristocrats of the Radnorshire hills. The contrasts feature such heavy emphases as to appear laboured, and he returns to the central theme as to a sore place at which he had to pick. He was not entirely at home in the world of Clifford Priory, even though the background and education he shared with its guests was complemented by just the congeniality he relished.[24] A greater sense of acceptance was his in the 'kindly hospitable houses' of farms he visited around Clyro.[25] What they and, to an extent, the Priory had in common, was a classlessness that was also relatively free of the trammels of Victorian etiquette. In these passages he seems to be reaching out for an experience of family in which class factors and tensions are absent. Relationships between brothers and sisters are egalitarian in that there exists generally no principle of authority which automatically subordinates one individual to another, except where poisoned by primogeniture amongst gentry families. Parental authority over children and servants was a different matter; in that area Kilvert was completely orthodox, as has been shown. It was the family unit which most adequately expressed the kind of community he wished society to be. Family relationships at their best are easy, natural, non-threatening, non-hierarchical, and the love found within them is readily given, one does not have to deserve it, or win it, or take risks to secure it. The fact that in general Kilvert favoured a traditional hierarchical society illustrates that there were contradictions in his outlook. His 'sleeping friends' *Diary* entry had at its centre the assumption that in life the members of the rural family would be separated by rank, even if they achieved parity in death.

In asserting that ordinary people could possess an innate gentility that made them the equal even of the highest gentry, Kilvert was not embracing a genuinely democratic viewpoint; society's natural leaders would for him always be aristocrats and gentry,[26] and the idea that the working-class could be politically on a par with his own class always remained for him a preposterous idea. Nor was he challenging the notion of gentility itself. In fact, he was confirming a gentility that existed irrespective of political status, of wealth, of education, of social position. Such a concept was a counterweight to the spread of democracy and egalitarianism. Kilvert's main motive in endorsing it was not, in the passages examined, primarily a political one, though that dimension has a place in the complex of feelings surrounding it. The repeated emphases are in one sense an attack on the excessive pride in rank, often accompanied by snobbery, heartlessness, and a concern to use the rigid rules of etiquette to keep inferiors in their place, that was condemned directly in *A Week in a French Country House* and indirectly in Kilvert's visit to Chieflands. Kilvert also asserted the value of innate gentility in order to rationalise the guilt he felt at the social and psychological unease he experienced in the homes of the grander gentry. And, finally, he expressed through it the anger and frustration associated with the homelessness he suffered because he lacked wife, family, household, and settled social position.

His lack of these blessings, plus most of the elements that have appeared in the *Diary* passages examined so far in this chapter, come together in the last in the sequence. Shortly before it had occurred, Kilvert had looked after Clyro parish for three weeks when Venables was away, and when Kilvert left he acknowledged Venables' generosity. He not only sent him £5 to pay his travel expenses but had allowed him to keep open house at the Vicarage. So again, we are reminded of Kilvert's dependent position. He had also had his worth confirmed by the welcome given him by his former humble parishioners. As a penurious curate, he was travelling three weeks later by third class carriage on the Wootton Bassett train to stay with friends near Swindon, and a chance meeting yielded an experience of profound significance, and one which adds a new dimension to the pattern of episodes involving women and girls. He saw 'a singularly beautiful child, lovely as few children are lovely, with a fair... complexion, beautiful flaxen curls... and eyes of the deepest blue'. She was nearly three years old and her beauty, fine clothes, and manner ('so distinguished') made him wonder that she was travelling third class. He found himself holding her and from that moment 'a great happiness came over me. I had thought my heart was growing hard and that I was no longer capable of such emotion'. He recognised again what he had always known—'there was only one thing in the world and that was love'. He saw 'she was no ordinary child... She might have been a king's daughter'.[27]

The elements this encounter has in common with the earlier ones need no additional underlining; the new element is the transcendental nature of the experience for Kilvert. It reveals again how much he followed Kingsley's Evangelicalism because the values and attitudes in it all have their counterpart in *Yeast* and *Alton Locke*. In *Yeast*, Lancelot reflects on how an individual learns the nature of love and the ability to love and decides that if one is to come to love mankind, one must start by loving one person. The infant learns love at its mother's breast by 'looking into loving human eyes, by feeling the care of loving hands ... to have found the key to one heart is to have found the key to all.'[28] The thought that one's heart was growing hard held particular terror for an Evangelical because Christianity was the religion of the heart, the heart was its 'special residence', and to have a hard heart meant in effect that one was not a Christian at all.[29]

The closest parallel in Kingsley to the *Diary* entry concerning the child on the Wootton Bassett train is to be found in *Alton Locke*. Kilvert had begun to read it only a month before and carried its key ethic in his head and his heart so that in the meeting with the child he was irresistibly reminded of it. Early in the book, Alton makes a passionate declaration of the divine principle of love which animates the universe, in order to show that the harsh Evangelical conception of redemption, that was touched on in chapter 4 in relation to Kilvert's feelings of hostility towards his father, was a total contradiction of God's love, which 'shines out in every tree and flower and hedge bird'.[30] Alton believed it was a crime to put that conception, with all its emphasis on original sin, before working men, who, 'in the smiles of their innocent children, see the heaven which they have lost'. When Kilvert came to write up the episode of the girl on the train, he found himself using very similar phrasing to this Kingsley passage. As he contemplated her beauty and innocence, he too was transported, he said, into heaven, and, just as the smiles of their children were, for Alton's working men, 'the messages of baby-cherubs, made in God's own image', so for Kilvert 'the way the angel child looked into my eyes and soul' meant that 'she had a message, that she was God's sweet unconscious messenger'. Kilvert knew what the message was: it was love and the capacity to love was the source of all human happiness and goodness. The angel child had been sent to remind him of the fact and her coming was no accident: 'How strange is this *seemingly* chance crossing of paths', he wrote.[31] For Alton Locke the failure to emphasise sufficiently the principle of love was the cause of Christianity falling into contempt, especially in the minds of the working-class. In that principle alone could they find the true democracy that gave 'equal hopes, claims, and deliverances to all mankind alike', and that was the only form of democracy that Kilvert could embrace.

Another daughter of a Radnorshire farmhouse, the one belonging to the Hill family where Kilvert had felt so much at home, excited the same response in him as the angel child had. The girl was Florence Hill, whom he had taught at Clyro School and had always found heart-wrenchingly beautiful. By this time he had left Clyro and she was about 15 years old and her beauty was nearer that of a mature woman, but her appeal included his memory of her as a child. She has much in common with the 'angel child'. She, too, had fair hair, wonderful eyes of 'soft dark tender blue', and aristocratic features. She looked at him lovingly as had the girl on the train. Once more he knew the heaven on earth that could come only from the experience of love. 'As she stood and lifted those blue eyes, ...it seemed to me as if the doors and windows of Heaven were suddenly opened. It was one of the supreme moments of life'.[32]

A much more subordinate, but not irrelevant, part of the angel child's meaning turns on the fact that she was in a third class carriage: a daughter of the gentry would be unlikely to be found there. Was she gentry or not? In one sense, it didn't matter for Kilvert because her message was the same, and she, like Carrie Gore, Mrs. Jones and Florence Hill, might as well have been gentry. Nevertheless, the confusion nagged at Kilvert. Now it was the railways, along with other developing forms of public transport, that were mixing social classes together in a way found very disturbing by those, like Kilvert, who were anxious about their own genteel status. They wanted to place a barrier between themselves and lower-class persons. Kilvert objected to the way cheap rail travel enabled the latter to visit places he preferred to be exclusive to his class.[33] He had compounded the problem of the 'angel child' by travelling 3rd class himself, thus contributing to the merging of social distinctions, complained of by the novelist Surtees: '...all people are put so much on a par by the levelling influence of rail'.[34]

Kilvert was only 32 when he was expressing joy at still being capable of the intense emotion he felt for the beautiful child in the Wootton Bassett train, but he was clearly anxious that age would bring a diminution of the love he was desperate to channel into marriage and children. Six months before, his mind had been focused on the ever more pressing need to achieve the conditions required to realise that dream. There was a possibility that the living of Disserth in Radnorshire would be offered him.[35] However, he was still torn between the dream of marriage and his characteristic inertia. He reflected that he felt very settled as curate to his father in Langley Burrell but that, if he turned Disserth down, he would be throwing away 'a fair chance of making myself a home and run the risk of finding myself adrift in the world, still a curate in middle age'. The *Diary*, especially the later parts of it, is filled with entries recording his delight in home and family; it is superfluous to refer to more than a few. Staying at the home of his Wadham friend, Mayhew, he was captivated by his pretty infant daughter; he took particular delight in the Crichtons of Wye Cliff, Clyro: 'I found the Crichtons at home with all their children, a lovely happy family group'; full of envy of these parents, he described himself as 'hungry at heart' for the delights they experienced.[36]

Kilvert's poem 'The Highest Of Women' contains a picture of the woman he hoped to marry and it reiterates many of the attributes characteristic of the women he admired who appear in the *Diary* entries examined earlier, and adds a few more. It begins by emphasising naturalness and lack of affectation:

> She who prefers adorned to be
> In unadorned simplicity,
> And wears that brightest, loveliest dress,
> The robe of self-unconsciousness.

The new emphasis in the poem is most apparent in the way the 'highest of women' is pictured as a true Christian, whose 'pure spirit'

makes her 'a sweet handmaiden to her Lord'. Her constant compan-
ions are 'Faith, Hope, and Love' and she never puts her 'love of
husband, friend, or child' before the 'higher love' of Christ. She is all
kindness and charity, 'ever bent on love's service' and 'freely gives as
God hath given', thinking of herself 'last of all'. Above all, she has a
heart 'soft with tender ruth', and, though possessed of great courage
and a stern sense of duty, she is 'all gentle, sweet and womanly'. He
had met real women who he thought came close to this ideal. There
was Mrs. Hockin, whom he had known in Langley Burrell, later living
in Cornwall and, of course, there was Mrs. Crichton.

Mrs. Crichton was admired by Kilvert exactly because she represented the feminine qualities underlined in the passages noted
earlier. He had found an article in the *Saturday Review* in November
1870, under the title 'Great Girls', which, he said, 'described Mrs
Crichton to the life'. The 'great girl' of the article was valued principally for the naturalness and intensity of her emotions. She was 'ready
to love', and while 'intellectually as well as emotionally alive', she
retained the spontaneity of girlhood.[37] Such a woman was Kilvert's
gateway to the 'heaven' of home and family, especially of pretty
daughters.

His love of pretty young girls is frequently merged in *Diary* entries
with the attraction of older women, who might be mother to his
daughters. Aware of his own erotic affinity for female children, he
experienced some guilt, which is caught in the cryptic entry of 20
June 1871: 'An angel satyr walks these hills'. He saw himself as an
'angel' because he was able to feel positive about his intense love for
children and theirs for him, yet recognised the 'satyr' element in his
response. Guilt over the illicit feelings young girls engendered in him
led him to fear that the paradise of home and family would be denied
him. He once recalled an idyllic outing to Aberedw with a party of
children, but its rocks, which formed the gateway to paradise, were
guarded by 'the angel with the flaming sword' and he was denied
entry.[38] The way in which his meetings with girl children were
charged with sexual passion is illustrated by the *Diary* entry for 23
August 1871, when he called at Hannah Burton's. 'Hannah's beautiful seven year old child gradually stole up to me and nestled close in
my arms. Then she laid her ... soft round cheek lovingly to mine and
stole first one arm and then the other round my neck. I stroked back
her fair curls'. The child then kissed him 'again and again. Then

came the old, old story, the sweet confession as old as human hearts, "I do love you so. Do you love me?" "Yes", said the child ... Time was of no account. An hour flew by in seconds. I was in heaven'. In the entry for the following day when Kilvert saw the child again, he referred to her as 'my lover' and took a lock of her hair. His comment that the token was 'in happy and holy remembrance of a child's love' indicated both his conviction that such moments were heaven-sent and his need to exculpate himself of guilt.

Little girls, however, while representing sexual temptation, were 'safe' compared with adult women whose unpredictability, artificiality, and lack of simple, natural feelings, frightened him. His enjoyment of a picnic with the Hockins in Cornwall in July 1870 was marred by the uncertainty he felt at the behaviour of some young ladies who were in the party: 'Young lady affectations, peculiarities, vagaries, etc, etc, unintelligible'. (The picnic began badly for Kilvert when he 'unhappily mistook butter for cream'. Earlier that month, in consequence of another social gaffe, he had commented: '...if there is a mistake to be made I invariably make it'.) Little girls, he stated, behaved 'so nicely... much better than most young ladies'.[39] What Kilvert found delightful and reassuring about the naturally aristocratic women of the humbler classes, such as Carrie Gore and Mrs. Jones, was that in the simple sincerity of their manners, they resembled children, just as the adult poor often did for him. It was a quality Wordsworth had recognised in country people, and Kilvert was most fully Wordsworthian in sharing it.[40]

The relative rarity of such women in his own class was another barrier denying him entry to the heaven of home, wife and family. On one occasion when he had become attracted to two promising specimens (the Miss Halls—'so natural and genuine') and they departed suddenly, he wished he had the means of 'hardening [his] heart' in order to reduce his susceptibility.[41] But the barrier he came up against again and again was the barrier of English gentry manners. Kilvert had to go on meeting young women, stunted in their capacity to feel by their upbringing and hedged about by artificial rules of behaviour, with his vulnerability to their charms and his craving to be married undiminished. 'The English, more than any other people', J.S. Mill had written in 1869, 'not only act but feel according to rule'. Kilvert rebelled against this state of affairs, and, in a vague way, recognised that it was women who were most in thrall as a result of it.

Brought up as simple, innocent creatures, whose sexuality had to be battened down because it posed a threat to morality, women were regarded by Victorian society in much the same way as children were. The latter were seen as 'pure and innocent but [they] inherited a fallen nature... [and] ought to be punished for doing or saying anything not refined or modest'.[42] Strict rules regulated the behaviour of children and women and manifested themselves in the form of manners. 'Manners were the clearest evidence of a mid-Victorian wish to do the right thing... Manners were social control which kept others out, confined them to their place; and manners - in the form of refined, honed etiquette - were social emulation assiduously pursued'.[43] Even in the broad-minded, intellectual Stanley family, Kate Stanley chafed against the restrictions: 'one's whole education is a state of repression of all strong feelings or wishes... one is hemmed in on all sides'.[44]

Kilvert was haunted by a desperate anxiety about his own or others' actual or potential gaffes in a society so dominated by rules. *Inter alia*, they are concerned with lack of skill at dancing, card games and chess, being late for meals, wearing the wrong clothes for particular occasions, badly organised social arrangements, clergymen's use of slang, ineptitude at carving joints of meat, being insufficiently attentive to ladies, nodding off after dinner, arguing and losing one's temper, and forgetting, as he once did, the number of his hotel room and nearly ending up in a room occupied by a married couple. Their frequency in the *Diary* as a whole,[45] seen in conjunction with the explicit contrast Kilvert made between easy, natural manners and the more artificial code he encountered in the country house, shows a conflict, which, while common enough in the period, was all the more severe for a man of uncertain social position, who also possessed a passionate, impulsive temperament. Mill believed that the English situation had become so distorted that it was not a question of following natural inclinations under the control of rule, but of being so conditioned that people had no inclination but that of following a rule. They had lost touch with their natural selves. Gay noted that in the vast Victorian literature of advice about manners, one factor stands out: the need for self-control. He commented: 'It demands nothing less than the triumph of reason over passion...'.[46] If Kilvert had any hope of finding a marriage partner, it was to women thickly hedged around by 'manners' that he had to present himself, and in their company he not only often felt awkward and ill at ease, but an actual failure. His lack of wealth, of position, and of assured social confidence, would make him seem so in gentry eyes. His fear that he would be a curate all his life is the most obvious aspect of his own feeling that he was a failure.[47] He felt this less in lower-class homes where the relative absence of social constraints and of concern for rank released his personality so that he was both less awkward and more lively.

In praising women who were by nature refined, Kilvert endorsed a notion of 'breeding'.[48] That he believed in it firmly is clear from the veneration he had for his own genteel origins and his concern for armorial bearings. He told one of his Clyro country women, Hannah Whitney, that he could see 'her good blood in her face'. Though fallen on hard times, she, like him, came from a line of squires. However, breeding was not simply a question of rank but of values and attitudes: one could be 'well-bred' and come from a line of hill farmers (like the Jones) or of Wiltshire yeomen (like the Frys). The urge to rise in society, the fear of not winning the approval of those superiors to whose position one aspired, and of being categorised with those whom one considered one's inferiors, were causes of the lack of ease and simplicity Kilvert found in his society. It was these elements among others which gave rise to the cumbrousness, stiff-ness, vulgar extravagance, and artificiality of it. Kilvert's reference to 'vulgar extravagance' suggests that he was also sickened by the mate-rialism he observed in the fine houses where he was a guest.

The growing materialism of society that commentators noted earlier in the century, was still sufficient of an issue to feature in the *Cornhill Magazine* in 1860. The author of the article on 'Luxury' in the July number believed it was entirely appropriate to refer to the society of the time as 'luxurious' in the sense that excessive importance was attached to material possessions.[49] As the wealth of the nation had increased, so had there grown up a taste for refinement in domestic comfort. The hope of social advancement and the desire for the money to promote such advancement had 'bitten deeply into the minds of mid-Victorians'.[50] (It is worthwhile here to remember that Kilvert's youth and early maturity coincided with a great surge in national pros-perity).[51] Wealthy parents could afford education which encouraged the development of expensive tastes and domestic comfort had, in consequence, become 'the object of idolatry' in the minds of the comfortable classes. Because there was both a demand for and a supply of appealing, quality goods in the booming Britain of 1860, luxury did exist. What, in essence, the *Cornhill* writer was describing was the early growth of consumerism, which is now an accepted feature of contemporary society. Kilvert's antipathy to commercialism is another instance of his rejection of the modern world; it is also a significant element in his romantic attachment to the past.

His father belonged to the generation which experienced in the post-Waterloo years that turning back to the past to which reference has already been made. The Kilverts, father and son, subscribed to that feeling. Robert showed it in his strong penchant for Scott's novels. It is very likely that Robert also knew Kenelm Digby's *The Broad Stone of Honour*, which had a profound influence on young men in the 1820s and was very widely known. In addition, it not only appeared just before Robert began at Oriel, when its impact on undergraduates must have been considerable, but was fervently recommended by Copleston, the man whose patronage opened the door of that college to him and who was Provost during his time there. Copleston saw the book as the antidote to the commercialism of the period. It was, he said, 'designed to revive the principles of loyalty and generosity and honour that were almost extinct among mankind'.[52] It seems likely, therefore, that Kilvert's romantic attachment to the past was in part nurtured by his father, and that, in his Evangelical upbringing, he would regularly hear condemned by paternal authority the material prosperity in which the Kilvert family did not share. The loss of what material comfort the family did possess, as a result of the failure of the coachbuilding business, may have deepened the resentment towards those who enjoyed wealth.

The Broad Stone of Honour made a particular point of attacking luxury: '...mark how contrary to the spirit of a gentleman ...are those pompous luxuries, effeminate refinement, which are now so generally the attendants upon wealth'.[53] Just like Kilvert and his father, Digby was ambivalent about the highest aristocrats because they always stood in danger of becoming so corrupted by luxurious living that they neglected their duties. One explanation for Kilvert's lack of worldly ambition and relatively passive acceptance of his humble status may be that the notion of a gentleman expounded by Digby (but also an element in the standard Victorian concept of it) included the idea that genuine nobility of character was the most important thing about a man and that had nothing to do with social position, or property, or wealth. In the opinion of the writer of the *Cornhill* article, the 'exaggerated appetite for solid advantages' which was the form luxury took in 1860, made the attainment of genuine nobility of character all the more difficult because it restricted man's vision of life's possibilities to the mean and the material. Kilvert's hatred of materialism, democracy, crowds, tourists and some aspects of urban life, had its roots in sentiments such as these, which were current when his father was an undergraduate at Oriel and he an undergraduate at Wadham.

Though the pace of life would have been slower in Radnorshire than in the cities, the mania for luxury and the desire for social eminence would not have been significantly less, as he had discovered to his cost. It seems certain that he would have encountered also in that society the provincialism and conformity of which the *Cornhill* writer spoke. It was suggested at the beginning of the chapter 'Kilvert and *A Week in a French Country House*' that it would be largely the gentry social circle of Clyro which gave rise to his criticism of English country house life. There are several reasons for this. It was for a start more extensive than that which he encountered in Wiltshire: there were almost a dozen upper-class homes in the neighbourhood of Clyro which he was visiting regularly when the *Diary* record began in January 1870, and which he had presumably visited for the five years of his curacy there before that date. Secondly, his visits to some of them certainly were the more intensive because he was a bachelor living away from home and there was a tendency for some families—the Baskervilles, Thomases, and especially the Venables and Bevans[54]—to involve him in their activities for this reason, whereas in Wiltshire he had his own family. Thirdly, when he made the *Diary* entry about reading *A Week in a French Country House*, his social life to all intents and purposes *was* that furnished by Clyro.

The *Diary* had to be the recipient of his observations on domestic country life because they constituted an attack on his friends there, and the very ethos that was his target forbade such frank observations and held him in check. It was hardly more possible for a gentleman in Victorian society to make observations on that subject than it was to talk openly about such personal and controversial subjects as love or religion. Even if Kilvert had had either the temperament or the confidence to launch into the intellectual and cultural issues raised by Sartoris' novel, the social ethos of the time ruled it out of account. Looking back to the days when to be a gentleman a man had also to be a poet, Mason observed that in Victorian times that quality would have been distinctly suspect. 'It was quite the thing to be philistine' because involvement with the arts or with any intellectual activities was mistrusted. 'The emphasis is now on character, on avoiding excess...'.[55] Kilvert's romantic nature, though not 'morbid' like that of the protector of Judith, Sartoris' eponymous heroine, represented 'excess' for the gentry of Clyro.

Lord Ernest Hamilton had illuminating things to say about drawing room conversation in the period of Kilvert's *Diary*. He belonged, of course, to Society with a capital 'S' and experienced a life altogether more metropolitan and sophisticated than that of Kilvert's Clyro society, but the latter would inevitably take its lead from the former. Hamilton believed that men and women of the upper-classes were more 'enlightened' in the later part of the century than they were in the late 1860s and early 1870s, the period of his earliest memories (he was born in 1858). Girls were more natural, conversation was less 'vapid', sentiments were more real, and there was less humbug; in the 1860s, a strong vein of humbug ran right through Society. By 'humbug' he meant affectation of manners, the over-refinement of which was a reaction against the crudities of the manners of the Georgian period, but this was waning during the 1860s as the cult of manliness gained ground. Mid-Victorian girls were 'as natural as their mothers allowed them to be, but the habit of artificiality was still too strong to be entirely shaken off in one generation', Hamilton concluded.[56]

The extent to which women were denied a life and an individuality of their own can be gauged partly from the nature of conversation during this period. Hamilton stated that it consisted mainly of anecdotes, which was inevitable in a society in which people did little actual work themselves and had servants or paid professionals to attend to the practical business of life. The gentry of Kilvert's acquaintance were more heavily involved in the practical affairs of county administration and of estates than was the case with Hamilton's set, and when Kilvert recorded in June 1870 that after the picnic lunch at Snodhill Castle, the gentlemen talked 'local news and politics and the ladies wandered away by themselves', one feels that he was registering a fairly typical pattern.

Hamilton noted that much interest was taken in his circle in election results but that the interest went no further than declarations of partisanship. No attempt was made to discuss principles or to analyse 'party propaganda'. This, too, like the predominance of anecdotes, seems to correspond to what can be deduced about the conversation in Kilvert's society. Apart from these elements, conversation in Hamilton's world 'revolved around the simple topics of food, health, and the weather, and in no case was an attempt made to soar above accepted generalities'.[57] Original ideas, imagination, artistic and intellectual interests were all viewed with suspicion in spite of the fact that they were recommended as the most desirable topics by some manuals on the art of conversation.[58]

Thackeray had indicated in 1856 the way things were going in polite society: 'It is not learning, it is not virtue, about which people enquire... It is manners... What is wanted... is that folks should be as agreeable as possible in conversation and demeanour'.[59] A year later Milne's study of women's position in society appeared in which he underlined the difficulty middle-class men experienced in forming relationships with women of their own class: 'The stiffness and reserve between the sexes, in the middle ranks, brought about by the separation of their education, of their daily interests and pursuits, cause young men to undervalue women of their own rank; and finding little pleasure in their society, little room for the natural flow of impressions and feelings, they seek such vent elsewhere; in the more unrestrained and artless intercourse of a lower rank'.[60] These observations help us to see more clearly into Kilvert's social predicament, pictured at the start of this chapter, as he deliberately sought out lower-class women and girls with whom to flirt. By the 1870s, blandness and reticence had become the norm. Conversation then was, according to Benson, full of 'reticences and reserves', which were observed in recognition of the laudable principle that, since social enjoyment between men and women was the object, a certain 'outward form of dignity and politeness' should be preserved. It produced, he said, a 'mid-Victorian society tradition of frozen pompous dignity...'.[61]

Almost everything was denied to young women of the upper middle-class during this period. The lives of Edward Carpenter's sisters were as circumscribed as those of the Thomas girls of Clyro and others of Kilvert's circle. Carpenter was a little younger than

Kilvert and lived in what he called the 'would-be fashionable world' of Brighton, which he hated for its artificiality, 'heartless convention-alities and silly proprieties' and his sisters' predicament in it elicited his compassion. They lived a life of idleness and boredom, allowed to do nothing but paint and play the piano. Housework was for the servants and working in the garden was held to be 'unladylike'. The life of the young woman in the 1860s, said Carpenter, was 'tragic in its emptiness... There was absolutely nothing... to do or live for'.[62] Her state was the result of changes in the model of femininity. At the beginning of the century, it had been the 'perfect wife', an active participant in the family, fulfilling a number of vital tasks. This had been replaced, however, by the ideal of the 'perfect lady', which had little connection with any functional role in society, and which was most fully developed in the upper middle-class society of Kilvert's time. The social/intellectual growth of the young girl who was its victim was confined to the family and close friends. The education she received was designed to bring out her 'natural' submission to authority and to her maternal instincts.[63]

Victorians exalted 'pure-mindedness' and 'inherent purity' in women and to achieve it, they required daughters to be brought up ignorant of their own sexuality. That was the state of Thackeray's daughter, Minny, when Leslie Stephen married her in 1867, and he was delighted at it. It was assumed that such girls had no or little sexual feeling. Kept well away from the coarser experiences of life, they could be expected to possess a sexual innocence which would shield them from the predatory male. When Kilvert came across the daughters of the Vicar of Newchurch castrating lambs, it was quite at variance with his expectations of what girls from such a background should be doing.[64] It was daughters of the poor normally who had to confront similar (or worse) realities and they, therefore, stood in most danger of sexual contamination. Kilvert's words to Daisy when he had virtually abandoned his courtship of her—'Rest, happy child, guileless and unspoilt'—indicated his confidence that her lack of sexual drive and inherent purity would ensure her equanimity. Respectable daughters needed men to help them remain innocent of their sexual desires and Kilvert could feel that he had behaved with propriety in not encouraging Daisy's. It seems clear that his guilt over Ettie Meredith Brown was the result of his having encouraged her desires.[65]

Carpenter was prepared to spell out the consequences of sexual repression in the case of his sisters, and his comments fully and effectively sum up the tragedy of Llanthomas, which, the closer one draws to it, comes more and more to resemble a play by Eugene O'Neill. When Carpenter returned to Brighton from Cambridge early in the 1870s, he was always overwhelmed by 'the idiotic social reserve and Britannic pretence' that enveloped his home and condemned his unmarried sisters to a life which, by ignoring 'the obvious facts of the heart and of sex', left 'the primal needs of life unspoken and unallowed'. The state of society 'set up gold and gain in the high place of the human heart' and the result was 'the nerve ruin of thousands and thousands of women, and even of a considerable number of men'.[66] Daisy Thomas and her sisters ended up in a society which had a great surplus of women over men. Their father's actions had, of course, stacked the marital odds even more heavily against them, because of his obsession with 'gold and gain'. Their sufferings hardly bear contemplation. Some degree of the 'nerve ruin' referred to by Carpenter must have been experienced by all of them; in the case of Grace Thomas, Daisy's sister, its consequence was the asylum.

Cominos' analysis of the mechanism of sexual and emotional repression facilitates an understanding of their predicament and of other young women in Kilvert's world.[67] An upper-class girl was in permanent conflict between repressive conscience and sexual desire. Any true sense of her own personality was denied her by the model of female behaviour she had to follow. She had to identify herself so much with the life of the family and her limited social roles that she was completely effaced as an individual. 'All the moralities tell women it is their duty... to live for others, to make complete abnegations of themselves, and to have no life but in their affections'.[68] Daughters were brought up to be so clinging and dependent that inevitably they had a defective sense of responsibility. Brothers, husbands, and especially fathers, took responsibility for them; morally they were innocents. Their social training was designed to bring out their 'natural' submission to male authority, and since a girl's father was her first authority figure, in terms both of chronology and emotional significance, he would loom very large. As Cominos puts it, 'the daughter's first love was authoritarian'. When her sexual feelings emerged, they should have been the means by which freedom from parental authority and true individuality were attained. With the repression of sexual instincts, the fusion of feelings of affection and sensuality characteristic of normal development tended not to be achieved. The result was that the daughter was 'disembodied affection without sensuality. The sensual part belonged to her father'. Daughters consequently formed neurotic attachments to their fathers.[69] If a daughter married, she would be likely to transfer this turmoil of feelings to her husband. To the Thomas girls' turmoil was added their awareness that their father was deliberately blocking their chance of obtaining husbands.

It is hard to find any evidence in the *Diary* which suggests that conversation among Kilvert's Clyro friends went much beyond the 'accepted generalities' referred to by Hamilton. Although Kilvert records scenes of visits to gentry homes, one looks in vain for evidence of what was actually discussed and of any sense that he found the conversation stimulating. It is noticeable that for all his interest in and knowledge of poetry, he was able to discuss it with only a handful of people, and they were usually not members of the society he regularly encountered but strangers and visitors. It is true that the *Diary* records reference to the connection Wordsworth had with the Dew family. Henry Dew, Vicar of Whitney, had married Mary Monkhouse, whose father was a first cousin of Mary Hutchinson, Wordsworth's wife. Such a connection should have made possible a shared interest in the poet between the Dews and Kilvert, but conversation was limited to the family links and hardly touched upon the poetry or the poet's social and political ideas.

As a romantic himself, Kilvert understood the motives that impelled people to make literary pilgrimages; his visits to William Barnes and to Yaverland were of this kind. He would rightly have resented the notion that he was a mere tourist. However, the interest shown in September 1870 by Jane Dew (aged 24) and Emily Dew (aged 22) seemed overly touristic. They had, Kilvert noted, 'just returned from the Lakes full of Wordsworth, Rydal and Grasmere and with a store of photographs, ferns and other plants collected from places connected with the poet'.[70] There is a suggestion here that he felt that they were insufficiently 'full' of Wordsworth's poetry. An even more telling moment occurred a few weeks later at a ploughing match dinner, most probably at Whitney. At the dinner, Arthur Cheese, a friend of the Dews, made a speech in which he quoted, rather condescendingly, 'Let not ambition mock their useful toil' from Gray's 'Elegy' but he attributed it 'complacently' (Kilvert's word) to Goldsmith. 'I looked round in undisguised amazement', said Kilvert, 'but no one seemed to have noticed anything particular'.[71] Clearly, his look of amazement was aimed at the other gentry present, among whom doubtless were the Dews; he would not have expected the local farmers and labourers to be familiar with Gray and Goldsmith. He was, however, alone in his reaction.

When Kilvert does refer to a conversation about Wordsworth (and Tennyson and the Holy Grail),[72] it was with the visitor, Mr. Barton, as they walked one day in July 1870 to Clifford Priory. He made particular note of the fact that Barton was 'a clever well-read man', almost as though he was a rarity among 'the usual set' that was assembled at the Priory, where conversation of his kind was not pursued. Instead it was 'great fun on the lawn, 6 cross games of croquet and balls flying in all directions'. After tea, 'a young gentleman caused some amusement by appearing on the lawn in full evening dress, tail coat, white tie and all'.[73]

This is one of those moments in the *Diary* when the sense of peering through the looking glass into a quite other kind of society is especially strong. It was a society in which people, even those of an educated and moneyed background, seemed, by comparison with their equivalents today, easily amused. Frances Cobbe found that one of the chief contrasts between the society of 1840 and that of 1890 manifested itself in the greater simplicity of character of the older generation. Of course, writers, philosophers and politicians exhibited subtlety of thought and feeling but ordinary ladies and gentlemen, even intelligent, educated ones, seemed childlike by comparison with later generations. On the basis of the evidence cited above and that of the *Diary*, not a great deal of change had taken place by 1870, at least in rural areas. Conversation then apparently bore at least some resemblance to that of the 1840s, which Cobbe described as 'downright and matter-of-fact, and rarely if ever concerned with critical analyses of impressions'.[74] In 1840, when she was 18, she found the young men whom she met at balls in Dublin were marked by an 'extraordinary inanity' and 'really marvellous silliness and dullness'.

George Venables, brother of Kilvert's vicar, counted Llysdinam as his home but since he lived and worked in London, he had the status more of a visitor, making only a few appearances in the *Diary*. As a barrister and a literary critic he brought with him, therefore, perspectives on to a wider social and intellectual world. He had actually taken tea with Wordsworth at Rydal Mount and passed on to Kilvert some anecdotes of the visit, though he was capable of a more serious exchange on the subject of Wordsworth's poetry.[75] A more permanent member of the local society was Mary Bevan, daughter of the Rev. W.L. Bevan of Hay Castle. She mixed in a wide circle of people, some of them titled, and was a woman of some intellectual stature, having written some poetry and articles on aspects of Welsh history. She once lent Kilvert a copy of the poems of Mrs. Barrett Browning, and he read his 'Colva Ballads' to her (Colva is a village near Clyro). However, the *Diary* reveals no further contact with her on the subject of poetry or any other intellectual topic, and her local activities were of the standard kind pursued by upper-class ladies: sketching, croquet, and appearances at flower shows, bazaars, harvest festivals and Hereford Hunt Ball. Some exchange in the area of poetry occurred between Kilvert and Katharine Heanley yet the simple but rewarding activity he shared with her—'comparing notes... about our beloved "In Memoriam" and showing each other our favourite passages and poems'—was not one that he indulged in with any of his Clyro friends, male or female. In May Dimsdale of Lady Verney's *Fernyhurst Court*, Kilvert had an example of a daughter of the country house capable of discussing books and ideas with men, who also took an interest in field sports. She recognised that 'it was a crime ...in many English [country] houses to be caught sitting still, "only thinking"'.[76] It is revealing that, George Venables excepted, there were no local *men* with whom he shared his interests in literature, nor were the articles he read in periodicals on literary topics the subject of any conversation with them, on the evidence of the *Diary*. If there had been any exchanges it seems certain he would have recorded them, as he did those he had with 29 year-old Lewis Williams, son of a Clyro farmer, who 'had read a good deal, Shakespeare all through, is very fond of poetry and writes verses'.[77] He was able to talk to Williams about Byron, Scott, Wordsworth, Pope, and Clare.

Such interest as there was in intellectual matters among Kilvert's circle was taken by the local clergy, the most prominent among whom was the Rev. Bevan. He was a particularly devoted and progressive supporter of the cause of education and had helped to make the Hay National School one of the most respected. It was this kind of enthusiasm that drove him to revive the Hay Literary Institute in 1851.[78] It had been established ten years before and had struggled for eight years before expiring. Local clergymen supported his efforts to promote an interest in literature but other gentry were largely indifferent. The Rev. R.L. Venables was the President of the Institute, and the Rev. Webb of Hardwick gave several talks, such as the one of 4 November 1861 on the comet of that year. George Venables spoke on the American Civil War in December 1861 and 'the School Room was literally crammed', but not with the gentry.

Subsequent soirées and ordinary meetings repeated the general pattern: support came mainly from the clergy and their families and a few of the lower gentry. None of the men from the Baskerville, Thomas, De Winton or Devereux families took an interest in the venture, although Baskerville and Thomas women often attended. The reporter who covered the annual soirée of January 1864 noted that those who lived in country towns knew that certain meetings were held which 'everybody of any pretensions to respectability is supposed to attend'. Clearly the upper gentry were above any necessity to prove their respectability or that they loved reading, not that the Institute's programme included much that was genuinely literary. Venables approached it with some condescension, referring to it as '"The Mechanics' Institute", or as I believe they style themselves, "Literary Institute"'.[79] His remark revealed the true nature of Bevan's initiative, which was an example of the desire on the part of the ruling class to provide 'improving' entertainment for their inferiors, while simultaneously denying them the chance of expressing their autonomous needs. And what of Kilvert's support for Bevan's initiative? His name did not appear in any of the reports of meetings in 1865, his first year in Clyro, nor was he at the January 1866 soirée, but he did attend on 18 May that year when the Hay Choral Society gave their annual spring concert. In a programme described as 'very select', was the song, 'An English Wife for Me', which was an eccentric choice for an audience that was probably half Welsh. The Bevan and Dew families were there in force, a Miss Baskerville, and the Rev. Tom Williams of Llowes. That it was probably Kilvert's first visit to an Institute meeting is given some credence by the fact that the reporter of the event was so unfamiliar with his name that he set it down as the 'Rev G. Kilbert'.[80] His lack of support may at bottom reflect his hostility to working-class organisations or his awareness that there was little of a literary character in the programme. There was more in the Clyro Penny Readings, which he probably felt obliged to attend anyway because the audience were his own parishioners.

In addition to his tireless work on behalf of the Literary Institute, Bevan also was responsible for the first Penny Reading at the Hay National Schoolroom on 10 December 1864, and did the first reading himself. It was announced then that Venables would do a reading at the next one. It was typical of Rev. Bevan to have acted so promptly to establish Penny Readings in Hay following the first local meeting of promoters of the Penny Reading movement in Hereford in early October that year. The *Hereford Times* reporter of the promoters' second meeting a week later observed that the way to raise the intellectual level of the working-class was not to pander to their existing taste but to whet their intellectual appetite by offering fare just beyond it. A letter to that edition of the paper gave these as the criteria for selecting material for Penny Readings: amusement, interest, morality, instruction. However, during Kilvert's first month in Clyro (January 1865), a correspondent to the *Hereford Times* rejected upper middle-class condescension in the matter of Penny Readings. They were intended for the working-class, he said, but too often the available space at them was taken up by their social betters, who also did all the readings; this was the situation at Bevan's Hay readings, and at the Clyro ones.

Both Bevan and Venables, as well as the Rev. Thomas of Llanthomas and Captain Devereux, were committee members of the Cambrian Archaeological Association. Neither Walter Baskerville nor his brothers involved themselves in such activities; their interests seemed to be entirely sporting, as has been noted.[81] There was one cultural event—an annual one—which attracted some local sportsmen: we find that Tomkyns Dew, Walter Baskerville, and several men of the Hopton family into which Walter would later marry, attended the Three Choirs Festival that was an institution in the English border countries. In general, however, they remained true to the manly ideas of the English country gentleman to which a deferential local farmer paid tribute in a letter of 10 June 1865 to the *Hereford Times*: 'In plain truth a good landlord and a good sportsman should mean much the same sort of thing... There is no higher character for an Englishman that that which is embodied in these two congenial qualities...'.

In a society in which 'landlord' and 'sportsman' could be regarded as 'qualities' of a gentleman's character, it is obvious that Kilvert would be out of place. Adelaide Sartoris would have found it ludicrous that they could have been considered as such, and would have concluded that the observation reflected much that was wrong in English society. To confuse the social position of landlord and the social activity of field sports in this way with moral qualities would have seemed a prime example of English smugness and philistinism. As an earlier chapter has made clear, Kilvert had no sympathy with field sports, and would have resented the suggestion that merely to indulge in them was a guarantee of being a 'good type'. Sportsmen were valued for their vitality and dash but coolness and restraint were equally prized because they differentiated the gentleman as much as possible from the lower-classes, whose feelings were seen as disturbingly out of control. (It was that which was the basis of the prevalent fear of the 'mob' and Kilvert shared it). Thus, Mrs. Braddon describes Henry Dunbar as 'a gentlemanly creature ... not often disturbed by any vulgar demonstration of his own feelings'.[82] However, while Kilvert was intent on the lower-classes recognising their inferiority in this respect, he himself was a man whose personality, like that or Ursula Hamilton, contained much spontaneity and impulsiveness, and he would fret in a society that gave them few outlets for expression, apart from the arena of manly sports. The gentlemanly code of the period had as its aim the production of an essentially conformist authority figure, who would not disturb the surface of society with passionate feelings or with radical ideas, whether religious, political or artistic.

There was little room in the country houses Kilvert knew for the kind of sensitivity which was such a feature of his personality and that of Adelaide Sartoris. She had herself a particularly sensitive nature and was very aware, as Kilvert was, of how people could suffer in company from the crassness and coldness of others. She was fond of complaining that nobody ever spoke frankly about what they thought and felt except herself and her sister, Fanny Kemble. She once observed in one of her essays: 'Now, to love anything sincerely is an act of grace, but to love the best sincerely is a state of grace'.[83] It is a sentiment that goes, literally, to the heart of Kilvert and to the heart of the complaint he was making about English manners. He, too, had the 'quick emotions' of Adelaide Sartoris; on several occasions his

Diary shows how perilously close to impropriety his passionate, impulsive nature brought him. That and his artistic sensitivity were not qualities that were valued by the manliness cult that permeated the society of his day. 'Manliness meant both physical and moral fibre; or as Carlyle put it "sheer obstinate toughness of muscle; but much more what we should call toughness of heart". The qualities of Tennyson's "great broad-shouldered genial Englishman" were on the way up; sensitivity, gentleness, a sense of beauty were on the way down'.[84] It was this which made Kilvert an outsider or at least a misfit in the society of the country house, as, to a degree, it had made him an outsider at Oxford.

Kilvert's hostility to the manners of the English country house was a confirmation that the values which Taine found so dominant there—hierarchy, authority, subordination, inequality, deference, stiffness, emotional repression and frugality—had been successfully passed on to the next generation. The three decades 1820-1850 were the period in which the greatest snobbery was experienced at Eton and at other public schools; it was the period in which the majority of the landowning men of Kilvert's *Diary* had their schooling. Mack, the historian of the public schools, found that class consciousness and materialism were very strong in the public schools from the middle of the century onwards. Kingsley saw that the 'great spirit' of the 19th century was to make as much money as possible and to retire to 'luxurious ease and suburban villas'.[85] There was something of that spirit abroad in deepest Radnorshire and Breconshire, and it showed itself not in the building of suburban villas but of mansions. A desire for domestic luxury and for a house whose grandeur was commensurate with his family's status played an important part in Rev. Thomas' plans and effectively wrecked Kilvert's.

Kilvert found that all these qualities combined to create a dead and suffocating atmosphere in the country houses he visited. On occasion, of course, they were stimulating and refreshing places but the emphasis he placed on the qualities of naturalness, warmth and ease that made them so, indicates that those occasions were comparatively rare. Though it was women who caused him most anguish, it was also usually women who possessed the naturalness and the warmth which made him feel at home. In Adelaide Sartoris' novels it is women who speak out against life-destroying codes and attitudes of mind; Kilvert's enjoyment of *A Week in a French Country House* was centred in 'dear Ursula'. Whenever it was possible for Kilvert to share his love of literature, it was women who were his confidantes; the 'manliness' of most of the men was likely to have repelled him, and he would have been unable to join in conversations about field sports. The anti-intellectual bias of their society would have set limits on those facets of his personality which he could safely reveal in company. He may have tended to become one of the 'mutes' which Taine said were produced by English manners; this would have given him additional motivation for keeping his *Diary*. That he hardly figures in the diary kept by Mary Bevan or in Venables' letters is the result partly of his lack of social stature but also of the fact that he felt unable to be fully himself in some of Clyro's country houses, and therefore made little impact.

He did take some interest in the physical side of life which was of such importance in the world of men; he did some fishing and enjoyed watching cricket. A.L. Rowse observed that Kilvert's physical side expressed itself especially in walking, 'that favourite pursuit of the intellectually-minded', but he added, 'Not that he was an intellectual... He was something more and better than that; he was an artist, with a passionate love of life'.[86] It was that passionate love of life which was the root of his protest against the deathliness of life in the English country house. Those who love his *Diary* recognise that it is the vitality and energy proceeding from that source which are the supreme qualities of the man. 'It is comparatively speaking, minutiae that fill it, the deepest, remotest, richest provincialism that speaks, yet the voice is neither quaint not old-maidish but young, direct and vital'.[87] A truly artistic vision of life, such as Kilvert possessed, is inevitably the enemy of conformity and it was perhaps conformity above all which, in Kilvert's experience, created the stiffness and unnaturalness he loathed.

There was no Victorian more conscious than Kilvert of the pressure to conform; his natural conservatism, attachment to custom and tradition, humble status, hatred of upstart behaviour, and timidity, made him the perfect subject for social prescriptions. Some of his unease in the English country house stemmed partly from his fear of transgressing them. It was the spontaneity of consciousness he shared with Ursula Hamilton and her creator that, on his death, prompted his Bredwardine parishioner to say '...his *living* was good, his *heart* was good, and he was *all* good...'. He was loved, in other words, because he was a gentle, simple being and it showed in his deep Wordsworthian love of children. He believed, with the poet, that heaven lay about them in their infancy and that they came into the world trailing the 'clouds of glory' which indicated their divine origins. Deeply conscious of hierarchy and rank though he was, and committed to their preservation in a society showing more and more tendencies to become egalitarian, he ended up as a sacrificial victim to his beliefs.

Among the questions that could be posed to test whether a man was a snob, said Thackeray, were these: whether he was uncharitable, whether he was proud of his narrow soul, and how he treated a great man and a small man. Kilvert was small man blessed with a wide soul. From that stemmed all the ambivalence that characterised his experience in the English country house. He had a romantic attachment to it and all that it stood for, yet aspects of its life disturbed him greatly. It was the home of men whom he regarded as the natural leaders of society, but many of them and their women repelled and frightened him. He knew he should seek a wife among its daughters. They were, however, surrounded by rules designed to trap and demoralise social inferiors such as he, and while he resented the way they constrained women emotionally, he simultaneously hoped to find a wife who was so 'girlish' as to be almost a child.[88] Though he liked to discuss literature with women, and enjoyed Ursula Hamilton as a fictional companion, both she and Adelaide Sartoris would have frightened him because they challenged conventional manners. He would have been out of his depth in their cultural milieu. He found he was invariably happier with the women of the farmhouse than with those of the country house, but the criterion by which he judged them superior was the aristocratic one of 'breeding'; it had nothing to do with the democratic tendency of society. He had found the key to the hearts of farmhouse people and when the time came for him to depart from Clyro they confirmed it to a degree which humbled him. Overwhelmed by the tears his departure occasioned in one farmer's wife, he wrote: 'What have I done? What am I that these people should so care for me?' And he felt, as Lancelot did in *Yeast*, that he was 'gaining more real acquaintance with English society' in their homes than 'by dawdling... in exclusive drawing rooms'.[89] Nevertheless, he continued to seek his future wife among country house girls who were strong in the quality of 'heart', and thus reinforced the conventional view that women should leave intellectual matters to men. He expected women to defer to men. There is no suggestion from him in the *Diary*, when Daisy Thomas's father denied her any voice in the matter of a husband, that she should do anything but obey.[90] When Kilvert was confronted by the 'anguish' of Daisy's soul reflected in her face, he asked 'What could I do?' There is no doubt what Ursula Hamilton's answer would have been: she would have upbraided him both for failing to confront Rev. Thomas a second time and for abiding by his insistence that he said no more to Daisy of his love. Had she been *sure* of it, she might have worked on her father as Frances Grenfell did on her relatives when she was determined to marry Kingsley. By keeping quiet, Kilvert played into the Rev. Thomas' hands.

If Thomas had been capable of recognising that the suitor for his daughter's hand was a good, loving man and had, on the strength of that recognition, make her an allowance sufficient for them to marry and to set up a home, Kilvert would have been a father and Daisy a mother. Thomas had subordinated 'heart' to commercial considerations but was entirely typical in doing so.[91] There is a multiplication of references in Kilvert's *Diary* from the middle of 1873 onwards to his desire for a wife and family, and of moments of emotional and sexual frustration. A consistent melancholy strain appears and there were bouts of mysterious illness which may have been signs of the 'nerve ruin' referred to by Carpenter. At the time of Kilvert's death, a letter written by his sister to Mrs. Venables stated that he had never recovered from his disappointments in love: 'I feel more and more sure that he had been slowly passing away from us ever since his terrible sorrow ... his health was quite broken up'.[92]

The Rev. Thomas seemed bent on ensuring that none of his daughters married, whether for money or for love, and there is further evidence to show that the life of another of them (ie. in addition to Daisy, Charlotte and Grace) was blighted by his actions. In a letter dated 4 June 1886 to Rev. Venables, Louisa Bevan, wife of Rev. Bevan, wrote that her husband had just left to take the funeral of Mary, the eldest Thomas daughter. Louisa Bevan expressed concern about the Thomas family: 'We have all been much distressed for the Llanthomas people. Mary had never been well since her mother's death and I fancy she has had much anxiety lately, and had felt the rooms being stripped of all pictures and books and all the plate being sent off to London to be sold very much'. Mary had complained of a chill the previous Monday and had gone to bed. The next day, Dr. Williams pronounced her dangerously ill. She seemed to rally by the end of the week but later deteriorated and died the next Tuesday night. 'Colonel Thomas and Walter feel her loss bitterly and she was certainly the most loveable of the sisters'.[93] We shall probably never know what crisis compelled Rev. Thomas to sell off some of the contents of his luxurious house but it indicates that the money he had saved on marriage settlements had not produced financial stability. It is equally unclear what the other elements were which brought on, or exacerbated, his daughter's illness and led finally to her death at the age of 42.[94] Louisa Bevan and others of her family knew that something was terribly wrong at Llanthomas. Mary Thomas' death provides the final, melancholy postscript to the family's history, and to Kilvert's relationship with the English country house.

'The common people... said [I] had "done well for [myself]" because [I] had married the daughter of one whom they thought one of the great ones of the earth - a landed proprietor of old family, with county connections'.

Kilvert's father, reflecting on his marriage, *Trevellyk*, p.74

'The old feudalism of England - the state of things when there were yet serfs, and when the lords of the soil were almost a different order of beings - still colours the relations of the rich and poor'.

Article on 'The Agricultural Labourer', *Saturday Review*, September 1865

'The land of England was monopolised by a few hundred thousand eldest sons year after, century after century, since the Conquest, whilst the millions are left without a yard of land to stand on...'.

Letter to the *Hereford Times*, 3 July 1869

'The feeling of isolation and loneliness, so characteristic of modern man, first appeared in the nineteenth century. With the break up of a long-established order and the resulting fragmentation of both society and thought, the old ties were snapped, and men became acutely conscious of separation'.

W.E. Houghton, *The Victorian Frame Of Mind, 1830-1870*, p.77

EPILOGUE
The Strain of Keeping Things Fixed

In the Prologue to this book it was noted that the germ of Kilvert's *Diary* lay in his desire to pay tribute, in a period of profound social change, to traditional rural society, and the gentleman farmer's home of Chieflands was shown to be a symbol for Kilvert of all that was best in that society. Kilvert's story ends as it began with reflections on landed property and its importance. In a very real sense, the *Diary* is about property and the significance—economic, social, political, aesthetic, moral—of it. When it is possible to see deeply into Kilvert's personality, we find on so many occasions that his strongest thoughts and feelings centre on properties of different kinds.

Because of its social origins, the Kilvert family belonged firmly to the landed interest and identified itself with its fortunes. It was, in truth, a humble member of that community, certainly as far as its yeoman background was concerned, but its descent from two lines of squires made it cling all the harder to the tradition of the English country gentleman. The family's pride in belonging to that tradition derived from a belief that the country gentleman was a person of special qualities, culturally as well as socially. At its best, the tradition was epitomised by Rev. Venables' lifetime of service to rural administration, while at its worst it was summed up by the empty snobbery of his youngest brother, Henry. When debts of £16,500, accumulated by their father, threatened in 1856 that the Llysdinam estate would have to be sold, he wrote to Venables expressing his horror at the possibility, which the latter was entertaining, that the family would have to move to the town of Hay. To him the loss of social prestige would be catastrophic. It was, he said, unthinkable to be 'planted for life in a little dirty town with a few gooseberry bushes behind and a dirty station wagon in front, with no occupation, no prospect, no interest, no amusement of any sort'.[1] His brother, George, was also violently opposed to a move to Hay. As the eldest brother and heir to the estate, Venables had to make a more realistic assessment of the family's position, but the view of the country house and its status put forward by Henry was substantially the same as that which he himself had expressed in his book on Russia. Kilvert indicated his allegiance to it in his eulogy to the Clutterbucks and the 'influence of property' wielded by them. His romantic nature also found in country house tradition a rich source of delicious myths and picturesque locations that fulfilled a deep need in him. When he came across moral defects in the landowning class, especially its higher echelon, he felt his own position as a country gentleman compromised, but that did not lead him to question the ultimate value of the landed family as an institution. He was like his father in regarding the country house as his 'second home'.

For all their 'improvement' of landscape with mansions and parks, landowners generally did not present a glowing example of moral improvement. In Kilvert's *Diary*, the estates of Maesllwch, Tregoyd, Penoyre, Moccas, and Clyro Court, in addition to Llysdinam, all ran into debt.[2] There were some landowners, usually the wealthiest and most aristocratic, who did invest in drainage schemes and in decent housing for their dependants, but the income of many was too often directed towards dowries, extravagant living, and the building of mansions. And yet it was the landowning class which Kilvert steadily looked to for the moral and political framework of a contented, harmonious, Christian society. On the occasion of his homecoming from honeymoon, he replied to the good wishes of his parishioners with these words: 'It has ever been... the aspiration of my heart that we may live in confidence, and love one another as members of one great Christian family'. The emphasis on living together in love and confidence is revealing, as though by that stage of his life, his own confidence that this was a realisable goal was less strong than ever. He was enunciating the principles of love that Kingsley had expressed inspiringly through his life and his writings. It was the message of Chieflands and of Kilvert's country churchyard elegy about squires and peasants, landlords and labourers, lying peacefully side by side in the bosom of Mother Earth. He tried desperately hard to believe in the essential, fruitful connectedness between the inhabitants of country houses and the humbler folk of their communities, but the

348

tendencies among landed gentry making for superiority and exclusiveness were always too strong. Real contact between its various members was limited and controlled, and while it was true they had some important interests in common, others were productive of conflict, as has been shown earlier. The whole order of the landed interest was held together in 'a violent love-hate relationship'.[3] Social institutions express the moral values of those who endorse them. The landed gentry, in endorsing field sports, quarter sessions, the public schools, and the family seen in terms, not of a group of individuals united in affection, but of a 'house' representing superior lineage, were sowing the seeds of division between themselves and others.

In an essay written in 1887, looking back to the period just before Kilvert's death, Richard Jefferies spelt out why it was no longer possible for members of the rural community to live together in love and confidence, and he based his analysis on Kilvert's own county of Wiltshire. A series of changes was, he said, transforming rural society. As modern capitalist agriculture impinged increasingly on rural life, the static community with its traditional relations which Kilvert had celebrated in Chieflands was steadily disrupted: 'labouring men more and more think simply of work and wages. They do not want kindness—they want coin'.[4] They would no longer be held on their 'good behaviour'. That attitude, exacerbated by improved education, was unsettling in a way previously unknown. Most men were unwilling to hire themselves and their labour to a farmer for a whole year and the cottage tied to the job was no longer the means of tying the labourer to the community. Half of the labouring population was 'nomad' because it went in search of higher wages; the custom of living all one's life in the same village was going.

All of these changes produced a situation that Kilvert feared. Jefferies described it in terms of 'an air of freedom and independence' and as 'the altered tone of the entire country', and summed up the basis of it thus: 'no men, not even with families, will endure what they once did'. The condition of 'unfixedness', which J.S. Mill had identified as the mark of a democratic society, had come at last to the traditional rural community: 'that entire unfixedness in the social position of individuals ...that habitual dissatisfaction of each with the position he occupies...'. The 'ancient structure' of England was, Mill declared, being destroyed by the 'mobility and fluctuating nature of individual relations - the absence of permanent ties, local or personal'.[5] The society Kilvert struggled to preserve was doomed before he was born, therefore, because Mill was writing these words in 1840. The 'permanent ties' to which Mill referred were the ones Kilvert especially valued: the attachment of tenants to landlords, of servants to masters, of individuals to their native locality. His Oxford course, his choice of novels and his interest in Wordsworth, Crabbe, and Barnes indicate that he possessed a developed understanding of field sports, the role of squires, and the lot of the small proprietor. He had only a limited *intellectual* grasp of these issues but felt them deeply and passionately. They were integral to his wider conception of 'home'—the capacity of a community to provide a sense of identity and belonging to an individual. However, his traditional community was hierarchical and it was the respect habitually given to 'superior' persons that was declining. No longer could men be kept subject by fear of their social superiors.

Land reform had been an issue throughout the 19th century but it had become a burning one by the year Kilvert died, largely because of middle-class hostility to the landed interest and its power and privileges, as is made clear in the quotes that preface this chapter from the *Saturday Review* and the *Hereford Times*. Changes in the land laws would produce changes in the way property was distributed and therefore in the entire structure of society. One of the key laws was the one so dear to Venables—primogeniture, the settling of an estate on the eldest son. Kilvert implicitly endorsed it when he ecstatically greeted the news of the birth of Venables' son and heir in April 1874: 'There is at last a son to inherit the estate and the grand old name', he wrote. Primogeniture itself had an ancientness that would inevitably be endearing to one prone to revere all 'grand old' things. As a practice it began in the 13th century as a means of avoiding the division of estates by contending members of families. By the end of the 17th century the legitimacy of it was being challenged because it was inequitable and 'repugnant to a new concept of equal rights to family affection...'. One of its consequences was that it actually fomented division within families by favouring eldest sons at the expense of their siblings, and encouraged the idea of 'a family as a society in which personal feeling played no part, as "a house"' (i.e. a symbol of tradition, rank and power).[6] Thus, at the centre of the landowning class lay a conception of family that was the polar opposite of the one held by Kilvert. Furthermore, it tended to produce precisely the wastefulness that he had been brought up to deplore. The examples we have seen of eldest sons incurring large debts in order, chiefly, to assert family pride—Venables' father and Viscount Hereford's father, Thomas Baskerville, Col. Watkins (of Penoyre), Rev. Thomas, and Captain De Winton—were all attributable to the temptations offered by primogeniture.

Concern with the conception of a family as a symbol of rank permeated the 19th century public school. At Charterhouse, where Venables went after Eton failed him, it was the custom for new boys to be quizzed about their name, home, and who and what their fathers were socially, as Thomas Mozley recorded. He was in no doubt about the deleterious influence of the custom: 'There was mischief in it to the nervous system, to the *heart,* and to the brain'.[7] The result in the view of another contemporary commentator on public schools was that 'boys became ashamed of speaking of their homes and families in the natural language of the *good heart*'.[8] Later in the century we have the pathetic spectacle of Charles Phipps, the 14 year-old son of the Wiltshire landowning family, writing to his mother from Eton: 'Sandbach is very civil to me and is a gentlemanly sort of fellow. Am I to have anything to do with him? I ask because I don't know what you think of them'.[9] He needed to have his mother confirm whether the Sandbach family was socially acceptable before he felt able to make a friend of one of its sons.

Kilvert's problems in mixing with public school men have been indicated earlier. Had he himself attended a public school, they would have been less, but he would then not have been the sensitive, warm-hearted man he was. The result of such an education was, as he discovered, a class notably lacking in human sympathy, the greatest barrier to which was its inability to see beyond itself. The lesser gentry with whom he moved were more prone to this weakness by and large than the aristocracy, who were more open to artistic, even radical, ideas, and were less narrowly conservative.[10] The aristocracy generally moved in a wider circle than their gentry brothers, part of whose problem was, as Dr. Arnold pointed out in 1836, their restricted life in the country and ignorance of city ways. He noticed it especially among country gentlemen of Tory persuasion, whose selfish, aggressive attitudes interfered 'even with private relations', and made them unsympathetic to anyone's distress but their own.[11] In essence, they were incapable of conceiving of any situation in which they were not at the top of the social pyramid. William Wilberforce had seen the landed gentry's 'profane self-sufficiency' as the source of the pride which was the vice 'most opposite to the ...spirit of real Christianity'.[12]

Some critics of landowners not unreasonably held primogeniture responsible for their widespread failure to invest in improvements in property. It was not likely that families which were encouraged to adopt selfish attitudes towards their own members would display more sympathetic ones towards inferior persons of their communities. Shortly after Kilvert came to Clyro, a government commission underlined the way in which the essentially self-regarding nature of the landed family meant that the improvement of the landed estate was a forlorn hope: 'So long as estates can be tied up for generations, loaded with settlements, and so parchment-hampered that the proprietors are more in name than in fact, society at the same time expecting them to live up to the standard of their supposed proprietorship, it is clear that estate improvement is out of the question'.[13] The result of this situation, the commissioners saw, was that, in order to maintain the life-style of landlords, their labourers had to be compelled to work on low wages and to live in cottage hovels. It has been shown earlier that the bitterness caused by Game Laws, low wages, denial of land to labourers, and Poor Laws that made poverty a crime and encouraged grudging, condescending attitudes to charity, produced deep divisions in rural society instead of the harmony claimed by landowners.

Even when change of the most fundamental kind had come to the countryside, after the reform of the Poor Law, the 1870 Education Act, three reform bills, the establishment of the National Agricultural Labourers' Union, one Wiltshire landowner, Walter Long, grandson of the one who was too superior to make social contact with Kilvert's father when he took up his curacy in Keevil, was totally incapable of recognising that the time of his class's supremacy had gone forever. In his memoirs, written just after World War I, he developed a lengthy polemic on behalf of the landed interest, arguing that it should be restored to the dominant position it had occupied in its 19th century golden age. The means to this end was to be a change in the way landowners' income was taxed. He advocated that taxable income should be that which was left after the expenses of an estate had been met. To make what he had in mind absolutely clear, he cited the example of two men with the same income. One had a country house and an estate to maintain, the other had neither. Long argued that to tax them both equally was unfair because the former had the responsibility of property while the latter did not. 'Ought not every possible inducement be given to taxpayers to reside in their own houses', he plaintively asked, 'and so to contribute, not only to the wages earned in the neighbourhood, but to the general prosperity... of that part of the country in which they live?'[14] Now that it was no longer possible for landowners to maintain huge country houses, he looked to the nation to subsidise their deer parks, game coverts and gamekeepers, hunters, servants, and all the extravagence and waste which, for the previous hundred years had been subsidised out of the pitiful wages of their employees.[15]

One of the ordinary people of a Wiltshire village, W.H. Hudson, was impervious to the appeal of the country house. He had all of Kilvert's reverence for the 'humble, unremembered lives' of village communities, but because he had neither the social nor the psychological need of the Diarist to identify with landed gentry, he avoided his split in consciousness. He had no need for the illusion, which Kilvert worked so hard to maintain, that close bonds of affection and common interests united gentry and working people, and recognised that the inherent conservation and physical aloofness of country houses meant that they were essentially isolated from village life. 'The life that is in them does not mix with or form part of the true native life', he wrote.[16]

In 1830, Dr. Arnold was writing to the father of the barrister who would have the unenviable task of revealing the Tichborne Claimant as an impostor with this warning against conservatism: 'There is nothing so revolutionary, because there is nothing so unnatural and so convulsive to society as the strain to keep things fixed, when all the world is by the very law of its creation in eternal progress'.[17]

During the last phase of Kilvert's life, which may be seen as the period following his departure from Clyro, the strain 'to keep things fixed' began to tell. In a real sense, the *Diary* he began to keep from the first of January 1870 represented part of that effort. The clue to why he began keeping it is to be found in that date. Begun very probably as a New Year's resolution at the end of the first full year after the Second Reform Bill came into effect and at the beginning of the year in which a government bill threatened to take elementary education out of the hands of the Church, the *Diary* was his hymn of love for old things, and he demonstrated that love by his integrity and by the artistry he brought to the depiction of his society. As the last years went by and more and more developments threatened the stability of that society, he became increasingly unhappy, and the dark mood of this period was occasioned partly by this and partly by his anxiety that he would never achieve preferment, a wife and children. In the prospect of marriage at least there was hope for the future and this sustained him in this period when he increasingly looked towards the past.

His *Diary* comes to an end five months before he married so that we have no picture of his wife nor of his married life; his widow was determined that all reference to herself be excised from the *Diary*. He had first met Elizabeth Rowland in spring 1876 during a tour of Paris, organised by his Wadham friend, Mayhew, partly perhaps in an effort to help him recover from disappointment at the failure of his relationship with Ettie Meredith Brown. That year was a transitional one for Kilvert. Ettie now belonged to the past and the second relationship with Katharine Heanley began to flourish. He had become Vicar of St. Harmon, Radnorshire, that summer, but he was to stay barely a year and he took the Bredwardine living in autumn 1877. Elizabeth Rowland was the daughter of John Rowland of Hollybank, Wootton, near Woodstock, Oxfordshire. He had first trained as a doctor but gave that up to become a landowner. It was perhaps inevitable that Kilvert, like his father, would marry into a landowning family. The Rowlands had owned a small estate in Wootton from 1760 and the new, large, gentleman's house of Hollybank was built for Elizabeth's father during 1862-3. The changes that were coming over the countryside were affecting Wootton; in 1872 it was the centre of agricultural unrest, though poor housing, unemployment, and low wages had caused disaffection before that. A branch of the NALU had been formed at the very early date of May 1872 and a fight began to raise labourers' wages from 11s to 16s a week. John Rowland was prominent in a Farmers' Defence Association, formed to protect themselves against Union action.[18]

Though perhaps the least attractive of Kilvert's lovers, Elizabeth matched him in her simple piety. The motto on her family crest, 'Piety strengthens families', might have been that of the Kilvert family, and she came, as he did, from a large family of brothers and sisters. She was loved by the villagers of Wootton for her devoted visiting of the parish's poor and sick. After Kilvert's death she returned there to continue that work, never marrying again and dying in Eastbourne in 1911. Their marriage took place in Wootton on 20 August 1879, and they travelled to Scotland for their honeymoon, from which they returned on 13 September. The homecoming celebrations in Bredwardine took the form so beloved of Kilvert of tables spread under a tree (a very fine cedar of the kind that graced Wadham's gardens), at which the ordinary people of the village sat down to tea. The tables were supervised by, among others, Kilvert's brother-in-law, the Rev. Smith, Rev. Andrew Pope, Rev. Bishop, the curate of Moccas, and Miss Palmer of the Eardisley landowning family which had supplied one of the Jarvis Charity Trustees. Local farmers and cottagers had clubbed together to buy wedding presents and a band of labourers met Kilvert's carriage, took out the horses, and pulled it themselves to the Vicarage door. The wedding gifts from the farmers were presented by Frank Evans, the farmer who had been so critical of the appointment of the gentry Trustees of the Jarvis Charity. The social status of the village schoolmaster, Mr. Bates, whose son Kilvert had tutored in Greek, is clearly underlined by the fact that he was deputed to present the cottagers' gift. In his reply to Bates' address on their behalf, Kilvert said he was particularly touched by the generosity of it because he knew it came from 'slender incomes and pockets not very deep'.

The day after the celebration was a Sunday and Kilvert took both services at Bredwardine and Brobury as usual. He was feeling ill by the evening and continued so through the following day. His father was concerned and came over from Langley Burrell to see him on the following Sunday, the 21st, and took the morning service, while Kilvert's friend, Pope, stood in for him at Brobury in the evening. Kilvert was no better on Monday and was so bad on Tuesday that his doctor, Dr. Giles of Staunton-on-Wye, sent for Dr. Debenham of Presteigne. Twenty minutes after Debenham arrived, Kilvert died of peritonitis.[19] He was 38 and had been married for scarcely five weeks. It is possible to see a parallel between the tragic brevity of his marriage and the fate of traditional rural society: both were denied any further significant flowering.

The day of his funeral, 27 September, was as wet and gloomy as the day of his homecoming. The newspaper report paid tribute to his power of touching the hearts of those who heard him and to the 'quiet gentlemanly way' in which he did his work. To the poor, he was 'an unostentatious friend, a comforter, and a benefactor'. Venables read 'very touchingly' the first part of the burial service but the sermon was preached by Sir George Cornewall, who took as his theme the determination of the true Christian to spread Christ's word and to encourage faith in ultimate immortality. When he spoke of the way in which God made clear 'in a thousand ways... that this earth is not our home', he came closer to Kilvert than he realised. The tribute was, however, the conventional one paid to a deceased clergyman and we shall never know what Sir George's actual feelings were. He might have warmed to Kilvert's artistic nature if he had known about it because he was himself a painter, a musician, and an antiquary. There was no mention of Kilvert's literary interests. Sir George would have known little of them and nothing of the fact that he was the author of a huge diary. No one of his regular acquaintance knew of that, not even Kilvert's father, until some time after his death.[20] The *Diary* contained, among other private thoughts, comments that were critical of such as Sir George. The world of the imagination was as important to Kilvert as the world of the Christian religion because ultimately they were indivisible: it was his very soul that was fed by his experience of the manor house of Yaverland while the more modest house of Chieflands fed both heart and soul. His passion for literature and for beauty was an integral part of his spirituality, a wholeness underlined by Father Luff, who noted that Kilvert's spirituality 'was intrinsic to the mere fact, the mere act, of living'.[21] There was almost nothing in Sir George's sermon that evoked a sense of Kilvert as a man; it may have been strong in terms of theology but was decidedly weak in terms of warmth of feeling. Did Sir George feel closer to Kilvert because the possibility had been raised that he could be a relative? If he was prepared to welcome Kilvert as a full member of his class, was it that class he had in mind when he urged Kilvert's mourners to think of 'those who make this world their home, and think only of its pleasures and honours'?

Paradoxically, the mild-mannered, conservative curate of Clyro had proved himself in several ways a rebel. He had protested against the life-destroying codes of propriety of the English country house; he had allied himself with those who opposed death-dealing sportsmen; he had defended the small against the large proprietor;

he had condemned the 'unclean heart' of Venables; and finally he had taken a stand against aristocratic irresponsibility in the shape of De Winton. In recognising that Kilvert was a covert rebel, we touch upon the attraction that he held at the outset for his discoverer, William Plomer, for it was not simply the perfect picture of Victorian rural society contained in the *Diary* that he wished to bring before the public. He also admired the personality that he found there. Among *Diary* features that he singled out was 'the sense of character of which I am conscious', and it was this that made him feel particularly well qualified to undertake the editing of the *Diary*.[22] The picture that we have of Kilvert is, to a very high degree, that vouchsafed to us by Plomer's editing because he retained not only those parts of the original 22 notebooks that he considered would have most public appeal, but also those facets of its author's personality that appealed to him most. One consequence of this was, as Peter Alexander has remarked, to make Kilvert 'more like his editor: less interested in God and more concerned with sex'.[23] Plomer in fact had a number of traits in common with the obscure Victorian clergyman he discovered: passivity, poetic sensitivity to landscape, indifference to fame and wealth, and a deep compassion especially towards those in society 'unprotected by money or power'.[24]

Of special importance to Plomer was the 'surprising frankness about himself' displayed by Kilvert. In his preface to the first volume of the *Diary*, Plomer underlined again the honesty of Kilvert's record of his life. What Plomer had especially in mind were Kilvert's 'natural male appetites constrained by his priestly status and sense of responsibility, by his sense of sin, by social decorum'.[25] Plomer's own homosexuality and natural reserve forced him into what Alexander called 'a watchful self-isolation'.[26] Plomer recognised that Kilvert too had repressed sexual desires (Plomer called them 'certain peculiarities'[27]) which distinguished him from others. There is no doubt that Plomer felt a certain affinity between himself and Kilvert in this regard. He used his writing, as Kilvert did, as a repository for his most intense personal feelings and this bred a secretiveness in both men. Plomer did this from schoolboy years and as he grew up, he was able to proclaim himself through his writing in a way that Kilvert could not. The intellectual integrity that Plomer admired so much in Kilvert's writing fell victim to the social constraints of the period: 'Victorians repressed the truth whenever it seemed socially unacceptable', wrote

Robert Pirsig.[28] In all of Plomer's writing he showed a steady interest 'in people set apart from others by personality, philosophy, gifts or circumstance ...'[29] and he felt himself to be one of those people and warmed to the Kilvert he discovered in the *Diary* because he felt him to be one too. The perception that Plomer had of Kilvert supports, therefore, the picture of him presented in these pages as something of an outsider in his society.

In considering the question of where and what his true home was, we come closest to understanding the 'secret' of Kilvert, his unique balance of contradictions and paradoxes. His particular brand of Christianity had given him an especially acute sense of the way in which this world is not the home of the individual soul, and he expressed it in the family motto he invented: 'We are strangers'. In the Church and in his work as a parish priest he found comfort for this sense of isolation. At Wadham, he had assimilated the 18th century picture of nature as an ordered beautiful system that provided clear evidence of a creative and benevolent intelligence, which could only be divine.[30] His own kindly nature responded to this picture and confirmed him in his priestly role. His *Diary* contains only one direct reference to the prevailing religious scepticism of his day. However, the entry that records his admiration for the Bishop of Derry's sermon at the 1873 Bath Church Conference shows how he shielded himself from doubt. Among three things in it which, he said, struck him with particular force was the statement that 'natural laws are not chains bound about the living God, but threads which He holds in His hand'.[31] This was clearly a reaction to the scientific viewpoint, which had steadily gained ground during the Victorian period and which held that the physical world was subject to invariable natural laws. It pictured nature as a vast mechanism of cause and effect, a battleground in which individuals and species fought for existence. Kilvert had glimpsed the kind of endless meaningless struggle characteristic of such a world in the South Wales miners' strike. It had become, he said, 'a desperately bitter and obstinate struggle with the masters, a struggle to be fought out now to the death and till one party or the other is utterly exhausted'.[32]

It was natural that the shy and sensitive Kilvert would retreat from such experiences into the world of the rural parsonage because it, like the Church of which it was a part, was a home secure from what the Bishop of Derry had called 'the assaults of unbelief'. His profound awareness of the nature and value of innocence—in young children, in the old and infirm, in animals—made him unusually sensitive and provided the counterweight to his strong sense of sin. When parishioners demonstrated their love for him, he was taken aback: 'What is it? What do they all mean? It is a strange and terrible gift, this power of stealing hearts and exciting such love'.[33] Walter Baskerville recognised this gift in Kilvert, though he translated it into terms that made sense to him: 'It is a pity you don't stand for the county', he told Kilvert. 'You would have the suffrages of everyone here'.[34] It was the basis of his success as a parish priest. With the picture of the ideal wife that Kilvert had painted in his poem, 'The Highest of Women', is merged an idealised portrait of a clergyman, which obviously represents Kilvert's notion of how he would like to be seen. Although in the poem all the qualities listed are attributed to the noble woman who is its subject, several of them relate more properly to a parish priest and tell us something about Kilvert's sense of himself and of his role. Thus, the priest is 'merciful to those that stray' and his 'prayers and alms-deeds back are shed / In double blessing on [his] head', which reminds us of Kilvert's stance towards the poor that was outlined in chapter 8. It is not hard to see his situation vis-à-vis Venables in the lines about deriving comfort for his own 'smart' from 'comforting each sorrowful heart' and 'shrinking, though [his] own cause be strong,/ From proving others in the wrong', and being 'nobly unapt to take offence'. Aware continually of his own humble social position, Kilvert could nevertheless 'afford with grace/ Cheerful to take the lowest place', and could reconcile himself to the fact that 'remembering all' he might be 'perhaps by none remembered'.

'Religion is the empire over the human heart', Bulwer Lytton had written and Kilvert ruled the hearts of many of his parishioners, but by no means all of them. To the men of his parishes, especially the younger labourers, and to such as Josiah Evans, the Clyro schoolmaster, and John Couzens, he was too much identified with the gentry class, and with the way in which it showed kindness mainly to the 'deserving' and deferential poor. Evans and Couzens could recognise the 'enthusiasm for humanity' in Kilvert which, he said, brought him to tears once when he heard the congregation of St. Paul's lift their voices in the hymn 'Sweet Saviour bless us ere we go'.[35] They could, however, also recognise his hostility to change of any kind and his assumption that everyone should keep their appointed place.[36] The areas in which he served as a clergyman were characterised by relatively high levels of church attendance,[37] so it was easier for him to remain sanguine about the future of religion. The way in which the Church contributed importantly to his search for security may be gauged from the *Diary* entry in which he recorded the comfort he obtained from hearing a choir boy in Canterbury Cathedral sing an anthem which included the lines: 'I will lay me down in peace... For it is Thou, Lord, only that makest me dwell in safety'.[38] It is noticeable that Kilvert wrote the lines twice as though he found the mere act of doing so reassuring.

The country house was another place where he looked for reassurance. His Evangelicalism might have made him much more critical of its society than he was, but according to that religious outlook the purpose of Christianity was to soften 'the glare of wealth' and to moderate 'the insolence of power'.[39] He was too much bound by the attitudes of his class to condone radical criticism of gentry. He was also too much in love with the life of the land. However, he did not feel at home in the country house because it denied the validity of the major concerns of his life: piety, literature, a love of and a respect for ordinary people, and a love of nature. The *Diary* entry which perhaps most fully expresses his situation is this one: 'It is a fine thing to be out on the hills alone. A man can hardly be a beast or a fool alone on a great mountain. There is no company like the grand solemn beautiful hills... one has a feeling and a love for them which one has for nothing else'.[40] It is one of the most purely Wordsworthian passages of the *Diary*, identifying as it does genuine piety with a love of the eternal forms of Nature, the human and temporal were as nothing by comparison with them.

Kilvert, like all men, lived in a human and temporal world but struggled to find any sense of home there. Like many Victorians, he sought escape from anxiety in the thought of an idealised home. However, even in his search for such a home, which was the main object of his life, Kilvert once again encountered conflict. Strong as his need was for a home of his own, when the opportunity of the St. Harmon living was offered him, he stepped back because he felt it would be a terrible wrench to leave the 'dear old home' of his family. When he was alone on a mountain, he felt safe, not only because of the strength he derived from being in touch with the infinite, but because the possibility of appearing a 'beast or a fool' was removed. The 'beast' may have been the unfulfilled sexual passion within him, the 'satyr' self which, he knew, existed alongside the 'angel' self. Perhaps it stood for his dread of behaving in an ungentlemanly way, of displaying the crude, lower-class passions of an Arthur Orton, or the philistine ones of the 'sporting' gentleman. His fear of appearing a fool reminds us of his social uncertainty in the face of gentry codes that placed so many pitfalls in the path, especially, of the more spontaneous individual. One of the many paradoxes about him is that, although extremely sociable himself, he was driven by his fears to shun company. The desire to be alone can be seen, not only as an escape from weaknesses but an escape into the discipline of the solitary figures he much admired, who had renounced the world. This formulation helps us to understand why a parish priest with a fervent love of humanity could acknowledge that he found it easier to love mountains than to love people.

The price of 'alone-ness' can be loneliness, and it has been seen how, in various facets of Kilvert's life, he experienced a sense of isolation, even of alienation. His yearning for the security of home was one indication of it. He wished to be as close to Venables as he was to his own father, whom Venables closely resembled, but there were things about the Vicar of Clyro which repelled him. He was unable to draw as close to the poor of his parishes as he would have liked. His lack of wife and children was a consistent element in his feeling of loneliness. (It is noticeable that the only companion he could contemplate having on a mountain, who would not have spoiled his solitude, was a child). And, finally, the higher gentry of country houses, whom he admired in so many ways, seemed to him to inhabit a moral and cultural vacuum. They were the acknowledged leaders of a social system he venerated but they and it were unworthy of the trust he placed in it. The historian Best observed of country house society: 'How large a proportion of the gentry at any one time were kindly and hospitable, is a question that only the local historian will be able to answer'.[41] As far as the gentry of Kilvert's parishes are concerned, the evidence of kindness is not very impressive. It was kindness, the generous heart, which Kilvert most wanted from them, but one feels that, on balance, he must have been disappointed. One of the many fine qualities of his *Diary* is his ability to write about tenderness of feeling of various kinds, and it is a reflection of his deep need, as a Christian, a moralist, and a man, to believe in the possibility of a society in which all classes could live together in love and harmony.

The period from his first curacy in Clyro to his death was that in which modern society, the modern, democratic state, was emerging and his *Diary* represents his attempt to define both the older society it was replacing and himself in relation to it. His sense of alienation from his rapidly changing society led him to attempt to evoke the qualities of the older order and, by recording them, to preserve them in some sort. Readers are drawn to the *Diary* because it pictures in fascinating living detail a world unchanged in most important respects since medieval times yet, paradoxically, its steady theme is awareness of change. It is a particularly representative and powerful example of memoirs that reflect a profound shift in human consciousness that occurred in the 19th century. The structure of feeling in such memoirs Williams called 'significant and indispensable' because it provides 'a perception and affirmation of a world in which one is not necessarily a stranger and an agent, but can be a member, a discoverer, in a shared source of life'.[42] The world in which one was a stranger and an agent Williams identified with the modern world—capitalist, industrial, bureaucratic, impersonal—that threatens the small-scale world epitomised by the village community, which offered a much greater possibility of sharing, of mutuality, of 'direct relationships, face-to-face contacts'.[43] Kilvert's *Diary* similarly stands for this latter kind of world and that is one of the main reasons for its popularity with 20th century readers. The tragedy for Kilvert was that in his society hierarchy and the obsession with rank worked steadily against mutuality and close relationships among classes and individuals.

The tragedy for Kilvert readers is that more than two thirds of his *Diary* was destroyed so that our picture of him will always be an incomplete one. There were originally more than 22 notebooks placed in Plomer's hands by Kilvert's nephew, T. Perceval Smith; some had already been destroyed by Kilvert's widow. Plomer makes it clear that in his editing he rejected on average about twice as much material as he retained.[44] He believed that his chief task as editor was to select Kilvert's most characteristic traits and attitudes as well as pieces of writing, and by this means let Kilvert 'speak for himself'.[45] In trying to assess what the original *Diary* contained, it is necessary to glean what we can about the criteria used in the sifting process to see what clues they provide about the parts that are lost. Plomer gave as his general aim in that process the elimination of everything of 'merely fugitive interest' and the retention of everything that seemed 'most worth preserving'.[46] Peter Alexander has told us that a good deal of what Plomer rejected was the material that any diarist found himself repeating: 'descriptions of picnic outings, for example, or lyrical writing inspired by the sight of the Welsh mountains under moonlight'.[47] In selecting which to retain Plomer was influenced by his own love of landscape and his knowledge of the Border Country. He must also have omitted passages which repeated visits to church bazaars, Volunteer Concerts, and Penny Readings; those he kept, since he was fascinated by Victorian society and by what he called Victorian 'literary country clergymen', would have been those most evocative of the period.

It is likely that he would have deemed entries relating to political events to be of insufficient interest. Although Kilvert's concern with politics was limited, one feels, for example, that he must have made more than one mention of the 1870 Education Act, whose repercussions, extending throughout the period of the *Diary*, had such overwhelming significance for him as a clergyman and teacher in village schools. Similarly, there is no reference whatsoever to the founding of the National Agricultural Labourers' Union, another event of great moment for him, and only one reference to a strike in its aftermath. A very serious agricultural depression hit the countryside in the late 1870s but we have no inkling of that either, probably as a result of Plomer's editing. If the complete *Diary* had shown more engagement with contemporary political events, it was no doubt counterbalanced by even more nostalgia for the past.

Alexander also noted that Plomer 'whether consciously or not, tended to cut passages in which Kilvert's passionate devotion to God showed itself at length ... and he included almost every passage indicative of another passion, that for young girls'.[48] As a man of considerable sensuousness himself, it is understandable that Plomer would take an interest in that aspect of Kilvert. If Plomer had had access to the notebooks destroyed by Kilvert's widow, he would certainly have retained the sexually explicit passages relating to Ettie Meredith Brown which they very probably contained. He enjoyed the physicality of Kilvert's descriptions of scenery and of people and was attracted to the 'magnetism' (Plomer's word) of Kilvert's personality that is caught in the words of a cousin of his who remembered him as 'very sleek and glossy and gentle, rather like a nice Newfoundland dog'.[49]

Plomer argued that since his selection was determined by a concern for what the general reader would find entertaining, he had to play down Kilvert's 'priestly functions'. Chapter 4 has referred to the way in which Plomer recognised the way this led to an under-valuing of Kilvert's devotion to the affairs of the parish. A number of other consequences may have sprung from this in terms of the impression created of the curate of Clyro. Firstly, he has tended to appear more leisured than he actually was. It is all too easy to imagine that his existence was a relatively pleasant one with parish visits inter-spersed with calls on gentry friends, shopping trips to Hay, and long walks in the country. Secondly, the sense of how much he rather than Venables carried the work of the parish would have emerged all the more strongly, and excised entries may well have revealed even more occasions when Kilvert sank under the strain of it and made protests in his *Diary*. Thirdly, in the 'prayers of supplication or thanksgiving', which, according to Alexander, Plomer cut from the notebooks, there would inevitably have been clearer indication of Kilvert's religious beliefs and their Evangelical bias, of the stern moral outlook that counterbalanced his affectionate, caring self.

Kilvert stated that he wished to preserve a record of his own humble, uneventful life and in this sense the *Diary* is his home because it is the place where he is remembered. It seems undeniable that few of the gentry would remember Kilvert. When his *Diary* was published, an old lady from one of the Wiltshire's grandest country houses, asked if she remembered him, replied 'Who would remember a curate?' The fact that Kilvert hardly figured in Mary Bevan's diary can be attributed to that outlook. There appear to be good reasons for believing that he mattered far less to Venables than Venables did to him. To him, too, Kilvert would always be a mere curate whose lack of rank entitled him to no recognition socially. Venables would have acknowledged the squire element in Kilvert's background; he would not have thought much of the yeoman side of his descent. He would have been as scornful of yeomen as was his life-long friend Sir John Walsh, MP for Radnorshire, who wrote to him requesting that he check out the social worth of one of Venables' neighbours who had been proposed as a JP for the local bench. Walsh said he remembered this man as a farmer or yeoman 'with no pretensions to being a gentleman', and therefore unsuitable to sit alongside Venables.[50]

There was a good deal of bitter irony in the fact that Kilvert's funeral sermon was preached by Sir George Cornewall. To have the living Sir George speaking solemn words over the dead Kilvert meant that the old men of Moccas, the ancient oaks whom Kilvert feared because they appeared destined to live forever, had triumphed again; they had waited and watched till he too went the way of all flesh. Sir George was their master and they symbolised his estate, which also seemed indestructible. The changing times were, however, already threatening to put an end to that estate's tradition because only six months after Kilvert's funeral, Lady Cornewall wrote to Venables' wife to tell her that they were going to shut up Moccas Court because they could not afford it anymore and were going to live abroad.[51] The Cornewall family fortunes had never recovered since the slave rebellion of 1795 on the island of Grenada where its sugar plantation was located. By 1818, the estate debt stood at £21,800. The family received £4,000 in compensation in 1835 for slaves freed two years before but the market for sugar steadily declined in the 1840s. In 1849 no profits were forthcoming. This decline in fortunes was accelerated by two family disputes which resulted in expensive law suits, one over who had a right to the compensation, the other over inheritance. They signified everything Kilvert loathed about gentry families; family affections were forgotten in fights over money, prestige and precedence.

What he loved most was a humble but loving family home such as his own or Chieflands and the tradition he most wanted to be part of was not the one represented by one lord of the manor succeeding another, but that represented by the holes in the stone floor made by the feet of old Mr. Fry of Chieflands as he sat year after year in his farm kitchen. The worth of that tradition was to be measured not by size of acreage or of rent roll or length of pedigree but by the amount of loving kindness shown by one member of a family to another. It was the *Diary* that enabled him to have the last laugh on the superior people for whom a curate was a mere nobody, for while they might not choose to remember him, the world knows of them only because they appear in his *Diary*. And the *Diary* will be significant when the last of the country house families has ceased to be so.

References

A number of abbreviations are used in the notes to chapters to designate certain sources.

DNB: *Dictionary of National Biography*
HRO: Hereford Record Office
LWRO: Llandrindod Wells Record Office
WRO: Wiltshire Record Office

The Llysdinam Collection is the body of Venables family papers. It consists of 135 volumes of diaries, journals and letters divided into six classes. Class B consists of 3,000 letters. Five bundles of Richard Lister Venables' sermons make up Class F.

Preface
1. *The Autobiography of William Plomer*, p.365
2. Mrs Essex Hope did, in fact, preserve three notebooks, one of which has been published by the National Library of Wales; another is in the possession of the University of Durham Library; the wherabouts of the third is unknown
3. Kilvert's *Diary*, Vol. 3, p.107
4. A.L. Rowse. *The English Spirit*, p.237

Prologue
1. L. Le Quesne, *After Kilvert*, p.122
2. G.F. Best, *Mid-Victorian Britain 1851 -1875*, p.254
3. W. Bagehot, *The English Constitution*, p.248
4. W.L. Burn, *The Age of Equipoise*, p.16
5. *Ibid*, p.329
6. W.D. Arnold, *Oakfield*, (1853), p.119
7. The Department of the Environment volume of Wiltshire Listed Buildings (1985) described it as a mid-18th century farmhouse on an earlier core. See photograph
8. It seems there were several variants of the name: 'Cheverdon', 'Chievelands' and 'Chiverlings' also existed
9. Kilvert's mother's cousin
10. Kilvert's *Diary*, Vol. 2, p.403
11. WRO 1305/306
12. Son of Joseph Neeld
13. Kilvert emphasised in the case of the freeholder squatters of Seagry village that what little they possessed came from their own resources: '...every man sits under his own vine and under his own fig tree'. (Kilvert's *Diary*, Vol. 2, p.414)
14. J.A. Froude, *The Uses of a Landed Gentry*, pp.413-4
15. J.L. and B. Hammond, *The Village Labourer*, p.6. This account of the medieval village and the changes it experienced is drawn from that source
16. That structure was in fact in place by the end of the 17th century. What was different by the end of the Napoleonic Wars in 1815 was that the divisions between the tiers were marked by greater rigidity and an increased spirit of hostility. The decline in number of small owner-occupied farms exacerbated this trend. At the start of the 19th century, 20% of all farms between 1-300 acres or more were owner-occupied; by the end of the century only 12% were. (R. Williams, *The Country and the City*, p. 225)
17. B. Colloms, *Victorian Country Parsons*, p.21
18. F.M.L. Thompson, *English Landed Society in the Nineteenth Century*, p.7
19. B. Kerr, *Bound to the Soil. A Social History of Dorset 1750-1918*, p.17
20. Colloms, *op.cit.*, p.22
21. P. Horn, *Labouring Life in the Victorian Countryside*, p.11
22. It consisted of 84 acres in 1851; by 1952 it had grown to 143 acres. (WRO 1932/3)
23. Many smaller landholders did not and valued land as a source of social status or as an investment. At the time of Kilvert's *Diary*, only 10% of land was farmed by owner-occupiers. (F.M.L. Thompson, *op.cit.*, p.116)
24. Lord Ernle observed that 'yeoman' was used in the 16th century to include tenant farmers as well as owners of land and that the restriction of it to farmer-owners belonged to the 19th century. (*English Farming Past and Present*, p.296). Mingay also noted that 'yeoman' referred in the 18th and early 19th century to tenants. (See J.R. Wordie, 'Social Changes on the Leverson-Gower Estates 1714-1832', *Economic History Review*, Vol. 27, No.4, 1974, p.594)
25. Grice, *Francis Kilvert and his World*, p.106

26. R. Williams, *op.cit.*, p.322
27. W.A. Armstrong, 'The Countryside', in *The Cambridge Social History of Britain 1750-1950*, Vol. 1, p.123
28. D.W. Howell and C. Baber, 'Wales', in *The Cambridge Social History of Britain 1750-1950*, Vol. 1, p.284
29. D.W. Howell, 'The Regions and Their Issues', in G.E. Mingay, *The Victorian Countryside*, p.72
30. Kilvert's *Diary*, Vol. 3, pp.105-7 and pp.38-40. These are dealt with in a later chapter
31. M. Halford, 'Kilvert's Shropshire Ancestry' in *A Kilvert Symposium*, pp.5-6. Kilvert also had a middle-ranking businessman in his background in his grandfather, who was a coachbuilder in Bath
32. Kilvert's *Diary*, Vol. 3, p.401. His pleasure in his family's hereditary arms also identified him with land holding. F.M.L. Thompson, *op.cit.*, p.109, noted that it was automatic for geneaologists to include all gentlemen entitled to arms with peers and baronets as landowners.
33. Robert Kilvert, *Memoirs of Robert Kilvert, 1804-1882*, p.21
34. The Neelds were an example of a family which bought its way into the landed interest. Joseph Neeld, Sir John's father, inherited a fortune of £900,000 in 1828 from a great-uncle, who was a silversmith and jeweller, and immediately bought Grittleton House and estate in Chippenham to register his new status. He linked himself to the aristocracy by marrying, in 1831, Lady Caroline Ashley Cooper, daughter of Lord Shaftesbury, but six months later the marriage was in ruins. She petitioned him for restitution of conjugal rights while he charged her with 'acts of misconduct' and 'extravagant and vexatious spending of money'. Deciding that he could better play the part of landowner by becoming a county MP, he sought the support of other wealthy men of Chippenham and was elected Tory Member for the town in 1832 with 139 votes. He was elected unopposed for the next 17 years. His son, John, (created baronet in 1859), was MP for Cricklade (1835-59) and for Chippenham (1865-8)
35. F.M.L. Thompson, *op.cit.*, p.16
36. It was only the Ground Game Act of 1880 that gave tenant farmers this right
37. Wordsworth, 'Lines composed a few miles above Tintern Abbey, on revisiting the banks of the Wye'
38. Alun Howkins, 'The Discovery of Rural England', in R. Colls and P. Dodd, *Englishness, Politics and Culture 1880-1920*, p.69. Howkins cited W.H. Hudson, George Bourne, and Edward Thomas as examples of writers in this tradition
39. W.E. Houghton, *The Victorian Frame Of Mind, 1830-1870*, p.79
40. Williams, *op.cit.*, pp.356-7
41. *Ibid*, p.48
42. William Cobbett, quoted in John W. Osborne, *William Cobbett: His Thought and His Times*, pp.48-9
43. E.P. Thompson, *The Making of the English Working Class*, p.255
44. F. Thompson, *Lark Rise to Candleford*, p.143. Kilvert's relish for folklore, old sayings, and the dialect poetry of William Barnes was part of his desire to maintain contact with an 'older, sweeter country civilisation'
45. It seemed of some importance to Kilvert to locate the time precisely. Of course the story of Sleeping Beauty specified that she slept for 100 years but Kilvert mentioned that twice within five lines. It is also worthwhile to point out that the Chieflands passage has all the marks of a carefully wrought piece of writing in which he sought to make a considered statement
46. Not all of that can be laid at the door of Sir John Neeld. The overgrown orchard and garden were Fry's responsibility. Some of his neglect might be attributable to demoralisation in the face of his landlord's lack of interest, some to his own advancing years and eccentricity (his insistence on keeping a small menagerie, including a peacock)
47. Nathaniel Kent had in 1796 included the labourer among the 'three persons who have a natural tye upon each other: the gentleman of landed interest - the farmer - and the labourer'. He underlined their interdependence: 'Protection is due from the first - humanity from the second - obedience from the third'. (Quoted in W.A. Armstrong, 'The Countryside', in the *The Cambridge Social History Of Britain 1750-1950*, p.92). Already the labourer was being relegated to the totally subordinate position he would occupy for the whole of the next century
48. Nor is it noticeably 'tall'. It has only two floors, though there is a high pitched roof. It is built of stone with stone roof tiles. The accommodation comprises two reception rooms and four bedrooms. There are four first floor windows with the stone porch directly beneath the second from the left so that the front aspect presents an asymmetrical, unbalanced picture. There is no depth to the front garden and a pond is situated to the left of the house.

Chapter 1

1. The seriousness of the family's plight was brought home to him when, as a schoolboy of 13, he was taken to see his dying father whose mind had become unhinged over these losses. He laid his hand on Robert's head and said, 'Be a good boy and God will bless you'. (Kilvert's *Diary*, Vol. 3, p.248)
2. Robert Kilvert, *Memoirs of the Rev. Robert Kilvert*, p.34
3. J. Wroughton, *King Edward's School at Bath, 1551-1982*, p.50

REFERENCES

4. John Wade listed King Edward's among the many grammar schools which had existed partly for the free use of poor scholars, but which had become boarding, fee-paying establishments. (*The Extraordinary Black Book*, p.44)

5. K. Symons, *The Grammar School of King Edward VI Bath*, pp.254-5

6. At Eton, eight Latin declamations a year were mandatory. The prospectus of King Edward's was also careful to point out that the Eton Latin Grammar was used

7. W.L. Burn, *op.cit.*, p.197

8. One old boy stated that Morgan was 'kind' and 'attentive' as a teacher

9. Robert Kilvert, *op.cit.*, p.35. Phipps came from a wealthy family, which held estates in Somerset and Wiltshire

10. *Ibid*, p.44

11. The academic links that existed between King Edward's and Oriel College may also have helped

12. It was the genteel middle-class, to which Robert belonged, who were the principal beneficiaries of patronage. (J.M. Bourne, *Patronage and Society in Nineteenth Century England*, p.133)

13. J. Wroughton, *op.cit.*, p.60

14. W.E. Houghton, *op.cit.*, p.184

15. J. Sterling, *The State Of Society In England*, pp.25-6

16. G.M. Young, *Victorian England. Portrait Of An Age*, p.6

17. Quoted in L. Elliott-Binns, *Religion in the Victorian Era*, p.80

18. J. Lawson and H. Silver, *A Social History of Education in England*, p.216

19. R. Kilvert, *op.cit.*, p.57

20. It was possible in the 1820s to combine old-fashioned High Church opinions with distinctively Evangelical notions. (P. Allen, *The Cambridge Apostles. The Early Years*, p.25)

21. I. Bradley, *The Call to Seriousness. The Evangelical Impact on the Victorians*, p.51

22. L. Davidoff and C. Hall, *Family Fortunes. Men and Women of the English Middle Class, 1780-1850*, p.81 and p.83

23. R. Furneaux, *William Wilberforce*, p.152

24. Quoted in W.J. Copleston, *Memoir of Edward Copleston D.D. Bishop of Llandaff*, p.34

25. Chadwick wrote of him: 'If he wanted to declare some statement true, it was enough to declare it was what his father thought'. (O. Chadwick, *The Victorian Church*, Vol. 1, p. 67)

26. Houghton, *op.cit.*, p.133

27. Quoted in M. Trevor, *Newman. The Pillar Of The Cloud*, p.84. Newman found the Senior Common Room at Oriel 'a place of the dullest conversation'. (O. Chadwick. *Newman*, p.8)

28. R. Kilvert, *op.cit.*, p.61

29. T. Mozley, *Reminiscences of Oriel College and the Oxford Movement*, Vol. 2, p.412

30. Anne Mozley referred to the 'martinet manner then in fashion with college tutors. (A. Mozley, *Letters and Correspondence of J.H. Newman*, p.153)

31. O. Chadwick, *op.cit*, Vol. 1, p.67

32. R. Kilvert, *op.cit*, p.58

33. Pattison, *op.cit*, p.143

34. Quoted in A. Dwight Culler, *The Imperial Intellect*, p.53. These gentlemen-commoners were a dominant group, numbering 20 out of Oriel's 50 or so students

35. *Ibid.* p.54

36. Pattison said that tutors and gentlemen-commoners 'kept up a style of living... usual in a large country house'. (Pattison, *op.cit*, p.68)

37. R. Kilvert, *op.cit*, p.48

38. E. Christian, *Observations on the Sale of Game*, (1821). Quoted in H. Hopkins, *The Long Affray. The Poaching Wars In Britain*, p.88

39. The summarising of sermons was an Evangelical practice. It is not without significance that in the Oriel tasks Robert Kilvert mentioned, form was everything, and content virtually nothing. It was the same with the Latin orations at King Edward's. Symons noted that no one bothered about the content of the one delivered by Francis Kilvert, Robert's brother

40. Wroughton, *op.cit*, pp.84-5. This headmaster had been compelled by the Charity Commissioners to reinstate the free scholars required under the School's statutes

41. D. Spring, *The Clapham Sect: Some Social And Political Aspects*, Victorian Studies, Sept. 1961, p.46

42. Elliott-Binns, *op.cit*, p.47

43. G.M. Young, *op.cit*, p.1. Robert Kilvert was, of course a little older than this young man; he was 28 in 1831. He would, however, be no less subject to the influence of Evangelicalism

44. R. Kilvert, *op.cit*, p.62

45. The 'we' referred to his one servant and, later, his sister, who kept house

46. Mozley, *op.cit*, Vol. 2, p.372. Its author was the Vicar of Fulham. It provided examples of piety among the poor. The first volume was published in 1826. Such was its popularity that the first edition sold

out very quickly, as subsequent ones did. Volumes two and three appeared in 1827 and 1828. Wilberforce had a particular penchant for death-bed scenes

47. R. Kilvert, *op.cit*, pp.67-8
48. Kilvert's *Diary*, Vol. 3, p.126
49. W. Wilberforce, *A Practical View*, p.20
50. Kilvert's *Diary*, Vol. 3, p.216
51. *Ibid*, Vol. 3, p.127
52. *Ibid*, Vol. 3, p.243
53. *Ibid*, Vol. 3, p.437
54. *Ibid*, Vol. 3, pp.125-6
55. *Ibid*, Vol. 3, p.138
56. Only after the turn of the century did women wear undergarments. (Steven Marcus, *The Other Victorians. A Study of Sexuality and Pornography in Mid-Nineteenth Century England.* p.99)
57. Kilvert's *Diary*, Vol. 3, p.218
58. *Ibid*, Vol. 2, p.339
59. *Ibid*, Vol. 2, p.444
60. Kingsley was particularly forthright in asserting the 'pure woman' image. (See Houghton, *op.cit*. pp.350-1)
61. Kilvert's *Diary*, Vol. 1, p.168
62. *Ibid*, Vol. 1, pp.173 - 4. Kilvert expressed the same hope about Daisy Thomas. (See Chapter 5)
63. *Ibid*, Vol. 2, p.356
64. The texts he was reading were not, it appears, devotional ones
65. Sir Samuel Romilly. Quoted in H. Hopkins, *op.cit*, p.79.
66. R. Kilvert, *op.cit*, pp.65-6
67. William Cobbett, *William Cobbett's Illustrated Rural Rides 1821-1832*, p.21
68. W.R. Ward, 'County Government *c*.1660 - 1835', *Victoria History of Wiltshire*, Vol. V. pp.187-8. The countryside was governed between 1790 and 1830 with 'counter-revolutionary licence'. (E.P. Thompson, *The Making of the English Working Classes*, p.246)
69. E.J. Hobsbawm and G. Rudé, *Captain Swing*, pp.78-80
70. Since this *Diary* entry is dated Oct. 1874, this would place the riots in 1829. Kilvert may have been happy with this rough reckoning or it may indicate his casual approach to historical fact. The full text of the *Diary* may have included other references to the Swing riots
71. Clergymen were particular targets for labourers' anger because they sided with landowners; of 82 threatening letters sent during the riots, nearly one quarter were addressed to clergymen
72. Quoted in L. Davidoff and C. Hall, *op.cit*, p.92
73. Letter to William Money, 8 May 1824, WRO L14/329. Emma was grandmother of the Harriet Money-Kyrle who married Andrew Pope, one of Kilvert's closest friends, on 9 September 1874. Kilvert was best man. William Money's son, also William, was briefly a contemporary of Robert Kilvert at Oriel in 1826
74. Kilvert, when visiting Longford Park, home of the 4th Earl of Radnor in south Wiltshire, was told by a gatekeeper there that he 'ought to have bought a ticket'. Kilvert wryly noted that the Earl was currently spending £60,000 on his castle. (Kilvert's *Diary*. Vol. 3. p.221). The Earl had told labourers, starving on 8s a week, who wanted to rent allotments from him on which to grow food, that he would let them have land but at rents double those paid by farmers. 'Why should land be let to one man for less, when another was ready to give more?' the Earl asked, (*Letters of SGO*, Vol. 2, p.47). By 1890, the expenditure of the 5th Earl of Radnor on Longford Castle was £13,000 a year and he was having to make retrenchments in the face of hard times. (D. Cannadine, *The Decline And Fall Of The British Aristocracy*, p.99). Kilvert's attitude to landed gentry is discussed further in chapters 2, 5, 9 and 10
75. R. Kilvert, *op.cit*, p.62
76. *Ibid*, p.48. Wilberforce was fascinated by the Queen Caroline case and deeply disturbed as Robert was by the royal depravity that came to light
77. Bulwer Lytton believed that the people supported Queen Caroline, not because they thought her guiltless, but because they felt that she was persecuted as they felt themselves to be. The old woman, Prissy Price, in Kilvert's *Diary* (Vol. 3, pp.418-9), took this view
78. G. Best, *op.cit*, pp.169-170
79. A. Hare, *The Years With Mother*, p.79
80. She herself was a Leycester, of the Cheshire 'county' family, and her sister had married into the wealthy, influential Stanley family of Alderley. Hare's real mother was descended from the Earl of Strathmore, from whom the present Queen Mother is also descended
81. The Hare family was known also to the Venables
82. A. Hare, *op.cit*, p.17

REFERENCES

83. *Ibid*, p.18
84. *Ibid*, p.37
85. Kilvert's *Diary*, Vol. 3, pp.58-60
86. A. Hare, *op.cit*, p.49
87. W. Warde Fowler quoted in D. Lockwood, *Francis Kilvert*, p.31
88. *Ibid*, p.27
89. Peter Abbs, Introduction to Gosse's *Father and Son*, p.12
90. A. Hare, *op.cit*, p.15
91. Phyllis Grosskurth, *Approaches to Victorian Autobiography*, quoted by Abbs in his introduction to Gosse's *Father And Son*, p.19
92. Hare attended the school from summer 1843 to Christmas 1846. It is uncertain when Kilvert left the nursery at Harnish Rectory and joined the boys' school
93. P. Abbs, *op.cit*, p.21
94. F. Grice, *Francis Kilvert and his World*, p.13
95. A. Hare, *op.cit*, p.38
96. *Ibid*, p.23
97. Introduction to *The Years With Mother*
98. Mrs E.J. Wyndowe, 'Rambling Recollections', in *More Chapters from the Kilvert Saga*, pp.86-7
99. R. Kilvert, *op.cit*, p.60
100. Quoted in W.E. Houghton, *op.cit*, p.127, Carlyle's italics. To the devout Evangelical, 'all refined worldly learning was a snare for the soul'. (E. Stokes, *The English Utilitarians and India*, p.30)
101. A. Briggs, *The Age of Improvement*, p.177
102. Lecky writing in 1860. Quoted in *Dickens* by Peter Ackroyd, p.904
103. Charles mentioned in a letter of 4 Dec. 1824 that he had visited Boyle at Oriel, though he admitted he was a more frequent visitor to Christ Church, the home of Oxford's most exclusive set. (*Letters of Sir Walter Scott. 1823 - 1825*, edited H.J.C. Grierson, pp.441-2)
104. T. Mozley, *op.cit*, Vol. 1, pp.94-5
105. W.E. Houghton, *op.cit*, p.325
106. Other romantic novels read by Robert to his family were *Les Misérables* and *Lorna Doone*; Kilvert called the latter 'that wild and powerful book'
107. G. Aguilar, *Home Influence*, p.386. Wilberforce had not ruled out the writing of literature by Christians. Providing it could be reconciled with the Bible, no calling, pursuit or art was forbidden. (W. Wilberforce, *op.cit*, p.117). Whether this applied to clergymen is not clear
108. R. Kilvert, *op.cit*, pp.7-8
109. In Aguilar's *Home Influence*, the head of the Evangelical Hamilton household declares: '...difference of fortune alone can never constitute inferiority', (p.172)
110. A. Haig, *The Victorian Clergy*, p.28
111. E.P. Thompson, *op.cit*, p.61
112. J. Skinner, *Journal of a Somerset Rector 1803 - 1834*, p.396. 'The present age', he wrote, 'is an age of insensibility; indeed, all feeling of men of the world is of a selfish kind'. One letter written to a clergyman on the Isle of Wight by a labourer during the Swing riots read: 'For the last 20 years wee have been in a Starving Condition to maintain your Damn Pride. What we have done now is Soar against our Will but your harts is as hard as the hart of Pharo...'.

Chapter 2

1. R. Kilvert, *Trevellyk*, p.75
2. *Ibid*, p.77
3. Kilvert's *Diary*, Vol. 1, p.84. This relationship is dealt with in Chapter 5
4. Mrs E.J. Wyndowe, *op.cit*, p.103
5. *Ibid*, p.95
6. L. Davidoff and C. Hall, *op.cit*, p.108. Dr. Arnold, Thomas Hughes, and Charles Kingsley advanced a model of the Christian gentleman whose strength lay in his spiritual integrity. Its influence on Kilvert is explored in the chapter, 'Kilvert and Manliness'
7. Robert says nothing in his *Memoirs* about the influence of Newman, probably because he disapproved of his joining the Catholic Church. In the Harnish nursery, being sent to the 'naughty' corner was referred to by Robert as 'going to Oxford', i.e. doing what Newman and other Oxford dons had done
8. Kilvert's *Diary*, Vol. 2, p.441
9. Handley Moule, *Memories Of A Vicarage*, p.62
10. *Ibid*, p.47
11. Kilvert's *Diary*, Vol. 1, p.200
12. *Ibid*, Vol. 1, pp.207-8

13. *Ibid*, Vol. 1, pp.304-5
14. One who attended these regularly was Robert Kilvert's Melksham colleague, the Rev. George Shuldham Hume
15. Mrs. E.J. Wyndowe, *op.cit*, p.102
16. E. Gosse, *Father And Son*, pp.48-9
17. E. Wyndowe, *op.cit*, p.89
18. P. Turner, *Victorian Poetry, Drama and Miscellaneous Prose 1832 - 1890*, p.409
19. Gillian Avery, *Nineteenth Century Children's Heroes and Heroines in English Children's Stories 1780 - 1900*, p.39
20. F. J. Harvey Darton, *Children's Books in England*, p.212
21. L. Salway, *A Peculiar Gift: Nineteenth Century Writings on Books for Children*, p.320
22. L. Davidoff and C. Hall, *op.cit*, p.181
23. G. Aguilar, *Home Influence*, p.288, her italics. She worked on the book and its sequel, *A Mother's Recompense* in the 1830s. It is significant they are set in the immediate post-Waterloo years when society was most threatened by political unrest, though neither contains any reference to it
24. L. Davidoff and C. Hall, *op.cit*, p.74
25. W.E. Houghton, *op.cit*, p.344
26. Kilvert's *Diary*, Vol. 2, p.241
27. *Ibid*, Vol. 2, p.445
28. *Collected Verse* by the Rev. Francis Kilvert, p.31. This theme appears also in 'In Loving Remembrance of Little Davie', 'The Sleep of Annie Hargest', 'The Harbour', and 'Paradise Clyro'
29. Kilvert's *Diary*, Vol. 2, p.192
30. *Ibid*, Vol. 2, p.445
31. Bulwer Lytton (*op.cit*, Vol. 2, pp.246-8) said it coloured the national character, pervaded every level of society, and permeated literature, the arts, and the sciences
32. E.C. Mack, *Public Schools and British Opinion 1780 - 1860*, pp.108-9
33. G. Aguilar, *A Mother's Recompense*, p.527
34. She was born in 1770 and was the grandmother of Thomas Hughes, author of *Tom Brown's Schooldays*, that striking example of 'romantic attachment'. Hughes' father, John, was a student at Oriel where his tutor was Copleston. Mrs. Hughes, a 'true-blue Tory soul' according to her grandson, W.H. Hughes, had known Scott from an early period of her life
35. Mrs. Hughes, *Letters And Recollections Of Sir Walter Scott*, p.46
36. Kilvert's *Diary*, Vol. 2, pp.213-6
37. *Ibid*, Vol. 3, p.36
38. *Ibid*, Vol. 3, p.183
39. *Ibid*, Vol. 2, p.328
40. *Ibid*, Vol. 3, p.36. Nunwell and Yaverland became connected when Robert, a son of the Norman lord, Richard d'Orglandes, Nunwell's alleged founder, married Roberta Russel of Yaverland
41. *Ibid*, Vol. 3, p.38. My italics. Sir Bernard Burke gave a fanciful account of the Oglander family in 1863 in *Vicissitudes of Families*, Volume 3
42. Jane Austen had ridiculed this mania in *Northanger Abbey*. Mrs. Hughes liked Abbotsford because it was 'so admirably old', with 'so many towers and turrets... and all that one ever reads of in ancient story, that it is hardly possible to conceive of oneself in a modern residence...' (Mrs. Hughes, *op.cit*, p.59). Kilvert loved the panelling at Draycot House and its (Royalist) Civil War associations. (*Diary*, Vol. 2, pp.396-7)
43. G. Aguilar, *Home Influence*, p.78. In Scott's statement that the combination of scenic beauty with ancient ruins produced in him 'an intense impression of reverence', may be found the link between Aguilar and Kilvert. (Quoted in H. Pearson, Walter Scott, *His Life And Personality*, p.15)
44. Some of Mrs. Hamilton's qualities are present in Mme. Olympe (see the chapter, 'Kilvert and *A Week in a French Country House*'). Kilvert owed part of his attitude to the poor to Mrs. Hamilton, as the chapter on that aspect shows
45. Mrs. E.J. Wyndowe, op.cit, p.93
46. SGO (Sidney Godolphin Osborne) had posed the question in November 1844. Raymond Williams (*The Country and the City*, pp.78-9) pointed out that the notion of 'traditional relations' between classes, symbolised by the landed estate, was an illusion. The landed gentry lived 'by a calculation of rents and returns on investment of capital', and it was for this end that the 'ideology of improvement' existed. 'Social relations which stood in the way of this kind of modernisation were ...steadily and at times ruthlessly broken down'
47. S. Daniels, 'The political iconography of woodland in later Georgian England', in *The Iconography of Landscape*, edited by D. Cosgrove and S. Daniels, p.48
48. Kilvert's *Diary*, Vol. 3, pp 263-4
49. A later chapter considers the implications of this in connection with the idea of manliness
50. J. Gathorne-Hardy, *The Public School Phenomenon*, p.126

REFERENCES

51. W. Wordsworth. 'The Prelude', Book 1, lines 398-400
52. Clergymen tended to do this more and more during the century. (B.A. Bax, *The English Parsonage*, p.133)
53. Kilvert's *Diary*, Vol. 3, pp.345-6
54. *Kilvert's Cornish Holiday. Further extracts From Kilvert's Diary*, p.20, 21,29, 32
55. D. Morris, *Thomas Hearne and his Landscape*, p.24
56. D. Morris, *Thomas Hearne 1744 - 1817. Watercolours and drawings*, p.10
57. D. Morris, *Thomas Hearne and his Landscape*, p.28. Kilvert visited seven historic sites between June 1874 and April 1876. This activity is another aspect of his looking backwards
58. *Ibid*, p.66
59. *Ibid*, p.125
60. Kilvert's *Diary*, Vol. 3, pp.202-3
61. S. Seymour, S. Daniels, and C. Watkins, *Estate And Empire: Sir George Cornewall's Management of 'Moccas', Herefordshire and 'La Taste', Grenada, 1771-1819*, p.40
62. W.E. Houghton, *op.cit*, pp.64-5
63. Revisiting Oxford produced a bout of deep sadness, as he noted that no one had any recollection of him and he felt shut out as from an old home. After an illness in March 1874, he reflected on the number of illnesses he had had and added: '...some day will come the last illness from which there will be no convalescence'. He expressed the hope in December 1874 that, if he was 'spared another year', he might 'spend it better than the last'
64. J.A. Froude, *The Nemesis of Faith*, p.100. Kilvert had achieved success by becoming Vicar of Bredwardine in November 1877, but was still unmarried and without a wife and family. His melancholy was partly attributable to this fact and partly to his social unease. A later chapter deals with these issues
65. Kilvert's *Diary*, Vol. 2, p.280
66. Robert Kilvert, *op.cit*, p.58
67. *Observations on the Effect of the Manufacturing System*, quoted in R. Williams, *Culture and Society 1780 - 1950*, p.44
68. R.H. Tawney, *Religion and the Rise of Capitalism*, p.195
69. Dr. H.J. Hunter in the seventh report of the medical officer of the Privy Council, (1864), quoted in Richard Heath, *The Victorian Peasant*, p.30
70. Rev. J. Fraser, First Report of Commission on the Employment of Children, Young Persons, and Women in Agriculture, 1867, p.35
71. 'Easterly' in *Collected Verse* by the Reverend Francis Kilvert
72. Coleridge quoted in Roberts, *op.cit*, p.32
73. Kilvert's *Diary*, Vol. 3, p.153
74. *Ibid*, Vol. 2, pp.393-4. To the modern reader there is something grotesque about the kind of power that allowed a family to employ yeomanry - virtually its own private police force - to 'guard' from local people, some of whom would never taste meat and most of whom would be hungry, a roasting ox that was to be their treat
75. *Ibid*, Vol. 2, p.25
76. *Ibid*, Vol. 1, p.109
77. *Ibid*, Vol. 1, p.79
78. He had an interest in folklore and dialect words
79. Kilvert's *Diary*, Vol. 1, p.348
80. My italics. Kilvert was careful to underline the difference between his party and the tourists
81. Quoted in C.A. Bodelsen, *Studies in Mid-Victorian Imperialism*, p.202
82. J.A.R. Pimblott, *The Englishman's Holiday: A Social History*, p.87
83. F. Crouzet, *The Victorian Economy*, pp.288-290
84. Eric Hobsbawm in a BBC television programme, Oct. 1993
85. P.S. Bagwell, 'The Decline of Rural Isolation', in *The Victorian Countryside*, Vol. 1. (edited Mingay), p.33
86. Commentators have generally assumed that his knowledge of poetry was attributable to his uncle Francis, the antiquarian, and his Claverton Lodge school, as was noted in the previous chapter
87. Kilvert's *Diary*, Vol. 2, p.89
88. The preacher was 'unskilful to fawn, or seek for power.../Far other aims his heart had learned to prize,/More bent to raise the wretched than to rise.../His ready smile a parent's warmth exprest...'. It is amusing to think of Kilvert stumbling through these lines (as he admitted he did), prompted by Venables, 'who had the book'
89. Goldsmith knew of a village consisting of 100 cottages that had been destroyed along with church, vicarage, and ale house to make way for the mansion and park of a London merchant. (J. Ginger, *The Notable Man. The Life And Times Of Oliver Goldsmith*, p.264)
90. Kilvert was familiar with Crabbe's poetry and recorded that his father had actually met the poet in 1830 when he was Rector of Trowbridge, Wiltshire. Kilvert read the article on Crabbe in the *Cornhill Magazine* in October 1874

91. 'Hours in a Library. Crabbe's Poetry', *Cornhill Magazine*, October 1874, p.463. Raymond Williams (in *The Country and the City*, p.115) called 'The Village' a 'counter-pastoral'

92. Kilvert made a hero out of a labourer, John Hatherell, who survived such conditions to a ripe old age and managed to avoid the workhouse. See the chapter, 'Kilvert and the Poor'

93. Raymond Williams saw this as 'a pathetic retreat'. The same idea occurs in Kilvert's *Diary*, (Vol. 3, p.258). This entry is examined in 'Kilvert and the Poor'

94. Kilvert's *Diary*, Vol. 2, p.439

95. W. Wordsworth, 'The Excursion', Book IV, 1207 - 1217. Historically, this active sympathy was seen as a counter-balance to the industrialism and materialism of the age

96. Kilvert's *Diary*, Vol. 1, p.83

97. *Ibid*, Vol. 1, p.307. His lack of ease in social gatherings is explored in 'Kilvert and the English Country House'

98. W. Wordsworth, 'The Prelude', Book 1, 465 - 474. Kilvert's *Diary* has other examples of such 'visions'. e.g. Vol. 1, p.374, Vol. 2, p. 158, Vol. 2, p.433

99. The leech-gatherer appears in 'Resolution and Independence'. Wordsworth's interest in solitary figures is seen also in 'The Old Cumberland Beggar' and 'Michael'

100. Bulwer Lytton (*op.cit*, Vol. 2, p.97) saw Wordsworth's significance for his age in terms of his ideas which, reflected '...refined... Toryism, the result of a mingled veneration for the past...'.

101. W. Wordsworth, 'The Excursion' Book IX, 238 - 241

102. 'In the 50 years after 1830 the worship of the hero was a major factor in English culture'. (W.E. Houghton, *op.cit*, p.310). At a Penny Reading at Clyro on 23 Jan 1872, Kilvert read three heroic poems: 'The Battle of the Baltic', 'Ye Mariners of England', and 'Hohenlinden'

103. G.M. Young (*op.cit*, p.75) noted Tennyson's moral conservatism and the tendency of his 'In Memoriam' (a favourite of Kilvert) to decline to follow any arguments that did not lead to pleasant conclusions

104. Quoted in H. House, *The Dickens World*, p.153. The outlook expressed in those lines was shared by Kilvert. (See the chapter 'Kilvert and the English Country House')

105. Asa Briggs observed: 'Dickens' morality owed nothing to Evangelicalism'. (*The Age of Improvement*, p.464)

106. Rosalind Billingham, *The Reverend R.F. Kilvert And The Visual Arts*, p..

107. H. House, 'Man and Nature: Some Artists' Views', in *Ideas and Beliefs of the Victorians*, pp.224-5. He cited Frith as the Victorian painter who most clearly exemplified 'the practical domestic vision'

108. *Ibid*, p. 224

109. 'Victorian sentimentality is largely the imposition of feeling as an afterthought upon literalness'. (*Ibid*, p.223). The pre- and early Victorian veneration of Scott's novels may be seen as an example of investing so-called historical 'fact' with an excess of romantic feeling. Bulwer Lytton considered him to be most unreliable in the matter of historical accuracy

110. Kilvert's *Diary*, Vol. 2, p.109

111. *Ibid*, Vol. 1, p.59. He liked another pre-Victorian painter, Cuyp, and his 'View on a Plain', which showed cows grazing at sunset

112. Collins' son, Wilkie, the novelist, was named after him

113. J. Barrell, *The dark side of the landscape. The rural poor in English landscape painting 1730 - 1840*, p.90 and pp.98 - 100

114. Rosemary Treble, 'The Victorian picture of the country', in G.E. Mingay, *The Rural Idyll*, p.53

115. L. Lambourne (*Victorian Genre Painting*, p.19) commented on its lyrical Wordsworthian quality. Collins had in fact met the poet

116. These are dealt with in 'Kilvert and the English Country House'

117. For example, Murillo's 'The Good Shepherd' and Doré's 'Andromeda'

118. Quoted in *The Pre-Raphaelites*, Tate Gallery, p.221. His italics

119. Recounted in B. Colloms, *Victorian Country Parsons*, pp.257-8

120. W.E. Houghton, *op.cit*, p. 77. This nostalgia is shared by many of today's readers of Kilvert's *Diary* and the reason for it unites them with the Victorians: modern life appears threatening. For some Kilvert devotees the *Diary* and its locations are 'home'

Chapter 3

1. G.M. Young, *op.cit*, p.100

2. *Ibid*, p.101

3. Kilvert's *Diary*, Vol. 3, p.99

4. E.C. Mack, *Public Schools and British Opinion since 1860*, p.xi

5. Fox-Davies, in his *The Right to Bear Arms*, stated flatly that they were 'the distinctive privilege of the nobly born' and that a landholder was automatically a gentleman. Robert Kilvert, when he went to Oriel, had the option, because of his antecedents, of styling himself 'son of an esquire' or 'son of a gentleman' but chose the latter because he would pay 'lighter fees'

REFERENCES

6. G. Best, *op.cit*, p.268. By 1850, Tennyson thought 'the grand old name of gentleman' was 'defamed' and 'soiled'

7. J. Wells, *Wadham College*, p.174

8. Basil H. Jackson, *Recollection of Thomas Graham Jackson. 1835 - 1924*, p.104

9. P. Wright-Henderson, *Glasgow And Balliol And Other Essays*, p.14

10. W.M. Thackeray, *The Book of Snobs*, p.146

11. He also made a point of noting men who had Christ Church in their background. Mr. Phillips of Abbey Cwm Hir and Mr. Lucas, friend of Mr. Crichton of Clyro, are two examples. Kilvert's neighbour in Langley Burrell, Sir John Awdry, was also a Christ Church man, as Kilvert probably knew

12. Lord W. De Broke, *The Passing Years*, p.30

13. E.G.W. Bill and J.S.A. Mason, *Christ Church and Reform. 1850 - 1867*, p.137

14. Thomas Baskerville was increasingly ill at this time and died in 1864. Walter deputised for him at the cutting of the first sod of the Hereford - Brecon railway in April 1860

15. J.A. Bridges, *At 'The House' In The Fifties*, p.65 and p.74

16. Report, pp.23-7

17. 'University Life at Oxford', *Cornhill Magazine*, Vol. II, 1865, pp.223-232

18. Report, pp.28-9

19. *Ibid*, p.71

20. P. Wright-Henderson, *op.cit*, p.32

21. Partly because of Congreve's presence at Wadham as a Fellow, the College attracted Rugby men. Congreve left before Kilvert arrived

22. F. Harrison, *Autobiographic Memoirs*, Vol. 1, p.108

23. C.S.L. Davies and Jane Garnett, *Wadham College*, p.17. Kilvert's place at the High Table had been secured by the influence of his old Wadham friend, Mayhew, with whom he was staying. Mayhew was doing research in philology at Oxford. Later, he became Wadham's Chaplain

24. T.G. Jackson, *Wadham College*, p.182

25. Basil H. Jackson, *op.cit*, p.23

26. *Ibid*, p.24

27. C.S.L. Davies and Jane Garnett, *op.cit*, p.45

28. The reference Venables sought about Kilvert, prior to appointing him as his curate in Clyro, came from Canon Shirley of Christ Church

29. Basil H. Jackson, *op.cit*, p.39

30. A. Smith, *The Wealth of Nations*, Book III, Ch. 1

31. *Ibid*, Book III, Ch. 2

32. *Ibid*, Book IV, Ch. 9

33. Examples are to be found in chapters 4 and 9

34. See the chapter 'Kilvert and the Poor'

35. A. Smith, *op.cit*, Book IV, Ch. 9

36. *Ibid*, Book IV, Ch. 9

37. P. Gay, *op.cit*, p.146

38. W. Paley, *Reasons for Contentment Addressing To the Labouring Part of the British Public*, p.18

39. F.H. Lawson, *The Oxford Law School of 1850 - 1965*, p. 23

40. Professor Baden Powell, 'On the Study of the Evidences of Christianity', in *Essays And Reviews*, p.95

41. F. Harrison, *op.cit*, Vol. 1, p.104

42. Dean Stanley, review of 'Essays And Reviews', *Edinburgh Review*, April 1861

43. Kilvert's *Diary*, Vol. 3, p.143

44. C. Kingsley, from the poem 'The Bad Squire' in *Yeast*

45. C. Kingsley, *Alton Locke*, p.303

46. *Ibid*, p.49

47. *Twenty-five Village Sermons* (1849) was reviewed in *The Times*; *Sermons on National Subjects* appeared in 1853; *Sermons For The Times* in 1858

48. B. Colloms, *Charles Kingsley*, pp.361-2

49. Mrs. Kingsley, *Charles Kingsley. His Letters and Memories of his Life*, p.88

50. *Ibid*, p.155

51. C. Kingsley, *Alton Locke*, pp.363-4

52. *Ibid*, pp.377-8

53. These are the words of Kingsley's first curate, quoted in Mrs. Kingsley, *op.cit*, p.52. Other material in this paragraph comes from G.E. Mingay, *Rural Life In Victorian England*, pp.155-6, and from B. Colloms, *op.cit*, chapter four

54. Kilvert's *Diary*, Vol. 2, p.99

55. Kingsley in a letter of 17 Dec. 1866 to Professor Lorimer of Edinburgh, quoted in Mrs Kingsley, op.cit, pp.278-9

56. Quoted in B. Colloms, *op.cit*, p.278
57. *Ibid*, p.245
58. Letter to his wife in 1866, Mrs Kingsley, *op.cit*, p.272
59. Kilvert's *Diary*, Vol. 3, p.165. It is of some relevance to note that Kingsley and others of his Christian Socialist group were in the habit of describing themselves as knights
60. Quoted in J.A. Mangan, 'Athleticism: A Case Study of the Evolution of an Educational Ideology', in B. Simon and I. Bradley, *The Victorian Public School*, p.148
61. Kilvert's *Diary*, Vol. 3, p.22
62. K.A.P. Sandiford, 'Cricket And The Victorian Society', *Journal of Social History*, Vol. 17, 1983-4, pp.303-314
63. T.G. Jackson, *op.cit*, p.28
64. P. Wright-Henderson, *op.cit*, p.92 and p.32
65. *The Life And Correspondence Of Arthur Penrhyn Stanley, D.D.*, R.E. Prothero and the Very Rev. G.G. Bradley, Vol. 2, pp.2-3
66. Kilvert did not make any study of theology
67. Quoted in R.E. Prothero and G.G. Bradley, *op.cit*, Vol. 1, p.231
68. Report, pp.150-1
69. Inevitably one thinks of Kilvert in the light of this observation. His relationship with the poor forms the subject of a later chapter
70. R. Kilvert, *op.cit*, p.65
71. Kilvert's *Diary*, Vol. 3, p.23
72. These were Lord Melbourne's words, quoted by Redesdale
73. Lord Redesdale, *Memories*, Vol. 1 pp.95-6. It should be noted that Redesdale was not a particularly religious man; his concern was with loss of power
74. F. Meyrick, *Memories of Life at Oxford and Elsewhere*, p.172
75. One wonders, nevertheless, whether Kilvert learnt at Wadham that George Eliot was a supporter of the Positivists and avoided her novels for that reason
76. F. Harrison, *op.cit*, Vol. 1, p. 146. These words were written before Kingsley's 'conversion'
77. G.M. Young, *op.cit*, p. 85
78. C.S.L. Davies and Jane Garnett, *op.cit*, p.148

Chapter 4

1. Chadwick was so impressed by their accuracy that he consistently quoted them throughout *The Victorian Church*
2. A. Trollope, *Clergymen of the Church of England*, pp.57-63
3. Kilvert's *Diary*, Vol. 2, p.270. Venables then ran 3 miles back to Clyro arriving just in time to preach.
4. Robert Kilvert was born in 1803; Venables in 1809.
5. This is true of all the local gentry with whom Kilvert had contact. Whether this meant that there was such a close match between his outlook and theirs that he found no purpose in recording conversations, or whether nothing was said that he found challenging, is not clear. This issue is explored in later chapters.
6. Le Quesne gave no examples. Kilvert expressed almost identical criticisms of the Russian practice of employing foreigners as tutors and governesses to those of Venables. (*Diary*, Vol. 1, p.267-8). He gave as the source of his information a lady he had met on a train who had lived in Warsaw but her opinions may have gained weight because he had initially heard them on Venables' lips.
7. Kilvert actually lodged at Ashbrook, home of Mrs. Chaloner, widow of Peter Chaloner, sometime agent of Thomas Baskerville (late squire of Clyro) and, afterwards, Venables' estate manager
8. R.L. Venables, *Domestic Scenes in Russia*, p.42
9. *Ibid*, pp.132-3
10. H. Taine, *Notes on England*, p.179
11. Kilvert's *Diary*, Vol. 2, p.42
12. Quoted in C.H.E. Zangerl, 'The Social Composition of the Country Magistracy in England and Wales, 1831 - 1887', Journal of British Studies, Vol. XI, Nov. 1971, p.118. Gentry made up 75% of the magistracy's personnel
13. Kilvert's *Diary*, Vol. 2, pp.88-9
14. H. Hopkins, *The Long Affray. The Poaching Wars in Britain*, p.201
15. Llysdinam Collection, F 84
16. *Ibid*, F 53.
17. *Ibid*, B 646. Letter from Thomas Baskerville to Venables. The date of the letter is probably 20 March 1848; the last number is illegible
18. Kilvert's *Diary*, Vol. 2, p.21
19. Llysdinam Collection, B 1235, B 1234, B1236. The letters were all written to George Venables in 1848

REFERENCES

20. *Ibid*, B 1352, Letter to George Venables
21. *Ibid*, B 1361, Letter to George Venables, 17 January 1865
22. A. Haig, *op.cit*, p.27
23. Information taken from Stapylton's Eton Lists. The figure for 1889 was a mere 3%. The same decline was apparent in other public schools—see T.W. Bamford, *The Rise of the Public Schools*, p.210
24. A. Haig, *op.cit*, pp.49-51
25. For example, St. Bees in 1816, Lampeter 1822, St. Aidans 1846, Chichester 1839, Wells 1840. The first three were non-graduate institutions. The shortage of clergy in Wales would have been even more serious than it was without the men supplied by Lampeter
26. F. Meyrick, *op.cit*, p.333
27. Llysdinam Collection, B 708, Henry Dew to Venables
28. *Ibid*, B 742, Viscount Hereford to Venables, 25 July 1868
29. *Ibid*, B 648, Letter of Walter Baskerville to Venables, 1 October 1875
30. One of Kilvert's successors in Clyro, the Rev. Hughes, came there not from Oxford but from Lichfield Theological College
31. L. Le Quesne, *The Venables Diaries*, Oswin Prosser Memorial Booklet, Kilvert Society Publications, p.44
32. Llysdinam Collection, C 776
33. The choice of this name is interesting. Cavendish was the family name of the Dukes of Devonshire. They were the seventh largest landowners in the country, owning 198,667 acres, producing the second largest rent roll of £180,750 in 1883. The 11th Earl had been Venables' contemporary at Eton, probably in the same year. A summary of the Earl's character might well have been that of Venables himself: 'A naturally silent man, of almost excessively reserved disposition, with warm family affections and a high standard of conduct'. The Digby family were also landed gentry, far less wealthy, but had produced Kenelm Digby, author of the highly influential *The Broad Stone of Honour*, a set of rules of behaviour for the gentlemen of England. It is very likely that Venables read it as a young man
34. Llysdinam Collection, B 1419
35. Quoted in Mrs Kingsley, *op.cit*, p.127
36. Houghton, op.cit, pp.394-5. A later chapter will engage with all three in the context of Kilvert's response to the novel, *A Week in a French Country House*
37. Douglas Woodruff, 'The Aristocratic Idea' in *Ideas and Beliefs of the Victorians*, p.284
38. Bulwer Lytton, *op.cit*, Vol. 1, p.309
39. Kilvert's *Diary*, Vol. 2, pp.276-7
40. Next to the Venables, it was his family that had opened their home most completely to Kilvert while he was curate of Clyro
41. Kilvert's *Diary*, Vol. 2, pp.151-2
42. Robert Kilvert, *op.cit*, pp.43-4
43. Kilvert's *Diary*, Vol. 3, p.348
44. *Ibid*, Vol. 2, p.93
45. *Ibid*, Vol. 2, p.216
46. *Ibid*, Vol. 2, pp.364-5
47. *Ibid*, Vol. 2, p.446
48. *Ibid*, Vol. 3, p.92
49. *Ibid*, Vol. 3, p.211
50. *Ibid*, Vol. 3, p.382
51. J.M. Bourne, *op.cit*, p.89
52. Kilvert's *Diary*, Vol. 2, p.190, my italics
53. P.L. Berger, B. Berger, H. Kellner, *The Homeless Mind: Modernisation and Consciousness*, p.80
54. Introduction to Vol. 3 of the *Diary*
55. David Bentley-Taylor, 'The Strengths and Weaknesses of Kilvert's Christianity' in *Kilvert Society Newsletter*, Feb. 1984
56. W. Wilberforce, *op.cit*, p 24
57. B.A.M. Finlayson, *The Seventh Earl of Shaftesbury*, p.49
58. W. Wilberforce, op.cit, p.86
59. Kilvert's *Diary*, Vol. 2, pp.71-2
60. Other *Diary* entries show Kilvert choosing Biblical texts that helped him to reconcile himself to unpleasant, testing circumstances. (See 'Kilvert and the Poor' chapter). Perhaps the use of such texts to counteract the 'poison' of the Venables was seen by Kilvert as a means of 'baffling' them
61. Kilvert's *Diary*, Vol. 1, p.327
62. *Ibid*, Vol. 2, pp.194-5
63. *Ibid*, Vol. 2, p.182
64. *Ibid*, Vol. 1, p.325

65. *Ibid*, Vol. 2, p.233
66. The *Diary* yields these further occasions: Vol. I, p.34, Vol. 2, p.48, Vol. 2, p.123. On this last occasion, the text Kilvert chose for his sermon, significantly entitled 'Love and Duty', was I. John iii. 18 and it summed up very aptly Venables' failing as Kilvert saw it: 'let us not love in word and speech but in deed and truth'. Kilvert said he delivered the sermon 'with great satisfaction to myself'
67. Mark 3.29. The Holy Spirit is synonymous with the Holy Ghost. Luke 12.10 makes it clear that a characteristic form of 'blasphemy' against the Holy Spirit is covetousness, the laying up of material, instead of spiritual, goods
68. Kilvert's *Diary*, Vol. 2, p.57
69. This was made possible by an Act passed in 1813
70. Rev. J. Williams, *History of Radnorshire*, pp.251-2
71. LWRO. RC/E/CLY/2/86
72. G. Himmelfarb, *Victorian Minds*, pp.276-7
73. A. Trollope, *op.cit*, p.28
74. Houghton, *op.cit*, p.395
75. Himmelfarb, *op.cit*, p.278
76. Houghton, *op.cit*, p.406
77. Mrs. Kingsley, *op.cit*, p.50
78. Trollope, *op.cit*, p.65
79. Llysdinam Collection, B 1469
80. Bulwer Lytton, *op.cit*, Vol. 1, p.310
81. Back at home and facing highly autocratic behaviour from Squire Ashe over the purchase of a harmonium for the church, he praised the generous contributions made towards it by the Venables. 'What a difference in the spirit ...of Llysdinam and Langley House'. (*Diary*, Vol. 3. pp.111-112)
82. The passage is on pp.80-4 of *Practical View*
83. R. Kilvert, *op.cit*, p.19
84. G.B.A.M. Finlayson, *op.cit*, p.49
85. C. Kingsley, *Alton Locke*, p.12
86. Bradley (*op.cit*, p.28) refers to the way Evangelicalism's life-denying, negative values of discipline and self-control were in opposition to the altruism and generosity of spirit it recommended
87. W. Wilberforce, *op.cit*, pp.22-3, 40, 46, 77
88. B. Lytton, *op.cit*, p.310
89. Llysdinam Collection, B708, the letter was dated 2 March 1873
90. Kilvert's *Diary*, Vol. 2, p.246
91. Llysdinam Collection, B 786, no other letter in the Collection mentions Kilvert's death around the time that it happened
92. *Ibid*, A 86, the diary entry was dated 24 September 1879
93. *Ibid*, B 1524, the letter in which Venables recorded the discovery of the missing one was dated 4 May 1880. This missing letter was dated 18 October 1877 and it had fallen behind a cushion on the ottoman in the hall at Llysdinam

Chapter 5
1. Kilvert's *Diary*, Vol. I, pp.178-9. 16 July 1870
2. W. S. Blunt, *My Diaries*, p.388. He knew France well, having served up to December 1869 at the British Embassy in Paris under the crusty Lord Cowley, who resented ordinary people, such as Kilvert, skating on the lake of his Draycot home. Blunt confirmed this impression of the noble diplomat and pictured him as the kind of Englishman who might have been pilloried in *A Week in a French Country House*: 'a curiously silent man stiff and awkward, typically British in his anti-social manners, and ill at ease even in the bosom of his family...' (Quoted in Elizabeth Longford, *A Pilgrimage of Passion. The Life of Wilfred Scawen Blunt*, p.42)
3. E. Belfort Bax, *Reminiscences and Reflections of a Mid and Late Victorian*, pp.28-9
4. His younger brother, Charles Sartoris, was an Eton contemporary in 1838 of Velters Cornewall, elder brother of Sir George Cornewall of the *Diary*
5. A. Sartoris, *A Week in a French Country House*, p.60
6. Mrs. Ritchie in the Preface to *A Week in a French Country House*. Adelaide Kemble's mother was French and was born in Vienna into a family of musicians and dancers. Thackeray knew all the Kembles but his favourite was Adelaide, with whom he had a close friendship for over 25 years. After hearing her sing on one occasion, he remarked: 'She was passionate, she was enthusiastic, she was sublime, she was tender....the most....good-natured absurd clever creature possible'. (Letter to Mrs Brookfield. July 1849. *Letters and Private Papers of W. M. Thackeray*, edited Gordon N. Ray, Vol. 2, pp.559-560.) Thackeray was editor of the *Cornhill Magazine* when Mrs. Sartoris' novel appeared in its pages

REFERENCES

7. Preface to *A Week in a French Country House*
8. *Ibid*, pp.18-19
9. M. Mitford, *Our Village*, p.230
10. A. Sartoris, *op.cit*, p.82
11. H. Taine, *op.cit*, p.113
12. *The Diaries of Hannah Cullwick. Victorian Maidservant*, edited L. Stanley., p.282
13. F.V. Dawes, *Not in front of the Servants*, pp.62-4. T. Lummis and J. Marsh, *The Woman's Domain. Women and the English Country House*, p.187. F. Thompson, *Lark Rise to Candleford*, pp.163-4
14. H. Taine, *op.cit*, p.119
15. A. Sartoris, *op.cit*, p.142
16. Lady Verney., *Fernyhurst Court*, p.16
17. *Ibid*, p.29
18. *Ibid*, p.97
19. Kilvert's *Diary*, Vol. 2, p.152
20. *Ibid*, Vol. 2, p.186
21. *Ibid*, Vol. 2, pp.210-211. Kilvert, like many Victorian males, was moved to passionate indiscretions of this kind when travelling in trains
22. *Ibid*, Vol. 1, p.190
23. Richard Thomas, *Y Dduw Bo'r Diolch: A History of a Family of Mid-Wales Landowners*, p.63
24. Kilvert's *Diary*, Vol. 2, p.317
25. *Ibid*, Vol. 2, p.85. The book (dated 1869) by Mrs. Prentiss traces the spiritual progress of a young girl
26. D. Roberts, *Paternalism in Early Victorian England*, p.135
27. T. Lummis and J. Marsh, *op.cit*, p.79
28. F.V. Dawes, *op.cit*, p.19
29. T. Lummis and J. Marsh, *op.cit*, p.186
30. H. Taine, *op.cit*, p.195
31. Lady Warwick, quoted in J.F.C. Harrison, *Late Victorian Britain*, p.41
32. J.F.C. Harrison, *Early Victorian Britain. 1832 - 1851*, p.55
33. Kilvert's *Diary*, Vol. 3, pp.360 - 1
34. *Ibid*, Vol. 2, pp.349 - 50
35. *Ibid*, Vol. 2, p.374
36. Bredwardine parishioner, quoted in Kilvert Society Newsletter, February, 1980. His italics
37. Mrs. Hamilton suspected that Ellen, her sister's child, whom she was rearing within her own family, was guilty of stealing money. Convinced of her guilt, Mrs. Hamilton proposed banishing her to the penitential ethos of the home of Miss Seldon, a relative, who was fond of saying 'if a branch were in the slightest degree decayed, cut it off'. (*Home Influence*, p.294)
38. *Ibid*, p.100
39. *Ibid*, p.100
40. Houghton, *op.cit*, p.347. Houghton was paraphrasing Charles Kingsley
41. William Jay, *Autobiography and Reminiscences of the Rev. William Jay*, p.219
42. Lady Shelley noted in her journal in 1795 the origin of clothing clubs. Frightened by the French Revolution, the upper-classes of the time were fearful that the labouring masses of England might go the same way. Among the practical measures adopted to improve the condition of the poor were clothing clubs (*The Diary of Frances, Lady Shelley, 1787 - 1817*, Vol. 1, p.8)
43. Kilvert's *Diary*, Vol. 2, p.176
44. G. Aguilar, *A Mother's Recompense*, p.281
45. *Ibid*, p.313
46. G. Aguilar, *Home Influence*, p.363. Her 'strict watchfulness' echoes Wilberforce's phrase 'diligent watchfulness' that appears in his *Practical View of Christianity*
47. Kilvert's *Diary*, Vol. 2, p.180
48. Kilvert Society Newsletter, March, 1978
49. Houghton, *op.cit*, p.1. His italics
50. *Ibid*, pp.1-2
51. Kilvert's *Diary*, Vol. 3, p.66
52. *Ibid*, Vol. 3, p.229
53. *Ibid*, Vol. 3, p.260. Ettie's father stipulated in his will that, because he had lost his Christian faith, he was to be remembered not as 'the Reverend' but as 'Esquire'. He was, therefore, no more likely to have accepted a curate, especially an impecunious one, as his son-in-law than the Rev. Thomas had been
54. For other information about Kilvert and Katharine Heanley, I am indebted to L. Le Quesne's 'The Missing Year - Kilvert and "Kathleen Mavourneen"' in the Frederick Grice Memorial Booklet and to 'St. Harmon', edited by C.T.O. Prosser, in *Looking Backwards - A Kilvert Miscellanea*
55. C.T. Newton of the Newton family of Bredwardine wrote to Venables on 10 May 1872 inviting him to

become one of the trustees, (Llysdinam Collection B875). The 18 October 1877 letter (Llysdinam Collection B1524) was the one Venables failed to see until May 1880 (see end of chapter 4)

Chapter 6

1. B. Heeney, *op.cit*, p.87
2. Bulwer Lytton, *op.cit*, Vol. 1, p.280
3. In the week 11 - 15 Nov. 1878, he visited the school on each of four days; no entry exists for the fifth. The log book of St. Harmon's School shows that he regularly visited every day when he was vicar there
4. Sidney Ball, article in Kilvert Society Newsletter, Feb. 1985. One of Kilvert's pupils there was Henry Devereux, who was born in October 1848; he would have been of prep school age between 1856 and 1861. He was the brother of Lord Hereford
5. M. Sturt, *The Education of the People*, p.1
6. J. Skinner, *op.cit*, p.248. He was writing this in 1823
7. F. Meyrick, *op.cit*, p.333
8. Parliamentary Papers, Census Report on Religious Worship, Vol. LXXXIX 1852-3, p.132
9. P. Laslett, *The World We Have Lost*, pp.174-8. D. Roberts (*op.cit*, p.155) stressed the importance attached by early Victorian clergy to the Catechism. Keble of Oriel, for example, considered it a prime duty. For Kingsley it was 'the main point of instruction' in the education of the poor
10. Kilvert's Diary, Vol. 3, p.359
11. Llysdinam Collection, F. 34
12. This was the Special Minute of the Committee of Council for Education
13. J. Lawson and H. Silver, *op.cit*, p.270
14. Report of the Commission on the state of Education in Wales, 1847, pp.173-5
15. The Report as a whole was seen by the Welsh as an attack upon them and on Dissent by the Church and Anglican landowners. 'Though prejudiced and unsympathetic, the Commissioners were more ignorant than malicious', Maclure commented, and they simply repeated the reports they had been given. (J.S. Maclure, *Educational Documents. England and Wales. 1816 to the present day*, p.56)
16. This comment and the preceding ones from landowners and clergy are from reports 30, 38, 48, 52 and 63
17. It comprised Monmouthshire and the eastern half of Glamorgan.
18. Letter to Sir Thomas Phillips. 7 July 1846. E. Copleston, *op.cit*, pp.201-2
19. Connop Thirlwall. Charge of 1848, in J.J.S. Perowne, *Remains Literary And Theological Of Connop Thirlwall*, Vol. 1, pp.132-3
20. His wife had also contributed £20, as had the Bishop; Rev. Bevan, Rev. Henry Dew had each contributed £5; Henry Allen, Viscount Hereford, Captain De Winton, and Col. Wood of Brecon each gave £5; Venables himself gave £45 and his two brothers £20 each; £30 came from Sir John Walsh, the local MP. The Rev. Jones Thomas of Llanthomas gave nothing. LWRO R/C/E/CLY/5/131
21. *Hereford Times*, 27 April 1861
22. The Commission was set up to look into the provision of 'sound and cheap' elementary education
23. Kilvert's *Diary*, Vol. 1, p.371
24. It seems that the Rev. Bevan's school was not all that efficient at meeting the demands of the Revised Code
25. Kilvert's *Diary*, National Library of Wales (1989) edition, pp.56-8
26. *Ibid*, Vol. 3, p.289. Kilvert was visiting the place in May 1876 with a view to becoming, as he in fact did later that year, its vicar
27. Quoted in F. Smith, *A History of English Elementary Education 1760 - 1902*, p.263
28. M.K. Ashby, *Joseph Ashby Of Tysoe*, pp.17-18
29. P.H.J.H. Gosden, *How They Were Taught. Elementary Schools, 1833 - 1862*, p.31
30. She was Henrietta Coleburn of the Home and Colonial Institution
31. S. Frith, 'Socialisation and Rational Schooling: elementary education in Leeds before 1870', in P. McCann, *Popular Education and Socialisation in the Nineteenth Century*, pp.76-8
32. Quoted in Asher Tropp, *The School Teachers*, p.103
33. Venables' Visitation Return. Summer 1866
34. Report of Commission on Employment of Children, Young Persons, and Women in Agriculture, 3rd Report, 1867, pp.63-4. W.E. Forster, who brought in the 1870 Act, calculated that only 2/5 of working-class children between 6-10 and only 1/3 between 10-12 were attending school
35. Thirlwall's Charge of 1866
36. Kilvert's *Diary*, Vol. 1, p.285. The date was 21 Dec. 1870
37. *Ibid*, Vol. 3, p.98
38. *Ibid*, Vol. 1, p.109

REFERENCES

39. Llysdinam Collection, B 1432, letter of Venables to George Venables, 17 Dec. 1870
40. Kilvert stayed with Evans at his home of Llwynbarried in April 1870: 'a nice old-fashioned Welsh country house whitewashed or stuccoed with gables'. He was the squire of Nantmel and a JP, and Kilvert was impressed by his authority when he addressed the crowd at the opening of Hysfa Chapel and by their deference
41. Llysdinam Collection, B 1433, letter of Venables to George Venables, 22 Dec. 1870
42. Venables, in his Visitation Return of 1866, stated that either he or his curate catechised the children; in his 1869 one, he said it was 'chiefly done' by Kilvert. Rev. Henry De Winton in his Returns, assured the Bishop that he performed this office 'frequently', while the Rev. Tom Williams of Llowes said he did it 'very frequently'
43. Kilvert's *Diary*, Vol. 2, p.54
44. *Ibid*, Vol. 2, p.72. Albert Workman Headeach was a fellow student of Kilvert's at Wadham. He had been admitted the year before Kilvert arrived
45. *Ibid*, Vol. 1, p.237
46. B. Graham, *Nineteenth Century Self-Help in Education - Mutual Improvement Societies*, Vol. 2, pp.15-17. Radical and Dissenting material was to be found in reading rooms so that many Tories viewed their members as 'extremists and agitators' (*Ibid*, pp.36-8)
47. M. Sturt, *op.cit*, p.185
48. F. Smith, *op.cit*, p.181
49. H.G. Wells said that the elementary schools had 'specially trained, inferior teachers' whose job was to educate the lower-classes into suitably lower-class jobs. (Quoted in A. Briggs, *Victorian People*, p.265)
50. R. Sellman, 'The Country School' in G.E. Mingay, *The Victorian Countryside*, Vol. 2, p.550
51. F. Knights, *The Nineteenth Century Church and English Society*, p.192
52. Kilvert's *Diary*, Vol. 2, p.386, (my italics). There is, in fact, no evidence that Kilvert wrote to Evans
53. They were Boosie's sister Mary-Jane, two daughters of Clyro Court employees, three daughters of well-to-do farmers, and a clerk's daughter from Cusop
54. R.I. Morgan, Kilvert Society Newsletter, June 1978. There was no entry for the day Kilvert left Clyro because the school was on holiday
55. F. Grice, 'The Diary of Mary Louisa Bevan 1872-75', in the Frederick Grice Memorial Booklet, p.29
56. M. Sturt (*op.cit*, pp.250-1) stated that behind the Revised Code lay hatred, part of which was directed at the Church, though 'the greater part was directed at the teachers; and in this hostility churchmen and anti-clericals joined'
57. Entry for 18 August 1872
58. A. Tropp, *op.cit*, p.26
59. Article by F. Grice (Kilvert Society Newsletter, March 1978) on letters by Kilvert to Marion Vaughan. Grice stated that the prejudices shown in them were stronger than is implied by the *Diary*
60. D.O. Wagner, *op.cit*, p.95
61. P.C. Hammond, *The Parson And The Victorian Parish*, p.158
62. Kilvert's *Diary*, Vol. 2, pp.166-7. The frequency with which Kilvert used the phrase 'inextinguishable laughter' reinforces the impression that he meant literally what he said
63. M.K. Ashby, *op.cit*, p.95
64. Kilvert Society Newsletter, Feb. 1984
65. G. Bourne, *Change In The Village*, p.224. Elementary school log books in the last third of the century confirm this picture
66. Kilvert's *Diary*, Vol. 2, p.237
67. Kilvert also recounted the Hezekiah story to John Hatherell (see Chapter 8)
68. Rev. W.L. Clay, *The Prison Chaplain: A Memoir Of The Rev. John Clay*, p.557. SGO also thought that using the Bible as an 'every day hard lesson book' was deplorable; it was 'utterly destructive of reverence for God's word... and as injurious to the teachers as to the taught'. (SGO, *op.cit*, Vol. 1, p.99)
69. Rev. T. Mozley, *Reminiscences chiefly of Towns, Villages, and Schools*, p.271
70. Kilvert's *Diary*, Vol. 3, pp.422-3
71. *Ibid*, Vol. 3, p.368. An HMI's inspection of Clyro School on 1 July 1870, at which Kilvert was present, had begun with an examination of the Catechism, which included questions on sacraments, and one's duty to one's neighbour. (Kilvert's *Diary*, National Library of Wales, 1989, pp.56-8)
72. Kilvert's *Diary*, Vol. 3, p.121
73. E. Holmes, *What Is and What Might Be*, p.230
74. G. Kitson Clark, *Churchmen and the Condition of England*, p.139
75. *Ibid*, p.102
76. Joseph Arch, *The Autobiography of Joseph Arch*, p.28
77. SGO, *op.cit*, Letter of 1 Jan. 1857
78. Rev. W. Tuckwell, *Reminiscences of a Radical Parson*, p.19
79. T.W. Bamford analysed the educational origins of 70 leading figures in the administration of education

in the period 1870 - 1963, and showed that the overwhelming proportion came from public schools, a quarter from Eton, *The Rise of the Public Schools*, p.234

80. P.W. Musgrave, *Society and Education in England since 1800*, p.12. The Austro-Prussian War and the American Civil War had demonstrated the need for an efficient, modern system of education

81. It had provided an additional 1.5m school places by 1876. Correspondence between Rev. Venables and his solicitor in February of that year was concerned with the sale of half an acre of Venables' land for the building of a Board School

82. R. Jefferies, *Hodge and his Masters*, p.177

83. Even in 1880, in rural areas, there were still 6m people outside the bye laws governing attendance. It was only after the 1880 Act that all areas were required to enforce it

84. G. Kitson Clark, *op.cit*, p.284

85. D. Lockwood, *op.cit*, p.52

86. The attitude is clearly exemplified in a letter from George Venables to the Rev. Venables, dated 24 Aug. 1886. He was enraged by a pamphlet of Gladstone's because it contained 'more grievous nonsense about the oppression of Wales by England'. He himself had received an appeal for a contribution to a church which he was afraid would find its way into the hands of 'rascally Dissenters'. (Llysdinam Collection. B 1832)

87. Kilvert's *Diary*, Vol. 2, p.246

88. E. Carpenter, *My Days And Dreams*, p.286

Chapter 7

1. R. Kilvert, *op.cit*, p.10

2. *Ibid*, pp.48-9

3. Letter to Lady Portarlington, 22 Oct. 1802, *Letters of Lady Louisa Stuart*, p.134

4. Sir J.D. Astley, *Fifty Years Of My Life*, Vol. 2, p.22

5. Sir John Eardley-Wilmot, quoted in P. Mason, *The English Gentleman. The Rise and Fall of an Ideal*, p.83

6. Sir John Shelley, Cobbett's Parliamentary Debates, Vol. XL, 14 May 1819

7. R. Kilvert, *op.cit*, pp.9-10

8. Kilvert's *Diary*, Vol. 2, pp.287-8, his italics and question mark

9. H. Hopkins, *op.cit*, p. 60

10. Kilvert's *Diary*, Vol. 2, p.85

11. Lord W. De Broke, *The Sport Of Our Ancestors*, p.1

12. D.C. Itkowitz, *Peculiar Privilege: A Social History of English Fox-hunting 1752 - 1885*, p.24

13. Quoted in De Broke, *op.cit*, p.86. He claimed that when the poem, from which this verse comes, was read before the critical audience of the Bullingdon Club of Christ Church College, Oxford, the members were spell-bound. The sporting novelist R.S. Surtees (1803 - 1864) had referred to fox-hunting as 'the image of war without its guilt'

14. D.C. Itkowitz, *op.cit*, p.26

15. Lord W. De Broke, *The Passing Years*, p.55

16. Kilvert's *Diary*, Vol. 1, p.118, 27 April 1870

17. *Ibid*, National Library of Wales edition, 14 June 1870

18. *Ibid*, Vol. 1, pp.232, 20 September 1870

19. *Ibid*, Vol. 1, p.263, 23/24 Nov. 1870

20. Quoted in J.F.C. Harrison, *Early Victorian Britain 1832 - 1851*, p.97

21. John Freeman Blisset, son of the Rector of Letton, who was also a landowner

22. Kilvert's *Diary*, Vol. 1, p.335

23. C. Kingsley, *Alton Locke*, p.116

24. Kilvert's *Diary*, Vol. 1, p.329. Cf. the poem by Kilvert that prefaces this chapter

25. *Ibid*, Vol. 2, p.195

26. H. Hopkins, *op.cit*, p.84

27. Kilvert's *Diary*, Vol. 1, p.226, 6 Sept. 1870

28. Llysdinam Collection, B1226, letter to George Venables, 28 Jan. 1847

29. *Hereford Times*, 8 Nov. 1862

30. Mrs. Partridge was a devoted supporter of Clyro Church and was always to be found in the ranks of ladies who dressed it for harvest festivals. She also played a very moving rendering of 'Auld Lang Syne' at a Penny Reading

31. Kilvert's *Diary*, Vol. 1, p.129, 9 May 1870

32. E.A. Freeman had mentioned St. Anselm in 1 October article on 'The Morality of Field Sports'

33. *Ibid*, p.383

34. H.C.G. Moule, *op.cit*, p.37. Kilvert's brother, Edward, did not share his attitude to field sports. He was quite happy to shoot game birds

35. Kilvert's *Diary*, National Library of Wales edition, p.35

REFERENCES

36. *Ibid*, Vol. 1, p.333, May 1871
37. J. Hawker, *A Victorian Poacher*, pp.105-8
38. Kilvert's *Diary*, National Library of Wales edition, p.23, 23 June 1870
39. *Ibid*, Vol. 2, p.179
40. *Hereford Times*, 23 April 1864
41. Kilvert's *Diary*, Vol. 2, p.333. Her papa was squire of Cabalva, near Clyro
42. These entries record such occasions: Vol. 2, p.335; Vol. 2, p.389; Vol. 3, p.164
43. De Broke quoted this both in *The Passing Years* and *The Sport Of Our Ancestors*
44. Kilvert's *Diary*, Vol. 3, p.225
45. *Ibid*, Vol. 3, p.422
46. *Ibid*, National Library of Wales edition, p.44
47. The title of the article in which this claim was made was 'The English Gentry'. It appeared in the Tory *Blackwood's Magazine* and presented a highly flattering account of the worth of that class at the moment the new county councils were threatening the very existence of the country gentleman as a type
48. Kilvert's *Diary*, National Library of Wales edition, p.73. The date was 8 July 1870
49. Quoted in J.F.C. Harrison, *Late Victorian Britain*, pp.37-8
50. Kilvert's *Diary*, Vol. 3, p.426
51. *Ibid*, Vol. 1, p.194
52. *Ibid*, Vol. 2, p.303
53. *Ibid*, Vol. 1, p.377
54. Mrs Kingsley, *op.cit*, p.12
55. *Ibid*, p.68
56. Kilvert's *Diary*, Vol. 1, p.125. The idea and its phrasing owe something to 'To The Cuckoo' by Wordsworth, to whom Kingsley was also devoted
57. *Ibid*, Vol. 3, p.91
58. C. Kingsley, *Yeast*, p.14
59. Kilvert's *Diary*, Vol. 2, p.309
60. C. Kingsley, *Alton Locke*, p.116
61. Kilvert's *Diary*, Vol. 3, p.202
62. C. Kingsley, *Alton Locke*, p.181
63. N. Vance, *The sinews of the spirit. The ideal of Christian manliness in Victorian literature and thought*, p.44
64. Kilvert's *Diary*, Vol. 1, p.52
65. *Ibid*, Vol. 1, p.68
66. *Ibid*, Vol. 1, p.75
67. *Ibid*, Vol. 3, p.34
68. *Ibid*, Vol. 1, p.63
69. *Ibid*, Vol. 1, p.72
70. *Ibid*, Vol. 2, p.375
71. C. Kingsley, *Yeast*, p.7
72. *Ibid*, pp.19-20
73. Kilvert's *Diary*, Vol. 1, p.88
74. *Ibid*, Vol. 2, p.411
75. *Ibid*, Vol. 2, p.421
76. *The Hereford Times*, 5 May 1860,
77. A.C. Ainger, *Memories of Eton 60 Years Ago*, p.275. Eton began to set up a number of companies in 1860. Martin Tupper (*My Life As an Author*, p.302) spoke of 'the great scare of Napoleon's rabid colonels'
78. F.M.L. Thompson, *op.cit*, p.271
79. Bertrand and Patricia Russell, *The Amberley Papers. The Letters and Diaries of Lord and Lady Amberley*, Vol. 1, p.63
80. O.F. Christie, *op.cit*, p.90
81. In the preface to *Alton Locke*, Kingsley cited the Movement as one 'absolute proof' of the changed conditions between the upper and lower-classes, a sign of increased trust and goodwill
82. Lord De Broke, *The Passing Years*, p.268
83. Lord Redesdale, *Memories*, Vol. 1, p.163 and p.183
84. R E. Prothero and G.G. Bradley, *op.cit*, Vol. 2, p.407
85. Kilvert's attitude to the mutineers was as intemperately vengeful as Kingsley's. Both characterised them repeatedly as 'devils'. This was the reaction of most Victorians, including Venables, whose cousin died of wounds received in the Mutiny. He expressed the hope that one Indian leader of it had not escaped hanging by committing suicide. (Llysdinam Collection, B1311, Letter to George Venables, 17 Sept. 1857)
86. Kilvert's *Diary*, Vol. 3, p.429 and p.426

87. R. Furneaux, *op.cit*, p.322
88. J. Martineau, *The Life and Correspondence of Sir Bartle Frere*, Vol. 1, p.470
89. Sir B. Frere, *Remarks On The Organisation Of Missions To Uncivilised Populations*, Proceedings of the Bath Church Congress, Oct. 1873, pp.93-7
90. Sir B. Frere, *Christianity suited to all Forms of Civilisation*, Lecture given to the Christian Evidence Society, 9 July 1872, p.5 and p.23
91. Edward W. Said, *Culture and Imperialism*, p.127. George D. Bearce, *British Attitudes Towards India 1784 - 1858*, p.234; V.G. Kiernan, *The Lords Of Human Kind*, p.42
92. J. Morris, *Heaven's Command. An Imperial Progress*, p.334
93. Kilvert's interest in this particular campaign may have resulted from the fact that it was located in a part of West Africa relatively close to Sierra Leone and Abbeo Kuta, which his sister, Emily, noted were two areas of the mission field to which the family sent charitable boxes, (E. Wyndowe, *op.cit*, p.102). Abbeo Kuta is in western Nigeria, which borders on modern Ghana, home of the Ashanti
94. Kilvert's *Diary*, Vol. 2, p.411
95. Quoted in Morris, *op.cit*, p.398
96. A. Maitland, *Speke and the discovery of the Nile*, p.170
97. The Goldney family, which provided a succession of mayors for Chippenham and Kilvert's MP for most of his adult life, were long-established cloth merchants, trading with the West Indies. The Frere family, too, belonged in this social group. They were both landowners and manufacturers. They owned an iron works in Clydach, Breconshire
98. J. Martineau, *op.cit*, p.258 and p.244
99. Kilvert's *Diary*, Vol. 3, p.454. Col. Thomas was Daisy's eldest brother
100. Celebrated in the fine film 'Zulu'
101. M. Arnold, 'An Eton Boy', *Fortnightly Review*, 1 June 1882
102. Ian Knight, *Brave Men's Blood. The Epic of the Zulu War, 1879*, p.192
103. Brian Roberts, *The Zulu Kings*, p.335
104. N. Vance, *op.cit*, p.115
105. L. Davidoff and C. Hall, *op.cit*, p. 112
106. The words are Martineau's, in Mrs. Kingsley, *op.cit*, pp.120-1
107. W. Houghton, *op.cit*, pp.385-390
108. P. Ackroyd, *op.cit*, pp.528-9
109. Kilvert's *Diary*, National Library of Wales edition. Again, he was recording this experience in April 1870, when he was especially disturbed at the cruelty of field sports
110. Pets were an important part of Kilvert's Harnish home. His sister Emily recalled ponies, dogs, cats, rabbits, and birds
111. Kilvert's *Diary*, Vol. 2, p.86. Kilvert referred derisively to the gamekeepers and beaters accompanying Baskerville as a 'posse comitatus' (technically the body of men whom a sheriff of a rural country could raise to suppress riots). In Kingsley's *Yeast*, the same phrase is used to mean the men a squire could rely on to guard his covers against poachers
112. See P. Gay, *op.cit*, p.82
113. P. Bailey, *Leisure And Class In Victorian England*, p.86

Chapter 8
1. Brian Heeney, *A Different Kind of Gentleman. Parish Clergy as Professional Men in Early and Mid-Victorian England*, p. 71
2. Osborne, *op.cit*, p. 200
3. Heeney, *op.cit*, pp. 71-2
4. The Rev. J.T. Becher, *The Anti-Pauper System*, quoted in P. Wood, *Poverty and the Workhouse in Victorian Britain*, p. 60. Becher was particularly influential in Poor Law development in his own area of Nottinghamshire
5. These were the worst aspects of the workhouse in the view of D. Roberts, 'How Cruel Was The Victorian Poor Law?', *Historical Journal*, VI, 1963, p.103
6. A. Digby, *Pauper Palaces*, p.143
7. Kilvert's *Diary*, Vol. 3, p.156
8. *Ibid*, Vol. 1, p.135
9. *Ibid*, Vol. 1, p.367
10. The agriculturalist, W. Cubitt, speaking in 1863 of Norfolk labourers' cottages. Quoted in R. Heath *The Victorian Peasant*, p.39
11. Kilvert's *Diary*, Vol. 1, p.233
12. *Ibid*, Vol. 1, p.372
13. *Ibid*, Vol. 1, p.379
14. J. Fraser. Assistant Commissioner. Commission on Employment of Children, Young Persons and Women in Agriculture, 1876. Quoted in R. Heath, *op.cit*, p.29

REFERENCES

15. G. Kitson Clark observed that poverty was so commonplace that even a humane man would not find the extent of it all that remarkable or susceptible to much amelioration. (Clark, *op.cit*, p.38)
16. Wordsworth, Ecclesiastical Sonnet XVI
17. *Ibid*, Ecclesiastical Sonnet XXVIII
18. Kilvert's *Diary*, Vol. 1, p.89
19. G. Aguilar, *Home Influence*, p.124. Wilberforce, too, had emphasised this spiritual benefit
20. Kilvert's *Diary*, Vol. 3, p.31
21. *Ibid*, Vol. 3, p.387
22. *Ibid*, Vol. 3, pp.441 - 3
23. *Ibid*, Vol. 3, p.94
24. B. Harrison, *Peaceable Kingdom: Stability and Change in Modern Britain*, p.229
25. Kilvert's *Diary*, Vol. 2, p.393
26. B. Heeney, *op.cit*, p.36
27. R. Heath, *op.cit*, p.24
28. Le Quesne, *op.cit*, p.46
29. Kilvert's *Diary*, Vol. 2, p.249
30. G.F. Best, *op.cit*, p.290
31. D. Cannadine, *The Decline and Fall of the British Aristocracy*, p.36
32. Quoted in O. Chadwick, *op.cit*, Vol. 2, pp.171-2
33. Kilvert's *Diary*, Vol. 3, p.426
34. *Ibid*, Vol. 2, p.79
35. *Ibid*, Vol. 3, p.450
36. *Ibid*, Vol. 2, p.189
37. F. Grice, *op.cit*, p.121
38. Kilvert's *Diary*, Vol. 3. p.297
39. *Ibid*, Vol. 1, p.203
40. *Ibid*, Vol. 2, p.377
41. *Ibid*, Vol. 3, pp.258-9
42. Of the 193 pages of Volume Two of the *Diary*, from where he left Clyro to the end of the volume (i.e. pp. 255-448), approximately a fifth concerns locations other than Langley Burrell. Virtually every other page of the remaining text contains reminiscence. It is true that Plomer's editing, during which he rejected material, might have created this balance; the unedited *Diary* might have shown a different one. It is also true that entries show, not only Kilvert, but other people looking back, but that reinforces the point being made here
43. E.J. Hobsbawm and G. Rudé, *op.cit*, p.62
44. Kilvert's *Diary*, Vol. 1, p.60 and pp.128-9. Shoemakers were often the radicals in village communities
45. *Collected Verses* by the Rev. Francis Kilvert, p. 21
46. Kilvert's benevolence towards him can be seen as part of the shift in the latter half of the century to charity prompted by the 'good heart', rather than, as in the earlier decades, by a stern conception of Christian duty. However, his respect for honest toil is more a vestige of the latter and his Evangelical upbringing. It reflects what Clough had in mind when he wrote of earning one's bread 'honestly - in the strictest sense of the word "honestly" - to do work.....well and thoroughly'. His italics. Quoted in Houghton, *op.cit*, p.276
47. Charles Kingsley died at this time. It was an event felt deeply by Kilvert and appeared to him as a further weakening of the old values
48. Smocks were disappearing in the 1850s and by the 1870s only a few older men were wearing them. When they wore them, they looked and felt like children. As they grew in independence, they rejected the smock and the attitude of deference that went with it. (O. Chadwick, *The Victorian Church*, Vol. 2, p.154). Some labourers' children wore smocks until well into the last quarter of the century. (P. Horn, *The Victorian Country Child*, p.26)
49. Kilvert's *Diary*, Vol. 1, pp.213-4
50. Kilvert's criticism of Captain De Winton has been touched on in an earlier chapter. The specific charge of his drunkenness is dealt with in the next chapter
51. Kilvert's *Diary*, Vol. 3, pp.102-3. Kilvert showed some of his appreciation of Jefferies by obtaining for his daughter, Annie, a place as a maid at Venables' home of Llysdinam. (Vol. 2, p.362)
52. WRO 118/144
53. Kilvert's *Diary*, Vol. 3, p.109
54. She was a daughter of George Jefferies and a 33 year-old mother of two. Perhaps the strain of political resistance in her was the stronger because she was married, not to an agricultural worker, but to the railway labourer, William Hicks, who may have been a member of the railmen's union (Amalgamated Society of Railway Servants—later the NUR), founded in 1871. It quickly grew to have 17,000 members

55. Cf. the case of Anne Pugh in the chapter 'Kilvert and *A Week in a French Country House*'
56. Kilvert's *Diary*, Vol. 3, p.82
57. Data on wages are drawn from P. Horn, *Labouring Life in the Victorian Countryside*, p.118; P. E. Razzell and R.W. Wainwright, *The Victorian Working Class: Selections from Letters to the 'Morning Chronicle'*, p.10; Report of Commission on Employment of Women and Children in Agriculture, 1867, p.245
58. Kilvert's *Diary*, Vol. 1, p.283
59. *Letters of SGO*, Vol. 2, 14 August 1868
60. He was in the habit of leaving tracts against drunkenness in the homes of poor parishioners. He was exultant in October 1871 when the Clyro JPs closed down the New Inn, 'a happy thing for the village'. He was voicing the gentry view of a pub that was frequented largely by labourers. The resolve of the Clyro JPs may have been strengthened by the influential 1869 Church report on intemperance, which recommended reducing the number of pubs available to the working-classes. It was also a policy of the closed parish
61. He was Lord Sidney Godolphin Osborne, third son of Baron Godolphin, and had been educated at Rugby and Oxford
62. It is noticeable that the *Diary* makes no reference to any stand made by Robert Kilvert against Squire Ashe's tyranny, but, after all, he owed his living to the Squire.
63. SGO, *op.cit*, Vol. 2, 15 May 1865. Landowners did build estate cottages for their workers. They were built to enhance their estates, often in 'cottage ornée' style, in an attempt to create an impression of 'quaint, fairytale peasantry'. They were frequently too expensive for labourers and unsuited to their needs. An additional aim was to have deferential, respectable tenants. They represented the triumph of the principle of property because landowners effectively owned those who lived in them. (E. Gauldie, *Cruel Habitations: A History of Working Class Housing 1780 - 1918*, p.33.) Walter Baskerville built some in Clyro after Kilvert left. The latter hated them, declaring them to be 'huge and staring' and out of character. For him, they were only an aesthetic issue, not a moral and economic one
64. Hatherell would not have entered the workhouse. Those too old or infirm to earn their own living received outdoor relief. Life on the pittance of outdoor relief in a squalid, uncomfortable cottage could often be far harder than indoor relief. (A. Digby., *op.cit*, pp.161- 2)
65. SGO, *op.cit*, Vol. 2, 15 September 1863
66. *Ibid*, Vol. 1, 26 December 1849
67. W.L. Burn, *op.cit*, p.305. Joseph Arch, (*op.cit*, pp.126-7). G.C. Brodrick, *English land and English landlords*, p.85
68. J.F.C. Harrison, *The Common People. A History from the Norman Conquest to the Present*, p. 271 and p.276
69. The *Hereford Times* of 8 August 1863 reported a meeting there. After a church service, the Hay Volunteer Band led the procession to the pub where the members had dinner
70. P. Horn, *Life and Labour in the Victorian Countryside*, p.184
71. Kilvert's *Diary*, National Library of Wales edition (1989), pp.79-83. In Kilvert's description of a Foresters' parade in Langley Burrell, there is an element of ridicule, though not as marked as in the Oakfield account
72. T. Mozley, *Reminiscences chiefly of Towns, Villages and Schools*, p.358
73. Quoted in E. Selley, *Village Trade Unions in Two Centuries*, p.75
74. W. Cobbett, *Two-Penny Trash*, Vol. 2, No. 7, 1 January 1832
75. J.F.C. Harrison, *Early Victorian Britain*, p.121
76. G. Kitson Clark (*op.cit*, p.185) noted that many poor used clergy-run friendly societies and did not experience condescension
77. M.K. Ashby, *op.cit*, p.70
78. Kilvert's *Diary*, Vol. 3, p.353
79. *Ibid*, Vol. 3, pp.115-6. In 1876 his living was in fact worth £1,380. It was in the gift of Lady Lonsdale
80. *Ibid*, Vol. 3, p.363
81. *Ibid*, Vol. 3, p356. This was not a good example for the landed gentry Trustees to put before the poor, who were continuously criticised for improvidence. It was, nevertheless, a general situation: 'The total amount of debt.....on landed estates in the nineteenth century was.....substantial, and was probably on the increase.....especially during the prosperous mid-Victorian years'. (D. Cannadine, *Aspects of Aristocracy*, p.41. See also Lord Shaftesbury's words that preface this chapter.) Diary gentry families reflected this situation; debt was experienced by the Money, Baskerville, Venables, Devereux, De Winton, and Cornewall families
82. *Ibid*, Vol. 3, p.356. The living was in the gift of the Rev. Newton, a clergyman of some wealth, and Kilvert had been favoured with it by Miss Newton, whom he had known from his Clyro days. A bullet had been fired at night through the window of her sister's house in January 1878. A local schoolboy first admitted he was responsible but later denied it, so the mystery remained. The most likely explanation is that someone bore a grudge against the Newton family, as had been the case with

REFERENCES

Kilvert's great, great grandmother, who was shot at through the window by 'someone.....who owed her a grudge'. (*Diary*, Vol. 3, p.107.) One of Kilvert's parishioners also told Kilvert frankly one day that, as he was gentry, someone might very well take a shot at him. The shots were manifestations of the disaffection of the 'dark' village.

83. He is buried there in the same churchyard as Kilvert

84. In today's values the sum would be worth well over £3 million

85. Tomkyns Dew was the brother of Henry Dew, Rector of Whitney, near Clyro. Kilvert was very friendly with the Dew family

86. Freeman Blisset was the son of Henry Blisset, who, as a former Rector of Letton, had opposed the original plan to build schools. Like Walter Baskerville, his friend and neighbour, Freeman had gone to Eton at the age of 13 and then on to Christ Church, Oxford. He left as Walter Baskerville did without taking a degree, and lived as a squire. He was one of the Clyro Court rook-shooting party which so disturbed Kilvert

87. Kilvert's *Diary*, Vol. 3, p.404. A Charity Commissioner, Walter Skirrow, had been sent to this special meeting of the Trustees on 16 July 1878 to enquire into the Charity's workings. He told Kilvert he had been at Eton with Gladstone, a fact which Kilvert found impressive enough to record. Ironically, Gladstone was one of the Charity's severest critics

88. Phillott's background was Christ Church, Oxford (BA 1838) and some time as a master at Charterhouse. He collaborated with the Rev. W.L. Bevan on a work related to Hereford Cathedral's famous Mappa Mundi. Kilvert made a particular friend of Phillott's son, George

89. Kilvert's *Diary*, Vol. 3, p.385

90. John Hatherell was also lucky that he had escaped injury similar to that suffered by her husband

91. His unanimity with Sir George may have been influenced by the fact that he owed his living to him

92. Both Joseph Arch and Joseph Chamberlain had backed the cause of the local people.

93. D.O. Wagner, *op.cit*, p.61

94. While Kilvert was not prepared to criticise the clerical Trustees, he felt able to criticise their leaders within the confines of his *Diary*. He heard the Bishop of Hereford, James Atlay, (present at Kilvert's first meeting of Trustees) preach the sermon at the reopening of a local church. Kilvert thought it a dreadful effort, a mere 'screed', and quite inappropriate to the occasion. The sermon of the archdeacon, Lord Saye and Sele, at another reopening was more suitable but still a 'rigmarole'. In an effort to display local knowledge, he became hopelessly confused. (Kilvert's *Diary*, Vol. 3, pp.374-5). It is evident that the bishop and the archdeacon were in touch neither with local people nor with their own clergy. The *DNB* entry on Atlay casts about somewhat desperately for some clear and positive qualities with which to credit him. He was, it said, 'a conservative in politics' and 'a high churchman of the old school', with great 'geniality' and 'earnestness of character'. To his clergy he was a 'trusted counsellor and guide'. Successive Bishops of Hereford remained consistently silent in House of Lords debates. The record of their episcopal brethren was hardly more impressive: of 70 who sat in the Lords from 1850 - 1872, 20 never spoke at all in debates, while a further 19 spoke less than six times each. In the Lords and Church assemblies, most of the issues debated were quite unconnected with social questions; they concerned ritual, foreign missions, Church finance. (D.O. Wagner, *op.cit*, pp.67-70)

95. For the foregoing account of the Charity, I am indebted to Richard Pantall's *George Jarvis (1704 - 1793) And His Notorious Charity*.

96. A. Digby. (*op.cit*, p.5) claimed that two classes of poor were created partly as a result of gentry's favouring of this system and partly through charging high farm rents, which encouraged farmers to pay low wages to labourers.

97. Hatherell spent his working life in the estate system, which was in conflict throughout the century with the yeoman farmer enterprise Kilvert so much admired. Closed parishes (those dominated by estates) attempted to reproduce the personal relations of traditional rural communities but were in reality pseudo-communities. (D.R. Mills, *op.cit*, pp.138-9)

98. Independence, the virtue which, according to Squire Ashe and Kilvert, enabled Hatherell to stand proudly above the undeserving poor, was ironically the virtue in which he was most deficient

99. SGO, *op.cit*, Vol. 2, 14 August 1868

100. *Ibid*, Vol. 2, 3 March 1845

101. *Ibid*, Vol. 2, 18 September 1847

102. Kilvert's poem 'The Pilgrimage'

Chapter 9

1. J. Hart, 'Nineteenth Century Social Reform: A Tory Interpretation Of History' in *Past and Present*, No. 31. July 1965, p.53

2. *Ibid*, p.54

3. Parliamentary Papers. Report of Commission on Employment of Children, Young Persons and Women in Agriculture, 1867, 3rd Report, p.86

4. Charles Knight in *Farmer* (1844), quoted in Report on Employment of Children, Young Persons, and Women in Agriculture, 1st Report, 1867, p.xliii
5. Lord Ernle, *op.cit*, p 306
6. Kilvert's *Diary*, Vol. 3, p.199
7. Mrs. Hamilton praises Collins, who had, in the midst of poverty, shown 'the very loftiest virtues' (G. Aguilar, *Home Influence*, p.371)
8. Lord Ernle, *op.cit*, p.298
9. Kilvert's *Diary*, Vol. 2, p.161
10. *Ibid*, Vol. 2, pp.441-2
11. Stokes, *op.cit*, p.13. Rev. Venables had been prepared to give a small plot of land to his fictional cottagers in *The Poacher*, but in his book about Russia he had declared his aversion to every cottager becoming a 'petty farmer'. It was one way in which his more aristocratic background differentiated him from Kilvert
12. Kilvert's *Diary*, Vol. 1, p.87
13. *Ibid*, Vol. 2, p.425
14. *Ibid*, Vol. 2, p.160
15. *Ibid*, Vol. 1, p.378. Kilvert did not witness this exchange and regretted that he didn't. He had received his invitation late and typically anxious to avoid the embarrassment of arriving after lunch had started, decided not to go. The fact that he heard all about the exchange between De Winton and the guest shows how much the former's doings were the subject of talk
16. *Ibid*, Vol. 2, p.131. Bovill (*English Country Life 1780-1830*, p.9) confirmed that large-scale felling of trees was a sure sign of landowners seeking to pay off debts. Kilvert recorded similar felling on Clyro Court lands too. (Vol. 1, p.41)
17. Kilvert's *Diary*, Vol. 3, pp.225-6
18. The account of it that follows is largely based on the *Hereford Times* for 6 April 1867
19. Kilvert, on a walk in spring 1870 to his beloved Aber Edw rocks, had got lost and ended up in the village
20. The piece of land was insignificant in extent. See map
21. If the strip could be proved to be common land, De Winton, as lord of the manor, was entitled to it
22. D.R. Mills, *op.cit*, p.167. Kilvert's parish of Clyro was border territory. Mr Price, a landowner of Builth, considered Radnor Forest, the Clyro Hills, and the Begwyns as the boundary of English and Welsh farming (Parliamentary Papers, Report of Commission on the State of Education in Wales, 1847, pp.170-1)
23. Kilvert's *Diary*, Vol. 2, p.224. As he told the story, there was 'a merry twinkle in his eye'
24. D.W. Howells and C. Baber, *op.cit*, p.297
25. Charles Stretton, *Memoirs of a Chequered Life*, p.3
26. H.J. Perkins, in *Land Reform And Class Conflict In Victorian Britain* (in J. Butt and I.F. Clarke, *The Victorians And Social Protest*, p.187), noted that the popular conception at this time was that 'bribery, tenant bullying, and place-hunting were the characteristic contributions of the landed interest to political life'
27. P. Horn, *Labouring Life in the Victorian Countryside*, p.166. Kilvert's border area, in contrast to Welsh upland areas, had a very high density of church, as opposed to chapel, attendance. (Alan D. Gilbert, *op.cit*, pp.45-6)
28. Gilbert, *op.cit*, p.48. A Poor Law Commissioner was writing of Wales in 1843: 'The landlords are most of them of the old Church - and - King school - the tenantry are almost all Dissenters'. (Quoted in D.W. Howell, 'The Regions And Their Issues: Wales', in Mingay, *The Victorian Countryside*, Vol. 1, p.73)
29. Copleston, Robert Kilvert's patron, went on from Oriel to become bishop of Llandaff. Thirlwall was bishop of St. David's. Louisa Bevan, wife of Rev. Bevan, expressed the hope to Rev. Venables that an Englishman would be appointed to replace the Rev. Jones Thomas, who had just died, in the living of Llanigon. (Llysdinam Collection, B668, 27 Feb. 1886)
30. LWRO. RD/JGW/23/6
31. Report of Chester trial, *Hereford Times*, 17 August 1867
32. The pattern was well established from the late 17th century: 'If you grew up under the shadow of the castle or outside the walls of the lordly park, you knew who ruled England, even if the place was in the hands of tenants'. (P. Laslett, *op.cit*, p.63)
33. The original 'encroachment' took place in 1807
34. Letter of Walter Wilkins (1742 - 1828) to Edward Jones, solicitor, of Llandovery, 26 Feb. 1792. (National Library of Wales, D.T.M. Jones, 8736). This action was pure vindictiveness on Wilkins' part. He was unable to strike at Howarth, against whom he had some grievance, because he was dead, so he punished Griffiths, who may well have bought in good faith. The fact that Griffiths was 'a little cottager' made no difference. (Vaughan was hardly more—his Glangwye farm comprised a mere 8 acres)

REFERENCES

35. *Hereford Times*, 1 Jan. 1862, The JPs who heard the case were the Rev. Venables and Henry Allen
36. It was not lack of money that prevented Vaughan from having QCs; De Winton had undertaken to pay all the costs of the Chester trial
37. The Talbots were descended from Norman barons who became pillars of the establishment. Several Talbots fortified castles in the Welsh Marches from Chester to Monmouth during the 13th century, including Builth Castle and other Breconshire ones. From the 15th century, the Talbot name was associated with the Earldom of Shrewsbury. De Winton's friend, Charles Talbot, was to inherit the title. He was two years older than De Winton but they overlapped at Eton during 1846-8. Frances Jessie was Charles Talbot's cousin. De Winton's link with the family may have been the reason for locating the second trial in their part of the country
38. C. Kingsley, *Alton Locke*, p.233
39. Kilvert's *Diary*, Vol. 2, p.190. The date was 18 April 1872
40. *Ibid*, Vol. 2, p.197
41. *Ibid*, Vol. 2, p.222
42. C. Woodham-Smith, *Florence Nightingale*, p.220
43. Lady Verney, *Fernyhurst Court*, p.4
44. When he inherited Claydon in 1827, it was seriously decayed but by great effort and self-discipline, he recovered it. He was a model landlord. Although he had renounced game preservation on his estate by 1846, Kingsley strangely chose to name his vicious game keeper Harry Verney in *Yeast* (1848). The book attacks the Game Laws for much the same reasons that the real Verney did
45. Lady Verney, *Lettice Lisle*, p.2
46. *Ibid*, p.9. Lady Verney wrote two factual accounts of the problems of small proprietors
47. *Ibid*, p.22. Kingsley had the same attitude to trees
48. Kilvert's *Diary*, Vol. 2, p.316. The middle-classes had been particularly enraged by reports of the intimidation and 'tyranny' of unions in 1866-7. (A. Briggs, *Victorian People*, p.189). Best noted that miners were not considered 'respectable' till the mid-1870s. (Best, *op.cit*, p.292)
49. Letter of 4 Feb. 1873 to Marion Vaughan, quoted in *Kilvert Society Newsletter*, Aug. 1985. As a young man, Kilvert would have noted with some alarm the formation in 1860 of the Agricultural Labourers' Protection Society at Highworth, 25 miles from Langley Burrell
50. Reports of Leeds Church Congress, 1872, p.362
51. They had begun in 1861 as a forum in which clergy and laity could discus important questions
52. John Fielder Mackarness, (1820 - 1889), Eton and Oxford. His speech is in the Report of the 1873 Bath Church Congress, pp.24-8. He was a notable pluralist and had deeply resented the reforms that undermined Oxford University as a clerical and aristocratic citadel
53. He also rejected the charge that the clergy were oppressors of the poor, and said it came not from labourers themselves but from their leaders, who were Dissenters. The leader of the NALU, Joseph Arch, had been a Methodist minister
54. P. Horn, *Labouring Life in the Victorian Countryside*, p.258
55. M.K. Ashby, *op.cit*, p.159. Houghton noted that Victorian society tried to have it both ways by refusing to interfere with the laws of supply and demand while simultaneously insisting that 'its heart was tender'. (Houghton, *op.cit*, p.277). Earl Nelson, in one of the papers that found favour with Kilvert at the Bath Congress, stated that employers never grudged a good day's pay for a good day's work
56. Canon Girdlestone, Report of Bath Church Congress, 1873, p.34
57. Canon Girdlestone, 'Landowners, Land and those who till it' in *Fraser's Magazine*, Dec. 1868, p.747. Subsequent quotations in this paragraph come from this source
58. *Hereford Times*, 8 Aug. 1868
59. *Ibid*, 19 Sept. 1868
60. It had been adjourned once before, to the annoyance of Rev. Jones Thomas, who was one of the JPs present (the others were Henry Allen, De Winton, and the Rev. Bold)
61. Kilvert's *Diary*, Vol. 2, p.146. The date was 7 March 1872
62. A connection with the prestigious Talbot family, into which De Winton had married, had been made by the marriage of the daughter of the 8th Tichborne baronet; she became the mother of an Earl of Shrewsbury
63. An ancestor of that family was Jane Seymour, briefly wife of Henry VIII
64. His uncle wrote to Lord Fitzroy Somerset, afterwards Lord Raglan
65. The Tichborne fortune was increased by the death of another Doughty cousin and by the Jamaican sugar wealth of Roger's uncle
66. Ruskin quoted in Houghton, *op.cit*, p.190
67. Douglas Woodruff, *The Tichborne Claimant: A Victorian Mystery*
68. Whereas Roger was only 9 stone at the time of his disappearance, the Claimant was already 16 stone when he left Australia. He was to become even larger
69. Kilvert's *Diary*, Vol. 2, p.151

70. Lord Maugham, *The Tichborne Case*
71. George Nugent Bankes, *An Eton Boy's Letters*, Letter VI. *Henry Dunbar* caught the public's imagination in the period when the talk was all of reform: it had gone through seven editions by 1865
72. Maugham, *op.cit*, pp.372-4
73. Woodruff, *op.cit*, p.255
74. *Ibid*, p.324. The foreman was Henry Dickins, of Dickins and Jones, the drapery establishment
75. Quoted in Burn, *op.cit*, p.315
76. It was one element in the mounting criticism of public schools that characterised the reform-conscious 1860s. Sir John was an Etonian. Three articles in the *Cornhill Magazine* in 1860 contained a swingeing attack on Eton. William Johnson Cory published his *Eton Reform* in 1861 and the *Edinburgh Review* article of April 1861, which reviewed both that and Sir John Coleridge's lecture, helped to provoke the setting up of the Public Schools Commission of 1862. The article stated flatly that the 'general education of the pauper school in Slough is considerably better and more useful to all... conditions of men than the education to be had at Eton College'.
77. Burn, *op.cit*, p.315
78. Kilvert's *Diary*, Vol. 3, p.134
79. F.B. Smith (*The Making of the Second Reform Bill*, p.54) stated that he was one of the 'Victorian intelligentsia' who supported the Bill on the side of the radicals, whose company included J.S. Mill and Thomas Hughes
80. *DNB*. This helps us to understand why his cross-examination of the Claimant imposed such a fearful strain on him
81. Woodruff, *op.cit*, p.xi
82. *Ibid*, p.xiii. Woodruff observed that in making that judgement, *The Times* was not summing up what had emerged from the trial, but stating what the public ought to think
83. Kilvert's *Diary*, Vol. 2, p.410. He was disturbed at the mere fact that a 'Radical' (ie. Liberal) candidate had appeared, though there had been one in 1865 and 1868
84. At Leicester, for example, 4,000 working men attended a meeting to express support
85. This identified him more with working-class men and less with gentlemen, who in theory should look finer and more handsome
86. Kilvert's *Diary*, Vol. 2, p.420
87. Letter to William Thirlwall Bayne, New Year's Day 1874, *Letters of Connop Thirlwall*, p.373
88. It was generally believed that it was written for him and that there was never any word of truth in it
89. Sergeant Ballantine, *Some Experiences of a Barrister's Life*, p.163 and p.167
90. Article in *The Englishman*, Vol. 1, 18 April 1874, p.18. *The Englishman* was a newspaper started by Kenealy to appeal to working-class readers. Wilfred Scawen Blunt, while a diplomat in Buenos Aires, met the explorer, Sir Richard Burton, whose constant companion at the time was Arthur Orton. Blunt found Orton, 'heavy lump as he was, the more gentleman of the two'. (Longford, *op.cit*, p.67)
91. Kilvert's *Diary*, Vol. 3, p.84
92. Robert Tracy, *Trollope's Later Novels*, p.73. The next chapter will deal more fully with Kilvert's fear of social and moral isolation
93. St. George, *op.cit*, p.20
94. Burn, *op.cit*, p.310. One wonders whether Dickens borrowed from this case the name of Provis for his transported convict character in *Great Expectations*
95. Kingsley. Preface to *Alton Locke*
96. *The Times*, 13 Feb. 1871
97. Kingsley. Letter to Professor Lorimer, 17 Dec 1866. Mrs Kingsley, *op.cit*, p.279
98. Report of Bath Church Congress, 1873, p.27
99. Its other main objectives were reform of the land laws, the democratisation of local government, and the disestablishment of the Church of England

Chapter 10
1. A. Sartoris, *op.cit*, p.86
2. Artists and performers enjoyed a degree of licence not granted to others. A parallel case to that of Adelaide Sartoris was that of the soprano, Jenny Lind: their 'foreign-ness' helped to excuse departures from social etiquette. Lind was able to enjoy a life-long friendship with A.P. Stanley, Dean of Westminster. (A. St. George, *op.cit*, p.117)
3. Lord Redesdale, *op.cit*, Vol. 2, pp.516-7. Her guests included Dickens, Matthew Arnold and Frederick Leighton, the painter. Charles Hallé would accompany Mrs Sartoris and other outstanding singers of the day
4. A. Sartoris, *Judith*, p.97. The country gentleman whom Mrs Sartoris had herself married formed, it appears, something of a contrast to this fictional creation. Edward Sartoris was wealthy (his estate yielded £5,000 a year) and, though he later became MP for Carmarthen (1868-74), in his younger

REFERENCES

days he led the life an 'idle man-about-town', according to G.N. Ray, who understood that he neglected his wife in spite of the fact that she was very affectionate towards him. Thackeray recorded that he left his wife in Rome to ensure that he was in London for the season, principally because he missed the company at Cremorne Gardens, a notorious place of popular entertainment in Chelsea. (Letter to Mrs Procter, 8 March 1853. *Letters and Private papers of W.M. Thackeray*, edited G.N. Ray, Vol. 3, p.340). However, Eleanor Ransome (in *The Terrific Kemble. A Victorian Self-Portrait*, p.170) quotes Thackeray saying of Sartoris: 'He is everything that is good. There never was such a kind creature'

5. A. Sartoris, *Judith*, p.181

6. E. Carpenter, *op.cit*, p. 321

7. Kilvert's *Diary*, Vol. 3, p.278

8. *Ibid*, Vol. 1, p.175

9. They were the clergymen Bevan, Dew, Thomas, Webb and some members of their families, plus Crichton, Morrell, the Wyatts, Bridges, Oswalds, and Trumpers. (Dr. Trumper was in practice locally)

10. W. Houghton, *op.cit*, pp.342-3

11. They were visiting their brother, Father Ignatius, at the monastery of Capel y Ffin.

12. Kilvert's *Diary*, Vol. 1, p.178

13. *Ibid*, Vol. 2, pp.399-400. My italics

14. Approval of a girl is invariably accompanied by this emphasis. Cf. his comments on Amelia de Winton: 'Her manner is very pleasant and good, so frank, open, simple and natural'. (Kilvert's *Diary*, National Library of Wales, 1989 edition, p.68). The Duke of Norfolk's two sisters were 'pleasant unaffected girls' (*Diary*, Vol. 2, p.328) and his neighbour, Mrs Adderley, was acceptable because of her 'simple, unaffected... gentle manner'. (*Diary*, Vol. 2, p.243). There was also Mrs Decie, 'a genial, impulsive cordial woman, simple-hearted, straightforward and genuine'. (*Diary*, Vol. 2, p.74)

15. The Gore family ran Whitty's Mill in Clyro and owned some land. They were, so Kilvert understood, 'very well off', making at least £200 a year

16. Kilvert's *Diary*, Vol. 1, pp.255-6

17. It is worth mentioning that it was to be found in Ursula Hamilton in *A Week in a French Country House*, which Kilvert had read four weeks before this visit

18. Kilvert's *Diary*, Vol. 1, p.133

19. Though the event was only a concert in a village school, followed by supper in the home of the local vicar, Kilvert's account indicates there was much sensitivity to rank and a high degree of formality

20. Lord Willoughby de Broke, who understood these things well, provided this list of country 'personages and classes, arranged in descending order: The Lord Lieutenant, the Master of Fox Hounds, the Agricultural Landlords, the Bishop, the Chairman of the Quarter Sessions, the Colonel of the Yeomanry, the MP, the Dean, the Archdeacons, the JPs, the lesser clergy, and the larger farmers'. (De Broke, *The Passing Years*, p.57)

21. The fact that he could 'fall in love' with the youthful Llowes songstress is partly explained by this and partly because a wife and a pretty daughter were merged in his mind as one entity

22. Mrs Elizabeth Jones, aged 51, and her husband farmed 100 acres with the help of one labourer and two farm servants. They had a five year old daughter, whom Kilvert invited to the party he organised earlier in the year to mark the birthday of Boosie Evans, daughter of the Clyro schoolmaster

23. Kilvert's *Diary*, Vol. 2, p.206. Kilvert also visited her on the 13 June 1870 and spoke of her 'magnificent sweeping courtesy' and of her 'hospitable house where there is still to be seen the ...simple, homely life of the freehold farmer'. (Kilvert's *Diary*, National Library of Wales, 1989 edition, p.8). In Chieflands, home of a similar farmer, he had found the same qualities. Taine, too, met a farmer's wife who shared them. She was 'full of gaiety... without any embarrassment... Excepting some shades in manners and talk, she is a lady; she is so wholly *in heart*'. (H. Taine, *op.cit*, p.159). My italics

24. He had pronounced a dinner there to be 'very nice [and] pleasant' with 'no constraint' and the house as one of the 'nicest most comfortable' in the area

25. One painting by William Collins with whose work Kilvert was familiar, is entitled 'Cottage Hospitality'

26. Cf. his view of the Clutterbucks in the chapter 'Kilvert and Home'

27. A man on the train told him she was the only child of Lord Stanley of Alderley, travelling with her nurse. Plomer dismissed this suggestion because the second Lord Stanley's daughters were all far too old. However, the man may have misunderstood the child's relationship to the family

28. C. Kingsley, *Yeast*, p.52

29. W. Wilberforce, *op.cit*, p.66. He had also written: 'It is the heart that constitutes the man', p.71

30. C. Kingsley, *Alton Locke*, p.12

31. Kilvert's *Diary*, Vol. 2, p.346. His italics. He believed that God's influence lay behind these moments in which 'two souls have touched ... The momentary crossing of a path ...It is the will of God'.

(Kilvert's poem 'The Pilgrimage'). This 'angel child' is the daughter he longed for but never had (cf. the prefatory quote to this chapter). She also has obvious links with the Bristol waif, and the 'loving fellow pilgrim' who accompanied him on his visits to the poor of Crafta Webb. (cf. 'Kilvert And The Poor')

32. Kilvert's *Diary*, Vol. 2, p.427

33. On this trip to Land's End, for example, he was indignant at having to share the location with 'a rude vulgar crew of tourists'. (Kilvert's *Diary*, Vol. 1, p.195). Thackeray wrote of a marchioness who disliked steam boats because one had to mix with all sorts of people. (*op.cit*, p.11)

34. Quoted in N. Faith, *The World the Railways Made*, p.234

35. Kilvert's *Diary*, Vol. 2, p.279. This was October 1872

36. The three *Diary* passages in which he admired these families are Vol. 3, p.322, p.275 and p.206 respectively

37. Quoted in F. Grice, *op.cit*, pp.68-9. Son was like father in admiring these qualities: as a young man, Robert Kilvert said how much he liked the 'amiable, lively and thoroughly natural' girls of the Marriott family. (Robert Kilvert, *op.cit*, p.53). The 1860s saw a flowering of interest in the status and capacities of women. The popular periodicals debated the issues, beginning with an article entitled 'The Girl of the Period' in the *Saturday Review* March 1868. The articles focused particularly on middle class women and Kilvert probably kept track of them all

38. Kilvert's *Diary*, Vol. 3, p.168

39. *Ibid*, Vol. 2, p.136. The occasion of this remark was the children's party he gave to mark the birthday of Boosie Evans

40. When Kilvert was emphasising the genuine gratitude of the little girl whom he looked after at the Llowes concert, he quoted Wordsworth's lines (from 'Simon Lee') about 'hearts unkind' responding to kind deeds with coldness, and commented, 'Dear old Wordsworth'. On another occasion, he observed that the poet 'did not care much for society and preferred the society of women... with men he was often reserved'. (Kilvert's *Diary*, Vol. 1, p.318). Kilvert might have been referring to himself. Roberts (*Paternalism in Early Victorian England*, p. 60) noted that Wordsworth was a paternalist whose poetry reflected his faith in 'intimate personal relations'. Many Victorians admired Wordsworth for this quality

41. Kilvert's *Diary*, Vol. 1, pp.324-5

42. Peter T. Cominos, 'Innocent Femina Sensualis in Unconscious Conflict', in M. Vicinus, *Suffer And Be Still*, p.158

43. A. St. George, *The Descent of Manners, Etiquette, Rules and the Victorians*, p. xvii. The treatment Kilvert received at the hands of Rev. Thomas illustrated just what the effects of such a concept of manners could be

44. Quoted in Bertrand and Patricia Russell, *op.cit*, Vol. 1, pp.124-5

45. Volumes 1 and 2 of the *Diary* are particularly full of entries of this kind (there are approximately 40 in each), probably because his status in Clyro made him that much more vulnerable. In volume 3 they are noticeably less frequent

46. Peter Gay. op.cit. p. 494. Cf. also his statement at the head of this chapter

47. Victorians were very sensitive about failure and saw 'character' as the means of avoiding personal 'ship wrecks'. St. George noticed a link between the Victorians' fear of failure and their obsession with shipwrecks, which Kilvert shared. (He mentions them more than a dozen times). Kilvert's fear of failure may have centred on what St. George called 'the steady drip of indolent afternoons inexplicably wasted' (A. St. George, *op.cit*, p.36), the solitary musings of what Grice called his 'Wordsworthian Dream'. At the age of 33 Kilvert joined a Mutual Improvement Society to improve his character and prospects

48. The word recurs repeatedly in his descriptions of them

49. It is possible that Kilvert had read this article in his youth. He referred to seeing an article on Crabbe's poetry 'this month', as though he habitually perused its pages. *A Week in a French Country House* also first appeared in the magazine, though he read it in book form

50. Best, *op.cit*, pp.98-9

51. E.J. Hobsbawm, *The Age of Capital 1848 - 1875*, pp.44-6. He noted that an economic boom began in Britain in 1850 and exports experienced a rise in the first seven years of the 1850s never surpassed. Figures for total gross income of the country also reflect the prosperity: between 1831 - 1851 it rose from £340m to £523m. (Harrison, *Early Victorian Britain*, p.22)

52. Quoted in M. Girouard, *The Return to Camelot. Chivalry and the English Gentleman*, p.63

53. Kenelm Digby, *op.cit*, pp.588-9

54. Kilvert, about to give up his curacy in Clyro, wrote of the Bevans' Hay Castle: 'a home to me for nearly 8 years and its inmates like brothers and sisters'. (*Diary*, Vol. 2, p.252)

55. P. Mason, *op.cit*, pp.144-5. Bulwer Lytton had noted this tendency earlier. It was women, he said, who set the tone of society, though they took their lead from men, and because men did not favour

REFERENCES

intellectual pursuits, women avoided them in case it frightened them off. Women tended to connect literature and intelligence with 'odd persons not in society'. In England, respect was paid primarily to wealth; in France, by contrast, writers might be found in the highest social circles. 'A literary man with us is often forced to be proud of something else than talents—of fortune, of connexion, or of birth— in order not to be looked down upon'. (B. Lytton, *op.cit*, Vol. 1, pp.148-9)

56. Lord Ernest Hamilton, *Forty Years On*, p.5
57. Hamilton, *op.cit*, p.8
58. A. St. George, *op.cit*, p.57
59. W.M. Thackeray, 'Mr Brown's Letters to his Nephew', in *Miscellanies*, Vol. 2, p.211
60. *Industrial and Social Position of Women in the Middle and Lower Ranks*, (1857) by John Duguid Milne. Quoted in *Victorian Working Women: Portraits from Life*, by M. Hiley, p.31
61. E.F. Benson, *As We Were*, p.85 and p.101
62. E. Carpenter, *op.cit*, pp.13-14 and pp.29-31
63. M. Vicinus, 'The Perfect Victorian Lady' in *Suffer And Be Still*, edited Vicinus, p.ix
64. Kilvert's *Diary*, Vol. 1, p.127
65. It was the existence of sexually explicit passages in the *Diary* in connection with Kilvert's earlier lovers that led to the destruction of portions of it by his widow and Mrs Essex-Hope
66. E. Carpenter, *op.cit*, pp.94-5
67. Peter T. Cominos, *op.cit*, p.158
68. J.S. Mill in *The Subjection of Women*, quoted in Cominos, *op.cit*, p.161
69. Cominos, *op.cit*, p.161 and p.169
70. Unpublished extracts from Kilvert's *Diary* relating to the Dew and Bevan families, (Kilvert Society publication), p.7
71. *Ibid*, p.8. Arthur Cheese was a solicitor of the wealthy family of solicitors with branches in Hay, Rhayader and Kington. He was Under-Sheriff to Walter Baskerville in 1868 when he was Sheriff of Radnorshire
72. Kilvert had read an article about this on 22 February that year in the Jan - April number of the *Quarterly Review*. The article was entitled 'The Holy Grail and Other Poems' by Tennyson
73. Kilvert's *Diary*, Vol. 1, p.175
74. F.P. Cobbe, *Life of Frances Power Cobbe As Told By Herself*, p.173
75. It is possible that Kilvert first heard of *A Week in a French Country House* during this conversation. It occurred on 28 September 1870 when he was out walking with George Venables. The latter knew both Mrs. Sartoris and her brother, John Mitchell Kemble, who was a Cambridge contemporary. Since Kilvert recorded that he was reading the novel only two days later, a copy of it may have been lent him by George Venables
76. Lady Verney, *Fernyhurst Court*, p.107
77. Kilvert's *Diary*, Vol. 1, p.64
78. His high principles owed something to his schooling under Dr. Arnold at Rugby
79. Llysdinam Collection, B1276, Letter of 4 Jan. 1855 to George Venables
80. The Institute was chronically short of funds and of support, and on 9 January 1869 the local paper announced that its programme of fortnightly meetings in the winter months had lapsed. Neither Kilvert nor Venables attended the soirée held on Monday 4 Jan. 1869
81. Basing his judgement largely if not entirely on the activities and interests of Rev. Bevan and his daughter, Mary, Grice asserted that 'the social circle in which Kilvert was fortunate enough to move during his stay at Clyro, was, far from being parochial and provincial, a remarkably enlightened and progressive community', (*Frederick Grice Memorial Booklet*, Kilvert Society, p.30). The evidence, including Kilvert's outburst apropos *A Week in a French Country House*, hardly bears this out
82. Mrs. Braddon, *Henry Dunbar*, p.57
83. All those points about the character of Adelaide Sartoris, and the quotations, come from the preface to *A Week in a French Country House*, pp.xxxviii-xlvii
84. M. Girouard, *The Victorian Country House*, p.35
85. C. Kingsley, *Alton Locke*, p.101
86. A.L. Rowse, *The English Spirit*, pp 233-4
87. Ronald Blythe, *From the Headland*, p.187
88. Daisy Thomas was a child and that was a substantial element in Kilvert's love for her. She was, he said, a 'happy child, content with a few simple innocent delights', (*Dairy*, Vol. 2, p.148)
89. C. Kingsley, *Yeast*, p.52
90. It was Tennyson, another of Kilvert's favourite poets, who wrote:
   'Man with the head and woman with the heart:
   Man to command and woman to obey:
   All else is confusion'.
   ('The Princess', Section V, pp.350-1, *The Poetical Works of Alfred Lord Tennyson*). An 1873 book of

advice to young married women observed: 'A woman can help her husband [most], perhaps, by BEING CONTENT'. (*Woman's Own Book.* Quoted in P. Gay, *op.cit*, p.575)

91. By the 1860s marriages based on money were, however, becoming less common. (W.E. Houghton, *op.cit*, p.385)

92. Letter from Fanny Kilvert, quoted in 'Llysdinam and Newbridge' by Owain Jones, *Brycheiniog*, Vol. XX, 1982/3, p.83

93. Llysdinam Collection, Letter B672, Colonel Thomas was the eldest son, Walter a younger son, of the family

94. She actually died on 1 June. Pneumonia was the direct cause of her death though she had suffered for two years from Addison's Disease, which Dr. Williams also gave as a contributory cause. The disease is characterised by weakness and muscle wasting, and results from deficiency of certain hormones produced by the adrenal glands. In Victorian times, TB was the most common cause of the decay of those glands. The disease had a slow onset but rises could be triggered by infection and other stresses. In the case of Mary Thomas, pneumonia and possibly emotional disturbance produced the fatal deterioration

Epilogue

1. Llysdinam Collection, B1072. Letter of Henry Venables to Richard Lister Venables, 16 May 1856. £16,500 was owing on a mortgage in 1853, interest on which exceeded the income from the estate, whose value then was £25,000

2. Clyro Court cost Thomas Baskerville a mere £11,500 to build in contrast to the £100,000 that went on the refurbishment of Penoyre, but, according to an old woman of Clyro, who lived as a companion to his widow, he overstretched himself to do it. (M.M. Morgan, *Kilvert's Clyro*, Kilvert Society Publications, p.2)

3. F.M.L. Thompson, *op.cit*, p.3. Jefferies (*Hodge and his Masters*, p.210) described the typical village as 'often a perfect battleground of struggling parties'

4. R. Jefferies, 'The Wiltshire Labourer' in *The Hills and the Vale*, p.252

5. J.S. Mill. 'De Tocqueville on Democracy in America.. II', in *Essays on Politics and Society*, pp.193-4.
   J. Berger *et al* (*The Homeless Mind*) have much to say that is relevant to the change in social reality Kilvert was experiencing, in particular the loss of the harmony that existed when 'the same integrative symbols permeated the various sectors of everyday life', (p.62.) The nature of this order was, significantly in relation to Kilvert, 'typically religious'. Absence of it has produced for modern man a state of what Berger *et al* call 'homelessness'

6. P. Ariés, *Centuries of Childhood*, p.359. Kilvert had read Adam Smith's evaluation of primogeniture during his Oxford course. In feudal times, Smith noted, when land was a source of power and protection for inferiors, it was thought better to pass it on to one child. In Smith's own time, its only virtue was to bolster family pride, (*Wealth of Nations*, Book III, Ch. 2)

7. T. Mozley, *Reminiscences chiefly of Towns, Villages, and Schools*, Vol. 1, pp.375-6, my italics. C. Eardley-Wilmot (*Charterhouse Old And New*, p.60) also referred to this 'ceaseless interrogation of new boys'

8. *English Boarding Schools*, Quarterly Journal of Education, January - April 1834, p.44, my italics

9. WRO. 540/286

10. F.M.L. Thompson, *op.cit*, p.20. R.J. Olney (*Lincolnshire Politics 1832 - 1885*, pp.231-3) noted the extent to which Lincolnshire rural gentry MPs, when addressing constituents, restricted their comments entirely to agriculture; they were blinkered with regard to other issues

11. Letter to W. Empson, 8 Jan. 1836. *The Life And Correspondence Of Dr. Arnold*, edited by A.P. Stanley. p.265

12. Quoted in D. Spring, 'The Clapham Sect: Some Social And Political Aspects', *Victorian Studies*, Sept. 1961, p.46

13. Parliamentary Papers, Commission on Employment of Children, Young Persons, and Women in Agriculture, 1867, 2nd Report, p.8

14. W. Long, *op.cit*, pp.184-7. Broderick stated that estates were held primarily 'for the sake of social position, territorial infuence, and legal privileges', *op. cit*, p.85

15. Cf. chapter 8 and the accounts landowners' agents had given SGO of the economy of estates

16. W.H. Hudson, *A Shepherd's Life*, p.110

17. Letter to J.T. Coleridge, 1 Nov. 1830

18. *Victoria History of Oxfordshire*, Vol. xi, p.264

19. Miss C. Hodgson, whose father was Vicar of Bredwardine from 1922, told how the villagers there under stood Kilvert's death to be due to pneumonia; no mention was made by them of peritonitis. (Kilvert Society Newsletter, May 1982)

20. He did show some *Diary* passages to his Wadham friend Mayhew in July 1875

21. Father S.G.A. Luff in The Clergy Review, quoted in Grice, *Francis Kilvert and his World*, p.232

22. William Plomer, *Autobiography*, p.365

23. Peter Alexander, *William Plomer. A Biography*, p.217

REFERENCES

24. Plomer's own phrase, *op.cit*, p.135
25. W. Plomer, *op.cit*, p.366
26. P. Alexander, *op.cit*, p.41
27. Introduction to Volume 3 of the *Diary*. He believed they grew out of the life of the boys in the school run by Kilvert's father at Harnish
28. Robert. M. Pirsig, *Lila. An Inquiry Into Morals*, p.272. He also observed: 'What held the Victorian pattern together was a social code, not an intellectual one ... the test of anything in the Victorian mind was, "Does society approve?"'
29. P. Alexander, *op.cit*, p.28
30. This picture was itself an inheritance from earlier centuries
31. The other two were: 'the papacy is the ghost of the Roman Empire sitting crowned upon its grave' and 'the earth is strewn with the wreck of Heaven's ideals'. Kilvert's *Diary*, Vol. 2, p.381
32. *Ibid*, Vol. 2, pp.320-1
33. *Ibid*, Vol. 2, p.338
34. *Ibid*, Vol. 2, p.427
35. *Ibid*, Vol. 3, p.336
36. Colloms experienced some difficulty in reconciling the contradictions in Kilvert. She noted that he was highly intolerant of miners, trade unionists, Dissenters and tourists mainly on grounds of snobbery. Yet he was, she said, 'tolerant [and] responsive to decency and sincerity in others no matter what their creed or social station'. However, he found it impossible to believe that radicals could have any decency or sincerity. 'In a word, he was a natural democrat'. (B. Colloms, *Victorian Country Parsons*, p.167.) Can a man be a 'natural democrat' and yet be a paternalist and a staunch believer in rank and hierarchy?
37. H. McLeod, *Religion and the Working Class in Nineteenth Century Britain*, p.13
38. Kilvert's *Diary*, Vol. 3, p.338, my italics
39. William Wilberforce, quoted in D. Spring, *The Clapham Sect: Some Social And Political Aspects*, p.47. Wilberforce assumed that all good Christians respected noblemen
40. Kilvert's *Diary*, Vol. 1, pp.349-350
41. G.F. Best, *Temporal Pillars*, p.168
42. R. Williams, *The Country And The City*, p.358
43. *Ibid*, p.203
44. Introduction to volume one of the *Diary*
45. William Plomer, *op.cit*, p.365
46. Introduction to volume one of the *Diary*
47. P. Alexander, *op.cit*, p.217
48. *Ibid*. p. 217.
49. William Plomer, *op.cit*, p.366
50. Llysdinam Collection, B.895. The letter was dated 5th February 1885
51. *Ibid*, B.1530. The letter was dated 1st June 1880. After 1915 Moccas Court was let and in the late 1940s its contents were dispersed. It is now in flats. In 1889 Louisa Bevan was telling Venables of other local country houses that had been empty for some time: Oakfield, Cabalva, The Moor, and Tregoyd (Lord Hereford's home). *Ibid*, B674, 23 Jan. 1889

Index

INDEX

INDEX

INDEX